CONFEDERATE
STRUGGLE
FOR COMMAND

TEXAS A&M UNIVERSITY

120

MILITARY HISTORY SERIES

CONFEDERATE STRUGGLE FOR COMMAND

GENERAL JAMES LONGSTREET AND THE FIRST CORPS IN THE WEST

ALEXANDER MENDOZA

TEXAS A&M UNIVERSITY PRESS
COLLEGE STATION

For my professors,
whose inspiration and guidance I can never repay
Dr. Alwyn Barr
Dr. Peggy J. Hardman
Dr. David L. Snead
Dr. Jerry D. Thompson
Dr. Steven E. Woodworth

CONTENTS

LIST OF ILLUSTRATIONS *ix*

ACKNOWLEDGMENTS *xi*

PREFACE *xvii*

1

"Our Best Opportunity for Great Results Is in Tennessee"

LONGSTREET AND THE FIRST CORPS'S ROAD TO THE WEST

1

2

"One of the Most Gallant Struggles"

OPERATION WESTWARD HO AND THE CHICKAMAUGA CAMPAIGN

27

3

"The Shafts of Malice That Have Been Hurled against Him"

LONGSTREET AND THE COMMAND CRISIS IN THE ARMY OF TENNESSEE

53

4

"It Is Hard to Keep up One's Spirits with an Empty Stomach and Wet Clothing"

THE FIRST CORPS AT CHATTANOOGA

75

5

*"No Men Who Are Determined
to Succeed Can Fail"*

KNOXVILLE, NOVEMBER 1863

104

6

*"I Long for Some Relief from This
Constant Toil and Anxiety"*

LEADERSHIP AND CONFLICT IN
THE FIRST CORPS, 1863–64

141

7

"Bitter Cold, Everything Frozen"

THE FIRST CORPS IN EAST TENNESSEE, 1863–64

171

CONCLUSION   *201*

APPENDIX   *211*

NOTES   *215*

BIBLIOGRAPHY   *251*

INDEX   *273*

ILLUSTRATIONS

Photographs

1. Lt. Gen. James Longstreet *9*
2. Gen. Robert E. Lee *15*
3. Gen. Joseph E. Johnston *17*
4. Sen. Louis T. Wigfall of Texas *21*
5. Longstreet's soldiers debarking from the trains below Ringgold, September 18, 1863 *35*
6. Gen. Braxton Bragg *56*
7. View of Chattanooga from Lookout Mountain, 1863 *81*
8. Brig. Gen. Micah Jenkins *86*
9. Brig. Gen. Evander M. Law *88*
10. Maj. Gen. Lafayette McLaws *111*
11. Fort Sanders, Knoxville, Tennessee *128*
12. Knoxville, Tennessee, from the south bank of the Holston River *130*
13. Assault on Fort Sanders, November 29, 1963 *134*
14. Pres. Jefferson Davis *155*
15. James Longstreet after the war *199*

Maps

1. Chickamauga *37*
2. Chattanooga Region, 1863 *79*
3. Lookout Valley *90*
4. First Corps Campaigns, 1863 *106*
5. Race to Campbell's Station, November 1863 *118*
6. Knoxville, 1863 *127*
7. Operations in East Tennessee, December 1863 to April 1864 *139*
8. Great Valley, East Tennessee *173*

ACKNOWLEDGMENTS

THIS STUDY, LIKE MOST OTHER WORKS OF HISTORY, COULD NOT have been written without the counsel, support, and encouragement of numerous individuals who gave generously of their time. I would like to offer my sincere appreciation for their assistance.

Anyone who deals with the history of the nineteenth century and the Civil War, in particular, recognizes the legions of archivists and librarians who are immensely skilled at what they do, but who too often remain unappreciated for their essential labors. Special thanks go to the library staffs and archivists who helped me find my way along during the various research trips I had to make while completing this study: the staffs at the University of North Carolina at Chapel Hill; Duke University in Durham, North Carolina; Center for American History at The University of Texas at Austin; Dr. Lynda L. Crist at The Papers of Jefferson Davis at Rice University in Houston, Texas; the Hill Special Collections Library at Louisiana State University; the Manuscripts Department at Tulane University in New Orleans; and Dr. John Coski at the Museum of the Confederacy in Richmond, Virginia. A note of appreciation also goes to the staffs at the additional libraries listed in the bibliography who corresponded with me and mailed me copies of pertinent material.

I am also indebted to the interlibrary loan staff at The University of Texas at Tyler for working diligently to help me track down relevant items and getting them to me as quickly and efficiently as time allowed. Penny Reynolds and Howard Rockwell were very helpful in my search for relevant items—Penny's methodical nature and Howard's diligence provided me with strong liaisons for those particularly elusive sources. Also at UT Tyler, our departmental administrative assistant, MaryEllen Holland, was extremely helpful with all university-related matters, which allowed me enough time for the final writing process.

My sincere thanks also go to several dear friends who were kind enough to read the entire manuscript and provide helpful critiques and ideas. Dr. Charles Grear, Prairie View A&M University, was one, who offered some insightful comments amid discussions over sports, the city of San Antonio, and other historically irrelevant topics. He also shared key documents dealing with Texas soldiers in the Civil War that proved invaluable. Dr. Mark Bradley, my friend and colleague from the U.S. Military Academy Seminar in Military History and author of *This Astounding Close: The Road to Bennett Place,* also took the time to read the manuscript and offered some sharp observations that greatly improved the final book. His thorough reading saved me from many embarrassing errors. Anyone who has been around Mark recognizes that his value and contribution to the study of the Civil War and Reconstruction era far surpasses the numerous honors and awards he has already received for his scholarly work. I am proud to call him my friend. Also, my longtime friend and former college roommate at the University of Texas at Austin, Robert E. Cantu, offered his perspectives, asking me to explain various lapses in my arguments. Even though Bob is more familiar with the military history of the twentieth century due to the nature of his own personal interests and teaching responsibilities, I appreciate his perspective of the highly political world of Civil War generals. I thank him for his friendship and his support.

I am also grateful to several individuals who provided help and guidance in the final stage of preparing this book for publication. Prof. William Garrett Piston of Missouri State University offered sound counsel and encouraged me to pursue my study. His work on Longstreet remains a stimulus to countless students who might be interested in the realm of the Civil War. Prof. Joseph "Chip" Dawson at Texas A&M University, former editor of Texas A&M University Press's Military History Series, also read the manuscript and made vital suggestions that improved the clarity of the study. A sincere thanks goes to Mary Lenn Dixon, Thom Lemmons, and the rest of the dedicated and professional editorial and production staffs at Texas A&M University Press, along with copyeditor Kevin Brock, for guiding me through the realm of academic publishing. At the University of Texas at Tyler, my academic home for the last few years, Dr. Daniel S. Murphree has regularly read and critiqued my work and has served as an indispensable guide for many historical matters. Even though he knows little about Longstreet, he has patiently listened to my stories while feigning great interest. Particularly helpful were our numerous discussions on the concept of leadership. UT-Tyler is fortunate to have him.

Individuals with a mutual interest in Longstreet, the Civil War, or military history in general were generous in sharing their information and their insights. From the awe-inspiring knowledge of Jim Ogden, the chief historian of Chickamauga and Chattanooga National Military Park, to the many formal and informal discussions with various people interested in the Civil War, I have gleaned valuable tidbits of information from conversations that have served as motivation when my own work seemed nearly overwhelming. Particularly helpful were Dr. Kelly Long, Dr. Bruce Daniels, Dr. Joseph King, Richard Pilcher, and Dr. Don Walker. Kevin Levine of Richmond, Virginia, was kind enough to send me copies of Capt. John Christopher Winsmith's 1863–64 letters, and Jonathan Hood shared some pertinent material on the Texas Brigade. I am very grateful for their help. Space precludes mentioning the many other people who in some way contributed to my views on scholarship and research, but I thank them nonetheless.

Additional friends jumped on the bandwagon of support during these last few years. In particular, Bill Hrncir; Steve Sisson and his father, Tom; and Luis Valdez have all expressed an interest in my work and, more importantly, in my sanity as deadlines loomed. Sometimes, unbeknown to them, the best thing they did for me was talk about something other than the Chattanooga or Knoxville campaigns. For that I thank them.

This book is dedicated to my professors, who inspired me with their courses, regularly read and critiqued my work, and encouraged me in ways they probably do not realize. As an undergraduate at the University of Texas at Austin, I was inspired by knowledgeable professors who really strived to make me think beyond names and dates. Particularly influential were the courses offered by Drs. Ricardo Romo, Michael B. Stoff, Clarence Lasby, Norman Brown, John Lamphear, and George B. Forgie. I only hope to be a fraction of the influence on others that they were on me.

The catalyst for my interest in the Civil War and Reconstruction era stemmed from Dr. Jerry D. Thompson's graduate course on the topic. He has since been a big supporter and has taken time from his own research projects to send me tidbits of information dealing with Longstreet. This particular study, however, actually grew out of an informal discussion on Civil War historiography with Dr. Peggy J. Hardman. She first encouraged me to begin to study Longstreet's military career in the Civil War's western theater. Since then Peggy has been a staunch supporter and a huge fan, reading my manuscript and encouraging me to move forward when I seriously considered putting it to rest. For that I thank her immensely.

Officially, Dr. Steven E. Woodworth was not my professor, but he might as well have been. He agreed to serve on my dissertation committee through a special dispensation from Texas Tech University's Graduate School, and his sharp critique of my study made it a better work. Dr. Woodworth might not have agreed with many of my conclusions, but his cogent comments made me hone my arguments and improve the final product. In a book he inscribed for me, he wrote: "To Alex Mendoza, Who I wish were my student." I can honestly say it should have been the other way around—I wish he would have officially been one of my professors, for his kindness and generosity are clearly recognized and appreciated. As I have told him before, I admire him greatly as a scholar, though more as a person.

At Texas Tech I was very fortunate to meet Dr. David L. Snead and have him agree to serve on my dissertation committee. I will never be able to repay him for his guidance and support during those stressful years. I realize now, years later, that I must have been a nuisance with all my questions on military history and unrelated matters. Yet he always kept his door in Holden Hall open and remained patient through our various intense discussions on college football, Virginia, and the topics of diplomatic and military history. I remain profoundly in his debt.

Nothing could have been accomplished, however, without the direction of Dr. Alwyn Barr. Not only did Professor Barr serve as my dissertation chair at Texas Tech, he also became a trusted advisor long after he affixed his signature to the title page of my work. He has been an inspiration, venturing far beyond his always positive outlook on life and academia. Despite my obvious shortcomings, I have tried to model myself after him in regards to his sharp intellect and his immeasurable sense of professionalism. Throughout the initial dissertation-writing process, his judicious use of a pencil—and thankfully not a red pen—to mark the many grammatical and syntactical errors I had made saved me from too many embarrassing blunders to mention. In the years since, he has continued to be a valued mentor, taking time from his own busy schedule to provide a sharp insight into the world of academia. I can honestly say that without his help and support, this book would not have been published. Yet for any errors I have made along the way, I alone am responsible.

Sometimes I think that most of my family, immediate and extended, still wonders what I do, exactly. My mother, Maria Guadalupe, always kids me for not appearing to go to work on a daily nine-to-five schedule and having what appears to her is an inordinate amount of time off during the Christmas holidays. Yet my mother and my late father, Delfino, were always encouraging to me and my siblings about our education and our interests. I only wish my father could have lived to see me complete this book. His recent passing has served as an emotional benchmark for me—I, like my siblings, recognize the value of hard work and the importance of education thanks to him. My sister, Elva Brewster, has been involved in the process of historical research for the sake of her younger brother, actually taking time from visiting her in-laws in Cleveland, Ohio in order to photocopy several important items. She and her husband, Charlie, provided food and shelter during my research trips to their homes in New Orleans and Austin. Her encouragement throughout the years has been significant, to say the least. I thank her wholeheartedly for all her help and her support.

Like most authors, I have imposed most of all on the time of the people who actually live with me on a daily basis. My wife, Punny, who is not only my best friend but also my sounding board, has provided a great deal of love and confidence. Anyone who knows us recognizes just how patient she must be for dealing with me. For that, and more, I thank her. At his young age our son, Justin, has no idea why his father is always working on a computer when there is so much more to do, such as picking dandelions and watching AC/DC videos, but he has generally resisted his impulses and refrained from dumping juice on my laptop. Hopefully one day he will be impressed with what his father has done. Finally, our dogs, Peanut and Pepper, have struggled to nap during the late night and early morning hours while I turned on the lights and typed away. They have been there during the entire process, from the writing of the dissertation, upon which this study is based, to the final revisions. I can only assume they are happy this project is done and they can sleep undisturbed.

Alex Mendoza

PREFACE

NYONE WHO STUDIES THE MILITARY ASPECT OF THE CIVIL WAR, particularly the eastern theater, must sooner or later deal with Lt. Gen. James Longstreet and his place in Confederate historiography. In some cases the interpretations of Longstreet have been as hotly contested as the campaigns themselves. Scholars have made a sport of pointing out Longstreet's most glaring weaknesses: his ambition, his proclivity for sulking and brooding, his lack of intelligence, his repeated tardiness on the battlefield, and his surliness. Historians generally criticize him as a petulant, ambitious subordinate who was an abject failure as a military commander without the supervision of his commander, Gen. Robert E. Lee. Revisionists, however, venerate him as a strategist and tactician whose vision transcended the Civil War.

A question that arises out of examining the plentiful literature on the Civil War and the Army of Northern Virginia is: how can history have been so critical of James Longstreet? How could a man who enjoyed such wide acclaim during the war come to be, in many circles, so widely despised by the time the Lost Cause movement had begun in earnest during the late 1800s? William Garrett Piston has skillfully chronicled the role of Southern partisans in the historical judgment of Longstreet, arguing that the general had criticized powerful combinations during his lifetime and lacked a sympathetic posterity due to the postwar associations he chose to make with the Republican Party and the Catholic Church. By the time he died, Longstreet had accumulated a score of enemies in defending himself against charges that he lost the Battle of Gettysburg. In sum, as Piston has argued, Longstreet was a pariah in his native region.[1]

The authors of the Lost Cause seemed to have influenced later scholars who supported the interpretations of these Southern partisans by lending credence to their arguments. Central to supporting the critical interpretation of James Longstreet was the work of Douglas Southall Freeman, a prominent newspaper editor and historian who studied Robert E. Lee and the Army of Northern Virginia. In his four-volume *R. E. Lee: A Biography* (1934–36), Freeman writes about a Christ-like Lee who fought for an honorable cause and exemplified attributes of the tragic hero. His work won the

Pulitzer Prize for biography and left a distinct interpretation that Longstreet had somehow cost the Confederacy the war for his poor performance at the Battle of Gettysburg. It was Freeman's interpretation of Gettysburg, the "High Water Mark" for the Confederacy, that sealed history's critical judgment of the once resolute lieutenant. Freeman followed his hagiographical account of Lee with a three-volume study of the Army of Northern Virginia, *Lee's Lieutenants: A Study in Command* (1943–45), which slightly tempered his earlier interpretation of Longstreet but still held him in contempt.[2]

The shadow of Freeman loomed large in Civil War historiography. Longstreet's first biographers, Hamilton J. Eckenrode and Bryan Conrad (*James Longstreet: Lee's Warhorse* [1936]), were strongly influenced by Freeman's work. Their interpretation of the First Corps commander as an overly ambitious general further detracted from Longstreet's reputation. While other scholars and writers supporting the Freeman school continued in this vein, Donald B. Sanger and Thomas Robson Hay's *James Longstreet: Soldier, Politician, Officeholder, and Writer* (1952) and Wilbur Thomas's *General James "Pete" Longstreet, Lee's Old Warhorse: Scapegoat for Gettysburg* (1979) attempted to absolve the general of all blame at Gettysburg. Because this battle's literature so dominates that of any other military operation in American history, it is understandable why students of the Civil War should concentrate on it.[3]

Accordingly, while examining Longstreet's military career, historians have focused on his role at Gettysburg. As a result, the general's transfer to the West in the fall of 1863 is often seen as an epilogue to the Gettysburg campaign. Biographies of Longstreet have glossed over his participation in the Chickamauga, Chattanooga, Knoxville, and East Tennessee campaigns in order to provide a more thorough account of his actions in the critical Pennsylvania campaign. For instance, his most recent biographer, Jeffry D. Wert, devotes four chapters to Longstreet's seven months west of the Appalachians—almost the same amount he devotes to the lieutenant general's three days at Gettysburg. Wert's explanation for his study's emphasis, however, is right on target. "The Gettysburg Campaign," he writes, "comprises a central feature of my book, for it is that operation which lies at the core of history's judgment of Longstreet."[4]

Even though the Lost Cause interpretation is all but dead thanks to modern scholarship and critical historians, negative images of Longstreet persist. More importantly, any analysis of Longstreet as a military commander is often overshadowed by the personal representations of the man as a nefarious scoundrel who knew no bounds in order to obtain career advancement.

Part of my purpose in writing this book is to provide a complete and detailed account of Longstreet's service in the West. But my intent is not merely a desire to elucidate the struggles Longstreet experienced. The transfer of the First Corps to the West, I believe, has never been chronicled fully or accurately. While Judith Lee Hallock's *General James Longstreet in the West: A Monumental Failure* (1995) offers a study of Longstreet's command under Bragg, the work falls short of serious historical scholarship. The author, also Bragg's most recent biographer, portrays Longstreet as an overly ambitious general who hurt the Confederate cause through his petulance more than he helped it. Hallock's concise study, however, fails to delve into the comprehensive research of manuscript collections and lacks citations. I thus try to fill that void.

The common soldiers of First Corps also receive attention here. Excellent campaign studies from Peter Cozzens, James Lee McDonough, and Steven Woodworth, to name a few, have analyzed the Army of Northern Virginia troops' participations in the battles for the West. Yet scholars have failed to maintain a continuous thread of analysis on the eastern troops as they made their way from Virginia to northern Georgia and, ultimately, East Tennessee. All too often, discussions of demoralization and privation dominate the traditional accounts of the First Corps veterans in the West. I argue that the morale of the rank and file was more complex than historians have generally maintained. While discouragement and hardship were clearly part of the soldiers' experiences, the spirits of the eastern troops more accurately reflected the momentum of the campaign or the hopes they maintained to return to Virginia, rather than a somber reflection of their views of Longstreet and his generalship. By and large, the men who traveled west were confident in their abilities and resolute in their devotion to the Confederacy.

My second goal is to provide a more balanced view of Longstreet's command in the West. The public's perception of James Longstreet is still one of a brooding, sulking commander who was willing to sacrifice the Confederacy's military prowess for his own ambitions. Obviously, he did himself no favors during his detachment from General Lee's army in the fall of 1863. Descriptions of Longstreet's deportment in Georgia and Tennessee range from the deplorable to outright pettiness. Before departing from Virginia, his disparaging letters regarding his new commanding general, criticizing Bragg's ability to lead and questioning his judgment, reflected poorly on the First Corps commander. His continued criticism and participation in an unseemly petition to oust his new commander further deteriorated any positive views historians and students of the Civil War could have mustered. Clearly Longstreet's behavior, which entered into the realm of insubordination, tarnished his image. Yet historians are far too eager to critique Longstreet while ignoring or absolving other generals who demonstrated comparable poor conduct. The Civil War is replete with instances of officers criticizing their commanders, utilizing scapegoats, and behaving as if they forgot that they were working within the confines of a military command structure. As such, I attempt to place Longstreet's actions within this context. In doing so, I probe the nature and extent of the challenges facing the general's relationship with his superiors and his subordinates. My explanation emphasizes the problems inside the First Corps that fostered the dissent and acrimony found during the unit's western campaigns.

A third goal is to highlight the many challenges facing Longstreet and the First Corps in Georgia and Tennessee. Historians have been quick to dismiss Longstreet's service in the West as an insignificant operation at best and as an absolute failure at worst. A few have argued that this detachment was destined to fail simply because of the general's ambitions and flawed personality. I do not absolve Longstreet in his performances at Chattanooga and Knoxville. But I do attempt to bring a sense of objectivity to understanding why he failed to accurately gauge the Federal operations around Lookout Mountain and why he erred so badly in ordering the ill-fated assault on Fort Sanders. Upon his arrival in North Georgia, Longstreet slipped into a whirlwind of acrimony and dissent that he was unprepared to handle. During the next few months, he and his First Corps would march dozens of miles, survive on scant rations, and endure a bitter winter, leaving most of the men both literally and figuratively numb from the experience. Yet Longstreet generally continued to enjoy the support of his troops. While desertions and grumbling certainly occurred in the corps, it was never as significant as it could have been considering the situation. Consequently, Longstreet's ability to maintain control was a significant achievement considering the dire situation his troops faced.

Finally, I try to reexamine Longstreet in light of recent scholarship that provides a more objective interpretation of the First Corps commander. Longstreet's participation in the Battles of Chickamauga and Chattanooga has been studied to varying conclusions by recent historians. It will be evident that the tone of this work is generally pro-Longstreet, a stance considered highly controversial at one time. But with works like Jeffry Wert's judicious military biography of Longstreet, Peter Cozzens's painstaking studies of the Chickamauga and Chattanooga campaigns, James R. Furqueron's meticulous tactical study of Longstreet at Chickamauga, and R. L. DiNardo's thought-provoking interpretation of Longstreet's approach to staff command, a more balanced view of the general's military career is now available. Taken individually, however, these studies, due to their specific nature, fail to examine Longstreet's service in the West as a whole.

The portrait that emerges of Longstreet is one of a resolute commander who dealt with military defeats and insubordination, endured an unbearably wretched winter in East Tennessee, quarreled with a few subordinates, feared that he had lost the confidence of the authorities in Richmond, but still found the resolve to keep fighting. I dare not suggest that he waged a perfect campaign in the West. It will be evident that Longstreet demonstrated a range of weaknesses as a commander in Tennessee. Yet I maintain that Longstreet was placed in a difficult situation by the swirling events around his command, and despite the long odds facing him, he maintained a resiliency that allowed him to keep his corps united amid great hardship. I have found that historians too often have used the negative images of Longstreet at Gettysburg and simply transferred them to the general's service in the West, placing too much blame solely on his shoulders. Doing so without a comprehensive analysis of the obstacles faced by the First Corps during their detachment to Georgia and Tennessee detracts from the study of Longstreet's struggle to command.

CONFEDERATE STRUGGLE FOR COMMAND

1

"OUR BEST OPPORTUNITY FOR GREAT RESULTS IS IN TENNESSEE"

LONGSTREET AND THE FIRST CORPS'S ROAD TO THE WEST

O N SEPTEMBER 9, 1863, THE FIRST COMPONENTS OF LT. GEN. James Longstreet's First Corps departed the Army of Northern Virginia's base along the Rapidan River destined for northern Georgia. Before leaving, Longstreet visited the army's commander, Gen. Robert E. Lee. Both men knew that the detachment of the First Corps would be disheartening to the Virginia army, yet mutual respect and admiration filled their meeting. As Lee walked with Longstreet to his horse, the conversation turned to the situation on the Tennessee-Georgia border, where Union major general William S. Rosecrans had maneuvered Gen. Braxton Bragg's Army of Tennessee out of Chattanooga and toward Lafayette, Georgia, approximately fifteen miles south of the city. "Now general, you must beat those people out West," Lee said. Longstreet's foot was in mid-stirrup, but Lee's comments caused him to dismount, stand firmly, and face his commander. "If I live," Longstreet promised, "I would not give a single man of my command for a fruitless victory." Lee vowed that any success in the West would be exploited by both Confederate armies. They bid farewell one last time, and Longstreet rode away.[1]

How Longstreet arrived at this point in the fall of 1863 was truly a remarkable realization. Supported by a faction in the Confederate government that had lobbied for a concentration of military forces in the western theater of operations, Longstreet himself had campaigned for a western concentration of forces and his transfer to the West since the fall of 1862. His negative comments about Bragg's generalship in a letter to Lee dated September 5, 1863, and his proposal for Lee and Bragg to switch places suggest that Longstreet coveted the command of the Army of Tennessee. But his desire to serve under his old chief, Joseph E. Johnston, the commander of the Department of the West, certainly overrode any other motives for the transfer. Ever since Johnston had covered for his subordinate's errors in the Battle of Seven Pines, Longstreet had demonstrated an intense loyalty for his former commander. Furthermore, members of the "western concentration bloc," particularly Sen. Louis T. Wigfall and Secretary of War James A. Seddon, had encouraged the general's belief in the necessity to reinforce Bragg's army. Longstreet, who was not entirely convinced of this proposal as late as May 1863, acquiesced to their entreaties and lobbied for his detachment from Lee's army.[2] Moreover, after the defeat at the Battle of Gettysburg, Longstreet sought to escape Lee's search for a decisive offensive victory to end the war and asked to serve under Johnston. If personal advancement coincided with his goal of transferring to the West, Longstreet would readily accept.

BY THE FALL OF 1862, LONGSTREET WAS CONSIDERED LEE'S "OLD Warhorse," but his rise to prominence in the Army of Northern Virginia resulted from a roundabout journey that took him through the U.S. Military Academy, the war with Mexico, and a stint in the antebellum army. James Longstreet was born in the Edgefield District of South Carolina on January 8, 1821. From his earliest recollections, Longstreet conceded that he preferred a military career as opposed to applied study or the life of a planter. Through perseverance and familial ties, the future general, whom the family called "Pete" or "Peter," obtained an appointment to West Point in 1838. James Longstreet's military career had begun.[3]

The cadet made no academic impression at the academy, choosing instead to ready himself for the life of a soldier rather than an engineer. At the age twenty-one, Longstreet graduated from West Point in 1842 ranked fifty-fourth in a class of fifty-six. While his low ranking disqualified him from the more prestigious branches such as the engineers, artillery, and dragoons, he received a commission as a brevet second lieutenant in the infantry, where chances for advancement during peacetime remained minimal. While modern scholars have diminished Longstreet's academic career, they fail to take into account that he attended a rigorous academic institution that in many respects was just as challenging—if not more so—than most traditional four-year institutions of the antebellum era and was better educated than the vast majority of America's population at that time.[4]

After a few years in the antebellum army, Longstreet was assigned to Brig. Gen. Zachary Taylor's Army of Observation on the Texas-Mexico border in 1845. The resulting conflict with Mexico took the young lieutenant to the city of Monterrey, where he fought admirably in the house-to-house fighting that marked this first major campaign of the Mexican-American War. For his actions at Monterrey, Longstreet earned promotion to first lieutenant and adjutant of the 8th Infantry Regiment before being trans-ferred to Maj. Gen. Winfield Scott's Army of Invasion, which was to at-tack the Mexican capital via Veracruz, a port city on the Gulf of Mexico. Longstreet, detained by a previous assignment, did not reach his regiment until February 5, 1847, but he was among Scott's 8,600 troops during the assault on Veracruz on March 9, going ashore three miles south of the city on specially built boats that served as landing craft. After taking Mexico's key port city, the Americans moved into the country's interior, fending off Gen. Antonio Lopez de Santa Anna's forces in the process. Undaunted by the task, Scott ordered his troops toward Mexico City, abandoning his line of communications in a risky venture designed to force the Mexicans to sue for peace. By August, the army had approached the gates of Mexico City, an unprecedented feat to many contemporary observers.[5]

On August 17 the Americans had reached the village of San Agustin, where the two routes to Mexico City led around the Pedregal, a large lava field south of the capital. The Mexicans blocked the direct road toward the city, which entered on the east, with strongly fortified positions. After a council of war, Scott decided to attack both flanks around the Pedregal simultaneously. He ordered Col. David Worth's 2nd Division to take the eastern road toward the town of San Antonio. There the brigades of Cols. John Garland and Newman S. Clarke overwhelmed the Mexican defend-ers, causing them to retreat to the town of Churubusco near the Rio Churu-busco. On the southern side of the river, the Mexicans constructed a "tete de pont," a two-sided earthwork protected by a moat, defended by more than 7,900 soldiers. Five hundred yards away stood the formidable San Ma-teo Convent, also protected by Mexican troops. The two strongholds stood as the main defensive points to the bridge at Churubusco. Scott, without employing detailed reconnaissance, ordered an immediate attack on the two bastions.[6]

As the Americans advanced toward Churubusco, enemy gunfire deci-mated Worth's men as they struggled in the surrounding irrigation ditches during the assault. Worth sent the 5th and 8th Infantry to attack the tete de pont's eastern flank while the 6th Infantry attacked it head on. The 8th Infantry, the only force to reach the earthworks, stalled in the bastion's surrounding moat. Carrying the regimental flag, Longstreet led his comrades while under a heavy fire from the Mexican defenders. As the Americans jumped into the ditch, they received an enfilade fire from the enemy troops within the enclosure. The attackers struggled to scale the fort's slippery walls with their bare hands and finally succeeded by standing on each other's shoulders. Once atop the wall, they engaged the Mexicans in fierce hand-to-hand fighting. After an intense struggle Scott's army won the day, and the Mexicans, recognizing that the enemy had pierced their defenses, retreated toward Mexico City. Longstreet received a promotion to brevet captain for his actions in the Battle of Churubusco. His superiors praised his "gallant and meritorious conduct" on the field.[7]

The successful attack on an apparently impregnable stronghold would profoundly affect Longstreet. Seventeen years later as a Confederate general, he would order an assault on Union-held Fort Sanders in Knoxville. That Tennessee stronghold, with similar high walls and also surrounded by water, proved a formidable obstacle to the Southerners. Calling for the assault to "be made with a determination which will insure success," Longstreet believed that it required the "entire support and cooperation" of his troops. In ordering an assault on a fortified position, he probably recalled his experiences during the Mexican-American War, where the courage and fighting spirit of his fellow soldiers had carried the day. Unlike the Mexicans, however, the Union defenders successfully repulsed the Confederates and won the day.[8]

Longstreet fought admirably in the rest of the Mexico City campaigns, receiving General Worth's commendation and a promotion to brevet major. In the charge to take the enemy bastions, Longstreet once again carried the regimental flag and led the 8th Infantry's assault. He was wounded in the right thigh during the charge on Chapultepec, the Mexican military academy and the key to the capital. Despite meeting heavy resistance, the Americans captured the stronghold and, with it, Mexico City. Longstreet recovered from his wound in an army field hospital and then later in the home of a Mexican family, the Escandóns, who cared for wounded American soldiers. He remained with the Escandón family until December 1847, his wound being slow to heal.[9]

During his convalescence, Longstreet probably reflected on his combat experiences. Although he left no written record during this time, it is likely that he had a great deal to digest. On the one hand, he had witnessed the success of the strategic offensive as Taylor and Scott defied logic and cut their supply lines to pursue a numerically stronger foe into the enemy's interior. Longstreet had been an active participant in a spirited charge against a formidably defended bastion at Chapultepec. He had witnessed how troops, if properly motivated, could overcome great odds and overtake a strongly fortified position. Yet he had also observed how Scott repeatedly utilized flanking movements against the Mexicans. Consequently, the young captain had learned to appreciate the value of a flanking maneuver in lieu of a frontal assault. Considering Longstreet's lackluster performance at West Point, he would be influenced more by his experiences in Mexico than by those in the classroom. This was not a unique phenomenon, for the war with Mexico served as a training ground for dozens of officers who rose to high command in the American Civil War.[10]

As the Americans and Mexicans negotiated a peace settlement, Longstreet, now twenty-six, left Mexico in December 1847 and returned to the United States, where after a brief visit with his family, he courted his first love, Maria Louisa Garland (the daughter of his regimental commander, Col. John Garland) at Jefferson Barracks, Missouri. Longstreet had asked Maria Louisa to marry him prior to his departure to Mexico, but her parents insisted that she wait several years. Louise, as Longstreet called her, soon accompanied her new husband to various posts on the Texas frontier. After a few years the War Department rewarded Longstreet's service on the frontier by promoting him to captain of infantry in the Regular Army, to date from December 7, 1852. The promotion and pay raise came at an opportune time, for the young officer's family was growing. Good fortune smiled on the Longstreets when authorities in Washington named Colonel Garland as the new commander of the Ninth Military District, with headquarters at Albuquerque, New Mexico Territory. Garland's new position allowed him to dispense favorable duties to his son-in-law. Despite incurring resentment at what some considered undue favoritism from his wife's father, Longstreet continued to perform admirably in various administrative duties for the Old Army until the secession crisis of 1860–61.[11]

A month after the election of Republican presidential nominee Abraham Lincoln, South Carolina seceded from the Union. Longstreet declared his allegiance to the South. Although he did not support secession, he considered himself a Southerner and believed in the concept of states' rights. Because he had received his appointment to West Point from Alabama, Longstreet wrote to political leaders from that state, hoping to be awarded a commensurate rank (based on his service in the U.S. Army) in the new provisional force being formed in the South. In December he contacted Alabama congressman J. L. M. Curry, asking him to consider his services if his state seceded. When he received no response, Longstreet wrote to Alabama governor Andrew B. Moore on February 15, 1861, and offered his assistance in case of war.[12] Unknown to Longstreet, the state had seceded on January 11. Delegates from six Southern states met in Montgomery, Alabama, on February 4 and formed the provisional government of the Confederate States of America. In the interim Governor Moore had endorsed Longstreet's initial letter to Curry and forwarded it to the recently appointed Confederate secretary of war, Leroy P. Walker. Moreover, the new Confederate president, Jefferson Davis of Mississippi, had received letters from Longstreet's brother, William, and several Alabama citizens recommending the major for a position in the new Confederate Army.[13]

Following the secession of the seven Lower South states, the nation waited to see how Lincoln would handle the showdown over three army bastions in South Carolina: Castle Pinckney, Fort Moultrie, and Fort Sumter. The Confederate Congress had demanded that the U.S. government remove all troops from the sovereign territory of the Confederacy. As a result, U.S. soldiers had abandoned Fort Moultrie and moved to the island of Sumter in Charleston Harbor. Soon afterward Lincoln received reports that the troops at Fort Sumter were beginning to run out of supplies. He ordered that the forts be resupplied by unarmed boats, placing the Confederates in a no-win situation—they could permit the ships to pass or fire the first shots of the war. On April 12, Confederate officials determined that the Federals in Fort Sumter must surrender. When Sumter's commander, Maj. Robert Anderson, refused terms, shore batteries opened fire on the island fortress. Neither side inflicted any casualties, but Lincoln's attempt to resupply the garrison triggered the Civil War. In the wake of his call for troops to quell the rebellion, four additional Southern states—Virginia, Arkansas, North Carolina, and Tennessee—seceded from the Union.[14]

Longstreet did not hear of the firing on Fort Sumter until the end of April, but he did not tender his resignation to the U.S. Army until May 9. Three weeks later, on June 1, the War Department accepted it. Although several officers tried to persuade the major to remain in the army, he and his family departed Albuquerque in early June. Longstreet left Louise and their four children with friends in El Paso while he traveled with a group to Galveston. There Longstreet met Thomas Jewett Goree, a Texan who would later become his aide de camp during the Civil War. From Galveston the party sailed to New Orleans, where they boarded a train for Richmond, Virginia, the Confederacy's new capital. Longstreet arrived there on June 21 and met Jefferson Davis the following day. Even though there is no record of the discussion between the two men, Goree observed that

Longstreet displayed ample self-confidence before meeting the Confederate president.[15]

Longstreet claimed in his memoirs that he only wanted an assignment with the Confederate paymaster's department, but his commission as a lieutenant colonel in the Alabama state army, to date from March 16, 1861, suggests otherwise. As his foremost biographer, Jeffry Wert, asserts, if Longstreet had truly intended to follow a peaceful existence as a paymaster, he forgot his initial aspiration and quickly acquiesced to a frontline command when Confederate officials presented him with the opportunity. Moreover, his resignation from the U.S. Army suggests that Longstreet flirted with treason during the secession crisis. Southern officials apparently had appointed Longstreet a lieutenant colonel in the infantry and mailed his commission to him while he was still with the U.S. Army in New Mexico. He accepted the commission on May 1, eight days before he resigned from Federal service. For obvious reasons, Longstreet did not mention this in his memoirs. Instead, in light of his omission of this episode, his later dialogue on how commissioned officers in the U.S. Army were bound by the terms of their enlistment seems disingenuous at best.[16]

An indication of Longstreet's true ambitions is revealed in his decision to travel to Richmond instead of Alabama. Although he had accepted a lieutenant colonelcy from Governor Moore, he instead traveled to the Confederacy's capital with his commission. Rather than answer the call of Alabama, as he had promised to Congressman Curry and Governor Moore, Longstreet headed straight for Richmond with the intention of serving the Confederacy. The fruits of his labor earned him a commission as brigadier general from President Davis on June 17, which he accepted eight days later. Davis's appointment, a result of political pressure to assign officers who could quickly organize a regiment, seemed sound. Longstreet immediately tried to raise a regiment of Texans, with Goree and the other members of his travel party benefiting from his newly appointed rank. When the War Department ordered him to command a brigade in the Provisional Army of the Confederate States, the brigadier general remembered his promises and appointed his Texas friends to positions in his new command. In Goree's case it would lead to a lifelong friendship.[17]

Longstreet assumed his new duties with a wealth of experience under his belt. He had lived a happy, carefree life in the Old South and West Point but had experienced the hardships and the brutality of combat during the Mexican-American War. Longstreet also recognized the importance of independence, self-reliance, and well-placed friends and acquaintances. He owed his appointment to West Point to his familial connections and later received select assignments from his father-in-law while he served on the Texas frontier. With this in mind, the new general sought patronage from Confederate officials in Richmond. It is understandable that an officer, after serving for years in a peacetime army, where promotions are slow and choice assignments scarce, would use every means at his disposal to gain advancement. When James Longstreet felt he deserved something, such as a general's commission in the Confederate Army, he did not hesitate to ask influential people for their assistance. This practice would continue during the war. Longstreet was not alone in his approach, for many of his fellow officers on both sides also sought political aid in receiving positions and promotions.[18]

Longstreet's Mexican-American War service also influenced his views as a military commander. Although the war had disenchanted him with the often-costly frontal assault, he believed that brave men, if properly equipped and motivated, could overcome almost any obstacle (as the Americans had with Churubusco's formidable tete de ponte). From Zachary Taylor and Winfield Scott he had also learned the importance of the strategic offensive. Witnessing Scott's flanking movements probably convinced Longstreet that it was better to outflank a strong position than to attack it directly. The young officer's experience in the antebellum army would also serve him well during the Civil War. With his strong will and abundant self-confidence, Longstreet encountered no difficulties in handling troops as an independent commander in Texas. He had acquired a wealth of experience as an adjutant, a garrison commander, a commissary officer, and a paymaster, not to mention his combat experience on the frontier. Above all, Longstreet did not allow his West Point education to restrict him to the traditional military thinking so typical of his fellow officers. While he recognized the advantages of interior lines and defeating an enemy's force in detail, Longstreet proved himself adaptable to changes if the tactical situation presented itself (as they would at Chickamauga and the Wilderness), in the process emerging as one of the foremost Confederate generals of the Civil War.[19]

In June 1861 Longstreet received orders to serve under Maj. Gen. Pierre G. T. Beauregard as commander of the 4th Brigade, which consisted of the 1st, 11th, and 17th Regiments of Virginia Volunteer Infantry. The 4th Brigade reported to Manassas, Virginia, a key rail center twenty-five miles southwest of Washington, D.C., as Beauregard's force of 18,000 men stood ready to face Union major general Irvin McDowell and his 35,000-man army. Longstreet immediately set out to train his raw and mostly ill-equipped troops. Many of the men had no military experience and often resented receiving orders. The common soldier of the Civil War grudgingly

*Lt. Gen. James Longstreet.
From the author's collection.*

respected authority, and officers often had difficulty earning their respect. Yet despite these initial shortcomings, on July 16, in anticipation of a Union advance, Beauregard ordered the 4th Brigade to protect Blackburn's Ford, a key point where the Centreville Road crossed Bull Run Creek between Manassas and Centreville.[20]

In his initial test as a Civil War commander, Longstreet did not disappoint. Dressed in civilian clothes and chewing a cigar, the general calmly deployed his men as Union soldiers advanced against his lines on the morning of the eighteenth. Longstreet had assumed a defensive stance on the south side of Bull Run and allowed the Federals to exhaust themselves with repeated attacks on the strong Confederate position. After easily repulsing these assaults, Longstreet ordered an artillery barrage and a counterattack that forced the enemy to withdraw and seek an alternative route of advance against the Confederates. The tactics Longstreet employed at Blackburn's Ford sharply contrasted with the bloody frontal assaults he had witnessed in Mexico. His troops had not only used the terrain of the creek to their advantage but also had enhanced it with earthworks constructed from logs, dirt, and driftwood. Unfortunately for Longstreet, his brigade did not participate in the Confederate victory at the Battle of First Manassas three days later. Afterward Beauregard ordered him to pursue the fleeing Federals and cut off their line of retreat, but Gen. Joseph E. Johnston, realizing that his own command was almost as disorganized as McDowell's, called off the pursuit because he believed an attack on the retreating force would have been costly and ineffective. Nevertheless, the victory at Manassas surprised many Confederates who had feared defeat just days before the battle. Despite the victory, Johnston and Beauregard took no further action against the Federals.[21]

Longstreet had little time to savor the victory, for shortly after Manassas, Beauregard ordered him to occupy Centreville a few miles north of Manassas Junction. For the next several weeks, Longstreet devoted his time to completing his staff organization and drilling his inexperienced troops. The Confederates remained in their camps for the next few months as both sides prepared for a long struggle.[22]

Frustration and boredom ultimately led the Confederate high command to hold a council of war. On October 1 President Davis traveled to Centreville to confer with Generals Beauregard, Johnston, and Gustavus W. Smith about the army's future plans for offensive operations. After his arrival on July 21, Johnston had assumed command of the Confederate forces around Manassas. A native Virginian and West Point graduate, the fifty-four-year-old general had served ably in the Seminole and Mexican-American Wars. Rising to quartermaster general of the U.S. Army, Johnston had resigned his commission and joined the Confederacy. In the fall of 1861, Davis ranked him in seniority behind Gens. Samuel Cooper, Albert Sidney Johnston, and Robert E. Lee. Fuming over what he considered a personal affront, Johnston wrote a disparaging letter to the president citing his grievances. The ranks remained unchanged, and neither man forgave the other for the perceived injustice: Johnston for his ranking, and Davis for being challenged on an administrative technicality. For the remainder of the war, Johnston remained distrustful of the president, while Davis believed that the general refused to cooperate with the government.[23]

The tension between the men was evident in the October 1 military conference at Fairfax Court House. The meeting addressed administrative matters and a proposed offensive into Union territory but accomplished nothing except to further the resentment between Davis and some of his subordinates. Despite the acrimony, Davis, Beauregard, and Johnston reviewed Longstreet's troops and spoke favorably of their performance during the campaign. On October 7 Longstreet received a promotion to major general and an assignment to lead the 3rd Division of Beauregard's Corps in Johnston's Army of the Potomac. Favorable reports from Johnston praising

Longstreet's actions at Blackburn's Ford probably influenced the promotion. Longstreet reciprocated by supporting Johnston during his conflict with the president. The two generals soon formed a strong friendship that lasted for the rest of their lives. Unfortunately, Longstreet did not keep his critical opinions of Davis's strategic views to himself. When Captain Goree remarked that the president might have had political motives for delaying an advance on Washington, the general retorted, "That may be very good politics, but . . . very poor fighting."[24]

Longstreet's opinion of Davis also became apparent to others outside his staff. In early November 1861 Davis ordered Mississippi politician Lucius Q. C. Lamar to report to Johnston as a volunteer aide on his staff. Davis had an ulterior motive in this assignment, instructing Lamar to eliminate any "ill feeling between the Potomac generals and the President." Lamar, Longstreet's cousin by marriage, immediately noted his kinsman's views. On November 11 he wrote his wife: "I fear that cousin James Longstreet is taking sides against the administration. He will certainly commit a grave error if he does." Lamar's concern for Longstreet's military career suggests that the authorities in Richmond were sensitive to the tension between Davis and Johnston. During his visit to Fairfax, Davis may have detected the hostility of many on Johnston's staff. Whatever effect Lamar might have had on Longstreet is unknown since he remained ill and confined to his quarters during most of his assignment.[25] There is no record that Lamar discussed the president's concerns with Longstreet, and if the latter's comments reached the president, it certainly demonstrates a serious lapse in judgment on his part. Clearly Longstreet forgot his military training and reverted to the mores of the frontier, where a man was expected to be blunt and outspoken. In the military, however, open criticism of the commander in chief borders on insubordination. Longstreet's gruff comments about Davis's political decisions and his condemnation of appointments in turn lowered the president's estimate of Longstreet.

Louis T. Wigfall, a South Carolinian by birth and a Texan by choice, led one of Longstreet's brigades in his new divisional command. Wigfall's military service proved brief, for in the fall of 1862, Texans voted him to the Confederate Senate. Wigfall and Davis shared a checkered past. During the secession crisis and the early months of the war, the two had established a cordial, if not friendly, relationship while Wigfall briefly served on the president's staff. Yet the harmonious relationship did not last long, for Wigfall, who had a fondness for drink and a habit of engaging in tirades, soon fell out of favor with the Davis family. Portents of trouble appeared in the summer of 1861 over personal matters involving their wives, but the discord soon became political when the Texan supported Johnston in the quarrel over rank.[26]

While the Confederate Army remained inactive, Longstreet continued to earn the commanding general's confidence. In January 1862, after Beauregard left for his new assignment in the western theater, Johnston embraced Longstreet as one of his most trusted subordinates. He demonstrated this in late spring when the authorities in Richmond recommended that Longstreet be transferred to North Carolina. Johnston's insistence on retaining the general's services proved prescient once the Confederates abandoned their position at Centreville on March 8 and retreated toward Richmond, establishing a defensive position near Yorktown behind the Warwick River on the Virginia Peninsula, formed by the York and James rivers. The withdrawal changed the strategic situation near the capital, prompting deliberations within the War Department. On April 14, 1862, Davis summoned Secretary of War George W. Randolph, Lee, and Johnston to discuss Johnston's desire to abandon the Yorktown line in favor of a position in front of Richmond. Johnston ordered Gustavus W. Smith and Longstreet to accompany him to the meeting. During the conference, Longstreet silently observed as Johnston and Smith proposed to abandon their position on the Peninsula. Davis, Lee, and Randolph rejected any retreat, arguing that it would place the capital in jeopardy. Davis then asked for Longstreet's opinion. Longstreet replied that he felt Maj. Gen. George B. McClellan and his Army of the Potomac would not advance until early May. Realizing that the president had asked his opinion out of mere courtesy, Longstreet reverted to his previous stoic silence. When the meeting adjourned, Davis maintained that the army remain at Yorktown.[27]

Regardless, it did not take long for Johnston to disregard Davis's instructions. On May 2 Johnston ordered his division commanders to retreat up the Peninsula, Longstreet commanding the army's rear guard as the Federals advanced toward the Confederate capital. On the fifth, near Williamsburg, five of Longstreet's six brigades engaged the enemy in a rear-guard action that became a full-scale battle. Afterward the Confederates resumed their retreat up the Peninsula to the town of Fair Oaks, less than ten miles from Richmond. The proximity of Union troops to the capital alarmed Davis. He and Lee urged Johnston to attack. Johnston did indeed devise a plan to strike the Federals, ordering Longstreet on May 31 to lead an assault on McClellan's left flank. Longstreet inexplicably took a wrong road and then quarreled with Maj. Gen. Benjamin Huger over seniority and whose troops had the right of way. The dispute delayed for several hours the early morning attack on the Federal Army. In the resulting Battle of

Seven Pines, Longstreet performed poorly. Not only did he become lost but also acted indecisively during the second day of fighting by giving imprecise orders to his subordinates. Although Johnston failed to provide written orders for the attack on the thirty-first, Longstreet failed to carry out his superior's oral instructions, and his dispute with Huger showed him at his worst. In blaming Huger for his own errors, Longstreet made several misleading and self-serving statements that Johnston accepted, thereby gaining Longstreet's loyalty for the rest of the war.[28]

The debate over who was at fault during these critical moments of Seven Pines began on June 7, when Longstreet wrote Johnston (who was in Richmond recovering from a serious wound suffered during the battle) blaming the unsuccessful Confederate attack on "the slow movements of General Huger's command." But he failed to mention the two incidents that caused Huger's delay: Longstreet's division taking the wrong road, and his quarrel with the general over seniority. Johnston accepted Longstreet's version of events and blamed Huger for the delay. Huger protested the report and supplied his version of the events at Seven Pines, blaming the holdup on Longstreet's blundering onto the wrong road and their subsequent quarrel over seniority. He also demanded that Longstreet "correct the errors" in his account.[29]

Huger asked Johnston to investigate the matter. The disgruntled general also wrote Secretary Randolph and President Davis to demand a court of inquiry to prove his innocence. Despite Huger's protests, the War Department failed to form the requested court, and Johnston continued to acquiesce with Longstreet's effort to make Huger the scapegoat for the botched assault, going so far as assuming the blame for the mix up and asking General Smith to delete certain parts of his report that criticized Longstreet. Ultimately, since Longstreet failed to answer Huger's assertions, the War Department dropped the matter. Even in their postwar accounts, Longstreet and Johnston adhered to their version of events, both men blaming Huger for the failure at Seven Pines. Johnston's biographer, Craig Symonds, suggests that the commanding general had two reasons for distorting the facts. First, Johnston wanted to protect Longstreet, whom he had come to respect and rely on during the previous year. He acknowledged Longstreet's support during his quarrel with Davis and probably sought to reward him for his loyalty. Second, Johnston felt responsible for Longstreet's misunderstanding of orders, reasoning that if he criticized Longstreet for the confusion, he would in fact be criticizing himself for giving such unclear instructions. Johnston's vanity would not allow that.[30]

Historians have used Longstreet's poor conduct at Seven Pines to criticize him for using scapegoats to absolve himself of purported incompetence. But blaming another for one's own mistake was not out of the ordinary for Civil War generals. The history of the war is replete with instances of commanders unfairly blaming subordinates. Ulysses S. Grant wrongly blamed Brig. Gen. Lew Wallace for perceived insubordination at the Battle of Shiloh, while Maj. Gen. Thomas J. "Stonewall" Jackson unfairly castigated Brig. Gen. Brooke Garnett during the Shenandoah Valley campaign of 1862. Even though Longstreet's treatment of Huger cannot be defended, Longstreet was no worse than his contemporaries and not alone in blaming others for his failures.[31]

Despite Johnston's extensive communications with the War Department and his subordinates, his wound kept him from returning to active field command. Davis realized that the army would have to be given to another full general. On June 1 he appointed Robert E. Lee to command the force that Lee would soon rechristen the Army of Northern Virginia. Lee took over under unfavorable circumstances. Earlier in the war, soldiers had dubbed him "Granny Lee" and "Evacuating Lee" after an unsuccessful campaign in western Virginia. Now they called him the "King of Spades" for ordering them to entrench and fortify their defensive positions around Richmond. The truth was that the Southerners knew very little about him. They knew he had served honorably in the Mexican-American War and in the peacetime army, but his Civil War record up to Seven Pines was sketchy. His promotion to commander of the principal army in Virginia thus caught many Confederates off guard and displeased others.[32]

Lee soon quieted his critics by launching a series of assaults on McClellan's army that became known as the Seven Days Battles. In a series of assaults, the Confederates drove the Federals back to Harrison's Landing on the James River, about thirty-five miles from Richmond. The often uncoordinated attacks caused by poor timing and faulty staff work resulted in heavy casualties for the Army of Northern Virginia and rendered it unable to pursue the reeling Army of the Potomac. Realizing the need to reorganize his command, Lee evaluated the performances of his subordinate generals. Many times during the Seven Days, subordinate generals failed to carry out orders. Lee's assessment of Longstreet, however, was favorable, and he valued his subordinate's self-confidence and common sense during the campaign. Unlike his performance at Seven Pines, Longstreet handled his troops well, offered sound advice, and provided reliable reconnaissance for the army. Lee, like Beauregard and Johnston before him, placed much confidence in Longstreet. So, without issuing promotions or titles, Lee divided his army

Gen. Robert E. Lee, commander of the Army of Northern Virginia, maintained a warm relationship with Longstreet.
LIBRARY OF CONGRESS
(LC-B8172-0001)

into "Longstreet's Command" and "Jackson's Command," a de facto two-corps arrangement, and considered Longstreet his second in command.[33]

The Confederate victories in the Seven Days Battles had saved Richmond, but the campaign had cost the army more than 20,000 casualties—losses that the Confederacy could ill afford. The Army of Northern Virginia briefly rested before resuming offensive operations on July 13, with Lee ordering Jackson north to meet a new Union army under Maj. Gen. John Pope. The resulting victory in the Battle of Second Manassas reaffirmed Lee's confidence in Longstreet and Jackson, as the Confederates defeated the latest Union advance toward their capital. This battle solidified Longstreet's belief in defensive tactics, specifically, allowing the enemy to attack a fortified position, then counterattacking the weakened foe. First employing this tactic with success at Blackburn's Ford, Longstreet grew even more confident after the impressive Confederate triumph at Second Manassas. He also believed that Lee's combination of the strategic offensive and the tactical defensive had reaped immense rewards. Years later Longstreet would regard the Second Manassas campaign as the Army of Northern Virginia's greatest achievement. As his foremost biographer, Jeffry D. Wert, suggests, Longstreet would attempt to replicate the concept of a resolute defense followed by a rapid counteroffensive, a goal that would elude him for the remainder of the war.[34]

Soon after Second Manassas, Lee proposed an invasion of Maryland to attempt to fight a decisive battle that would force the Union to sue for peace, earn diplomatic recognition from Europe, and allow his army to forage beyond Virginia. McClellan's extreme caution (even with Lee's orders in his hand) allowed Lee time to gather his divided forces at Sharpsburg, Maryland, near the banks of Antietam Creek. On September 17, 1862, the Confederates survived repeated assaults until finally repulsing a final Federal attack on their right flank. Lee wanted to resume the offensive the next day, but Longstreet and Jackson convinced him that the army must retreat to Virginia, and the Army of the Northern Virginia withdrew on the nineteenth.[35] The commanding general's fondness for Longstreet became apparent to those around them on the evening of the seventeenth, when the major general failed to report to army headquarters. "But where is Longstreet?" asked a visibly concerned Lee. Unknown to the general and his staff, Longstreet had stopped to help a family whose house had been set on fire by an artillery shell. When at last he arrived, calmly chewing a cigar, a relieved Lee grasped him by the hand and said, "Ah! Here is Longstreet; here's my old war-horse!"[36]

CLEARLY LEE AND LONGSTREET HAD ESTABLISHED A WARM RELAtionship, a friendship that grew stronger after Longstreet's promotion to lieutenant general and command of the First Corps after the Antietam campaign. Yet Longstreet still yearned to serve under his old commander, Joe Johnston. On October 6, while the Army of Northern Virginia camped near Winchester, he wrote Johnston, appreciatively thanking him for a photograph before discussing the latter's appointment to command the Department of the West:

> *I can't become reconciled at the idea of your going west. I command the 1st Corps in this army; if you will take it you are more than welcome to it, and I have no doubt but the command of the entire army will fall to you before spring. . . . If it is possible for me to relieve you by going west don't hesitate to send me. It would put me to no great inconvenience. On the contrary it will give me pleasure if I can't relieve you of it. I fear that you ought not to go where you will be exposed to the handicaps that you will meet with out there. I am yet entirely sound and believe that I can endure anything.*[37]

Before he was wounded at the Battle of Seven Pines on May 31, 1862, Gen. Joseph E. Johnston was Longstreet's commander and mentor. By the fall of 1862, Longstreet yearned to serve again under Johnston, the newly appointed commander of the Department of the West.
LIBRARY OF CONGRESS
(LC-B813-2109)

While these words could be interpreted as a selfish quest for independent command and personal glory that his enemies so often imputed to him in their postwar writings, Longstreet's letter merely reveals his attachment to his former commander.

One Longstreet biographer has argued that this letter represented an "extraordinarily unfavorable assessment of Lee's ability." Longstreet, however, did not overtly criticize his commander. The Antietam campaign had cost the Confederates more than 10,000 casualties that Longstreet knew the South could ill afford. This realization drew him to Johnston, a commander who shared his conviction in defensive tactics. Second Manassas had solidified his belief that the Confederacy's most likely road to military success lay in defensive tactics and that Lee's quest for the decisive battle—as shown by the Maryland campaign—would deplete the South's meager manpower resources. Yet the offer to switch places with Johnston does seem odd, considering that Johnston led an army before his wounding at Seven Pines and his pride would have not allowed him to accept what amounted to a demotion in his former command. Longstreet's proposal was a clumsy attempt to express his gratitude to Johnston for his guidance and for sustaining him in the controversy with Huger following Seven Pines rather than a means to escape Lee's authority. Longstreet thought that Johnston, a native of Virginia, would want to remain in the eastern theater, but he did not consider the impossibility of Johnston accepting a demotion in rank or responsibilities.[38]

The Army of Northern Virginia's extended stay at Winchester allowed Longstreet to write letters to old acquaintances. He wrote his old friend Louis T. Wigfall to inquire about the senator's feud with President Davis: "It is no business of mine, but I would like to take the liberty to beg you not to allow anything to bring about any differences between you [and Davis]. We think that all of our hopes rest upon you and the hopes of the country rest upon the Army." Once more Longstreet had taken it upon himself to write an influential politician to discuss matters that, in reality, were none of his concern, attempting to flatter Wigfall by suggesting that the hopes of the Confederacy depended on him. Although the general left no record as to why he wrote Wigfall during the fall of 1862, William Garrett Piston has demonstrated in his study of Longstreet's antebellum military career that Longstreet was motivated by his pursuit of professional advancement. Thus during the Civil War, he probably felt that the Texas senator could help promote his career. But Longstreet remained blissfully unaware of the intensity of the feud between Davis and Wigfall. Unlike Lee, who witnessed firsthand the collapse of Davis's relationship with Johnston, Longstreet never understood the president's character nor the wisdom of avoiding the anti-Davis faction. He also failed to realize his own association to the Wigfall-Johnston opposition camp.[39]

Although Davis expressed no disapproval of Longstreet's relationships with Wigfall and Johnston, he probably did not trust the First Corps commander because of his outspoken criticism. If he caught wind of Longstreet's comments, it probably provoked two of the president's personality traits—his inability to accept uninvited criticism gracefully, and his tendency to equate opposition to his policies as disloyalty to the Confederacy. Furthermore, shortly after the surrender of Forts Henry and Donelson in 1862, Longstreet had reportedly criticized the strategy of Gen. Albert Sidney Johnston, the ranking general in the West. If accurate, then he committed a third sin by criticizing one of the president's idols. Davis apparently had admired Sidney Johnston since their West Point days during the 1820s, establishing a close friendship that lasted until the general's death at Shiloh on April 6, 1862. Davis regarded any criticism of his friends as criticism of himself.[40]

In addition to his alliance with Wigfall and Johnston, Longstreet also received the support of Alabama congressman Jabez L. M. Curry, Vice Pres. Alexander Stephens, and Brig. Gen. Robert Toombs, three political adversaries of President Davis. Curry had endorsed Longstreet in his initial bid to earn a commission from Alabama in the spring of 1861. The congressman, who regarded Davis as cold and distant, severed his connection with the president in 1862 and soon aligned himself with anti-administration critics. Longstreet also had come to Stephens's attention through the vice president's fellow Georgian, General Toombs. An influential lawyer, Toombs had served as the Confederate secretary of state until his resignation in the summer of 1861 to lead a brigade under Longstreet. When he failed to receive a promotion after Antietam, Toombs resigned his commission and returned to Richmond, where he spent most of his time railing against the Confederate government in general and Davis in particular. He sang Longstreet's praises to his good friend and political ally, Stephens, who came to view Longstreet as positively as Toombs did. By late 1862 the vice president had detached himself from Davis's camp and began writing letters and speeches criticizing the president.[41]

WHILE LONGSTREET RECKLESSLY ASSOCIATED WITH ANTI-administration politicians, in November 1862 the Army of Northern Virginia had to face yet another threat from the Army of the Potomac, now led by Maj. Gen. Ambrose E. Burnside. The urgency of the situation forced Longstreet to put aside any notions of politics or trading places with Johnston as Lee ordered the First Corps to Fredericksburg on November 19 to meet the latest advance on Richmond. After several weeks and many delays, the Federals crossed the Rappahannock on the morning of December 13 and moved through Fredericksburg toward Lee's army, which was positioned on the high ground overlooking the city. Burnside's men attacked the Confederates, only to meet disastrous results. After a truce to bury the dead on December 15, the Federals withdrew across the river. The Fredericksburg campaign made a deep impression on Longstreet, highlighting the importance of field fortifications and battlefield reconnaissance. Above all, it reinforced Longstreet's belief in the inherent strength of a well-chosen defensive position.[42]

Following Fredericksburg, Lee was content to remain where he was and await the next Union move. Longstreet used the time to renew his correspondence with Wigfall and Johnston. After appointing Johnston as commander of the Department of the West, Davis had decided on a complete reorganization of the Confederacy's western forces after the failed October offensive into Kentucky, which convinced him of the need for a unified command west of the Appalachians. In his new position, Johnston would command all Confederate troops from the Appalachians to the Mississippi River, including the Army of Mississippi under Lt. Gen. John C. Pemberton and the Army of Tennessee under Gen. Braxton Bragg. Davis designed Johnston's authority to enable him to shuttle troops to any threatened point within his command. Johnston disagreed with the president's strategy and instead advocated a concentration of forces to ward off an enemy offensive. The two strong-willed men thus held divergent views as to how the newly created super-department should be run.[43]

Soon after arriving at his new headquarters in Chattanooga, Johnston began to confer with Wigfall on political matters and military strategy. Each man used Johnston's new position as theater commander to promote his own personal agenda. In Johnston's case, he knew that Wigfall had befriended the new secretary of war, James A. Seddon, and worked diligently to have the senator persuade Seddon to advance the general's strategic concepts. For his part, Wigfall gladly acquiesced, since supporting Johnston gave him an opportunity to challenge Davis's military policies. They and Seddon exchanged a series of secret letters proposing a western concentration of forces, thus assuming prominent positions in what historians Thomas Lawrence Connelly and Archer Jones have called the "western concentration bloc."[44]

In January 1863, two months after Johnston received his appointment as theater commander, Longstreet approached Lee with a plan to hold the Rappahannock line with a corps while the rest of the army reinforced the West. The commanding general rejected his lieutenant's proposal, but Longstreet persisted, and each time Lee ignored Longstreet's pleas for sending troops west. On February 4 Longstreet wrote Wigfall and told him about his plan. He denied seeking the glory of an independent command but believed that he "should make suggestions to my commander whenever I think it my duty to do so." The general maintained that in "the far west, there appears to be opportunities for all kinds of moves to great advantages."[45]

Several scholars have cited Longstreet's correspondence about a western concentration and attributed his desire to serve in the West solely as a selfish bid to obtain an independent command. One historian has asserted that Longstreet was "chafing to get out of the shadow of Lee and win more glory for himself." Another has suggested that the general was anxious to escape Lee's army, which was replete with pro-Virginia bias. Longstreet, however, did not loath serving under Lee's command but was worried

Louis T. Wigfall, Confederate
senator from Texas, was
a member of the "western
concentration bloc" and a strong
ally of Joseph E. Johnston
and James Longstreet.
LIBRARY OF CONGRESS
(LC-B813-3874A)

about Lee's aggressiveness. Longstreet was principally concerned that the Virginia army had suffered a high number of casualties under Lee, a pattern of losses the Confederacy could not maintain and win the war. Certainly, Longstreet desired personal advancement. Yet that ambition, when placed within the context of the Civil War and the generals of both the Union and Confederate armies, was not out of the ordinary. Whether they were politically appointed amateurs or West Point graduates, many generals—North and South—repeatedly sought to advance their careers. In many cases the military profession was shaped through the use of benefactors and political patronage. Longstreet's aspiration to go West was thus a combination of his desire for promotion and the respect he had for his former commander, Joe Johnston—the fact that Johnston was a proven commander whose defensive proclivities mirrored Longstreet's own were additional benefits. He assumed, however, that if Bragg failed again, Johnston would likely appoint Longstreet to command the Army of Tennessee.[46]

In February 1863 he put aside his discussions on grand strategy upon receiving orders from the War Department to command the Department of Virginia and North Carolina so to protect the southern approaches to Richmond and to forage for the Army of Northern Virginia. While Longstreet's force scavenged for food in the southeastern corner of the state, on April 29

the Army of the Potomac launched a spring offensive across the Rappahannock. That day Lee ordered him to return to Fredericksburg with his two
divisions. Difficulties kept Longstreet from arriving in time to reinforce Lee
for the Battle of Chancellorsville, a decisive but costly victory for the Confederates, who suffered more than 12,000 casualties, including the loss of
Stonewall Jackson (who died on May 10).[47]

Afterward Longstreet met with Seddon. He continued to lobby for a
concentration in the West, where Maj. Gen. Ulysses S. Grant had recently
advanced against the Army of Mississippi, stationed at Vicksburg. As he
had done in February, Longstreet proposed using interior lines to transport
reinforcements to the western armies—that if his corps could be sent, he
and Johnston could join Bragg and move against the Federals in Middle
Tennessee. Once the Confederate juggernaut defeated the Union armies,
Longstreet reasoned, it could then move up through Kentucky and into
Ohio in a more successful version of Bragg's 1862 Kentucky campaign. He
argued that as a Confederate force advanced into Union territory, Grant's
army would be forced to abandon its campaign against Vicksburg to meet
the Southern threat. Seddon but was unconvinced, believing that an attack
on Washington, D.C., would probably bring about the same results.[48]

Longstreet's discourse on grand strategy continued into the second
week of May as he conferred with Lee to plan for a summer offensive. As
he had discussed with Seddon, Longstreet advocated a reinforcement of
Bragg's army in Tennessee by detaching his corps from the Army of Northern Virginia, with the intention of advancing into Union territory. According to Longstreet's postwar recollections, the two men conferred at length
about the proper course of action for the summer of 1863. Lee countered
Longstreet's western concentration proposal by advocating an offensive
into Pennsylvania and Maryland. Longstreet objected because while the
northern campaign unfolded Vicksburg might fall. Lee, however, was determined to pursue his plan for a northern invasion. Writing years after
the Lost Cause advocates had made him a virtual pariah in the South,
Longstreet maintained that he agreed to the Pennsylvania offensive only
because Lee's assurance that the Army of Northern Virginia would invade the North, take a formidable position, and then compel the Federals to attack.[49] Longstreet's postwar recollection of his May meeting with
Lee might have been influenced by his desire to challenge his status as the
scapegoat for the Gettysburg debacle. A letter he wrote to Senator Wigfall
on the day of the last meeting with Lee, casts doubt on his postwar account.
In his correspondence with the Texas senator, Longstreet did not mention Lee's acquiescence to a northern invasion based on defensive tactics.

Instead, the First Corps commander informed Wigfall that Lee's plans for a summer offensive had changed his outlook on a concentration of forces in the West. Longstreet appeared enthusiastic about the potential for an all-out offensive into the North. "If we could cross the Potomac with one hundred & fifty thousand men, I think we could demand Lincoln to declare his purpose," he wrote. In conclusion, Longstreet told Wigfall that if the Confederate War Department did send troops to the western theater, they should go to Johnston, not Pemberton, because he doubted the latter's "fighting ability."[50]

Longstreet ultimately failed to commit to the western concentration bloc as did Wigfall, Johnston, Beauregard, and Seddon. Although he had sought an assignment in the West, he remained dedicated to serving under Lee and fighting for the Confederate cause in the East. Longstreet's letter also indicates that he appeared less adamant about obtaining an independent command than some historians have argued. As for his criticism of Pemberton, this perhaps reflected Lee's views, given that Lee had known the general while serving as Davis's military advisor in South Carolina. (At that time Pemberton commanded the Department of South Carolina, Georgia, and Florida.) As Longstreet intimated in his postwar recollections, he remained Lee's close confidant.[51]

Lee met with Davis and his cabinet on May 14 to propose his plans for an invasion of the North. After several days of talks, the president approved the proposal. Accordingly, Lee reorganized the Army of Northern Virginia into three corps under Longstreet and two new lieutenant generals, A. P. Hill and Richard S. Ewell, who led divisions formerly commanded by Stonewall Jackson. The Confederates began their northern advance on June 3, taking a circuitous route to avoid contact with Union forces. On July 1, the day after a brigade of Hill's Third Corps had first encountered a Union cavalry patrol near Gettysburg, Pennsylvania, both armies fought for control of the town and the nearby high ground. A small skirmish soon escalated into a fierce battle. After being routed north of town, the Federals seized control of Cemetery Ridge south of Gettysburg as the day ended. The next morning Lee ordered Longstreet to turn the newly arrived Union army's left flank. Although the late-afternoon assault shattered a Federal corps, the northern army held its position. On the third Lee ordered an assault on the Union's center. This attack, spearheaded by Maj. Gen. George E. Pickett's division of Longstreet's corps, reached the crest of Cemetery Ridge, but after suffering heavy casualties, the survivors retreated to their original position. On the Fourth of July, Lee rested his battered army before beginning the long retreat to Virginia on the fifth.[52]

Lee and his principal subordinates performed poorly during the Gettysburg campaign. Yet following the battle, the commanding general assumed the responsibility for his army's failure in Pennsylvania and broached the idea of resigning. Davis, however, refused to entertain any discussion of Lee's removal and instead requested the general to travel to Richmond to discuss future Confederate strategy. Like Lee, Longstreet also felt he had fought the Battle of Gettysburg against his better judgment, acknowledging his poor performance in a letter to his uncle Augustus Baldwin Longstreet. A week later, on August 2, Longstreet told Senator Wigfall that the Army of Northern Virginia had lost the battle because the Confederates faced a numerically superior Union army. He also wrote Secretary of War Seddon later that month and repeated his request to be sent to the western theater. This he reiterated in a second letter to Wigfall on the eighteenth. Longstreet assured the Texas senator that he had no personal motives in the transfer, instead claiming only a desire to be "second to Johnston," whose defensive philosophy mirrored his own.[53]

On August 31, during his conference with President Davis, Lee wrote to Longstreet, instructing him to "prepare the army for offensive operations."[54] Distressed with the prospect of another advance against the Army of the Potomac, the First Corps commander responded with a letter reiterating his earlier views on a western concentration:

> *I don't know that we can reasonably hope to accomplish much here by offensive operations, unless we are strong enough to cross the Potomac. . . . I know little of the conditions of our affairs in the west, but am inclined to the opinion that our best opportunity for great results is in Tennessee. If we hold the defensive here with two corps[,] and sent the other to operate in Tenn. with that army[,] I think that we could accomplish more than by an advance from here. . . . I know of no other means of acting upon that principle at present except to depend upon our fortifications in Va. and concentrate with one corps of this army and such as may be drawn from others, in Tennessee and destroy Rosecranz [sic] army. I feel assured that this is practicable, and that greater advantages will be gained than by operations here.[55]*

Longstreet stressed his view in another letter three days later, acknowledging that he questioned Bragg's competency. "I doubt if General Bragg has confidence in his troops or himself either. He is not likely to do a great deal for us." Yet Longstreet assured Lee that he had no ulterior plans in seeking a transfer.[56]

President Davis actually wanted to send Lee across the Appalachians to take charge in the West. Following the fall of Vicksburg on July 4, Union forces under Maj. Gen. William S. Rosecrans had maneuvered Bragg's army out of Middle Tennessee, out of Chattanooga, and finally out of the state altogether. By early September the Confederates had retreated to northern Georgia and awaited the next Federal advance. Desperate for some success in the West, Davis asked Lee to take part of the Army of Northern Virginia and personally lead the western army. Lee responded that he would do whatever was best for the Confederacy, but he disagreed with Davis's proposal. The president respected Lee's opinion, and although he acquiesced in Lee's opposition to a transfer, he insisted that Bragg needed reinforcements from the Virginia army. The two men finally agreed to send Longstreet and his corps to the West.[57]

After conferring with authorities in Richmond for about two weeks, Lee returned to the Army of Northern Virginia on September 7. That day he ordered Longstreet to reinforce Bragg with two divisions of the First Corps. Longstreet proposed two days as "ample time" for the move. While the First Corps commander readied his command, Davis grew uneasy. On the eighth the president wrote Lee that his "presence in the western army would be worth more than the addition of a corps." Lee was also having second thoughts, but for a different reason. He realized that without Longstreet's troops, the Army of Northern Virginia would be reduced to only 45,000 men, leaving it vulnerable to a Union offensive. The general wrote Davis on the ninth, advising that Rosecrans "ought to be attacked as soon as possible" and that Longstreet should be returned to the army. Two days later Lee reiterated his previous point to the president.[58]

Despite the ambivalence of Davis and Lee, Longstreet enthusiastically prepared for his western operation. On September 9 the first components of the First Corps departed for northern Georgia. Longstreet had lobbied for a western concentration and his participation since the fall of 1862. Although historians have attributed his desire to join Bragg's army to a selfish search for independent command, his goals appear more complicated. Longstreet's negative comments about Bragg's generalship in his September 5 letter to Lee and his earlier proposal that Bragg and Longstreet switch places suggest that he coveted the command of the Army of Tennessee. Yet while Longstreet did seek personal advancement like many of his peers, his desire to serve under Joe Johnston also influenced his desire for a transfer west. From the day Johnston had covered for his errors during Seven Pines, Longstreet had demonstrated an intense loyalty to his old commander. Furthermore, members of the western concentration bloc, particularly Wigfall and Seddon, had encouraged Longstreet's belief in the necessity of reinforcing Bragg's army, something that the First Corps commander factored into his notion of obtaining a promotion. Longstreet, who was not entirely convinced of a western concentration as late as May 1863, acquiesced to their proposals and lobbied for his detachment from Lee's army after the defeat at Gettysburg, asking to serve under Johnston.[59] Above all, the general sought to escape Lee's costly search for a decisive victory to end the war. If personal advancement happened to coincide with these other goals, so be it.

As Longstreet corresponded with influential politicians while pursuing his transfer to the West, he focused on the notion of serving under Johnston rather than Braxton Bragg. Although the criticism of Bragg's generalship was in poor taste, especially given his status as a senior officer in the Confederate Army, Longstreet's views were shared by a large segment of the Southern populace in the fall of 1863.[60] Yet he failed to fully recognize the magnitude of conflict and dissent in the command structure of the Army of Tennessee. Dissension had festered in the Confederacy's foremost western army since the failed Kentucky campaign of October 1862. The army's corps commanders had criticized Bragg and urged his removal. Davis and Johnston had failed to stem the discord. When Longstreet arrived in northern Georgia, he did not appreciate either the volatility of Bragg's detractors or the determination of Davis to maintain Bragg in the field while keeping Johnston chained to an administrative desk.

2

"ONE OF THE MOST GALLANT STRUGGLES"

OPERATION WESTWARD HO AND THE CHICKAMAUGA CAMPAIGN

THE MILITARY SITUATION IN THE WEST WAS PRECARIOUS ON THE eve of Longstreet's transfer to the Army of Tennessee. On August 16, 1863—while Davis and Lee discussed Confederate strategy—General Rosecrans had ordered his Army of the Cumberland from its base near Tullahoma toward Chattanooga, where Bragg had retreated earlier that summer. Rosecrans, in the next phase of his design, relied on a flanking movement to maneuver the Confederates out of Chattanooga. Intending to deceive Bragg as to his crossing site on the Tennessee River, Rosecrans advanced three corps in different directions to avoid revealing his intentions. He also hoped Bragg would assume that Burnside's Army of the Ohio, at that time advancing toward Knoxville, would unite with the Army of the Cumberland. The ruse worked. On September 8 Bragg ordered his troops to abandon Chattanooga and concentrate near the town of La Fayette, Georgia, about fifteen miles south of the city. While the Army of Tennessee fled south, Burnside advanced against Knoxville, sixty miles northeast of Chattanooga. Believing that he faced a numerically superior foe, Maj. Gen. Simon B. Buckner abandoned the city on September 2. His 7,000 troops later united with Bragg at La Fayette.[1]

The fall of Knoxville altered the approach route to Tennessee long advocated by Longstreet and other members of the western concentration bloc. By abandoning Knoxville, the Confederates relinquished control of the East Tennessee and Georgia Railroad, the most direct route from Virginia to Tennessee. That railroad would have taken the First Corps from Lynchburg, Virginia, to Bristol, Tennessee, then on to Knoxville and Dalton, Georgia. Instead, Longstreet's troops would be forced to take an eight-hundred-mile roundabout journey through the Carolinas and Georgia before reaching Bragg's army. Using hindsight, President Davis criticized this route. A week after Longstreet's troops left, Davis lamented that he should have sent the First Corps to attack Burnside at Knoxville instead of reinforcing the Army of Tennessee. As it was, the transit from Virginia to Georgia would require sixteen railroad companies and considerable shuffling of dozens of freight and passenger schedules.[2]

THE SOLDIERS OF LONGSTREET'S CORPS TRAVELED WESTWARD with renewed spirits. Following the army's defeat at Gettysburg, the men had been swept up in a religious fervor while camped along the Rappahannock. The "Great Revival" in the Army of Northern Virginia had actually begun in the spring of 1863 but was interrupted by the Pennsylvania campaign. The army's rekindled religious devotion came in part from its commander, Robert E. Lee. Feeling the sting of defeat after Gettysburg, the Confederate chieftain issued a declaration in August 1863 urging his men to put the recent loss behind them, declaring: "Let us confess our many sins, and beseech Him to give us a higher courage, a purer patriotism, and more determined will; that he will convert the hearts of our enemies; that He will hasten the time when war, with its sorrows and sufferings, shall cease, and that He will give us a name and a place among the nations of the earth." Lee's message coincided with Davis's proclamation of August 21 as a day of prayer and fasting in the Confederacy. Both leaders hoped that their messages would influence Southerners to see the recent defeats as tests of their loyalty and faith, not as punishments from God.[3]

The Confederate high command had little difficulty in appealing to Johnny Reb's religious feelings since most Southern soldiers shared a strong Christian upbringing. Consequently, the Great Revival gained a wide following. A soldier in the First Corps observed, "A considerable revival of religion has been going on in our Brigade for the last two or three weeks." Another in Lee's army declared: "We air [sic] having a great Rivival here in my Brigade and I am glad to See it going on. I hope it may accomplish much good and that many So[u]ls may be converted to God." The increased attention to faith became evident throughout the army. The Gettysburg campaign had convinced many soldiers to turn to religion, and the

Great Revival did much to restore morale in Longstreet's corps and prepare the troops for their new mission in North Georgia.[4]

THE FIRST ELEMENTS OF LONGSTREET'S COMMAND BROKE CAMP along the Rapidan River on September 9. He planned to take the divisions of Maj. Gens. John Bell Hood, George E. Pickett, and Lafayette McLaws to the western theater. Once the First Corps arrived in Richmond, however, Lee and Longstreet decided to reshuffle some of the brigades. Both men agreed that Pickett's Division would remain in Virginia to recover from its devastating losses at Gettysburg; in its place would go the brigade of Micah Jenkins. Hood's Division consisted of the brigades of Brig. Gens. Evander M. Law, Jerome S. Robertson, Micah Jenkins, George T. Anderson, and Henry L. Benning. The brigades of Joseph L. Kershaw, Benjamin Humphreys, William T. Wofford, and Goode Bryan made up McLaws's Division. In addition, Col. Edward Porter Alexander's twenty-six-gun artillery battalion accompanied the infantry. About 10,000 men from Lee's army soon were en route to Bragg's Army of Tennessee. Their departure disconcerted some members of the Army of Northern Virginia, including Maj. Walter Taylor, Lee's chief of staff, who believed that no "better troops could be found anywhere than those under General Longstreet."[5]

The massive troop transfer taxed the scant resources of the Confederacy. "Never before were so many troops moved over such worn-out railways," observed one of Longstreet's staff officers, Col. G. Moxley Sorrel. "Never before were such crazy cars—passenger, baggage, mail, coal, box, platform . . . used for hauling good soldiers." Due to the conditions of the Southern railroads, Longstreet's men departed from Virginia in piecemeal fashion. Hood's Division led the contingent of reinforcements to the Tennessee-Georgia border. The authorities in Richmond gave precedence to the infantry, with the artillery units following later. The First Corps initially traveled on two different routes, the first running from Richmond to Weldon, North Carolina, then to Florence, South Carolina; the second going via Raleigh, North Carolina, and Columbia, South Carolina—they converged at Kingsville, South Carolina. From Kingsville the Confederates would then travel to Atlanta, and the Western and Atlantic Railroad would take them on to northern Georgia, where Bragg prepared to fight Rosecrans.[6]

Given the dilapidated conditions of the railroads, it should come as no surprise that there were several delays. Most resulted from mechanical failures. A soldier in the 5th South Carolina recalled that his train arrived several hours late because the engine broke down. Another South Carolinian noted that the locomotive pulling his train had to make several stops to allow the engineer to work on its steam engine. The troops also had to contend with overcrowded rail cars. Boxcars were so full that, rain or shine, many soldiers had to ride atop the car. One officer claimed that his men were "packed in so tightly that there was no room to sit down and many stood from Virginia to Georgia." Riding on the roofs caused a number of casualties as shaky railcars and overhanging branches knocked several men off their precarious perches, sometimes resulting in serious injury or death. North of Atlanta a head-on collision killed eighteen soldiers and injured sixty-seven others, closing the Western and Atlantic Railroad for a precious day.[7]

In addition to the hardships resulting from mechanical failures and other problems of mid-nineteenth-century rail travel, the troops of the First Corps also had to deal with the weather. As the soldiers moved through Georgia, they found that the weather had turned cold. To keep warm, some started fires on the floors and roofs of the boxcars, using sand to insulate the fires from the wooden vehicles. They also used these fires to cook rations. Others, packed into standing-room-only boxcars, did not have to worry about keeping warm since the crowded conditions resulted in hot and stuffy cars. Consequently, many of these men used their knives and axes to pry apart the boxcar walls for ventilation. Augustus Dickert, the historian of Kershaw's Brigade, recalled that the cars soon became "little more than skeleton cars" after the troops had worked on them.[8]

THE TRIP FROM VIRGINIA TO GEORGIA WAS MEMORABLE FOR MORE than its hardships and sacrifices, and even the soldiers in overcrowded boxcars managed to enjoy gazing at the passing scenery. Several veterans recalled that civilians came out to greet them. Met by crowds bearing food and cheering them on to victory, the soldiers of the First Corps endured the journey's hardships but also rejoiced at the citizens' hospitality. "The journey through the States from Virginia was a continuous ovation to the troops," Sorrel recalled. "They were fed at every stopping place and must have hated the sight of food. Kisses and tokens of love and admiration for these war-worn heroes were ungrudgingly passed around." According to Col. William Oates, the commander of the 15th Alabama Infantry, any time civilians came out with food along the travel route, the trains stopped and the men feasted. One officer serving on

Longstreet's staff noted that upon reaching South Carolina, "we received attentions which had long ceased to be common in Virginia." "At Sumter, South Carolina," he later wrote, "a number of ladies were waiting for us on the platform, armed with bouquets of flowers and with well filled baskets of cake, fruit and more substantial fare."[9]

Sumter also had a special reception for Colonel Alexander's artillery battalion, which followed the infantry. The residents treated the entire battalion to a meal, the men sharing their reward at one long table. Later in Atlanta, Alexander's sister, the wife of the superintendent for the Western and Atlantic, treated her brother's staff to "a good supper, & . . . a delightful evening." Other soldiers also received the added attention of female observers as they passed through Southern towns. Lt. Rufe Goodson, a member of the 44th Alabama Regiment, became the object of a young lady's affection. While passing through Covington, Georgia, Goodson tossed a letter to a young woman standing near the railroad tracks. Much to his surprise, the lieutenant received a response from the woman, starting a correspondence between the two. Richard Lewis of South Carolina's Palmetto Sharpshooters also noted that many Georgia women were not content with simply feeding the troops, many throwing bouquets of flowers at the men. Maj. Gen. Lafayette McLaws, a native Georgian, even complained to his wife that Georgia citizens had often requested for him to "Show myself to the assembled multitude as the ladies wanted to see a Georgia general."[10]

While his troops traveled to Georgia, Longstreet had stopped in Richmond on September 12 and learned of the loss of East Tennessee. The general soon after expressed mixed feelings about his transfer to Bragg's army. Although having petitioned for a reinforcement of the West since January 1863, he seemed to regret parting with Lee. "If I did not think our move a necessary one," Longstreet wrote Lee on September 12, "my regrets at leaving you would be distressing to me." That same day he wrote to Senator Wigfall and expressed disdain for serving under Bragg: "I don't think that I should be under Bragg. And would fight against it if I saw any hope of getting anyone in the responsible position except myself. If I should make any decided opposition the world might say that I was desirous of a position which would give me fame. So I conclude that I may be pardoned if I yield my principle under the particular circumstances." Longstreet also expressed his relief at being free of Lee's aggressive tactics: "I am also gratified to find myself in better spirits under adverse circumstances than my friends are. I have learned after much experience that one must after expressing views, fight for them if he hopes to have them adopted. So I shall hereafter contend with more pertinacity for what I know to be right."[11]

Despite his less-than-honest statement of regret at having to leave Lee's army, Longstreet remained determined to avoid another offensive campaign and hopeful of serving again under Johnston. While his regard for Lee might excuse him expressing regret over leaving the Army of Northern Virginia, his trenchant comments to Wigfall about Bragg's shortcomings reveal the First Corps commander's true opinions. Although he had likely heard reports of Bragg's failures as a commanding general from Lee and other generals, he probably received encouragement in his thinking from Wigfall, who had little confidence in the Army of Tennessee's commander, having advocated replacing Bragg with Johnston. Confessing his apprehension about serving under Bragg—even in a private letter—portended trouble for Longstreet, who entered his new assignment with a low opinion of his new superior before they had even met.[12]

As the general penned his letters to Lee and Wigfall, the First Corps met its initial test even before arriving on a western battlefield. The first contingent of Hood's Division reached Raleigh, North Carolina, one of the major stops en route to Bragg's army. Soldiers of Benning's Brigade decided to demonstrate their displeasure with one of the capital's newspapers, the *North Carolina Standard,* published by William Woods Holden. Holden's editorials had long been critical of President Davis and his policies, even supporting a negotiated settlement to the war. These veterans and many Southern citizens believed that the *Standard* had expressed disloyal sentiments that harmed the Confederate cause. Holden had also received criticism from some for encouraging soldiers to desert in order to force the Richmond government to negotiate a peace. Early in September 1863 North Carolina governor Zebulon Vance had issued a proclamation against individuals who promoted resistance to Confederate laws and urged a separate peace settlement by the state. General Lee had even expressed his concern to Secretary of War Seddon that the peace movement in North Carolina was detrimental to the morale of his army. Members of the 48th North Carolina Infantry even held assemblies to reaffirm their loyalty to the Confederacy and denounce the *Standard.*[13]

While government officials had stopped short of muzzling Holden's paper, some of Longstreet's men took matters into their own hands. On the evening of September 9, Benning's Brigade pulled in to the Raleigh depot. Consisting of the 2nd, 15th, 17th, and 20th Georgia Regiments, the unit was commanded by Brig. Gen. Henry L. "Rock" Benning. Arriving on flatcars and boxcars, the Georgians detrained between nine and ten o'clock. When Benning arrived, he sought transportation for the next leg of the journey and then fell asleep near the tracks. While the general slept, some of his soldiers, apparently guided by a detachment of North Carolina troops, went to Holden's home. Warned of the approaching rabble, Holden fled the premises and sought safe haven. Not finding the editor at home, the Georgia and North Carolina troops went to the *Standard* office and forced their way in. The men tore down the front doors, scattered the type on the floor, and painted the office with printers' ink. The damage proved so great that the paper had to suspend operations until early October. The next morning a pro-Holden mob destroyed the presses of the *State Journal*, the pro-Confederate newspaper in Raleigh, outdoing the damage of the Georgia and North Carolina soldiers.[14]

After the vandals had vacated Holden's office, Governor Vance fired off a telegram to President Davis demanding that no more troops be allowed to enter Raleigh. Although Davis complied with his request, the governor wrote him later that day complaining that other troops had threatened Raleigh and urging the president's assistance. The following day Vance wrote a more detailed letter that warned of anarchy in the state capital unless the Richmond authorities helped him restore order. He even threatened to recall North Carolina soldiers to protect the state.[15]

Benning and his Georgia troops became the targets of scathing criticism from the *Raleigh Progress,* the state capital's only newspaper to escape the mob violence. The *Standard* cast its own barbs when it resumed publication in October. After hiding out in the countryside for several days, Holden returned to Raleigh and blamed the vandalism on the "Georgia soldiers" and "the course pursued by the Richmond *Enquirer,* the Raleigh *Register,* the [Raleigh] *State Journal* and Charlotte *Bulletin*," which "had repeatedly called for mob law against the *Standard.*" Vance personally blamed Benning for the violence that tore through the city and demanded justice. President Davis turned the matter over to Adjutant General Cooper and requested a detailed report of the incidents.[16]

Benning's version of events was markedly different from Vance's account. Writing on September 28, the general explained that after arriving at Raleigh, he had made preparations for the next leg of the journey and then rested near the railroad tracks. He also refuted Vance's assertion that one of his subordinates, Lt. Col. William S. Shepherd, had participated in the riot, informing the War Department that Shepherd had actually aided in stopping the destruction and restoring order. Benning placed the blame for the entire affair on a group of North Carolina troops who "avowed themselves the authors of the deed, and claimed credit for it." He explained that the soldiers had received his permission to hitch a ride with his brigade while en route to Salisbury, North Carolina. Upon arriving at Raleigh, they had led some of his men into the *Standard* office. Benning claimed, however, that his Georgia troops were "merely unorganized individuals, each acting for and by himself." He pointed out that the instigators had disappeared before he could question them further.[17]

Although Vance expressed doubts about Benning's story, he was persuaded by the general's denial of personal involvement, even apologizing for mistakenly accusing Shepherd of taking part in the attack on the *Standard*. Benning's version of events was endorsed by the Georgia press, which called the accusations against the state's troops dishonest. Later the *Raleigh Spirit of the Age* reported that a group of North Carolina soldiers appeared in the newspaper's office and confessed to instigating the riot.[18]

The actions of these First Corps troops toward the dissident opinions of Holden's *Standard* demonstrated a fierce devotion to the Confederate cause, despite the recent setback at Gettysburg. Several months after the events in Raleigh, Longstreet and his men were stationed in East Tennessee, where large portions of the local populace were Union sympathizers. Colonel Sorrel noted that in East Tennessee "hatred and revenge made their homes in the breasts of these farmers," and the First Corps found itself in a region where "burnings, hangings, [and] whippings were common." The fact that the soldiers would maintain their esprit de corps within such a hostile environment bears testament to the loyalty they held for their commander, their comrades, and their cause.[19]

If the layover at Raleigh became a disconcerting stop for one brigade of the First Corps, the rest of the trip proved equally distressing for the rest of Longstreet's command. In Atlanta the large number of troop trains arriving from Virginia and Mississippi caused a traffic jam. The soldiers resorted to camping out in the public square while waiting a day or two before continuing their journey. During the stopover at Atlanta, Law's Alabama Brigade received new clothing, hats, and shoes. Given their proximity to their homes, some of Law's men found the temptation to desert too great to resist. Less these, Hood's Division numbered 4,500 officers and men when it reached Bragg's army on September 18. The soldiers of the First Corps arrived at Catoosa Station, just a few miles south of Ringgold, Georgia. A courier greeted Hood upon his arrival and gave him Bragg's orders directing the First Corps to form on the army's right flank. Hood assumed command of the corps in Longstreet's absence, Law taking over the division.[20]

The reason for Longstreet's absence was that he had remained in Richmond until September 14. Leaving his artillery to take a later train, the general and his staff arrived at Catoosa Station at about 2:00 P.M. on the

LONGSTREET'S SOLDIERS DEBARKING FROM THE TRAINS BELOW RINGGOLD.
September 18, 1863.
They hastened from here into the Battle of Chickamauga, which was already raging.

*The First Corps debarking from trains below Ringgold, Georgia,
September 18, 1863. The two divisions traveled more than 800 miles
from Virginia to arrive on the eve of the Battle of Chickamauga.*
LIBRARY OF CONGRESS (LC-USZ62-61447)

nineteenth. Although his staff could hear the sound of battle fifteen miles
away, they remained at Ringgold because Bragg had failed to send guides or
mounts to meet them. One officer noted that this negligence angered the senior officers and left a bad first impression. The rest of the First Corps staff
and most of their horses arrived on another train two hours later. Longstreet and two staff officers mounted and rode toward their first meeting
with Bragg.[21]

Darkness overtook Longstreet and his officers as they rode through the
unfamiliar terrain of northern Georgia, making their journey even more
difficult. Sorrel later recounted how he and the general "wandered by various roads and across small streams through the growing darkness of the
Georgia forest in the direction" of army headquarters. Longstreet soon
found that following the sound of battle would not lead them directly to
Bragg. He and his staff officers also had to meet another challenge. While
riding through the Georgia wilderness, they stumbled into a Federal patrol
at a ford. When the pickets ordered the strangers to identify themselves,
Longstreet simply responded that they were "Friends." Further inquiry led

the general to determine that the pickets were Federal troops. Realizing the precariousness of their situation, Longstreet pretended to look for a better fording place and then galloped away to safety. Sorrel later recalled how the harrowing experience led to some "hard words" for Bragg.[22]

As Longstreet and his staff made their way to Bragg's headquarters near Thedford's Ford, they were unaware of recent events. During the opening days of the Chickamauga campaign, the Confederates had bungled opportunities on two occasions to destroy Rosecrans's army. Although Bragg had devised a sound strategy to defeat the Yankees, his rebellious subordinates had failed to carry out his orders. Following these botched efforts, Bragg decided to concentrate his army near La Fayette and attempt to outflank the enemy. Knowing the Federals had concentrated in the West Chickamauga Creek valley on September 15, he hoped to cut their lines of communication by moving around their left flank and advancing toward Chattanooga. This plan, if successful, would have forced Rosecrans to fall back to protect his line of supply. Bragg, however, suddenly became apprehensive and seemed unwilling to act decisively. His senior officers questioned his fitness for command, and their troops feared another retreat. Bragg waited until the evening of the sixteenth to order an advance against Rosecrans's army but then reversed himself the next day, issuing new orders to maneuver around the Federal left the next morning. On September 19, the day of Longstreet's arrival, the two armies finally collided west of Chickamauga Creek.[23]

Swallowing their displeasure at being left to fend for themselves at Catoosa Station, Longstreet and his staff at last reached Bragg's headquarters at 11:00 P.M. on the nineteenth, only to find their new commander had already retired for the evening. After being awakened, Bragg conferred with Longstreet for about an hour, describing the day's operations. Hood had participated in the fighting. Serving alongside Brig. Gen. Bushrod R. Johnson's division, Robertson's Texas Brigade had crossed Chickamauga Creek on the eighteenth, followed by the brigades of Benning and Law. The next day Hood entered the battle, his arm still in a sling because of his Gettysburg wound. His troops advanced a short distance at the cost of numerous casualties. As Hood attempted to turn what he thought was Union left flank, Bragg deployed reinforcements to the Texans' right, ultimately making Robertson's Brigade the center of the Confederate line.[24]

The fighting on the nineteenth ended at nightfall. Bragg's original plan had called for attacking the Union left and advancing toward the La Fayette Road, but this had come to naught when Bragg's subordinates failed to carry out his orders. Had the Confederates advanced on the La Fayette and Dry Valley roads, they would have controlled the most direct retreat routes

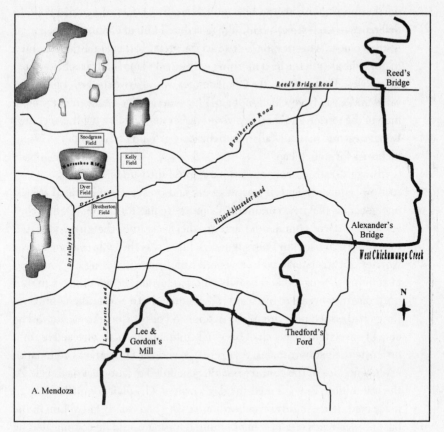

MAP 1. *The Chickamauga Battlefield*

to Chattanooga, enabling them to drive the Federals into McLemore's Cove. With the Army of Tennessee straddling Rosecrans's supply line to Chattanooga, Bragg expected to destroy the Union army.[25] When Longstreet arrived at headquarters, the commanding general was still determined to annihilate Rosecrans. With the reinforcements from Virginia, Bragg hoped to achieve the decisive victory that had eluded him for the past year.

If Bragg did not appear overjoyed to see Longstreet in North Georgia, that was probably because he was still feeling the stress of battle. Bragg's lengthy late-night meeting with him suggests that he wanted to take the newcomer into his confidence in a way that was no longer possible with some of his subordinates. He informed Longstreet that he intended to launch an attack on Rosecrans's left wing at dawn on the twentieth, hoping to drive the Federals southward and away from their base at Chattanooga. To accomplish this, Bragg divided his army into two wings. The right, or northernmost, wing would be commanded by Lt. Gen. Leonidas Polk. In deference to Longstreet's rank, Bragg ordered him to command the left, or southernmost, wing despite his late arrival on the battlefield. Bragg planned to open the assault the next morning with attacks launched en echelon from right to left. If successful, the Confederates would drive the Federals southward and away from Chattanooga. The general gave Longstreet a simple map of the terrain and then explained his strategy. Following this meeting, Longstreet and his staff "all took to the leafy ground under the tall oaks and hickories for some sleep."[26]

Bragg's restructuring of command amid the battle may have been correct procedure, given Longstreet's rank and prestige, but it grated at least one general. The new command structure reduced Lt. Gen. Daniel Harvey Hill, a corps commander and another veteran of the eastern theater, to leading a division in Polk's wing. But that was the least of Longstreet's worries, for his late arrival prevented him from inspecting his lines and examining the rugged and heavily wooded terrain; he would have to wait until dawn to organize his scattered command. To add to the confusion, Bragg had issued no written instructions to Polk or Longstreet, nor did he check to ascertain that each of his wing commanders had conveyed his oral orders to their subordinates. As a result, several of Longstreet's commanders had no idea of the coming assault, scheduled to launch at daybreak. At the last minute Bragg issued the day's orders. His plan compelled him to place confidence in several subordinates who had clearly failed him in the past. Longstreet's task of commanding his wing would be complicated by the fact that most of the field and staff officers had no horses, making command and control more difficult.[27]

Longstreet awoke at dawn on September 20 and immediately readied his troops for battle. His wing included the divisions of Maj. Gens. Thomas C. Hindman, Alexander P. Stewart, and John Bell Hood (commanded by Evander Law); Brig. Gens. Bushrod Johnson and William Preston; and two brigades from McLaws's Division under Brig. Gen. Joseph B. Kershaw. Longstreet arranged Stewart, Johnson, Hindman, and Preston from north to south and facing west. Each division deployed two brigades on the front and one in reserve. Behind Johnson's Division he placed Hood's Division, under Law, also with two brigades forward and one in reserve. He ordered Kershaw to deploy his own and Benjamin Humphreys's brigades behind Hood's line. Longstreet thus deployed eight brigades in a tightly packed column under the overall direction of Hood, one of the Army of Northern Virginia's hardest-hitting generals. The left wing would receive support from twenty-one batteries of the Army Reserve Battalion under the command of Maj. Felix Robertson. Due to limited visibility, Robertson's artillery would play a minor role in the day's fighting. The field of battle that the Confederates would traverse, Longstreet recounted, "was not a field, proper, but a heavy woodland, not adapted to the practice of artillery." He would command seventeen infantry brigades to Polk's fifteen.[28]

Longstreet's attempt to organize his forces in unfamiliar terrain was a formidable task. Some of his troops were not issued rations, and many were ignorant of the planned assault. Nevertheless, at first light on the twentieth, Longstreet informed General Stewart that Polk would launch the attack against the Federals from right to left and that Stewart would form on Polk's left, advancing when the division on his right moved forward. Stewart replied that there was no division on his right. Longstreet thus ordered Stewart to shift his division, consisting of the brigades of John C. Brown, William B. Bate, and Henry D. Clayton, to the right until he made contact with Polk's leftmost division (under Maj. Gen. Patrick R. Cleburne). Stewart moved more than a quarter mile to the north, across the Brotherton Road, stopping just shy of Poe Field. His troops then built breastworks. But Stewart soon discovered that part of his line now overlapped Cleburne's front, necessitating a hasty reorganization of the lines before the Confederates launched their attack.[29]

While Stewart tried to straighten out his position, Longstreet deployed the rest of his troops. Aided by Tom Brotherton, who lived in North Georgia before enlisting, the general quickly examined the terrain near Chickamauga Creek. The unseasonable cold morning brought about frost and dense fog that made reconnaissance even more difficult, but Longstreet's calm, methodical preparation inspired his fellow officers. He deployed his forces in the woods about three hundred yards to the east of the Brotherton Farm and the La Fayette Road. West of the main road to Chattanooga lay Bragg's main objective—elements of the Federal XIV, XX, and XXI Corps. Longstreet organized the remainder of his assault force, under Hood, into an attack column designed to utilize the battlefield's thick woods and poor visibility to his best advantage. "If the 1st and 2nd [columns] are broken and dispersed by the assault," Longstreet explained in a postwar letter, "then the 3rd in turn finds itself in full strength and force and near enough the enemy's lines to break thru [sic]." He thus aligned his divisions to serve as a battering ram against the Federal lines.[30]

Longstreet later asserted that he believed that an assault column required numerical strength and depth to overcome the defenders' advantages. He had witnessed firsthand the effect of all-out charges against formidable positions and knew the devastating firepower of massed rifled muskets. He now proposed to use topography to minimize the defenders' edge. The woods and uneven terrain of North Georgia would provide cover for his advancing soldiers until the assault column broke through the Union line.[31] Yet Longstreet's postwar analysis of the battle likely benefited from hindsight. On the day of the attack, he probably did not have time to reflect on tactical nuances. Rather, his troop dispositions proved fortuitous, for they would enable the left wing to exploit the weak point of the enemy forces confronting them.

While Longstreet considered his column a powerful ram poised to shatter the Union lines, the left wing, in fact, contained its own weaknesses. Of the seventeen brigades composing Longstreet's wing on the twentieth, ten had seen action the previous day. The divisions of Johnson and Stewart, for example, had suffered more than 30 percent casualties during the first day's fighting. As for the brigades from Virginia, they had yet to recover from their heavy losses at Gettysburg. The 1st Texas Infantry, for instance, was commanded by a captain, R. J. Harding. Worse yet, the First Corps soldiers had arrived ill-equipped and fatigued from their long journey through the Carolinas and Georgia. Maj. R. T. Coles of the 4th Alabama Infantry recalled, "We were in no condition whatever to go into battle." A South Carolinian reported that he and his comrades arrived on the battlefield "in an exhausted state."[32] Thus, out of Longstreet's 23,000 troops, many shared serious handicaps that placed the long-anticipated western concentration at a significant disadvantage.

Despite these shortcomings, Longstreet and his staff hustled to arrange their lines in preparation for Polk's opening volleys. Longstreet established his headquarters northeast of the intersection of the Brotherton and La Fayette roads. General Buckner, a Kentucky native who had recently joined the Army of Tennessee, aided him by placing his staff at the wing commander's disposal and helping him deploy his forces during the battle. Given that "Lee's Old Warhorse" had to issue orders with a skeleton staff, only four of whom were present, this assistance was invaluable. Buckner's familiarity with his own troops would prove advantageous later in the day when he received orders from Longstreet to take command of Preston's Division. Instructions accordingly went to General Preston, whose division's left-flank position remained the key to Bragg's plan to interpose his army between the Federals and Chattanooga. "The purpose of the commander in ordering the wheel to the left as pivot was to push in, from the start, between the enemy and his new base at Chattanooga," Longstreet later wrote.[33]

While Longstreet hurried to ready his troops for the advance, the expected daylight assault by Polk did not occur at the designated time. Given the responsibility of launching the en echelon attack, Polk retired on the night of September 19 before giving D. H. Hill specific instructions for the next morning's assault. Hill, for his part, made minimal effort to locate Bragg's headquarters at Thedford's Ford for further details. Although he had missed the commanding general, one of his staff officers received instructions for Hill to report to Polk, whose headquarters was near Alexander's Bridge, about three miles down Chickamauga Creek. For some reason, Hill decided to rest until 3:00 A.M. before departing for Alexander's Bridge. By the time of Hill's arrival, Polk's guides had left, and he failed to meet the wing commander. Inexplicably, Hill simply returned to his headquarters, unaware that he was expected to launch the daylight assault. As commander of the right wing, Polk was responsible for ensuring that his units received their proper orders, but he failed to inform Hill of his pivotal role. Hill, however, should have made every effort to locate Polk's headquarters. The two generals, thus, share responsibility for failing to execute Bragg's instructions.[34]

Polk and Hill's negligence foiled the intended morning assault. This delay gave the Federals precious time to construct breastworks for the anticipated onslaught. A Union officer later wrote that the Confederates failed to exploit some initial confusion in the Union lines by attacking early. "If he [Bragg] had done so," Brig. Gen. John Palmer later wrote, "with the force and energy with which the Rebel attack was [eventually] made, the battle would not have lasted an hour; we would have gone to Chattanooga on the run." Upon failing to hear gunfire at the anticipated hour, Bragg rode forward to investigate the delay. Arriving at Hill's position at dawn, he learned that Hill was ignorant of his crucial role in the daybreak assault. With the right wing in no position to attack as planned, Bragg and his officers had to realign the Confederate forces. By the time this was finished, the attack was running four hours late. At 9:30 A.M. Bragg finally ordered the advance. On the Confederate right, Maj. Gen. John C. Breckinridge's division attacked with ferocity, but the long postponement had allowed Rosecrans to reinforce his once-vulnerable left.[35]

While the delays on the Confederate right proved disastrous to the opening assault, the postponement nevertheless gave Longstreet additional time to prepare his troops and familiarize himself with the terrain. His divisions waited in the woods east of the Brotherton Farm for the order to advance. Exasperated by the day's events, Longstreet ordered a general advance across his entire front. Unaware of the situation on the Confederate right, the general sent a courier to Bragg around 11:00 A.M. "to suggest that I had probably better make my attack." While the messenger was away, heavy firing to the northeast startled Longstreet. Before he could investigate, he heard that Bragg had ordered an advance. Unknown to Longstreet, Maj. Pollock Lee of Bragg's staff had ordered Stewart's Division forward without delay. When the surprised Stewart informed Lee that he had received no orders from the wing commander, the major informed him that the commanding general had "directed him to pass along the lines and give the order to every division commander to move upon the enemy immediately." Embarrassed by these peremptory orders to advance, Longstreet failed to find Major Lee to inquire about the details but nevertheless ordered his units forward at 11:10 A.M. "I at once issued orders to attack to the troops not already in motion," he lamented.[36]

After Stewart engaged the Federals on the Confederate left wing's northern flank, Longstreet ordered Hood to advance and then rode south to instruct Hindman to move forward. The Confederates surged west and across the La Fayette Road only to meet heavy fire from Federal skirmishers. Longstreet still held Preston's Division in reserve because he believed it remained the key unit in the pivot to the south. As the his other units surged forward into the Union ranks, Longstreet unexpectedly benefited from a lapse by the Union high command that soon changed the direction of his assault.[37]

While miscues on the morning of the twentieth delayed the Confederate assault, Rosecrans became concerned with the stability of his left flank. Worried that Bragg would attempt to turn his left flank and cut him off from his base at Chattanooga, Rosecrans had reinforced his left. About ten minutes before Longstreet's column finally advanced, Brig. Gen. Thomas J. Wood, commanding the 1st Division, XXI Corps, received orders to move to the left and support Maj. Gen. Joseph J. Reynolds's 4th Division, XIV Corps. When Wood reached his assigned position, he discovered that Brig. Gen. John M. Brannan and his 3rd Division, XIV Corps stood on Reynolds's right. Rosecrans had incorrectly assumed that Brannan's division had shifted farther north to reinforce Maj. Gen. George H. Thomas and the vulnerable Union left flank. Wood's orders to move to the left and close on Reynolds's line made no sense because Brannan's division remained on Reynolds's right. Although the order struck him as illogical, Wood was still smarting from a dressing-down Rosecrans had given him for failing to obey orders. He therefore ignored advice from his subordinates to disregard the order, pulled his division out of line, and moved into position behind Brannan. This created a huge gap in the Union lines that Longstreet's command would eagerly exploit.[38]

As Wood abandoned his position and moved northward to reinforce

Brannan, Longstreet gave Hood the order to advance. Bushrod Johnson's Division ploughed through the quarter-mile opening in the Union lines, crossing the Brotherton Field and advancing more than three hundred yards east of the La Fayette Road. At the Brotherton House the division split, with Brig. Gen. Evander McNair's brigade passing north of it and Col. John S. Fulton's brigade passing to the south, both continuing to move westward through the Union lines. On Johnson's left Hindman's Division drove back the Federals along their front. Hindman reported that his brigades "drove the enemy from his breastworks, then pushed him beyond the La Fayette road, and charged his second line of breastworks, 300 yards farther on." As Johnson pressed on, he found Federal soldiers on both his flanks but encountered no opposition on his front.[39]

Heading due west, Longstreet's attack column swept across the Brotherton Field. On the right McNair's Brigade marched astride the Dyer Road, heading toward the Dry Valley Road; on the left Fulton's Brigade advanced toward the Dyer House. Just thirty minutes after stepping off, Hood's line had reached the edge of Dyer Field, almost a half mile from their point of departure. Brannan's Federals subjected the oncoming Rebels to a heavy fire. After briefly faltering, Fulton's men resumed their advance. McNair's troops also faltered but soon recovered when they made contact with Brig. Gen. John Gregg's brigade (Col. Cyrus Sugg had assumed command of the brigade after Gregg was wounded at the start of the battle). Despite the ease with which his command had advanced through the Federal gap, Hood realized that his column remained vulnerable to enfilading fire from the right even as it approached the Union army's rear. To eliminate this threat, the Texan ordered his troops to wheel to the right and meet the enemy head on. Although this shift right was a tactical necessity, it countered Bragg's original plan to wheel to the left.[40]

Meanwhile, on the left flank of Longstreet's wing, the Confederate advance met stiff resistance from Col. John T. Wilder and his "Lightning Brigade." Equipped with new Spencer repeating rifles, Wilder's command had been stationed south of the Federal lines on the morning of September 20. About noon, as the Union line buckled under pressure from Longstreet's assault, Wilder received orders to move north and attempt to stem the Confederate tide. His men reached the Widow Glenn House just as Hindman's Division was overrunning the Federal line and quickly concentrated their superior firepower on the Confederate left. This overwhelming fire struck the brigade of Brig. Gen. Arthur Manigault, on Hindman's far left, who ordered his regiments to retreat across the La Fayette Road. Manigault was furious to find his left flank exposed, having assumed that General Preston had advanced on his left in preparation for the pivot to the south. What began as an orderly withdrawal soon became a rout. Wilder's Brigade thus gained a brief respite by halting one of Hindman's brigades, but the effort could not prevent the collapse of the Federal right.[41]

After learning of Manigault's rout, Longstreet decided to follow Hood's lead and order his remaining brigades to wheel to the right instead of the left, then attack the Federal troops north of Dyer Field. "I was obliged to reverse the order of battle by retaining my right somewhere near the left of the Right Wing," Longstreet later observed. He instructed Hindman to move north and support Hood's column and also directed Maj. Gen. Joseph Wheeler, commanding the Confederate cavalry, to cross the Chickamauga and secure his left. After issuing further instructions to his subordinates, Longstreet rode northward to observe Hood and Johnson's advance.[42]

Despite the Confederates' success, the Federals remained a dangerous threat. Union artillery had begun to form north of Dyer Field, with infantry units in support. As the Confederates advanced across the southern part of Dyer Field, the fierce fighting momentarily unhinged Benning, whose brigade was following Bushrod Johnson. Benning's Georgians advanced alongside Law's Alabamians, suffering heavy casualties from intense musketry. His own horse having been killed, Benning now rode to meet Longstreet on a captured artillery horse. The frantic brigadier reported a catastrophic situation to his chief. According to Longstreet, Benning exclaimed, "General Hood killed, my horse killed, my brigade torn to pieces and I haven't a man left." Longstreet responded: "Nonsense, General. You are not so badly hurt. Look about you. I know you will find at least one man and with him on his feet, report your brigade to me, and you two shall have a place in the fighting line." Thus reassured, Benning returned to his brigade and advanced northward along the La Fayette Road toward the Poe House, a quarter mile from Dyer Field. Longstreet's pep talk might well have worked, for Benning's Brigade continued to advance. Having despaired of his brigade's survival moments earlier, he now saw his men overrun the Union position.[43]

While Benning struggled to control himself and his brigade, Johnson tried to remain focused on the task at hand. He had received his last order from Hood just after noon, his division commander simply telling him to "Go ahead, and keep ahead of everything." Hood then moved to the rear to bring up his old command, the Texas Brigade, led by Jerome Robertson. The Texans had begun to retreat when Hood, directing troops almost three hundred yards away, noticed his former brigade's difficulties and galloped to rally his men. As he and Robertson spoke, a minié ball struck Hood in the upper right thigh, shattering the femur. The general was carried to the rear, where army surgeons amputated his leg near the hip. Upon hearing of Hood's wound, Longstreet ordered Law to continue the advance. Longstreet noticed that Hood had "broken the enemy's line . . . and his own troops and those to his right continued to press the enemy with such spirit and force that he could not resist us." What the general failed to realize, however, was that the assault would become disorganized without Hood's guiding hand.[44]

The Texan's absence certainly hindered Joseph Kershaw's advance. Kershaw's Brigade had arrived on the battlefield at 1:00 A.M. on the twentieth, and the South Carolinians were eager for a fight. As Kershaw crossed the La Fayette Road and advanced westward, he remained unaware of the general movement to the right. "General Kershaw," Longstreet explained in his report, "having received no definite orders himself (being under the command of General Hood), was not advised of the wheel to the right and gained more ground to the front [that is, to the west] than was intended in the movement of his two brigades." Receiving instructions from Longstreet to watch his right flank, Kershaw complied, and his South Carolina troops continued to move forward, veering toward the right. Brig. Gen. Benjamin Humphreys, also of McLaws's Division, remained in awe of Longstreet's calm demeanor amid the raging battle. "I never saw him wear so bright and jubilant a countenance," Humphreys later wrote. Accordingly, his and Kershaw's brigades continued their northward advance past Dyer Field and toward Horseshoe Ridge, where George Thomas had rallied some Federal troops.[45]

Despite the crisis facing him, Thomas also maintained a calm and unflappable demeanor. His battered lines were bent back into a semicircle on Horseshoe Ridge, extending northward to Snodgrass Hill and Kelly Field. Thomas's left flank had withstood attacks from Polk's wing and Brig. Gen. Nathan Bedford Forrest's cavalry, while his right had repulsed Longstreet's men. But the greatest threat to the Federal position remained Longstreet's attacks from the south. Kershaw and Humphreys both advanced on Horseshoe Ridge, though only to be hurled back. After suffering several more bloody repulses, the two generals decided to hold their positions and await further orders. A veteran of the eastern theater, Kershaw called the contest for Thomas's position "one of the most gallant struggles" he had ever witnessed.[46]

While Kershaw and Humphreys waited on the right, Longstreet directed Hindman's Division, on the left, to form on Bushrod Johnson's left flank before launching an all-out attack on this last remaining Federal opposition. General Rosecrans and two of his corps commanders already had abandoned the field by noon and fled to Chattanooga without notifying Thomas. In his report Rosecrans declared that he had issued withdrawal orders to retreat to the city because he assumed that Longstreet would seize his supply wagons in an attack on the Union rear.[47] Despite his commander's actions, Thomas remained on Snodgrass Hill with whatever Federal units he could rally.

Longstreet realized Snodgrass Hill was the key to victory. As he waited for Hindman's northward advance against the Federals, the general established his headquarters at the Dyer House. About 1:00 P.M. Longstreet, accompanied by Buckner and his staff, rode along the Confederate line to observe the battle's movements. He instructed Buckner to bring up the reserve artillery on his right flank to enfilade the enemy's position. As the Kentuckian rode away, Longstreet and his staff sat down to a lunch of bacon and sweet potatoes. While the officers ate, Maj. William M. Owen of the Washington Artillery, the acting chief of artillery for Preston's Division, asked Longstreet if the Federals had been beaten. "Yes, all along the line," he assured him. Owen remembered that the general appeared supremely confident, promising the artillery officer as many captured cannon as he wanted.[48] Yet as he spoke, Longstreet was unaware that he had just missed a great opportunity.

Before lunch Longstreet and his staff had reconnoitered the Union line but had failed to notice a half-mile gap between Kelly Field and Horseshoe Ridge. It remained unnoticed until nightfall. Longstreet had plenty of troops in reserve to exploit the opportunity, which would have enabled him to cut the enemy position in two. Humphreys's Brigade sat idle along the Glenn Kelly Road, Law's troops rested near Dyer Field, and Buckner had just ordered Preston's Division to the Brotherton House to await further instructions. As obvious as this lost opportunity appears in retrospect, Longstreet's blunder is understandable in the context of challenges facing him on the battle's second day. The densely wooded terrain, in which the thick gunpowder smoke became trapped, limited visibility to a few hundred yards at most. Attempting a reconnaissance under such conditions would have been a dangerous undertaking. In addition, Longstreet typically delegated such responsibilities to his subordinates. He thus relied upon Hood to familiarize himself with the terrain and the enemy position in his front. When the Texan fell wounded just after noon, the Confederate advance simply lost cohesion.[49]

Despite the failure to detect this gap, the Confederates continued to enjoy success. Shortly after 3:00 P.M. Bragg sent for Longstreet. The lieutenant general rode to the rear to apprise the army commander—whom he had not seen since the morning—of the tactical situation. Longstreet confidently proclaimed success, reporting that his wing had captured more than sixty artillery pieces. He then suggested that Bragg send reinforcements from Polk's wing to seize control of the Dry Valley Road as well as McFarland and Rossville gaps, between Chickamauga Creek and Chattanooga, thereby cutting the Federals' line of retreat. But according to Longstreet, Bragg "was disturbed by the failure of his plan and the severe repulse of his right wing, and was little prepared to hear suggestions for other moves or progressive work." The general replied that he could not spare troops from his right wing, then left Longstreet in order to inspect the right flank and direct Polk to renew the assaults. Disappointed with Bragg's dismissal of his suggestion, Longstreet felt that "there was nothing for the left wing to do but work along as best it could."[50]

Longstreet left his conference with Bragg believing that the commanding general had failed to grasp the extent of the left wing's success against Rosecrans's army. "There is not a man in the right wing who has any fight in him," Bragg reportedly said when Longstreet asked him for reinforcements from Polk's sector. Although it is doubtful that the general would have used such language to describe the situation on the Confederate right, he did refuse Longstreet's request for reinforcements, remaining committed to his original plan of wheeling to the left across the Federals' line of retreat. When Longstreet, who had already abandoned the left wheel, suggested that Bragg modify his plan, the commanding general refused. Yet it is understandable if Bragg hesitated to follow Longstreet's advice, for after all, Longstreet had been on the battlefield only a few hours and not thoroughly familiar with the strategic situation.[51]

Bragg knew that by focusing on the Federal left, he would restrict Thomas to the La Fayette Road as his sole line of retreat. Hence, his insistence on turning the Union left. Bragg should have realized, however, that Longstreet still held Preston's Division in reserve and could have moved those troops to the Confederate right for an enveloping attack on Thomas's position. Longstreet did not use the division to reinforce of his own attack because he probably believed that using it against the Horseshoe Ridge position would offer him the best opportunity of success. In his official report Longstreet wrote, "I had but one division that had not been engaged, and hesitated to venture to put it in, as our distress upon our right seemed to be almost as great as that of the enemy upon his right." Bragg had abandoned control of the battle to his wing commanders when he altered his original attack plan and ordered all his divisions forward simultaneously. Since then, Longstreet was left to fend for himself. Moreover, two of his division commanders had been wounded during the fighting, adding further difficulties of command and control. Given the tactical situation, Longstreet's request for reinforcements from Polk's wing seemed reasonable. While the Confederate attacks on the right had failed, the left wing had driven back the Federals' line more than a mile. Longstreet's reluctance to commit troops to an uncertain situation appears understandable when viewed in this light.[52]

After Bragg departed, Longstreet returned to the situation facing him on Horseshoe Ridge. Shortly before 4:00 P.M. he ordered renewed assaults against the Federal position on Snodgrass Hill but failed to drive off the defenders. Realizing that his present force "was not strong enough for the work," Longstreet directed his reserve division under William Preston forward along with Stewart's Division, which had remained idle since early afternoon. For the next few hours, almost every brigade in Longstreet's wing made repeated attacks on Thomas's position, inflicting and suffering heavy losses. By nightfall the assaults at last "gained the line that had been held so long." Thomas and his men nevertheless retreated to Chattanooga in good order. The Confederates now had full possession of the battlefield. "The continued cheers of the army announced at dark that every point of the field had been gained," Buckner noted.[53]

As the last segments of Rosecrans's army retreated toward Chattanooga, Longstreet saw one final opportunity to inflict heavy damage on the enemy. He sent his chief of staff, Sorrel, forward to Stewart with orders to attack the Federal flank. Stewart refused. Determined not to be accused of disobeying orders, he requested a written order from Longstreet. This infuriated Longstreet, who knew that precious time was being lost. "Longstreet's thunderous tones need not be described when, in the first words of explanation, he sent me back with orders to Stewart to fall on the column with all his power," Sorrel later described. When Sorrel returned with the written orders, Stewart's troops advanced over the abandoned breastworks and hit the Federal rear guard, capturing nearly four hundred prisoners. Yet the Union troops had kept the Dry Valley Road open long enough to allow most of the Yankees to reach Chattanooga.[54]

The Battle of Chickamauga cost the Army of Tennessee more than 18,000 casualties, 8,000 from Longstreet's command, but the victory ended a string of disheartening losses for the western army. Longstreet's charge through the Union lines highlighted the Confederate success. Although preferring defensive tactics, he nevertheless led an attack under favorable conditions and proposed further offensive operations against Rosecrans's army. Contrary to Lee's open-ground assault at Gettysburg, Longstreet struck the Union positions while using thick woods as protective cover. Believing that the Army of the Cumberland was demoralized after its defeat, he devised an immediate pursuit. In his official report Longstreet praised the "steady good conduct" of his men and submitted a long list of names to be "distinguished for conduct and ability." The Army of Tennessee's soldiers reciprocated Longstreet's accolades, crediting the First Corps commander and his troops for leading them to victory. General Breckinridge, a Kentucky native and former U.S. vice president, reportedly rode along his line exclaiming, "Longstreet is the man, boys, Longstreet is the man." As word of the battle spread throughout the South, Longstreet became widely regarded as one of the key men responsible for the victory at Chickamauga. "Bragg, thanks to Longstreet and Hood," wrote Richmond socialite Mary Chesnut, "had won Chickamauga."[55]

In his memoirs Longstreet recalls his jubilation on seeing the two Confederate wings come together: "The left wing swept forward, and the right sprang to the broad Chattanooga highway. Like magic the Union army had melted away in our presence." In truth Longstreet and the Confederate high command did not realize that they had defeated the Federals on the twentieth. After his 3:00 P.M. meeting with Bragg, Longstreet returned to his wing and failed to communicate with his commander for the remainder of the day. Not until 6:15 P.M. did he finally write Bragg a short note describing the situation on the left, stating that he had "been entirely successful in my command today." His message failed to supply any essential details for Bragg, instead merely mentioning that he hoped "to be ready to renew the conflict at an early hour the next day." This suggests that Longstreet thought the Federals remained in position on Snodgrass Hill. His failure to detect the Federal withdrawal is betrayed in his failure to notify Bragg that the Confederates held the battlefield. Longstreet after the war asserted that he did not notify Bragg of the left wing's success because he felt that the "loud huzzas that spread over the field just at dark were a sufficient assurance and notice to any one within five miles of us." Yet orders leaving his headquarters on the morning of September 21 indicate that he was still unaware of events on his front. Not until 5:00 A.M. did he at last issue orders for Wheeler's cavalry to determine if the Federals had indeed retreated to Chattanooga. Ninety minutes later Longstreet ordered a line forward to seek the enemy. When Bragg requested a meeting that morning, Longstreet replied that he feared leaving his front line lest the Federals launch a counterattack.[56]

Bragg and Polk likewise shared Longstreet's ignorance of the tactical situation. At about 9:00 P.M. on the twentieth, Brig. Gen. St. John Liddell reported to Polk's headquarters to inform the right-wing commander that the "enemy had gone." Bragg rode up about the same time and entered into conversation with Polk. Liddell soon left frustrated with the Army of Tennessee's high command. Bragg ignored Liddell's report and notified Richmond that his army still faced Rosecrans near Chickamauga Creek. "After two days hard fighting, we have driven the enemy after a desperate resistance from several positions," Bragg wrote, "but he still confronts us." So while the senior officers in the Army of Tennessee pondered the whereabouts of Rosecrans and his army, the Federals continued to strengthen their position at Chattanooga.[57]

Longstreet and Bragg finally met at 9:00 A.M. on the twenty-first and determined that the Army of the Cumberland had indeed retreated to Chattanooga. They also discussed plans for future operations. According to Longstreet's official report, Bragg asked for advice on advancing against the Federals. The First Corps commander suggested two operations: First, the army could cross the Tennessee River above Chattanooga and cut Rosecrans's line of communications, thereby forcing the Federals out of the city. Second, the First Corps could advance against the Federals in East Tennessee and then strike westward toward Nashville. Longstreet claimed that Bragg concurred and prepared to issue orders for the move against Knoxville. Bragg later maintained, however, that Longstreet's "proposition was not even entertained" because "such a movement was utterly impossible for want of transportation." Fearing the loss of North Georgia, Bragg abandoned any plans to maneuver around the enemy's rear, preferring to surround the Federal army at Chattanooga.[58] His decision not to press the beaten Federals had merit. The Confederates had won a convincing victory but had suffered heavy casualties and lacked adequate transportation. In addition, the victorious army appeared confused and disoriented (perhaps because most of the officers and men were unaccustomed to victory). Longstreet and other senior officers in the Army of Tennessee criticized Bragg's reluctance to pursue the defeated enemy, however, and stood ready to resume the offensive.[59]

As Bragg considered his army's next move, Longstreet's command remained idle near Chickamauga Creek. On September 21 the rest of McLaws's Division arrived from Virginia. A native Georgian and a West Point classmate of Longstreet, McLaws immediately received orders to advance on Chattanooga in support of General Breckinridge. His division advanced toward the city as ordered and waited for a half hour for Breckinridge to appear, after which McLaws marched on, assuming that Breckinridge would join him later that night. The Confederates crossed Missionary Ridge and advanced to within two miles of Chattanooga before halting. McLaws held his position until 10:00 P.M., when Bragg ordered him to wait for the rest of the army. The next day the Army of Tennessee approached Chattanooga and positioned itself along Missionary Ridge, overlooking the town. The Federals had assumed a defensive position within the town, but Longstreet believed that McLaws should have attacked when he first arrived.[60] Bragg's decision to besiege the Federals suggests that he believed his army could ultimately capture the city without a fight. Having surrounded Chattanooga, Bragg now focused his energies on ridding his army of the dissident generals who had plagued his command since the fall of 1862.

The Army of Tennessee's senior officers were so absorbed in debating strategy that they failed to realize just how costly the victory at Chickamauga had been. The long-advocated transfer of Longstreet and the First Corps to Bragg's army had yielded the only major triumph for the Confederacy's main western army. Longstreet himself had fought admirably on the battle's second day. After a circuitous journey of more than a week, the general had arrived in northwestern Georgia ready to contribute to a victory in the West. Certainly, Longstreet's performance at Chickamauga was noteworthy. Although his surge through the Federal army's right flank depended on a serendipitous gap in the defensive line, Longstreet deserves credit for arranging his units into an attack column, which proved to be the deciding factor. Even though the general arrived late on the evening of the nineteenth, he succeeded in organizing his improvised left-wing command into an effective fighting force. He led his troops much as he had in Virginia, allowing his subordinates to direct the fighting while he plotted strategy. His free-handed approach led to a brief interlude in which he lost control of his units, but he soon recovered and directed reinforcements to areas where they were needed most.

Longstreet's performance at Chickamauga also demonstrated some of his weaknesses. Foremost, Longstreet arrived in northern Georgia with a negative opinion of the commanding general without having met him. His September 12 letter to Senator Wigfall suggests that he held a low opinion of Bragg and would refuse to cooperate with his new chief if things did not go according to plan. Thus when Bragg failed to send guides to meet him at the railroad depot, Longstreet and his staff immediately grumbled about the commanding general. This antagonism manifested itself on the twentieth when Longstreet met with Bragg to discuss the situation on the left wing and request reinforcements. When Bragg turned down his request to send troops from Polk's wing, Longstreet returned to his sector, disgusted with his superior. By the morning of the twenty-first, Longstreet and Bragg debated how best to exploit the Chickamauga victory. Although Longstreet gave various accounts as to what he and Bragg discussed that morning, one can deduce that the two men worked at cross-purposes.[61]

Beyond this antagonism toward Bragg, some historians have charged Longstreet with miscues on the battlefield. They have suggested that he remained aloof and indifferent to the events of September 20 and also claim that he was unaware of the situation on his front line. Yet Longstreet made sound dispositions and skillfully employed a successful style of command developed during his service in Virginia. He was aware of the critical situation on his left and shuttled reinforcements to key areas as the situation dictated. Some scholars have censured Longstreet for failing to recognize the gap in Thomas's line on Horseshoe Ridge. But his unfamiliarity with the terrain and the limited visibility on the thickly wooded battlefield explain this blunder. A few historians have even criticized Longstreet's altering of Bragg's original plan of wheeling to the left.[62] But when Bragg ordered a general advance, he inadvertently changed the tactical situation by shifting control to his wing commanders. Longstreet should not be faulted for seizing the opportunity that presented itself when a Union tactical blunder created a huge gap in the enemy lines to his front. Despite these critiques, Longstreet's performance at Chickamauga remains one of his most notable achievements. He overcame such handicaps as arriving only twelve hours before assuming battlefield command and having to lead troops unfamiliar to him. Yet he persevered and led the Army of Tennessee to its only major victory. For his efforts, Longstreet earned a new nickname from the western soldiers—the "Bull of the Woods."

3

"THE SHAFTS OF MALICE THAT HAVE BEEN HURLED AGAINST HIM"

LONGSTREET AND THE COMMAND CRISIS IN THE ARMY OF TENNESSEE

VACILLATION BY THE COMMANDERS OF THE ARMY OF TENNESSEE on September 21 exacerbated the internal tension that had plagued the army since General Bragg assumed command in the summer of 1862. Longstreet's transfer west did not relieve these problems. Indeed, the First Corps commander arrived in northern Georgia with a negative opinion of Bragg. For several months he had read and heard the criticism of Bragg's generalship and had himself advocated Joseph E. Johnston to command the Army of Tennessee. Longstreet's desire to serve under his former chief only fueled his dissatisfaction with Bragg. Like other members of the western concentration bloc who advocated a command change, Longstreet resented Bragg because he prevented Johnston from obtaining a field command. Yet the general remained unaware of the level of hostility between Davis and Johnston and of the dogged determination of the Confederate president to retain Bragg. As Longstreet told Senator Wigfall before arriving in the West, he would resist serving under Bragg for any extended period. After his arrival, Longstreet became yet another of the army's dissatisfied generals. He openly criticized his new commander, eagerly anticipated his removal, and hoped that Johnston would soon take over.

Longstreet's opinion of Bragg only worsened as he realized that the victory at Chickamauga had proved strategically barren. Union forces had managed to keep the main roads to Chattanooga open and succeeded in delaying the Confederates long enough to enable the Army of the Cumberland to retreat to the city. Anticipating a Confederate assault, Rosecrans immediately ordered his troops to establish a defensive perimeter.[1]

But Rosecrans was unaware that the Army of Tennessee was ill prepared to launch an attack on Chattanooga. The battle had cost Bragg's army about 18,000 casualties, and those soldiers who escaped death, wounding, or capture woke up on the morning of the twenty-first completely exhausted after two days of hard fighting. The initial success of Longstreet's attack had forced the Rebel troops to advance so rapidly that by the time they reached stiffening Federal resistance, they were spent. The final assaults against Thomas's position on Snodgrass Hill only added to the Confederates' mounting casualties. As Bragg later pointed out, the Army of Tennessee had suffered heavy losses and struggled with a shortage of food and transportation, only worsened by the addition of Longstreet's corps, which arrived in northwestern Georgia with neither provisions nor wagons. Worse yet, the army appeared confused and disoriented after the battle. The two wing commanders, Longstreet and Leonidas Polk, failed to verify that the Federals had left their front at dawn on the twenty-first. The commanding general fared no better. Not until later that morning did Bragg learn of his triumph. When he notified the War Department in Richmond of his victory, however, he warned that Rosecrans's army still remained a formidable foe.[2]

Although an advance against Chattanooga proved impractical, Bragg's subordinates criticized him for being indecisive and failing to exploit the victory at Chickamauga. Bragg in fact did not entertain the possibility of even reconnaissance toward the town. Rather, during September 21 and 22, he focused on minor details such as ordering the collection of weapons from the battlefield. Notified that "large numbers of arms and munitions of war [were] scattered throughout the country in front," the general instructed his corps commanders that "every effort shall be made to collect and save them." Even though Forrest reported on the twenty-first that the Federals appeared to be retreating from Chattanooga, Bragg did nothing. Forrest urged a pursuit of the enemy, but Bragg rebuffed him, citing a shortage of supplies. He then reportedly retorted, "General Bragg, we can get all the supplies our army needs in Chattanooga." Although ordering his generals to be ready to advance on Chattanooga on the morning of the twenty-second, Bragg did not move. He failed to recognize the demoralizing effect on his army of his defensive stance and his hesitancy in moving against the Federals. Rather than act, he blamed his subordinates for failing to rout Rosecrans's army. Bragg would ultimately place the blame for

Chickamauga's lost opportunities on three generals: Polk, Hindman, and D. H. Hill.[3]

On September 22, while news of the Army of Tennessee's victory spread throughout the Confederacy, Bragg wrote Polk and demanded an explanation for his failure to advance at dawn on the twentieth. That same day he wrote his wife a scathing letter criticizing Polk's inaction on the battle's second day. For some reason Polk failed to respond to his commanding general's missive. On the twenty-fifth, therefore, Bragg repeated his request. His adjutant, Col. George W. Brent, informed Polk that the general needed his report of the battle "without delay." Polk's intransigence caused Bragg to write Davis to request Polk's removal from command. He also described the failures of General Hindman for disobeying orders at McLemore's Cove and of General Hill, who "is always in a state of apprehension, and upon the most flimsy pretexts makes such reports of the enemy about him as to keep up constant apprehension, and require constant reinforcements." The commanding general stated that a want of transportation hampered military operations against the Federals, but he complained that the "greatest evil" frustrating his army remained "inefficient commanders." Bragg also hinted that Polk, a close friend of the president, might have to be replaced as a corps commander in the Army of Tennessee.[4]

While Bragg awaited a reply from Richmond, he received Polk's response to his earlier queries regarding the nineteenth. This detailed account of the morning of September 20 placed the blame squarely on D. H. Hill. According to Polk, he met one of Hill's staff officers and told him to relay a request for the general to meet with him at the wing's headquarters. When Hill failed to appear, Polk issued orders to his corps commanders to attack at dawn on the twentieth. His messenger returned later that night, however, unable to locate Hill. Polk then sent orders to Hill's division commanders to attack the Union lines as soon as their units went into position. At this point Hill finally became aware of Polk's orders to attack at dawn but warned that he would be unable to launch an assault until his troops received their rations. At 7:00 A.M. on the twentieth, Polk informed Bragg that he had to ride to Hill's sector to urge the advance and received yet another reason for delay: Hill had mistakenly assumed that Maj. Gen. Benjamin F. Cheatham's line stood at a right angle to his own, necessitating a delay to realign Cheatham's troops. Thus Polk shifted the blame for the failure to attack as planned to Hill. Dissatisfied, Bragg charged Polk with failing to attack the enemy as ordered, then cited Hindman for disobeying orders at McLemore's Cove. He suspended Polk and Hindman from command on September 29 and, to avoid further dissent in the Army of Tennessee,

Gen. Braxton Bragg, the much
maligned Army of Tennessee
commander and afterward
military advisor to Pres. Jefferson
Davis, feuded with most of his
subordinates during his tenure
as army commander (1862–63).
After his resignation from active
command in December 1863,
Bragg served in Richmond
and helped shape the War
Department's unfavorable
view of Longstreet in 1864.
LIBRARY OF CONGRESS
(LC-USZC4-7984)

sent them to Atlanta to await orders. As Richmond socialite Mary Chesnut observed, "Bragg always stops to quarrel with his generals."[5]

The origins of Bragg's quarrels could be traced back to the late summer and early fall of 1862 during the Confederate invasion of Kentucky. That June President Davis had appointed Bragg as commander of the Army of the Mississippi (later renamed the Army of Tennessee) after his predecessor, General Beauregard, had gone on medical leave. Upset with Beauregard's abdication of command and hesitant to trust the Creole general with the western army, Davis instructed Bragg to assume permanent command. Although the president faced widespread criticism for removing the highly popular Beauregard, he was determined to support Bragg, praising him for his past achievements in service to his country.[6]

Bragg's rise to command the Confederacy's foremost western army should not have surprised Southerners, for he boasted an impressive prewar record. Born in 1817 in Warrenton, North Carolina, Bragg graduated from West Point, ranking fifth in the class of 1833. He fought with distinction in the Mexican-American War at the Battles of Monterrey and Buena Vista. Following the war, Bragg served on frontier duty and then married Eliza Brooks Ellis in 1849. Seven years later he resigned from the U.S. Army to manage his two sugar plantations in Louisiana. At the outset of the Civil War, Bragg served as a major general in the Louisiana State Army before accepting a commission as a brigadier general in the Confederacy. An efficient administrator and strict disciplinarian, he assumed command of the Gulf Coast from Pensacola, Florida, to Mobile, Alabama, in the war's first months. President Davis rewarded Bragg's hard work and efficient service with a promotion to major general in September 1861. In early 1862 the War Department placed Bragg at the head of 10,000 men and ordered him to join Albert Sidney Johnston and Beauregard in northern Mississippi.[7]

As he entered to active field duty, Bragg took with him an earnest conviction in the offensive strategy taught at West Point by Prof. Dennis Hart Mahan. Too often he and many of Mahan's students ignored their professor's warnings of the tactical offensive. In the Battle of Shiloh, on April 6–7, 1862, Bragg launched frontal assaults on the Federals at the "Hornets' Nest," incurring heavy casualties in his command. After the Yankees repulsed his attacks, the Confederates flanked the position and expelled the defenders. As Bragg's foremost biographer, Grady McWhiney, has argued: "In his desire to drive back the Federals, he forgot Mahan's warning about the dangers of the frontal assaults on a strong position. Bragg had tried to overwhelm the enemy with the bayonet."[8]

Bragg received minimal criticism from the press and the authorities in Richmond for his costly tactics at Shiloh. Yet his soldiers began expressing their disapproval of their general's rigid discipline, a persistent complaint throughout his military career. Despite with his reputation as a martinet, Bragg did have his supporters. Foremost among them was President Davis, who ignored the criticism and promoted Bragg to full general, making him the Confederacy's fifth-ranking officer.[9]

Shortly afterward, Bragg proposed a late-summer invasion of Kentucky to drive the Federals from Middle Tennessee, feed his army, and inspire Rebel sympathizers in the state. If Kentucky could be added to the Confederacy, Bragg reasoned, the South might be able to win its independence. He therefore launched one of the Confederate Army's boldest offensives, utilizing six railroads to transport more than 30,000 troops nearly eight hundred miles on a circuitous journey through Alabama and Georgia to Chattanooga and then Knoxville. From Tennessee Bragg's army joined the Army of Kentucky under Maj. Gen. Edmund Kirby Smith as it advanced into the Bluegrass State.[10]

Bragg's bold offensive had the desired effect: Union forces under Maj. Gen. Don Carlos Buell retreated from southern Tennessee and northern Alabama to check the Confederate advance. Amid this struggle for control of Kentucky during the early fall of 1862, Bragg faced a myriad of problems, above all a lack of cooperation from Kirby Smith, who was not subject to his command. The campaign culminated in the Battle of Perryville on October 8, 1862. Although the Confederates had gained possession of the battlefield that evening, they believed a numerically superior foe remained, so Bragg refused to renew the offensive and retreated to Tennessee, rendering the invasion a disappointing failure. Consequently, Southern observers criticized the general's handling of the campaign and urged his removal from command. Bragg's subordinate generals, led by Polk, openly criticized their commander for the failure.[11]

As the army retraced its steps into Tennessee, the recriminations against Bragg intensified. Soldiers, politicians, newspapers, and citizens all joined in the anti-Bragg campaign. Polk remained foremost among Bragg's critics, however, exploiting his friendship with the Confederate president by openly criticizing the general. While attending West Point together back in the 1820s, Polk and Davis had struck a lifelong friendship. After graduating in 1827, Polk resigned from the army to become an Episcopal minister, returning to military service at the onset of war and receiving a commission from the Confederate government. Davis's fondness for Polk led the president to promote the bishop beyond his martial abilities. Maintaining Polk in command would be a mistake to which Davis would never admit.[12]

Polk also urged other generals to criticize Bragg. The bishop-general, whose talent for persuasion surpassed his military expertise, induced Kirby Smith to denounce Bragg's conduct of the Kentucky campaign. Kirby Smith informed the War Department that he would rather be transferred than serve under Bragg. Faced with a potential crisis, President Davis summoned Bragg and Polk to Richmond in late October to settle their dispute. After conferring with both men, the president decided to uphold Bragg.[13]

The failure in Kentucky, however, impelled Davis to appoint Joseph E. Johnston as overall commander of the western theater, including Bragg's army, now renamed the Army of Tennessee. Davis sought only to use the general's much respected expertise in military strategy, for although Johnston oversaw the Army of Tennessee and Lt. Gen. John C. Pemberton's Army of Mississippi, he commanded neither, acting more in the role of an advisor instead. Immediately, Johnston's military concepts clashed with those of Davis, deepening the discord between the two strong-willed men.[14]

While Davis and Johnston struggled over strategy, Buell's replacement, General Rosecrans, clashed with Bragg's army near Murfreesboro, Tennessee, about twenty-five miles southeast of Nashville, from December 31, 1862, to January 2, 1863. Although the Battle of Stones River resulted in a tactical draw, Bragg withdrew his exhausted and demoralized army. Like the aftermath of Perryville, the retreat following Stones River created dissension among Bragg's subordinates and disappointed the Southern populace. Maj. Gen. John C. Breckinridge, whom Bragg censured in his report, allegedly challenged his commander to a duel. The *Chattanooga Rebel* claimed that Bragg had lost the confidence of his army, "that a change was necessary & that the retrograde movement from Murfreesboro was against the advise [*sic*] of his general officers."[15]

The *Rebel*'s report particularly disturbed Bragg, leading him to write his senior generals and solicit their written opinions on his leadership and his decision to retreat from Murfreesboro. To Bragg's vexation, the responses to his missive generally called for the commanding general's resignation. Whatever vulnerability he might have displayed in sending out the letter evaporated with the replies. Bragg maintained that he only sought affirmation of his decision to retreat from Murfreesboro, stating that the letter "was never intended [to] go farther than the parties to whom it was addressed." He nonetheless prepared for what he believed to be his inevitable removal from command, explaining his decision to retreat in a note to Davis and offering his resignation to save the president the political embarrassment of having to support him.[16]

Davis responded by ordering Johnston to visit the army and examine the situation.[17] Johnston arrived at the Army of Tennessee's new base in Tullahoma on January 27, 1863, and after conferring with some senior officers, found that the army lacked confidence in its commander. Yet the general did not want to assume command himself because he feared that if he superseded Bragg, he would be accused of seeking an independent field command at the expense of a fellow officer. As historian Craig L. Symonds has noted, Johnston's sense of personal honor did not allow him to assume command of the army by recommending Bragg's removal. Even though he knew that the army had lost confidence in Bragg, Johnston gave Davis positive accounts to discourage the opinion that he sought active field duty. To avoid the impression that he coveted Bragg's command, Johnston defended Bragg's position with misleading reports of his leadership abilities. In addition to his acute sense of honor, Johnston's long-cherished hope of returning to the Army of Northern Virginia, his original field command, also influenced his actions. The report left Davis no choice but to retain Bragg in command.[18]

Davis's failure to resolve the Army of Tennessee's command problems ultimately harmed the Confederate war effort in the West. Critics of the president publicly censured Bragg to embarrass the administration's war policies, and their denunciation of Bragg convinced Davis that a conspiracy existed to supplant the controversial general. He felt that condemnations of his appointments indicated criticism of his administration. As a result, Davis intensified his support for Bragg.

Meanwhile, the ranking officers in the Army of Tennessee continued their feud with the commanding general. Depressed by his wife's illness and suffering from migraine headaches, Bragg added fuel to the fire by attacking those who had initially criticized him. This could not have come at a worse time, for in the mid-summer of 1863, Rosecrans's Army of the Cumberland, through a series of skillfully executed flanking movements, maneuvered Bragg out of Middle Tennessee and forced him to retreat toward Chattanooga.[19]

The Army of Tennessee arrived in Chattanooga on July 4, the day Pemberton surrendered at Vicksburg and the day after Lee suffered defeat at Gettysburg. Following those losses, the Confederate War Department again focused on events in Tennessee. In late July officials ordered 9,000 troops under Generals Breckinridge and William H. T. Walker, stationed in Mississippi, to report to Tennessee. Davis also promoted Daniel Harvey Hill to lieutenant general and ordered him to command a corps in Bragg's army. Furthermore, he directed General Hindman to replace Maj. Gen. Jones M. Withers as commander of a division in Polk's Corps. In August Davis further reinforced Bragg by ordering Buckner, commanding the Department of East Tennessee, to lead another corps in the Army of Tennessee.[20]

Although the Confederate government intended to improve the army's command structure, Bragg's working relationship with his new generals was poor and each of the men, for various reasons, would prove to be uncooperative. Thus this reorganization during Rosecrans's advance reflected a lack of knowledge in Richmond about the true conditions in the West. Although Davis's decision to reinforce Bragg appeared logical, his choice of replacements suggests a naïveté about the Army of Tennessee. Without considering the persistent discord between the general and his subordinates, the personnel Richmond transferred to Bragg's army practically ensured continued conflict and lack of cooperation. Breckinridge, Buckner, Hill, Hindman, and Walker each resented their new commander. While Buckner detested his demotion from independent command in Knoxville, Breckinridge disliked Bragg because he had criticized his fellow Kentuckians after Perryville. Hindman and Walker, loyal supporters of Joe Johnston, also had reservations about their new commander. With the imminent addition of Longstreet, also an ardent supporter of Johnston, most of the Army of Tennessee's corps commanders would be prejudiced against Bragg.[21] Despite Davis's best intentions, his reorganization and reinforcement of the Army of Tennessee would fail to unify its volatile command structure.

When Longstreet prepared to go west in early September 1863, Bragg had been struggling with dissension in his army for more than a year. The malcontents had incessantly lobbied influential Confederate politicians and spread their rancor toward Bragg to anyone who would listen to their grievances. The situation had so deteriorated that communication between Bragg and his lieutenants was almost nonexistent. In mid-August Rosecrans sought to exploit the paralysis affecting the Army of Tennessee by launching the Chickamauga campaign. Bragg's failure to stop the Federal advance resulted from the dissension in his army, which allowed Rosecrans to advance virtually uncontested into northern Georgia.[22]

Before Polk responded to Bragg's September 22 query on why he fumbled his daylight assault, Bragg decided to purge his army of the dissident generals. His letters to President Davis of September 25 indicate that decision, but he needed the president's assistance to instigate his plan. When Bragg received Polk's reply placing the blame for the delays of the twentieth on D. H. Hill, he declared it unsatisfactory and ordered both Polk's and Hindman's suspension from command nine days later, citing the latter's failure against the Federals at McLemore's Cove on September 10–12. Bragg knew that Polk was a popular figure in the Army of Tennessee and his removal would meet with disapproval. This is why he ordered both men to Atlanta, far away from the army. But Bragg did not realize that while he sought to place the blame for Chickamauga's lost opportunities on his dissident corps commanders, the army's other high-ranking officers continued to conspire against him.[23]

While Bragg maneuvered to suspend Polk, the bishop-general met with Longstreet, Hill, and Buckner on September 26 to discuss the "mismanagement manifested in the conduct of military operations in this army." According to one officer who met with Polk later that day, the generals "condemned [the] delay since Monday 21st and thought active pursuit would have been better." The generals agreed that Bragg had mishandled the victory at Chickamauga by failing to seize the initiative and resume the offensive against Rosecrans. The others urged Longstreet to write Davis and suggest Bragg's removal from command of the Army of Tennessee. Polk and his cronies probably assumed that Longstreet's reputation in Virginia and his close ties to Lee gave him great influence with the Confederate president. The support Longstreet received from the army's senior officers did not appear to be motivated by their desire to see him supersede Bragg, but rather to have Joe Johnston assume command. Probably remembering Davis's cold response to his opinion at the October 1862 meeting with Johnston, Longstreet demurred, proposing to write General Lee and Secretary of War Seddon instead. Polk then offered to write Davis once again to urge that Bragg be replaced with another general, preferably Lee.[24]

Longstreet wrote Seddon on the twenty-sixth, indicating that Bragg's command of the Army of Tennessee seriously impaired the Confederate cause. He began by proclaiming that Chickamauga proved "the most complete victory of the war." After a brief report of his actions during and after the battle, he turned to Bragg's generalship. Longstreet told Seddon that he was "convinced that nothing but the hand of God can save us or help us as long as we have our present commander." He cited Bragg's failure to "adopt and adhere to any plan or course" and expressed disdain for having to serve under him. "In an ordinary war I could serve without complaint under any one whom the Government might place in authority," Longstreet explained, "but we have too much at stake in this to remain quiet under such distressing circumstances." He then requested that Richmond send Lee to replace Bragg, suggesting that the Army of Northern Virginia could operate defensively while Lee led the western army and regained Tennessee. Longstreet also wrote Lee that same day and repeated many of his same arguments.[25]

In requesting his chief's services in the West, Longstreet already knew that he had rejected Davis's earlier request to assume command of the Army of Tennessee. The general may have believed that if Lee turned down the western command again, as Lee's senior lieutenant he stood next in line for the post—after all, Longstreet outranked every officer in the West except Bragg and Johnston. Meanwhile, on the same date that Longstreet wrote his letter to the secretary of war, Polk wrote to Lee also urging the Virginian's presence in Tennessee. He repeated many of Longstreet's same arguments, maintaining that Bragg had failed to exploit the victory at Chickamauga and that Lee could safely leave his army in Virginia on the defensive while he came west. For Longstreet, Polk, and the rest of the dissident generals, the central motive in requesting Lee's transfer appears to have been Bragg's removal, regardless of his successor. Polk, after his year-long effort to oust Bragg from command, seemed unlikely to yield to another commander he hardly knew. His alliance with Longstreet thus resulted from convenience more than from a genuine desire to see the First Corps chief assume command of the Army of Tennessee a mere week after his arrival.[26]

Several historians later described Longstreet's plea for Lee's assistance as a smokescreen to conceal his real goal of succeeding Bragg.[27] Longstreet, however, knew that if Davis appointed Johnston to army command, he would serve under a general who would allow him considerable latitude in his operations. Moreover, if Lee did accept command of the Tennessee army, Longstreet knew that it would be only a temporary measure— once Lee returned east, Longstreet probably reasoned that he stood a good chance of taking over the Army of Tennessee. Adding to the complex possibilities, McLaws, in a postwar account, suggested that Longstreet urged Lee to take command in Tennessee so Longstreet could assume the leadership of the Virginia army during Lee's absence. If that endeavor failed, McLaws reasoned, one of the dissident generals who sought Bragg's removal might even suggest Longstreet as a replacement for Bragg.[28] Regardless of the motive, Longstreet and his fellow conspirators flirted with mutiny in urging their commanding general's dismissal less than a week after a victorious battle. But if they expected Bragg's immediate departure, they were sorely mistaken.

Although Longstreet claimed that his criticism of Bragg reflected his concern for the Confederate cause, his professional behavior in Tennessee was deplorable. Not content with his official letters to the War Department, he continued to speak unfavorably of the commanding general and failed to dispel rumors that he would eventually supersede him. Upon arriving in the West, he continued to criticize Bragg. "Longstreet is talking about him [Bragg] in a way to destroy all his usefulness," observed Brig. Gen. William W. Mackall, Bragg's chief of staff. Mackall offered his candid views in a separate letter to General Johnston: "I think Longstreet has done more injury to the general [Bragg] than all the others put together. You may understand how much influence with his troops a man of his standing would have to the effect that B[ragg] was not on the field and Lee would have been."[29] Longstreet's blunt, outspoken disposition once again caused him problems. This time, however, he had joined a group of dissident generals who blamed their commanding officer for their own failures.

Bragg's attempt to stifle any protest arising out of Polk's removal had minimal effect, for once Polk arrived in Atlanta, the bishop launched a new campaign to oust his old nemesis. From his temporary exile, Polk wrote his fellow officers and requested their written statements to exonerate him. As he gathered evidence to support his case against the commanding general, his suspension caused additional insubordination in the army's high command; Bragg's attempt to suppress further rancor by ordering him to Atlanta thus backfired. Because of Polk's popularity in the Army of Tennessee, the discontent against Bragg escalated. Less than a week after Polk's removal, Longstreet, Hill, and Buckner met a second time, this time with

Breckinridge. Dissatisfied with conditions in the army and the removal of their fellow corps commanders, the malcontents wrote a petition requesting Bragg's removal to be circulated among the ranking officers.[30]

The disgruntled generals also wrote Davis and reiterated their earlier assertions that Bragg had proved an incompetent commander. Declaring that Bragg's health "totally unfits him for the command of an army in the field," the petitioners pointed out that the Federals in Chattanooga gained strength while the Confederates vacillated on Missionary Ridge. They urged Davis to "assign to the command of this army an officer who will inspire the army and the country with undivided confidence." Acknowledging that their joint appeal might seem "unusual among military men," they claimed that conditions in the western army compelled them to act. The conspirators subsequently circulated the document to the Army of Tennessee's senior officers and requested their signatures to support their allegations against Bragg. Originating at Buckner's headquarters, the document moved through the officer corps. Generals such as Breckinridge and St. John Liddell, a division commander in Hill's Corps, refused to sign it because of pending legal matters with Bragg or because no adequate candidate could take the commander's place. The petition nevertheless moved through Buckner's, Hill's, and finally Longstreet's corps, eventually bearing twelve signatures of corps, division, and brigade commanders.[31]

While scholars have debated the origins of the document, examination of it points to Buckner as the final author. The original four-page document bears Buckner's signature directly below the closing, includes Hill's signature fourth in line, and Longstreet's name at the upper left of a separate column of signatures. In his postwar account Longstreet concurred with Bragg's and Davis's 1863 theory that Hill wrote the document. He states that Hill, in a postwar letter, admitted to writing the petition. Hill, in fact, confessed to writing the original document but claimed that Buckner altered it without submitting the revisions to him. The positions of the signatures supports Buckner as the author, though Hill later acknowledged that he "signed the Petition readily." But this last part of Hill's account, composed more than twenty years after the war, does not coincide with a memorandum written by his adjutant, Col. Archer Anderson, less than two weeks after the event in question. According to Anderson, "Gen. Polk got it [the letter] up and it was written by Gen. Buckner." Hill told Anderson that he put "his name to that paper with great reluctance."[32]

Bragg learned of the petition the same night the generals wrote it. In a letter to his wife on October 5, Mackall confided: "Last night we found out that there was a petition to the President to relieve Bragg, circulating among the General Officers. It gave Bragg much distress and mortification. I do believe he thought himself popular." Wary about the effect of such an inflammatory letter on the troops, Bragg and Col. James Chesnut, Davis's envoy to the Army of Tennessee, wrote the president that same day and asked him to come to Chattanooga to calm the unrest in the army's high command. Chesnut learned of the discontent when Longstreet approached him on October 4, described the army's "distressed condition, and urged him to go on to Richmond with all speed and to urge upon the President relief for us."[33]

For over a year, Davis had ignored conditions in the West, thus allowing the situation to deteriorate beyond repair. He began to placate the dissent in Bragg's army by opposing the removal of his old friend Leonidas Polk. After Bragg suspended the bishop on September 29, he forwarded a message to the War Department informing them of his actions. Adjutant General Cooper immediately forwarded this dispatch to Davis. The president returned Bragg's telegram with an endorsement informing the general that he could not relieve an officer from duty without arrest. Moreover, if Bragg intended to arrest Polk, he would have to file formal charges against his subordinate in a court-martial. The following day Davis followed up his notation on Bragg's message with a short note encouraging the commander to recall Polk and Hindman and drop the matter. He also seemed to imply that Bragg's actions against the bishop had only further alienated his men. Perhaps if Bragg offered an olive branch to the dissident generals, Davis reasoned, the discord would fade away.[34]

Yet Bragg was adamant: Polk and Hindman must be punished. In a message to the president, he insisted that Polk's suspension resulted from a "flagrant" offense that was a "repetition of the past." "If restored by you to his command the amnesty should extend to all," Bragg argued. As a face-saving measure, he asked that if Davis reinstated Polk to at least send the bishop to Mississippi in exchange for Hardee. Davis responded two days later, still urging Bragg to restore Polk. The president pointed out how his earlier messages, suggesting that Polk not be placed in arrest, were with hopes of "avoiding a controversy which could not heal the injury sustained, and which I feared would entail further evil." He reminded Bragg that the "opposition to you both in the army and out of it has been a public calamity in so far that it impairs your capacity for usefulness." Davis maintained that Polk "possessed the confidence and affection of his corps," and it would probably be "better that his influence in your favor should be preserved by a lenient course."[35] Davis's efforts to reconcile Bragg to Polk clearly indicate his failure to grasp the state of bitterness in the Army of Tennessee.

After the president received Chesnut's telegram of the fourth, he decided
to travel to Chattanooga and investigate the situation personally. Davis departed for Missionary Ridge, the site of Bragg's headquarters, on October 6
but paused in Atlanta to confer with Polk about conditions in the Army of
Tennessee. During this meeting, he heard Polk's view of events and the
litany of Bragg's transgressions. The president tried to convince the bishop
that he should return to the army, but Polk declined, saying that he would
rather resign than serve under Bragg. Polk actually seemed disappointed
that the charges against him would be dropped since he hoped a court of
inquiry would vindicate him and demonstrate Bragg's incompetence. Ultimately, Bragg did not file charges; Davis approved Polk's transfer to Mississippi to serve directly under Joe Johnston. While the president conferred
with the bishop, he wrote Breckinridge on October 8 and requested that he
and Longstreet meet with him before he arrived at Bragg's headquarters so
they "could converse more fully on the road." On the appointed day the two
generals joined the president and his staff while Davis addressed crowds
in Atlanta and Marietta. Although there is no written record of their meeting, Davis probably heard critical assessments of Bragg from Longstreet
and Breckinridge as he traveled to Missionary Ridge with the hope that he
could eliminate the growing mutiny in the Army of Tennessee.[36]

Davis had actually formulated his plan to eliminate dissatisfaction in
the Army of Tennessee before he left Richmond. Dismissing the reports of
discontent as products of nervous anxiety, the president decided to retain
Bragg as army commander because he could not find a suitable replacement.
Despite Davis's earlier doubts about the general's fitness for command, he
now insisted that Bragg was the best man for the Army of Tennessee. Rul-
ing out Johnston, Beauregard, and Longstreet as possible successors, Davis remained unwavering in his support of Bragg. Consequently, within
twenty-four hours of his arrival, Davis informed the general that his position was secure. But to end the rancor in the army, the president planned
to gather the army's senior officers and ask them personally to declare their
allegiance before the commanding general. He felt that when in the presence of Bragg and himself, the generals would feel compelled to offer favorable assessments of their chief. Davis hoped that by asserting their loyalty,
they would boost their commander's confidence, which had sunk to a low
level since the victory at Chickamauga. The president, however, grossly
underestimated the breech between Bragg and his lieutenants. (Davis also
displayed a similar insensitivity to public opinion by traveling to Tennessee
with General Pemberton, a Northern-born officer thoroughly detested by
the Southern populace since his surrender at Vicksburg.)[37]

Arriving at Bragg's headquarters on October 9, Davis proceeded with his reconciliation plan by calling a meeting with the corps commanders: Longstreet, Buckner, Hill, and Benjamin F. Cheatham (Polk's replacement). The four generals assembled in Bragg's office, appearing anxious for the meeting to begin. Davis, with Bragg present, spoke first and addressed the issue at hand, the conduct of the Chickamauga campaign. He asked Longstreet for his opinion, but the First Corps commander hesitated. "I think that I understood the meaning of his question, but evaded it by a general answer," he later confessed. Remembering Davis's cold response to his opinion at a previous military conference, Longstreet answered that since he was a new addition to the Tennessee army, he "should not be called to an opinion." The president insisted, however, and Longstreet responded: "I said that my estimate of Gen. Bragg as a Field Marshall [is] not high, and . . . the little experience I had with him had not increased it." Buckner and Cheatham followed Longstreet, and they respectfully concurred with his account. Longstreet's criticism of Bragg, however, paled in comparison to Hill's scathing assessment. "Hill had carefully taken a seat off in a corner of the room, apparently trying to be overlooked," Longstreet later wrote. "But when forced to speak, took his chair up and moved out almost to the centre [sic] of the circle," offering his candid opinion of Bragg. Hill confessed to admiring Bragg when he first served under him during the Mexican-American War but concluded that "he was never so mistaken in his estimate of a man's character as a soldier."[38] Disappointed with the results of the meeting, Davis dismissed the generals to plan his next maneuver.

If Longstreet and the other petitioners thought that their assessments would induce Davis to remove Bragg, they too were mistaken. Embarrassed by the outcome of the conference, Bragg offered his resignation, but the president refused it because he felt that no "change for the better could be made in the commander of the army." Years later Davis recounted the meeting with Bragg and his lieutenants, lamenting "the painful fact . . . that there was not the harmony and subordination essential to success." Unwilling to concede failure to the western concentration bloc, which campaigned for Bragg's removal and the appointment of Johnston, the logical successor, the president "prevailed upon [Bragg] to stay where he was, assuring him of his support if it were needed in the future." Although some officers and men expected Davis to make sweeping changes in the Army of Tennessee, all remained as before—Davis kept Bragg in command despite overwhelming lack of confidence in his leadership.[39]

Determined to support Bragg and restore confidence in his command,

Davis resumed his inspection of the army and met separately with Longstreet and Buckner on October 10. He met first with Longstreet that morning. Riding along the Confederate lines, the two men spent most of the
day discussing military matters in general and the Chickamauga campaign
in particular. Ultimately, the subject of the army's leadership surfaced
once again. Longstreet, who left the only written account of the meeting,
remembered that the president's mood suddenly became sullen. Davis
asked the general who he thought should command the Army of Tennessee. Longstreet immediately recommended Johnston as Bragg's successor
but quickly received Davis's disapproval. "The suggestion of that name,"
Longstreet later noted, "only served to increase his displeasure, and his
severe rebuke." The First Corps commander noted the president's disappointment in his suggestion and offered his resignation, or at least a leave
of absence. Davis refused to accept either. Even though Longstreet recalled
that the meeting "was exciting, at some times warm," he remained wary of
the results. As the meeting ended, the president smiled and politely shook
the general's hand when he left. But Longstreet could sense that "clouds
were gathering about [the] head-quarters of the First Corps."[40]

Later that day Davis met with Buckner, a conference that proved equally
disappointing. As they rode along the crest of Lookout Mountain, overlooking the Tennessee River and the Federals in Chattanooga, Buckner
offered his assessment of Bragg's generalship. "General Bragg is wanting
in imagination," he declared, adding that when Bragg was faced with a crisis, he became so overwhelmed that he would "lean upon the advice of a
drummer boy." Other officers echoed Longstreet's and Buckner's opinions.
Colonel Chesnut even told Davis that "every honest man he saw out west
thought well of Joe Johnston" in a vain attempt to convince the president to
replace Bragg with Johnston.[41] Davis refused to yield to his political foes,
however, by appointing his old adversary to command the Army of Tennessee. But dissension in the army's high command was so strong that decisive
action appeared necessary.

Davis was surprised by the degree of animosity and dissent expressed
by Bragg's subordinates. "Mr. Davis got more than he came for," observed
one staff officer. Three separate interviews had elicited the same results:
blunt criticism of Bragg's generalship and an urgent request for his removal.
Davis, however, remained adamantly opposed to giving command of the
army to either Johnston or Beauregard. Furthermore, he was disappointed
with the conduct of Longstreet and Hill at his initial military conference.
Ignoring the critics, the president decided to uphold the commanding

general. On the eleventh Davis authorized Bragg to relieve any officer who failed to cooperate with him; Bragg eagerly planned to eliminate all of his hostile subordinates. "I want to get rid of all such generals," he declared. "I have better men in subordinate stations to fill their places." Bragg chose D. H. Hill as the first target of his housecleaning. On the day he received Davis's orders, the general relieved Hill, claiming that he "weakens the morale and military tone of his command." Before Davis left North Georgia, he officially approved this move.[42]

While Bragg maneuvered to eliminate all opposition within the army, Davis embarked on a public-relations campaign to sway troop sentiment in favor of their commanding general. On October 12 and 13 the president made several speeches in which he complimented Bragg and denounced the "shafts of malice that have been hurled against him." He also told the men they "were entitled to the gratitude of the country for their heroism, and assured them that the green fields of Tennessee would shortly be ours again." Although Davis hoped to increase morale by visiting several Confederate units near Chattanooga, most soldiers greeted him with indifference. According to a recent historian of the Chattanooga campaign, many of the army's rank and file resented the president's insistence on sustaining Bragg and the transfer of divisions and brigades to reduce the influence of the general's detractors. Likewise, the veterans of the First Corps did not care for Bragg, focusing their displeasure on their new commander and blaming him for the recent losses. John Percy Maloney of the 1st Texas Infantry expressed what seemed to be the general consensus. "Bragg is very unpopular with his troops, and justly so," he wrote. "He seems to vent his evil spleen at the causes of his unpopularity by arresting his generals."[43]

When Davis left the army on the fourteenth, he issued a proclamation urging the men to support their commanding general. After reminding them of their success at Chickamauga, the president urged them to remain focused on the Federals at Chattanooga, warning them not to fight among themselves. "He who sows the seed of discontent and distrust prepares for the harvest of slaughter and defeat," he asserted. "Crown these with harmony, due subordination, and cheerful support of lawful authority, that the measure of your duty may be full."[44] Thriving on the president's steadfast support, Bragg proceeded to reorganize his army and reassert his authority. In addition to relieving Hill, Bragg reduced Buckner from corps to division command and transferred Tennessee troops from Cheatham's Corps to reduce Cheatham's influence among the men. Only Longstreet, thanks to his prestige and his superb performance at Chickamauga, escaped Bragg's admonishment. Although Davis spoke favorably of Longstreet's ability as a military leader, he remained suspicious of the First Corps commander, who had aligned himself with the administration's critics.[45]

Despite Davis's solid support, Bragg's campaign against those who opposed him continued to create difficulties with some of his subordinates. General Liddell recalled, "Everything remained just as in the beginning." Others simply sought to be reassigned elsewhere. Forrest, the brilliant cavalry chief, arrived at army headquarters in early October, incensed that Bragg had transferred some of his troops to Maj. Gen. Joseph Wheeler's cavalry corps. Forrest confronted Bragg and, after criticizing the commanding general, threatened his life should he ever interfere with his own command again. On the thirteenth Bragg approved Forrest's request for a transfer. This displeased Colonel Brent, Bragg's adjutant. In his private journal Brent wrote: "This change is injudicious. Coupled with the existing discontents in the Cavalry it will tend materially to still further impair its usefulness."[46]

Forrest was not the only officer seeking a transfer out of the Army of Tennessee. William Mackall, Bragg's chief of staff, also had had enough of his commander. Since the spring Mackall, who had attended West Point alongside Bragg, had witnessed firsthand the deterioration of his classmate's command and yearned to serve elsewhere.[47] He felt that Bragg's personality did not suit him for army leadership. In a confidential letter to his wife, Mackall wrote:

> He [Bragg] is as much influenced by his enemies as by his friends, and does not know how to control the one or preserve the other. He is very earnest at his work, his whole soul is in it, but his manner is repulsive and he has no social life. He is easily flattered and fond of seeing reverence for his high position. Between ourselves, he has more than once issued orders for the movement of the army—would scarce listen to my objections, and yet I have gone to bed perfectly satisfied that the movement would never be made and had the orders revoked before morning. If he don't [sic] want news to be true, he will listen to nothing. "It can't be so," is his reasoning, and if it proves true, he is not prepared to meet it.[48]

On October 16 Mackall finally decided to leave Bragg and requested a transfer. The general lamented the loss of such an able assistant but thanked him for his services and approved the request.[49]

The transfers of Forrest and Mackall, however, did nothing to extinguish the discontent in the Army of Tennessee. In the next few weeks, Bragg moved against Generals Buckner and Preston, who had been critical of him in recent weeks. Shortly after the president left the army, Buckner received instructions from the War Department that his East Tennessee departmental command had been broken up. Despite Buckner's protests, the government instructed him to serve as a division commander under Bragg. Preston, however, received a transfer to Virginia to serve as a brigade commander. General Cheatham requested a transfer from Bragg's army but was denied by the War Department. Bragg did not focus solely on his senior officers; he also sought to break up factions among his rank and file. Bragg decided to reorganize his army, apparently to eliminate opposition from the Kentucky and Tennessee troops. He justified the reshuffling of his command while facing the enemy at Chattanooga by maintaining that several divisions in the army contained brigades from one state and that parceling them out would reduce the possibility of one state bearing an unfair share of the casualties. In reality, his efforts stemmed from his desire to reduce the influence of men such as Cheatham by eliminating large concentrations of soldiers from their home state. With Polk, Hindman, Forrest, and Hill out of the army and Buckner forced to accept a demotion, Bragg's ire now fell on Longstreet.[50]

The weeks after Chickamauga had been personally trying for Longstreet. Not only did he witness Bragg's failure to follow up the battlefield success but also encountered another commanding officer who failed to heed his advice. When he met with Bragg on the evening of September 20, the left-wing commander had requested reinforcements from Polk's wing only to be rebuffed in what he considered a discourteous fashion. When the two generals met again, Bragg rejected Longstreet's plan for an offensive to force the Federals out of Chattanooga. McLaws thought Bragg's failure to heed Longstreet's advice led to the latter's vendetta against his chief: "So it looks as if Gen. Longstreet's crucial test of the fitness of any one to command was his compliance or non-compliance with Longstreet's 'suggestions.' It was a sort of mania of his, and there can be no doubt that he was honest in that belief. For it seemed to make no difference who it was he advised; if he followed his advice he was worthy, if he did not he was not worthy." Despite McLaws's testimony, Longstreet actually held a poor opinion of Bragg even before he arrived in the West. As he traveled to North Georgia, Longstreet had written Senator Wigfall and expressed his displeasure at having to serve under the general. He did indeed fight against serving under Bragg, but his resistance only led to a bitter feud that would plague the two generals for the remainder of Longstreet's tenure in the West.[51]

Longstreet soon assumed a leading role in the anti-Bragg faction. Once Bragg had banished Polk to Atlanta, Longstreet filled Polk's position as the leader of the campaign to remove the commander. As he had done in Virginia, Longstreet spoke freely and bluntly in evaluating Bragg's negative effect on the Confederates' strategic situation in Tennessee. He knew that the Army of Tennessee could not succeed under Bragg, who after all had retreated in two of his major campaigns and then failed to exploit his victory at Chickamauga. Longstreet also knew that Bragg's lieutenants no longer tolerated their commander and hoped that the authorities in Richmond would replace him. His own reputation as a successful corps commander in the eastern theater and his desire to serve under Johnston thus further exacerbated the failing command structure of the Army of Tennessee. Longstreet's prominent role in forming and submitting a petition for Bragg's removal garnered him rancor from the commanding general and mistrust from the president.

Bragg could not rid himself of Longstreet—the savior of Chickamauga— by removing him from command as he did Hill. Unlike Hill, Longstreet held important connections with influential politicians and maintained the trust and affection of his former commander, Robert E. Lee. Following Chickamauga, Lee wrote Longstreet and offered him his "warmest congratulations," saying that "it was natural to hear of Longstreet and [D. H.] Hill charging side by side, and pleasing to find the armies of the east and west vying with each other in valor and devotion to their country." A month later Lee responded to Longstreet's letters requesting his presence with the Army of Tennessee. He lamented Bragg's failure to destroy Rosecrans. As for commanding the Army of Tennessee, he told Longstreet: "I think you can do better than I could. It was with that view I urged your going [to the West]." Such support from Lee, the most popular figure in the Confederacy and an influential confidant of Jefferson Davis, certainly added to Bragg's apprehension. Moreover, Longstreet was popular among the rank and file. It was no accident that his name surfaced as a leading candidate to replace Bragg. The commander therefore moved cautiously against Longstreet, reducing the latter's command to the two infantry divisions and one artillery battalion he had brought from Virginia. Bragg thus made it clear that he did not trust Longstreet.[52]

The uneasy relationship between Bragg and his chief lieutenant thus portended trouble for the Army of Tennessee. Bragg's biographer, Judith

Lee Hallock, presents Longstreet's conflict with Bragg as the "most serious and far-reaching" the army commander had yet experienced.[53] While Longstreet did play a prominent role in the increased discord, the problems had existed for almost a year before his arrival. Leonidas Polk had previously assumed the leadership role in the senior officers' efforts to oust Bragg, but with the arrival of Longstreet, the malcontents saw an opportunity to use him as a tool to influence the administration. While Longstreet did not remain guiltless in his efforts to oust Bragg, the blame should not fall solely on his shoulders. He may have been flattered by the generals' frequent mention of him as a possible successor to Bragg and subsequently failed to dispel rumors to that end. But Longstreet's supporters had not advocated a change in command for over a year only to have an outsider like Longstreet take over. Most likely they felt that they could use the newcomer's political connections and his influence with Lee to accomplish their goal of ending Bragg's leadership of the Army of Tennessee.[54]

Longstreet's role in these efforts proved a failure that reflected poorly on him. Flirting with insubordination, he and his fellow officers conspired to compose and sign a petition urging the removal of their commanding general. While they may have been correct in their assessment of Bragg, the generals had destroyed the solidarity of the army by waging a public campaign against their chief. Moreover, the bitter display of antipathy toward Bragg certainly displeased Jefferson Davis. Even though Lee held Longstreet in high regard and spoke favorably of his lieutenant, the president disliked Longstreet's involvement in political matters. As a Davis biographer has argued, by criticizing government decisions and by allying himself with anti-administration politicians, Longstreet had "pushed his brief familiarity with Davis too far." The president, who disliked strong-willed men who opposed his policies, privately labeled Longstreet a liability and regarded him as a "bitter disappointment."[55]

Davis and the generals of the Army of Tennessee had allowed their honor and pride to override their sense of duty. Firstly, the president would not remove Bragg and appoint Johnston or Beauregard because he disliked the latter two generals. Despite knowing that Bragg had failed as a commanding general, he refused to make a change, for it would be tantamount to admitting that his appointment of the North Carolinian had been a mistake. Secondly, Davis's requirement that the corps commanders confront Bragg with candid assessments of his generalship presented the subordinates with an unwinnable situation. Unaware of Davis's expectations, they spoke freely and denounced Bragg, only to earn the president's disaffection. Finally, Davis would have been spared this awkward situation had Johnston recommended Bragg's removal prior to the Chickamauga campaign and then assumed command of the army as ordered. Johnston failed to fulfill his duties as the commander of the Department of the West by offering a misleading assessment of Bragg's ability to lead the army in the spring of 1863. Had he identified Bragg's faults as a commander, the paralysis that gripped the Army of Tennessee probably would have been averted before the Battle of Chickamauga.

The resulting hostility only served to hinder the Army of Tennessee's high command on the eve of the Chattanooga campaign. Regrettably, Longstreet played a key role in this. The attitude of the First Corps high command filtered down to the junior officers and the rank and file. In early October Capt. John C. Winsmith of the 5th South Carolina lamented Bragg's dispute with his lieutenants: "It is unfortunate that such things occur, as they have a tendency to produce ill feeling and differences and have an unpleasant effect on the soldiers." Longstreet's men also struggled to deal with the perceived shortcomings of their new commanding general. A captain in the First Corps wrote: "Bragg ought to be relieved or disaster is sure to result. The men have no faith. . . . [If] Lee was at the helm [it] would be worth untold reinforcements. The belief that most men have in his infallibility of judgment makes them invincible." Longstreet's artillery chief, E. P. Alexander, observed, "Gen. Bragg [never] inspired any enthusiasm in his men—certainly nothing to be compared with what I was accustomed to see in Virginia." The morale of the soldiers continued to deteriorate in the weeks after Chickamauga as the siege on Chattanooga progressed into late October.[56]

4

"IT IS HARD TO KEEP UP ONE'S SPIRITS WITH AN EMPTY STOMACH AND WET CLOTHING"

THE FIRST CORPS AT CHATTANOOGA

WHILE LONGSTREET AND HIS FELLOW OFFICERS CONSPIRED to oust Bragg as commander of the Army of Tennessee, bitter rivalries and jealousies frustrated the internal harmony of the First Corps. The continuing siege of Chattanooga caused a deterioration of morale among Longstreet's men. The Army of Northern Virginia troops, who arrived in northern Georgia with buoyant spirits and received credit for leading the Confederates to victory at Chickamauga, witnessed bickering and discontent among their division leaders . The conflict grew so intense that it distorted the command structure of the corps and limited the unit's effectiveness. Along with this, Longstreet himself made significant errors that contributed to the reduced potency of Bragg's siege operations. Commanding the far left of the Confederate line at Chattanooga, he became convinced that the Federals intended to advance around his left flank and attack his rear. Consequently, he failed to deploy enough troops to defend Lookout Valley and prevent a Union force from seizing control of this gateway to the city. This allowed the Federals to open a line of supply. By the end of October 1863, Longstreet's mistakes convinced Bragg to order the First Corps into East Tennessee to operate against Union forces in that region.

The First Corps veterans traveled to northern Georgia with certain prejudices about their western counterparts. They had heard accounts of the failures of the Army of Tennessee and believed that Bragg had lost the confidence of his soldiers with the retreats following Perryville and Stones River. "It seems that he falls back every time he has a fight, which only serves to encourage the Yanks and prolong this war," an enlisted man in Hood's Division told his wife. A Georgia soldier regarded the failures of the western forces as "a most awful shock upon this army." He maintained that "the reverses in the West" demoralized the Army of Northern Virginia more than their recent "trip to Pennsylvania." Accordingly, some believed that the western armies had displayed poor fighting prowess. A veteran of the eastern theater wrote his father, "If the armys [sic] of the West were worth a goober we could soon have peace on our own terms." Eli Pinson Landers of Wofford's Brigade wrote his mother that he had little faith in the western troops. "I know it is bad to fight under officers without confidence," he noted. "I wish they had such officers as we have got." Another soldier boasted that "they were going to show them [how] the lick it [whipping the Yankees] is done with." J. B. Polley of the Texas Brigade may not have been as blunt as some of his compatriots, but he believed there was a difference between the two armies. He maintained that the eastern troops had a stronger tendency to charge the enemy, while the western troops were more inclined to "lie-down-and-shoot." Polley claimed that the easterners made the fight a bit more personal than the westerners. Even though he credited the western soldiers for maintaining their ranks in combat, he still thought that the Texas Brigade could overpower any of them.[1]

The senior officers of the Army of Northern Virginia shared the rank and file's views on the superiority of the eastern soldier. Lt. Gen. D. H. Hill noted the differences between the Army of Tennessee and his old command immediately after he arrived in Tennessee in the summer of 1863. In a postwar account he recalled a lack of confidence in Bragg among the enlisted men, attributable to the general's propensity to retreat. General Hood concurred with Hill's assessment of the Tennessee army when he arrived in the West in September 1863. He found Bragg's lieutenants speaking in "a sanguine tone" after the first day's battle at Chickamauga. The Texan conversed with General Breckinridge and told him that the Southerners would "rout the enemy the following day." Upon hearing Hood's optimism, Breckinridge exclaimed: "My dear Hood, I am delighted to hear you say so. You give me renewed hope."[2]

General Longstreet validated his men's conviction with his own views of the western armies. Before his transfer, Longstreet expressed confidence that he could lead Bragg's army to victory and quickly return to Lee. Although Lee concurred with his lieutenant, their attitudes suggest that the

Virginia army's high command underestimated the fighting quality of their western counterparts. Upon his arrival in northern Georgia, Longstreet met with the generals under his command. Hood informed him that after driving the Federals a mile on the nineteenth, they would continue to advance until they achieved victory. Hood noted that Longstreet responded "with that confidence which had so often contributed to his extraordinary success, that we would *of course* whip and drive him [the enemy] from the field." Hood then told him that he "rejoiced to hear him so express himself as he was the first general I had met since my arrival who talked of victory." After the battle Longstreet joked that if he had the rest of the Army of Northern Virginia, "we could have whipped them in half the time."[3]

Regardless of the views the First Corps veterans might have held toward their western counterparts, Bragg's army looked forward to the reinforcements from Virginia, despite some innate jealousies. In the summer of 1863, one Tennessee soldier lamented, "If only we had General Lee to lead us, the war might be won." Some Army of Tennessee veterans were wary that Longstreet and his men would arrive in the West and claim credit should the Confederates defeat the Federals. Lt. James H. Fraser of the 50th Alabama bemoaned that the Tennessee army "could not bear the idea for him to come from Virginia and gain all the glory of whipping 'Rosy.'" Despite some apprehension, a soldier in one Louisiana regiment welcomed the reinforcement. "Gen. Longstreet's corps of the Virginia army was sent to reinforce our army," Douglas Cater recalled. "They had arrived and we were very much encouraged because we certainly needed more men."[4]

For the Army of Tennessee, the influx of veterans from Lee's army was fortuitous. Although the easterners had suffered defeat—most recently at Gettysburg—their losses had been interspersed with major victories, while the Tennessee army had suffered repeated, demoralizing setbacks. Together these Confederates had participated in the largest battle in the western theater and earned the greatest victory for the Army of Tennessee. After the losses at Gettysburg and Vicksburg earlier that summer, the Federal defeat in northern Georgia had lifted Southern hopes and inspired the authorities in Richmond to attempt to regain Chattanooga and Tennessee. Newspapers lauded the victorious Confederate Army and many expressed a renewal of hope that the war would soon end. The Southern press viewed Chickamauga as a "great and glorious victory" as they printed highly partisan accounts of the defeat of the "abolition infidel foe."[5]

Yet the elation of the victory at Chickamauga soon transformed into bitter denunciation as the men of the First Corps blamed Bragg for not immediately pursuing the routed Federals. Although the eastern troops remained unaware of the complex history of problems that plagued the western army, their officers insisted that something must be done to exploit the victory lest it be in vain. Capt. Charles Blackford criticized Bragg shortly after the battle, claiming that the general's "suicidal policy" had spoiled the fruits of victory that Longstreet had won. "Our great victory has turned to ashes," he bewailed.[6] The Army of Northern Virginia's rank and file were far more scathing in their assessment of their new commanding general. A Georgia soldier wrote, "Incompetent fools were allowing the fruits of a great victory to fly from us." One South Carolinian argued that Longstreet could have annihilated Rosecrans's army if not for Bragg's interference on September 21. Another Georgian complained that his regiment had "been waiting for the order to advance or do anything else while waiting. Carry me back to ole Georgia or any where else." John C. West of the 4th Texas argued that if either Hood, Longstreet, or Lee had been in command, "half of Rosecrans's army would have been destroyed." West had no confidence in the commander of the Army of Tennessee. "I do not admire Bragg," he concluded.[7]

Nor did any of Longstreet's men as the Confederates approached the Federal fortifications around Chattanooga. The town had a population of about 2,500 in 1860, but its strategic importance in the war's western theater far surpassed its size. The railroads that bisected Chattanooga made it the "Gateway to the Confederate Heartland." Running to the northwest, the Virginia and East Tennessee Railroad provided an important link to Virginia and the East Tennessee valley. The Western and Atlantic connected Tennessee to Atlanta and other railroads south, while the Nashville and Chattanooga, which ran to the west and alongside the Tennessee River, connected the city with Alabama and the rest of Tennessee. The Nashville and Chattanooga was the most direct route into the city. Once the railroad crossed the Tennessee at Bridgeport, Alabama, it ran to the northeast to Shellmound, Tennessee, before turning to the southeast through Running Water Gap and reaching Wauhatchie, a small junction in Lookout Valley. Although the railroad trestles that crossed Running Water Creek had been burned, this route remained the most likely link between Chattanooga and the Union supply depot at Bridgeport.[8]

Chattanooga lies on the southern side of a bend in the Tennessee River and is surrounded by mountains. Overlooking the town from the southwest are Raccoon Mountain and Lookout Mountain, the latter rising more than two thousand feet above sea level and providing a dominant view of the area. South of Raccoon Mountain lies Sand Mountain, which runs in a northeasterly direction parallel to Lookout Mountain, creating a four-mile-

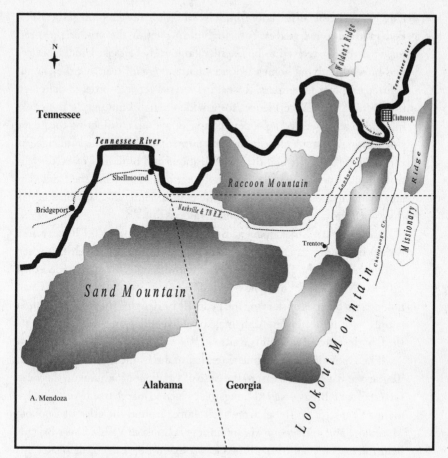

MAP 2. *The Chattanooga Region, 1863*

wide basin called Lookout Valley. On the opposite side of Lookout Mountain, the Chattanooga Valley lies to the east. Missionary Ridge towers five
hundred feet and overlooks Chattanooga from the east; it bisects the Great
Valley of the Appalachians west of the Blue Ridge Mountains. The Tennessee flows west as it approaches the town and then makes a ninety-degree
turn south at its eastern outskirts. At the base of Lookout Mountain, the
river turns north once again, passes Brown's Ferry, and then flows to the
west as it makes its way to Bridgeport. As it snakes through the Cumberland
Mountains, the river forms a peninsula, called Moccasin Point, to the west
of Chattanooga. The Tennessee River Gorge lies west of the city and sepa-
rates Walden's Ridge on the north and Lookout Mountain on the south.[9]

The Confederates approaching Chattanooga on September 23 found
the Army of the Cumberland in a three-mile semicircle around the city, oc-

cupying the same fortifications built by Bragg's army a month earlier. The Federals had confiscated every major building within the city and prepared for what they perceived to be the inevitable Rebel attack. Union soldiers had burned outlying homes around Chattanooga for fear that they might be used as refuge for snipers. Rosecrans and his generals ordered their men to fell trees, homes, and fences to provide enough kindling for the cooking and heat. It seemed a prudent course of action, considering the heavy skirmishing that took place in the days immediately after Chickamauga. As the Federals strengthened their fortifications and built new ones, despair turned into hope as the men regained their confidence and the Confederates made no attempt to attack. By the end of September, Union soldiers dismissed the possibility of a Confederate assault.[10]

Shortly after Chickamauga, Bragg attempted to cut off Rosecrans's retreat by sending a cavalry force across the Tennessee River. But when he realized that the Federals were not withdrawing, Bragg decided on a different course of action. The Army of Tennessee would lay siege to Chattanooga with hopes of starving the Federals by denying them access to their supply base at Stevenson, Alabama, about five miles southwest of town on the Charleston and Memphis Railroad.[11]

The Confederate siege line extended in a six-mile semicircle from the Tennessee River on the east to the base of Lookout Mountain on the west. On October 8 Bragg ordered Longstreet's men to march from West Chickamauga Creek to the Rebel army's left flank, around the edge of Lookout Mountain, and to Raccoon Mountain across Lookout Valley. Law's Brigade held the extreme left of the First Corps, extending a five-mile picket line along the southern bank of the Tennessee from the western edge of Lookout Mountain to the northern face of Raccoon Mountain, slightly beyond Brown's Ferry. To Law's right and across the valley stood the troops of Brig. Gen. Micah Jenkins, a recent arrival from service in South Carolina, who held his men on the eastern side of Lookout Mountain. Longstreet had placed Jenkins in command of Hood's Division while the maimed general recuperated from his Chickamauga injuries. McLaws's Division received orders to position itself on Jenkins's right, in the Chattanooga Valley west of Chattanooga Creek. With reinforcements, the First Corps had approximately 12,000 troops.[12]

Longstreet's men reached their positions along Bragg's siege line with the added equipment that a victory on the field of battle usually procures. Although they had reached northern Georgia with only the bare essentials, the eastern troops reaped the benefits of their victory at Chickamauga by scouring the battlefield for the guns, clothing, and other items soldiers

*View of Chattanooga, Tennessee, from the environs
of Lookout Mountain in the fall of 1863.*
LIBRARY OF CONGRESS (LOT 13464, NO. 2)

coveted during wartime. James K. Munnerlyn of the 2nd South Carolina proved his obedience to Bragg's directive to scavenge the battlefield by describing an abundant booty. "In a complete rout," he wrote, "we took all of their baggage and cannon." Even though he had lost a family bible, he claimed to have taken "several from the Yankees." Other First Corps soldiers corroborated Munnerlyn's experience. A soldier in Benning's Georgia Brigade wrote: "I saw a large mound of knapsacks which belonged to various Federal regiments and the 8th Indiana battery. I searched a number of them for the stationary and found some of the paper of that battery with the Indiana coat of arms and their battery name on it. . . . I have some of the paper now and use it in making reports, &c." Other soldiers maintained that their greatest reward was obtaining a pair of shoes and a blanket, which some claimed would enable them to endure the upcoming winter.[13]

The soldiers of the First Corps thus took their positions along Bragg's siege line with hopeful spirits. Even though Longstreet's men had participated in an unsuccessful siege earlier that year at Suffolk, they tried to remain optimistic that this strategy would prove victorious. A correspondent for the *Charleston Courier* reported that the Confederates were actually "growing stronger every day." At the very least the eastern veterans hoped that Bragg would not order a frontal assault against the formidable defenses. Lt. John B. Evans of the 53rd Georgia informed his wife that even though the Federals had taken refuge in Chattanooga, the "Yankees can't get out [of the city] with out fighting." In fact, a Texan wrote his father, "we are anxiously awaiting their approach." Another eastern veteran anticipated a desperate situation, given that the Confederates surrounded the Federals. "At this time the Yanks is still in Chattanooga," he wrote a week after Chickamauga, "but I think that they want to get out of there if they can." Col. John Bratton of Law's Brigade reconnoitered the Federal lines and ascertained that an attack would become impossible the longer they allowed the Yankees to fortify: "I am satisfied that we cannot take the place by a front attack, and do not think that it will be attempted." Another Alabamian, Pvt. P. T. Vaughn, confirmed Bratton's assessment, declaring that the Federals had "strongly fortified" their works around Chattanooga.[14]

After examining the extensive fortifications around Chattanooga, the Rebel high command determined that a frontal assault was out of the question. Instead Bragg ordered Longstreet to use his artillery, which had arrived from Virginia on September 24, in an attempt to shell the Federals out of the town. Longstreet in turn delegated that task to his artillery chief, Col. E. Porter Alexander, a twenty-eight-year-old West Point graduate and veteran of the Virginia theater. Alexander had arrived in the West with many of the same biases as other veterans of the First Corps. In addition to his partisanship, the artillery chief had no faith in Bragg's plan to shell the enemy out of his entrenchments. "Long range, random shelling is far less effective than it is popularly supposed to be," Alexander commented. Nevertheless, he supervised a three-day operation that involved hauling nearly two dozen guns up the narrow winding paths of Lookout Mountain to its summit, all the while being harassed by Federal batteries. Once the shelling began on the twenty-ninth, the lackluster results did not surprise the colonel. "We fired, mostly, at camps & wagon trains & we probably made some of them unhappy, but there was no result of importance to show," he later wrote. The constant bombardment from Alexander's guns failed to impress the Federals, most of whom carried on with their daily routines more amused than annoyed. After witnessing an ineffectual Confederate shelling, Union colonel Ferdinand Van Derveer joked, "I serve notice on Longstreet that if that is the best he can do, in spite of his successes on the Potomac, his laurels will soon wither in this climate."[15]

As the shelling of Chattanooga continued into October, the initial euphoria in the Army of Tennessee following the victory at Chickamauga soon turned to despondency as the Confederates too began to feel the effects of the siege. Even though the siege was demoralizing to the Federals, they still managed to maintain a tenuous supply line through an old wagon road that ran from Bridgeport north of the Tennessee River and across Walden's Ridge before entering Chattanooga. Yet the road did not provide adequate supplies for Rosecrans's 45,000-man army. The effects of short rations and limited provisions debilitated his soldiers, forcing many units to issue half-rations by early October. Starving men resorted to eating animal feed while the draft animals resorted to eating the bark off trees. The situation in the Army of the Cumberland became so precarious that officers had to post guards over the horses and mules while they ate to prevent the soldiers from stealing the few ears of corn available to them. Despite their hunger and being surrounded by the enemy, the Federal troops in Chattanooga had regained their optimism and anticipated reinforcements.[16]

In truth, the Confederates who surrounded Rosecrans's army suffered as much as the besieged Federals. The Army of Tennessee had depended on the Western and Atlantic Railroad and the depot at Atlanta to supply them with the necessary provisions, but they did not have enough railcars to provide the volume of supplies required by Bragg's 46,000 men. Politics and personal animosity added to the logistical problems of supplying the Confederacy's foremost western army. Col. Lucius B. Northrop, the commissary general of the Subsistence Bureau, disliked Bragg and favored Lee's army in Virginia, so he prioritized sustenance under his control for the eastern troops instead of the Army of Tennessee. Bragg made matters worse by irritating Northrop with his requests for additional food and supplies. When Bragg complained that the shortage of food hurt his army's morale, Northrop berated the general and urged him to recover East Tennessee for his subsistence.[17]

The food shortage demoralized the Confederates. Even the veterans of the Army of Tennessee, long accustomed to hardship, began to complain about their situation. Pvt. Sam Watkins of the 1st Tennessee Infantry was no exception: "In all the history of the war, I cannot remember of more privations and hardships than we went through at Mission[ary] Ridge." The soldiers in the First Corps also felt the brunt of scarce rations. "It is hard to keep up one's spirits with an empty stomach and wet clothing," observed John Blackford. Col. John Bratton noted that the region around Chattanooga was a "very poor country," making it hard to "supply ourselves with many of the little things that have invariably followed the army wherever we have been before." Private Vaughn of the 4th Alabama observed that while meat remained scarce, finding adequate bread rations was even more difficult. Pvt. William R. Montgomery of the 3rd Battalion, Georgia Sharp-shooters described the effect of the food shortage: "I am almost crazy for something to eat." When Montgomery acquired a stolen chicken, he was overjoyed. "You ought to have seen me eat chicken and dumplings," he boasted. "You may be sure they were good, though a little tough." By mid-October even the senior officers complained. McLaws confided to his wife that he despised his new assignment in the West. "This seems to be a most detestable climate and the men are suffering by the change from Virginia," he wrote, "where there was order and system and satisfaction and a fine country with a fine climate."[18]

The longer the siege continued, the worse conditions became for both sides. Pvt. John A. Barry of Wofford's Brigade described the barren region surrounding Chattanooga. "Sis, this is undoubtedly the poorest country in the world," he wrote. "I do not think there is a collard stalk in five miles of this place. The beef we get they have to lean it up against the fence to knock it in the head. The dogs up here are so poor it would take four to make a shadow." Years later Colonel Alexander recalled that the inadequate rations forced many of Longstreet's men to scavenge for food. "Rations among the infantry become scarce, some of them tore down an old cabin, & made a raft of the logs, & set out, through the woods, on a voyage to the other shore [of the Tennessee River]," he wrote. "After many hours they finally got back, too, with several boxes of hard tack & some bacon." Pvt. Frank Mixson of the 1st South Carolina also recalled that he had to chase rats and boil them for something to eat. But in the face of dire circumstances, some of Longstreet's men took the suffering in stride. Captain Winsmith of the 5th South Carolina told his sister that despite the conditions in Tennessee, he would persevere. Private West of the 4th Texas agreed. "We have eaten corn-bread half done, made with unsifted meal, accompanied with bacon raw or broiled on a stick, for three weeks at a time—yet I am well, perfectly well."[19]

Other members of the First Corps did not accept the adversity as cheer-fully as West. The weeks of inactivity added to the hardship of scant rations, and the rank and file became restless loitering in the hills surround-ing Chattanooga. The heavy rains that began on September 30 made the situation even more unbearable for Longstreet's men, as Chattanooga Creek flooded the valley and isolated the eastern soldiers from the rest of Bragg's army.[20] "We are in a complete slosh of mud," wrote a soldier in the 8th Georgia, "the muddiest little coop hole that mortals ever lived in." Morale declined, and soldiers began to desert. Although the First Corps's desertion rate never matched that of their counterparts in the Army of Tennessee, the Army of Northern Virginia soldiers still sought to escape the hardships of campaigning. In one case more than fifty men from the 11th Georgia deserted during the autumn of 1863. Most of these soldiers had arrived in northern Georgia after the Battle of Chickamauga, but they came from that region, found the Federal threat too close to home to ignore, and returned to their families. The proximity of their camps to their homes and Union-held territory allowed these men to slip away unnoticed. Other Georgia troops conspired to desert if the high command refused to grant furloughs. Pvt. Richard H. Brooks of the 51st Georgia Infantry told his wife he would see her during the upcoming winter. "If I cant come one way I will another," he promised, "if they wont give us furlows [sic] we will run away an[d] go home."[21]

Such was the condition and morale of Longstreet's corps when President Davis visited the army in early October to end the dissension among the senior officers of the Army of Tennessee. The Confederate president received loud cheers while he visited Bragg's army, but appearances may have been deceiving. As William W. Mackall observed, Davis only received empty plaudits. "The mob shouted, of course," Mackall noted sarcastically, "and they would have shouted just as loud if he had told them that their comrades' lives had been uselessly sacrificed and he would send them a better General." Colonel Bratton ventured his own observation of the presidential visit to Missionary Ridge. "Only one regiment cheered him," Bratton informed his wife. "It seems to me a cold reception, and I do not like it because it is no indication of the feelings of our army." When Davis left the Army of Tennessee on October 14, the morale of the First Corps had declined since its arrival from the East but still remained far better than that of the western army.[22]

As the Army of Tennessee resumed operations, Longstreet became embroiled in an internal feud between two of his subordinates that reduced the First Corps's effectiveness. The problem arose over who would command Hood's Division while the general recovered from his Chickamauga wounds. Even though Evander Law had assumed temporary command of Hood's brigades, Longstreet wanted Micah Jenkins to lead the division. Longstreet had long favored Jenkins, praising him in 1861 as "the best officer he ever saw." General Lee concurred with this assessment, praising Jenkins and recommending him for promotion after the Seven Days Battles. Jenkins served with Longstreet's corps in nearly all the major campaigns of the Army of Northern Virginia. Languishing on garrison duty near Richmond during the Gettysburg campaign, the South Carolinian eagerly

Brig. Gen. Micah Jenkins was a favorite of Longstreet, but his participation in the rancorous struggle to replace John Bell Hood as division commander led to jealousy and recrimination in the First Corps.
LIBRARY OF CONGRESS
(LC-USZ62-134005)

sought a return to Lee's army. Longstreet also worked to have Jenkins's Brigade transferred to Hood's Division for the trip to North Georgia.[23]

When Jenkins's Brigade arrived shortly after the battle, Longstreet placed his protégé in command of Hood's Division. Jenkins would have commanded the division when it journeyed to the Army of Tennessee if not for Hood being urged to return by his men. After Hood's wounding at Chickamauga incapacitated him temporarily, Longstreet sought to make the divisional command change permanent, confessing to McLaws that he had recommended Jenkins for the position. Longstreet's choice seemed logical considering that the South Carolinian ranked Law, the division's temporary commander at Gettysburg and Chickamauga, by two and a half months. Thus, he likely thought that in addition to his view of Jenkins as "a bright, gallant, and efficient officer," military protocol necessitated that he recommend the senior officer present.[24]

Yet Longstreet failed to consider how the men of Hood's Division would react to their new commander or how General Law would respond to being superseded. Law had a valid claim to the division in that he had personally led Hood's troops in combat on two occasions in the general's absence due to battlefield injuries. Longstreet was also probably unaware of an ostensible rivalry between the two South Carolinians that dated to their cadetship at the Citadel Academy and their tenure as faculty members of Kings Mountain Military Institute in Yorkville, South Carolina. After a brief period at Kings, Law had helped found a military school in Tuskegee, Alabama, prior to the war. In his adopted home state, he organized and served as colonel of the 4th Alabama, then rising to command an Alabama brigade composed of the 4th, 15th, 44th, 47th, and 48th Infantry. After being wounded at First Manassas, Law had recovered and led his brigade from the Seven Days to Gettysburg. At Gettysburg he had assumed command of Hood's Division after its commander was wounded during the second day of battle. Law led the division for two and a half months until Hood returned to the First Corps before the transfer to Tennessee. When Hood was wounded again at Chickamauga, Law took over during the battle and afterward believed that he would inherit permanent command of the division.[25]

Longstreet objected, however, to Law assuming command of the division. In addition to favoring Jenkins, he disapproved of the Alabaman as a division commander for several reasons. First, Law had earned Longstreet's displeasure during the siege of Suffolk in April 1863 when the Federals captured two of his companies. Although Longstreet did not file formal charges, he did point out that "there seems to have been a general lack of vigilance and prompt attention to duties on the part of most of the parties connected with this affair." The relationship between the two generals worsened during the Gettysburg campaign when, according to John Cussons, one of Law's military aides, Law questioned Longstreet's orders to attack the Federal left flank on Little Round Top after arriving late to his designated position. Cussons suggested that Longstreet felt the general's questioning of his orders bordered on insubordination. After the battle he failed to acknowledge the leadership and valor displayed by Law and mildly criticized him in his official report because the entire corps had to wait for his arrival on July 2, implying that otherwise the Confederates could have swept the Federal left.[26]

Longstreet had valid reasons to favor Jenkins over Law, but he failed to consider how the soldiers of Hood's Division would react to this after having served under Law through two critical campaigns. According to one account, Jenkins himself understood the volatility of such a situation. Col. Asbury Coward of the 5th South Carolina claimed that he met him in Chester, South Carolina, en route to Bragg's army, and the general ex-

Brig. Gen. Evander M. Law,
the popular commander of
the Alabama Brigade, became
embroiled in controversy
stemming from Longstreet's
support of Law's political rival,
Brig. Gen. Micah Jenkins, to take
command of Hood's Division.
ALABAMA DEPARTMENT OF ARCHIVES
AND HISTORY (LPP00396)

pressed apprehension about returning to the First Corps for fear of friction with Law. When Jenkins arrived in northern Georgia and Longstreet
proposed making him division commander, the veterans of Hood's Division protested the appointment, stating it was "against the wishes of a
large majority." The division's brigade commanders petitioned Longstreet
to leave Law in charge because he had "the confidence of all the officers
and men." But Longstreet did not acknowledge the petition and assigned
Jenkins the divisional command. Longstreet had dealt with animosity in
regard to favoritism and promotion in the antebellum army while stationed
on the Texas frontier, yet for some reason he failed to appraise the dynamics
of the citizen-soldier in comparison to the career soldier. He did not heed
the potential volatility of volunteers who might refuse to follow an officer
appointed to command.[27]

In addition to the conflict in Longstreet's corps, the Confederates faced
the impending reinforcement of the Federal force in Chattanooga. Dissatisfied with Rosecrans's performance at Chickamauga and concerned about
losing Tennessee, the Union War Department ordered additional troops to
Chattanooga and on October 19 appointed Maj. Gen. Ulysses S. Grant to
command of all Union forces west of the Appalachians. Grant in turn re-

lieved Rosecrans and ordered George Thomas to assume command of the army in the city. While the Rebel forces preoccupied themselves with internal affairs, Maj. Gen. Joseph Hooker moved toward Chattanooga with approximately 20,000 troops, and Maj. Gen. William T. Sherman advanced from Mississippi with an additional 20,000 men. With the imminent arrival of Grant, one of Longstreet's closest prewar friends, and additional units in Chattanooga, the Army of Tennessee had surrendered the initiative to the Federals.[28]

As Grant journeyed to Chattanooga, Longstreet returned to his headquarters on the eastern edge of Lookout Mountain. The general probably resumed his duties on the Confederate left with some apprehension. After President Davis upheld Bragg as commander of the Army of Tennessee, despite the critical opposition of his lieutenants, Longstreet knew that Bragg would hold him in disdain. Nevertheless, the First Corps commander and his staff enjoyed the idle moments of the siege. On October 20 he received the joyful news that Louise had given birth to a son in Petersburg, Virginia. "Old Pete" had not been happy since he lost three of his children to scarlet fever in January 1862. The news of his son's birth lifted his spirits and filled him with renewed vigor. He and Louise named their boy Robert Lee Longstreet in honor of his commander in Virginia. Years later Longstreet recalled that his correspondence with General Lee "about naming the son, was one of the few occasions of humor" during his service in the West. Longstreet, who had given up drinking and gambling since the death of his children, returned to these vices while at Lookout Mountain. His headquarters again became a center of social activity as guests arrived for evening meals and brandy.[29]

The movements of the Union army did not allow Longstreet to celebrate the arrival of a new son. When Grant arrived in Chattanooga, he immediately heard plans from the Army of the Cumberland's senior officers on to how to relieve their beleaguered forces. Brig. Gen. William F. Smith, the army's chief engineer, proposed to open the Tennessee River to supplies by means of a three-pronged attack on Brown's Ferry. Even though the Federals had maintained one supply route into the city via Walden's Ridge, the rains of early October had made the wagon trail impassable. Accordingly, they had to open a reliable line of supply that would sustain the army. Smith explained that he saw an opportunity to take Brown's Ferry and establish contact with the supply depot at Bridgeport. If they could gain control of Brown's Ferry and Lookout Valley, Smith reasoned, supply wagons could leave Bridgeport, use a pontoon bridge to cross the Tennessee at Kelly's Ferry, and take a road through Cummings Gap at the south

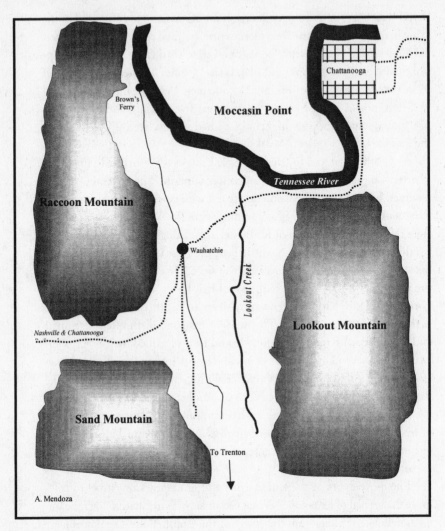

Chattanooga

Brown's Ferry

Moccasin Point

Tennessee River

Raccoon Mountain

Wauhatchie

Lookout Creek

Lookout Mountain

Nashville & Chattanooga

Sand Mountain

To Trenton

A. Mendoza

MAP 3. *Lookout Valley*

base of Raccoon Mountain all the way to Brown's Ferry. There they would cross the Tennessee and arrive at Chattanooga via another road running through the base of Moccasin Bend.[30]

To relieve the besieged army, the Federals would have to drive off the Confederate forces stationed at Brown's Ferry and along Lookout and Raccoon mountains. Smith had reconnoitered Longstreet's flank across the Tennessee River several days earlier and discovered that the Rebel position could be easily overpowered. He informed Grant that a detachment of troops could use pontoon boats to float past the Confederates on Lookout

Mountain and along the banks of the Tennessee River during a nighttime operation. Once across the river at Brown's Ferry, additional reinforcements could be sent to the landing site to oppose any counterattack. The second prong of the assault could be sent to march across Moccasin Point and provide cover while the vanguard built the pontoon bridge. Once the position at Brown's Ferry had been secured, Hooker's men at Bridgeport could advance as the third prong against Lookout Valley to protect the supply route.[31] Grant approved Smith's plan and ordered preparations for the attack.

The responsibility for Brown's Ferry and Lookout Valley rested with the First Corps. Longstreet positioned two regiments of Law's Alabama Brigade on the south bank of the Tennessee and instructed Law to reconnoiter the valley and ascertain how strong a force would be needed to protect the Confederate left. The brigadier spread his men along a five-mile picket line between the south bank of the river and the northern base of Raccoon Mountain up to Little Suck Creek. He deployed the 4th and 15th Alabama to picket the river while keeping the other three regiments in reserve, along with a section of artillery, on the western face of Lookout Mountain. Law also positioned sharpshooters in the woods on the south bank to harass the Federals on the opposite shore. These men were so accurate that they succeeded in "killing many mules" and "blockading the road completely." Members of Company F, 4th Alabama, the sharpshooters were equipped with English Whitworth Rifles, accurate at ranges up to four hundred yards. Lt. Robert T. Coles later wrote: "We had brought our Whitworth rifles from Virginia with us. These were placed down the river on our extreme left to shoot down the front teams, which after being done, the road was entirely blocked. We then proceeded in a leisurely manner to use our English rifles." Pvt. Turner Vaughn observed that his regiment's sharpshooters had "done considerable execution." Despite the sparse line on the Confederate left, Law felt confident that he could defend the valley with his brigade.[32]

The effectiveness of the Confederate marksmen had caused the Federals to search for an alternate route. It became apparent that the only other option would be access to Brown's Ferry and Lookout Valley. For this reason, on October 25 Bragg directed Longstreet to reconnoiter toward Trenton, Georgia, about fifteen miles southwest of Brown's Ferry. He had received reports of enemy activity across from Bridgeport and wanted Longstreet to ascertain the possibility of a Union movement up Lookout Valley behind the Confederate left. That same day Maj. James Austin of the 9th Kentucky Cavalry wrote Longstreet that the Federals were building a bridge across the Running Water Creek near Shellmound and requested reinforcements. Longstreet responded to Austin's missive and promised that help would soon arrive. This report also concerned Bragg, who ordered Longstreet to use Col. J. Warren Grigsby's cavalry brigade to reconnoiter in the direction of Bridgeport.[33]

Law later wrote that he foresaw the danger of a Federal movement up Lookout Valley toward Brown's Ferry, believing that the nature of the topography of the area would make it a viable enemy target. Despite this postwar claim, Law left his command on Lookout Mountain to visit Hood as the latter recuperated some thirty miles south in the Armuchee Valley of Georgia, seeking the general's aid to secure him the promotion to lead the division. Although Longstreet already had appointed Jenkins to lead Hood's Division, Law still entertained hopes of supplanting him.[34]

With Law's departure, Longstreet on the twenty-seventh ordered Jenkins to send a brigade to investigate the Federal movements around Running Water Creek and to cooperate with Grigsby's Brigade if necessary. Grigsby, who commanded three Kentucky cavalry regiments, received orders from Longstreet to hold the passes across Lookout Mountain. Grigsby's horsemen were some of the inadequately few remaining to the Army of Tennessee at this time. Bragg had detached General Wheeler on a mission to sever Rosecrans's line of communications in late September. After capturing several hundred wagons and wreaking havoc among the Federals in Middle Tennessee, Wheeler on October 9 limped back into Alabama, where he remained for several weeks to recuperate and await orders. Consequently, besieging Confederates possessed only one cavalry division, under Brig. Gen. John H. Kelly, to reconnoiter the Chattanooga region.[35] While Bragg's failure to provide sufficient cavalry patrols was significant, the lack of cooperation between the Rebel horsemen and Longstreet's headquarters proved a far greater transgression.

On October 30, after the battles for Lookout Valley, Longstreet complained that he had not heard from Grigsby since the twenty-seventh, fuming that he had received reports of the Federal movements on the twenty-eighth from his signal operators instead. He complained that Grigsby had not communicated with him for three days, operating under the impression that he was to receive instructions from Bragg and not him. Brent replied the same day, informing Longstreet that Grigsby's cavalry had been under Longstreet's direction and that no conflicting orders had come from Bragg's headquarters. A subsequent investigation maintained that Grigsby had indeed reported to Longstreet, only to receive orders to remain at Trenton. He claimed that his cavalry had reported enemy movements near Lookout

Valley but that Longstreet ignored their warnings and insisted on holding the mountain passes with dismounted cavalry. Grigsby further asserted that he received no instructions to reconnoiter toward Lookout Valley.[36] But this account is contradicted by the orders of Longstreet's adjutant, Colonel Sorrel. On the twenty-seventh Sorrel directed Grigsby to "ascertain the truth" of a report "that a force of the enemy" had advanced "from the direction of Bridgeport." If the enemy appeared too strong, the cavalry had instructions to hold the mountain passes until they received infantry support. Sorrel also ordered Grigsby to report the enemy's movements to Longstreet's headquarters. Despite these instructions to reconnoiter and hold the region, Grigsby offered minimal resistance to Federal troops advancing on Lookout Valley the morning of October 28.[37]

In regard to cavalry operations, the same pattern of miscommunication and recrimination that had plagued the Army of Tennessee continued to paralyze the Confederates besieging Chattanooga. While Longstreet may have issued discretionary orders to Grigsby, the *Official Records* contain no messages from the cavalry officer notifying the corps commander or army headquarters about Federal activity in Lookout Valley. Although it is possible that Grigsby's dispatches to Longstreet may have been lost en route, the lack of evidence shifts the discussion toward speculation. Moreover, if Bragg's investigation had determined that Longstreet neglected his duty in regard to the use of cavalry, the commanding general probably would have preferred charges against his corps commander. Instead Longstreet's October 30 message to Brent asserts that the general had received no reports from Grigsby. Although Longstreet failed to grasp the enemy's intentions regarding Lookout Valley, the cavalry remained responsible for notifying the army's high command of any Federal activity in the area. Regardless of the discourse between Longstreet and Grigsby, Bragg also bears responsibility for directing Wheeler to raid in Tennessee, thus depriving his army of adequate cavalry resources. He displayed poor judgment in assuming that Kelly's lone division could reconnoiter the Chattanooga region.[38]

In addition to struggling with the cavalry, the First Corps faced several problems with recent developments in the valley. First, Law's absence deprived the command of his knowledge of the terrain and Federal movements. Although Longstreet commanded the Confederate left, he was responsible for as much territory on the Rebel siege line as the rest of the Army of Tennessee, though with far fewer brigades.[39] Second, Longstreet failed to recognize the ongoing struggle between Law and Jenkins within Hood's Division. Although Jenkins had assumed command of the unit, the two generals' bitter rivalry led him to order three of Law's units—the 44th,

47th, and 48th Alabama regiments—to his own sector east of Lookout Mountain. Law believed there was no "rhyme or reason" in moving these troops from one side of the mountain to the other, but as Law's biographers maintain, the order was apparently meant to demonstrate to Law Jenkins's authority as division commander. After weeks of inactivity, the two South Carolinians probably never imagined that their rivalry would boil over as the Federals began moving in late October.[40] Third, Longstreet appears to have suffered from strategic myopia. Despite the warnings of Union movements to the southwest, the general seemed convinced that the activity near Bridgeport indicated that the Federals intended to march across the valley to the southern base of Lookout Mountain and advance along the crest toward Longstreet's rear. On October 14 he told McLaws that he expected an attack toward Trenton. Accordingly, Longstreet wanted to leave McLaws's Division on Lookout Mountain so he could fight the enemy "beyond Trenton or near there." Throughout the critical moments of the Federal advance, he did not focus on the threat to Brown's Ferry, instead regarding it as a diversion.[41]

There is no record explaining why Longstreet insisted that the Federals threatened Lookout Mountain and the move against Brown's Ferry was merely a diversion. Perhaps he remained miffed that, during the president's visit, Davis and Bragg had discounted his proposal to move against Bridgeport and "swing around towards the enemy's rear."[42] Since Davis's departure, Longstreet and Bragg had failed to discuss the army's intentions during the siege of Chattanooga. While Longstreet merits some blame for this lack of communication, Bragg bears greater culpability for not notifying his subordinate of his plans and supervising the siege more closely. After Longstreet had voiced his displeasure at serving under Bragg, the latter should have monitored the First Corps sector with greater scrutiny; the Chickamauga campaign should have taught him to do that. It is also conceivable that Longstreet simply made a mistake and gambled on predicting the enemy's intentions. With the birth of his new son and the president's fateful conference still on his mind, the general was guilty of not calculating all possible threats to his line. Although historians later argued that Longstreet's mistakes on Lookout Mountain resulted from his petulance in failing to obtain the command of the Army of Tennessee, the contemporary evidence fails to support this theory. If Longstreet merely sought advancement and glory, how could the failures around Lookout Mountain accomplish those goals? After all, he could not obtain a promotion or Bragg's dismissal by performing poorly at Chattanooga. In fact, the opposite held true—Longstreet needed to perform at his very best to possibly earn a promotion.[43]

While the Rebel high command pondered the intent of the forces near Bridgeport, Smith prepared his Federal flotilla to embark on its amphibious operation at midnight of the twenty-sixth. Brig. Gen. William B. Hazen would lead his 1,600 troops aboard more than fifty pontoon boats and ride the current of the Tennessee River around Moccasin Point and past the Confederate pickets on the opposite shore. Meanwhile, Brig. Gen. John Turchin would march his brigade and the remainder of Hazen's brigade (a total of 4,000 men) and a detachment of artillery westward across Moccasin Point. The nine-mile river voyage proved hazardous; not only would the Federal soldiers be vulnerable to the Rebel artillery and picket fire, but they also risked drowning in the river. By 3:00 A.M. Hazen's men pushed off and began their silent voyage down the Tennessee. The soldiers received instructions to shed their knapsacks and blankets and to remain silent to avoid alerting enemy pickets. About ninety minutes later the lead elements of Hazen's expedition landed on the west bank of the river and advanced against the Confederate positions nearby. Waiting to support the flotilla from the opposite shore would be Turchin's brigade.[44]

Although the operation remained a well-kept secret outside the Union high command, Federal activity across the river had alerted Colonel Oates of the 15th Alabama to the threat of an enemy expedition on the twenty-sixth. According to Oates, he reported to General Jenkins that "an attack was going to be made and asked for reinforcements." That same night the colonel claimed that he received another report of Federal activity toward Bridgeport and alerted Longstreet to an imminent attack, but his courier returned around midnight without a reply from the corps commander. "No other response came [from Longstreet], and I lay down and tried to sleep," he recalled. If Oates's postwar account is accurate, the colonel did not sleep long, for he received word of the Federal landing at Brown's Ferry at about 4:30 A.M. While Oates was being roused from his slumber, Law returned from his visit to Hood. Since Jenkins also went on leave, Law reported to the east side of Lookout Mountain to take temporary command of the division. Upon his arrival the general became angry with the news that three of his regiments had been recalled by Jenkins during his absence. Law immediately prepared to move his three regiments back to the opposite side of the mountain. By the time he reached Brown's Ferry, it was too late.[45]

Company B, 15th Alabama, under the command of Capt. Noah Feagin, manned the picket line at Brown's Ferry. The noise of gunfire and shouts that the Yankees were attacking awakened Feagin and his orderly. The advance element of Hazen's flotilla had landed its fifty-two men on the west bank of the Tennessee and easily overwhelmed the pickets near the shore. The Rebels fired a few shots before additional Yankee boats landed and overran the remaining pickets. Feagin's men were no match for the assaulting troops, and they retreated toward Lookout Mountain while the captain notified Oates to send reinforcements. While the Alabamans withdrew, other boats landed above Brown's Ferry, and the Federals seized the adjacent hills near the base of Raccoon Mountain. Hazen had ordered two men in each boat to carry axes, and once each pontoon landed onshore, these men disembarked to cut trees as the Federals quickly entrenched in anticipation of a Confederate counterattack.[46]

When a courier woke Oates early on the twenty-seventh, the colonel immediately issued orders to march his regiment to Feagin's support. He then left for Brown's Ferry, about half a mile away from his headquarters on the eastern face of Raccoon Mountain, with about one hundred and fifty men. Hearing the Federals constructing fortifications near the shore, Oates instructed two of his companies to seize their position. The Alabamans came upon seventy-five men under Lt. Col. James Foy at work building abatis. The Confederates opened fire, startling the Yankees and causing Foy, who believed he faced a force four times his strength, to order a withdrawal toward the river. As the two lead companies of the 15th Alabama plunged ahead, Oates led the other three companies toward the Federal right to cut off their retreat. As the Rebels swept over a ridge near the shore, they encountered the lead elements of the 6th Indiana Infantry, one of the first units ferried across the Tennessee. In response to the Confederates, Foy's men redeployed to the Indianans' left and fired a volley into the advancing line. Oates tried to rally his men, but to no avail. As he galloped toward the Union breastworks, a bullet ripped through his right hip and thigh. After the colonel fell, his men withdrew. The fight at Brown's Ferry had lasted about twenty minutes, costing the Confederates six men killed and fourteen wounded.[47]

By 7:00 A.M. the Southerners retreated toward Lookout Mountain, covering their retreat with artillery fire. Oates's Alabamans met with Law and the rest of his brigade up the valley, where the general positioned them near Lookout Creek to oppose any further Federal advance. Hazen's men moved forward cautiously, constructing fortifications for protection and building signal fires so that arriving reinforcements could find their position. Although Confederate artillery tried to harass the engineers as they built their bridge across the Tennessee, the shelling proved ineffective. By the early afternoon of the twenty-seventh, they had completed the bridge, and supplies began to flow across the river. Federal patrols reconnoitered Lookout Valley and prepared for Hooker's advance from Bridgeport. Brown's Ferry had been secured at the cost of twenty-one casualties.[48]

The early morning gunfire had alerted Longstreet to the Federal assault on his left. As the fog lifted, the general rode to the top of Lookout Mountain and observed hundreds of Federals building a pontoon bridge across the river. Inexplicably, Longstreet failed to report the activity in his sector to army headquarters. That morning Bragg asked General Liddell where Longstreet was. When Liddell informed him of the early morning musketry fire, Bragg "expressed great surprise." He told Liddell to go investigate since he had not had any messages from Longstreet. When the general reported his findings, Bragg was furious and immediately summoned Longstreet to discuss how to regain possession of Brown's Ferry.[49]

Longstreet made no attempt to regain the lost ground that morning. Instead he informed Bragg that he still believed that Brown's Ferry was a diversion for the real threat that lay to the south. He insisted that the Federals' advance on Lookout Mountain "seems to me to be more important, essential indeed, than any such partial move as his present one." That theory may have convinced Bragg, for he no longer believed that the First Corps could retake Brown's Ferry. Instead, he directed Longstreet to hold Lookout Mountain. Longstreet later informed Bragg that he had received reports of Federals advancing on Trenton. He proposed to send Jenkins's Brigade to cut off this Union movement and requested reinforcements to hold Lookout Mountain.[50]

The disputes of the twenty-seventh finally convinced Bragg that he and Longstreet were working at cross-purposes. The indecisiveness that had gripped Bragg in prior campaigns hindered him once more at Chattanooga. Although he initially had deferred to Longstreet's views, later that evening Bragg decided to meet with Longstreet to discuss strategy, arranging a conference on the crest of Lookout Mountain the next morning. At dawn on the twenty-eighth, Bragg rode to the top of the mountain, where for the first time since Davis's visit, he met with Longstreet. Years later Longstreet recalled that the acrimony that had characterized the October 9 meeting had not abated, noting that Bragg first complained of "false alarms" from Longstreet's sector before outlining his plans. While the two generals discussed enemy movements, one of Longstreet's signal officers reported that the Federals were advancing from Bridgeport. The breakdown in communications between First Corps headquarters and the Confederate cavalry had allowed a force of 7,000 Federals to march undetected down Lookout

Valley toward Brown's Ferry. This astonished both Longstreet and Bragg, who watched helplessly as Hooker's column advanced with beating drums and flags waving.[51]

Bragg ordered Alexander's artillery to harass the Union force, but they were out of range for the Rebel guns. The general was incensed: He had lost Brown's Ferry the previous day, and now it appeared that the Federals had succeeded in establishing a supply line into Chattanooga. He demanded that Longstreet do something to regain the initiative. Bragg returned to his headquarters on Missionary Ridge, complaining of Longstreet's "lack of ability" and "asserting him to be greatly overrated." This directive probably distressed Longstreet, for he considered attacking Brown's Ferry unreasonable because the Federals had already entrenched along the Tennessee. At Gettysburg he had witnessed the devastating effect of a headlong attack against a fortified foe, and he now tried to avoid repeating that fiasco. The solution to his dilemma appeared an hour after he witnessed Hooker reach the Federals at Brown's Ferry. A second Union force, the rear guard for the main column, appeared in Lookout Valley and bivouacked at Wauhatchie, about three miles from Brown's Ferry. The roughly 1,500 men, under the command of Brig. Gen. John Geary, would be the focus of Longstreet's counterattack.[52]

The general hastily devised a plan to strike Geary's five regiments. Longstreet instructed Jenkins's Brigade, under the command of Col. John Bratton and accompanied by General Jenkins, to advance on Wauhatchie while Law's and Jerome B. Robertson's brigades blocked the Valley (Trenton) Road from Brown's Ferry to prevent Hooker from reinforcing Geary. Since the Confederates were vulnerable to Yankee artillery, their attack would be made after dark to avoid detection and to take advantage of the Federals' confusion. Longstreet also ordered Benning's Brigade to provide support on Law's left, between his and Jenkins's brigades. The attack on Wauhatchie would require close cooperation between Law and Jenkins. When Law and Jenkins met at nightfall on the twenty-eighth, Law failed to endorse the plan to attack Wauhatchie, believing that the Confederates should instead attack the Federals at Shellmound the following morning. Even if successful at Wauhatchie, Law reasoned, daybreak would reveal the weakness of the Confederate position and invite a Union counterattack. Despite Law's insistence that his two brigades (and Benning's in reserve) could not hold the more than 10,000 Federals at Brown's Ferry, Jenkins maneuvered his former brigade into position around Geary's force during the early morning hours of October 29 while Law stationed his men parallel to Trenton Road, facing west, with Robertson's Brigade on the left.[53]

Although Longstreet later claimed that Bragg had promised him Mc-Laws's Division to support the operation, his postwar reminiscences are misleading. As corps commander, he was in charge of both divisions and thus had the authority to order McLaws forward. Moreover, Bragg already had informed the general earlier that day that he could use his entire corps to dislodge the Federals at Brown's Ferry. Regardless of Longstreet's postwar claims, Bragg acquiesced in the plan to attack Geary's detachment. He also offered to send one of Breckinridge's divisions from east of Chattanooga Creek to support the nighttime assault. George Brent, Bragg's chief of staff, noted the significance of the operation in his journal: "Should this effort to dislodge him [the enemy] fail I think we shall have to abandon this position."[54]

Amid this confusing situation, Longstreet and Jenkins rode down Lookout Mountain around midnight to reconnoiter the Federal position at Wauhatchie. The two generals failed to ascertain the enemy's flanks in the darkness, and Longstreet returned to his headquarters, apparently under the impression that the planned offensive should be called off. He instructed Jenkins to search for stragglers, abandoned wagons, and return to camp. "As we had no artillery, nor any means of getting any over," Longstreet explained on the thirtieth, "I did not think it proper to put a force out where it could be exposed to that of the enemy during daylight, and to have moved on at that late hour to attack the enemy's main camp would have kept us till after daylight."[55]

Whether Jenkins understood that the attack had been called off remains unclear. After the war Longstreet acknowledged that he failed to give him written orders canceling the assault. But Jenkins noted that Longstreet visited him at midnight on the twenty-eighth due to "the slowness of the movement" and because "various troops were scarcely in position." Regardless of instructions, Jenkins issued orders to proceed with the operation. As historian James Lee McDonough has noted, Jenkins "more than likely" understood Longstreet's intentions but decided to attempt the operation with his lone division because he saw "a good opportunity for personal advancement."[56]

Despite the confusion in the First Corps high command, the advance elements of Jenkins's Brigade, led by Bratton and accompanied by Jenkins, crossed Lookout Creek and marched south on the road toward Wauhatchie. Although surprise was an integral part of the Confederate plan, General Geary had observed Rebel movements during the day and prepared his men for a possible assault, ordering them to camp under arms. Between 12:30 and 1:00 A.M. on the twenty-ninth, Bratton's South Carolinians attacked Geary's position. The Federals had situated themselves in a semi-circle a quarter mile north of Wauhatchie, with their right along the Trenton Railroad and the Dry Valley Road and their left on Kelly's Ford Road. Instead of attacking the Federals quickly, Bratton's men advanced slowly, probably because of the darkness and their unfamiliarity with the terrain. This allowed the Yankees to react. The Rebels came from north and west of the Federals, who responded with musketry and artillery fire from Knap's Battery, positioned perpendicular to the Kelly Road. Although Col. Martin Gary's Hampton Legion turned the Union left and captured part of their wagon train, Bratton's men faltered.[57]

The musketry at Wauhatchie alerted Hooker's men of the danger to their rear. Hooker dispatched Brig. Gen. Carl Schurz's division to march to Geary's relief. Law's two brigades waited for the Federals along the Valley Road. Although Law received instructions to prevent reinforcements from reaching Geary, the Alabamans did not block the road itself. Instead, he positioned his men parallel to the road, facing west, in order to ambush the Federal left flank. As Schurz moved south from Brown's Ferry, Law struck the lead elements of the Federal column. During the struggle with the Yankee reinforcements, Law received the first of several messages from Jenkins to hold his position while he continued to attack the Union force at Wauhatchie. As the battle for the Valley Road raged, the 136th New York Infantry advanced between the Tennessee River and Law's right flank. If the Yankees succeeded in turning the Confederate right, they could march all the way to the Chattanooga Road and cut the Alabamans' only line of retreat. Faced with this predicament, Law ordered his men to withdraw.[58]

As the fighting raged along the Dry Valley Road, Jenkins received reports that the Federals had driven past the Alabamans and were advancing toward Wauhatchie. Facing a potential double envelopment, he ordered Bratton to withdraw toward Lookout Creek. The general realized that Bratton's retreat would take some time, so he sent a messenger to notify Law to "hold his position till I ordered him to retire." Before Bratton withdrew, Jenkins pointed out, "I received a message from General Law that he had begun to fall back." According to Law, before he issued his orders to withdraw, he had already received information that Bratton had pulled back. Regardless, by 3:30 A.M. the battle for Lookout Valley was over. The Confederates suffered 408 casualties to 416 for the Federals. Yet within the First Corps leadership, the battle had just begun.[59]

With the defeat of the Confederates at Wauhatchie, the Federals now maintained a supply line to the Bridgeport depot and could reinforce the Army of the Cumberland across Raccoon Mountain and Brown's Ferry.

For all intents and purposes, Bragg's siege of Chattanooga had failed. The responsibility for the loss of Lookout Valley rests with Longstreet, the commander for that sector. Since assuming command of the Confederate left in early October, he had failed to comprehend the strategic implications of losing control of the valley. Longstreet had neglected to reconnoiter the area and had failed to deploy a strong force to block Hazen's landing at Brown's Ferry. Law later claimed that from the outset, he knew that the Federals would attempt to reopen their line of supply through his area and that Longstreet had never deployed enough troops to hold the valley and Brown's Ferry. Longstreet's failure at Lookout Valley had cost the Confederates the opportunity of starving out the Federals in Chattanooga. Worse yet, the First Corps commander exacerbated his mistakes by shifting the blame onto others.[60]

After Wauhatchie, accusations and recriminations as to responsibility for the failure to regain control of Lookout Valley disrupted the First Corps. To no one's surprise, Jenkins blamed Law for falling back prematurely and forcing him to retreat. Law rejected this assertion, stating that since he felt that "the object for which my position was occupied had been accomplished, [so] I withdrew." Bratton's report appeared to confirm Law's version of events, but Longstreet sided with Jenkins, asserting that Law was responsible for the defeat. While acknowledging the conflicting testimonies of Jenkins and Law, he cited Law's withdrawal as the reason Jenkins had to recall his troops from Wauhatchie. Years later Longstreet claimed that Law "had said that he did not care to win General Jenkins's spurs as a major general." He wanted to have Law arrested, but further campaigning prevented him from filing charges. Consequently, the internal rivalry between Law and Jenkins that had begun prior to the battle in Lookout Valley developed into a bitter quarrel that ruptured the command structure for the First Corps.[61]

Ignored in all of this was Longstreet's decision to attack the Federal detachment in the first place. Bragg had repeatedly instructed him to retake Brown's Ferry on October 27 and 28. As Law indicated in his postwar memorandum, Longstreet's attempt to attack the Union rear guard at Wauhatchie with only one brigade served no purpose, for the numerically stronger foe could simply wait until daybreak and reopen their supply line. Moreover, Longstreet's decision to use only a total of four brigades (about 5,000 men) to attack a force of more than 10,000 men was illogical. Even though he tried to blame Bragg for failing to send McLaws's Division on the night of the attack, the responsibility for not using McLaws remained with Longstreet, the corps commander. Bragg had repeatedly told him that he could use his whole corps for any activity against the Federals. Longstreet's decision to blame Bragg suggests that he tried to relieve himself of the responsibility for losing Brown's Ferry and for the poor reconnaissance in planning the attack at Wauhatchie. Finally, if Longstreet's postwar account is accurate, his decision to return to headquarters on the night of the twenty-eighth, assuming he ordered Jenkins to call off the attack, contributed to the botched operation.[62]

Longstreet's hesitancy to attack the Federals from Lookout Mountain suggests that once the enemy had gained control of Brown's Ferry, he knew any offensive would prove impractical. By late October he was convinced that anything Bragg proposed must be wrong. Accordingly, when Bragg warned Longstreet of the threat to Brown's Ferry, the First Corps commander insisted that the real threat lay south toward Trenton. Of course, President Davis's conference had exacerbated a tense situation between the two men that made effective communication almost impossible. Longstreet had witnessed the removal or demotion of several generals who had opposed Bragg in the weeks following the Battle of Chickamauga. Since he had publicly denounced Bragg's generalship, it is likely that in his mind Longstreet believed that the Army of Tennessee commander hoped to see him fail. Thus Bragg's insistence to attack led him to make a halfhearted assault against the smaller of two enemy forces. Yet when Longstreet reconnoitered Lookout Valley, he decided to call off the assault and assumed that Jenkins understood the change of plans. He had seldom advocated the tactical offensive, and when faced with a numerically stronger foe, he probably thought it would be best to avoid excessive casualties. Longstreet returned to his headquarters thinking that an attempt to attack would probably accommodate Bragg and the two could then confer on a more prudent course of action.

The morning after the failure at Wauhatchie, Bragg wrote Davis to inform him of the army's movements near Chattanooga and requested that the president either come personally to the Army of Tennessee or at least send Colonel Chesnut or General Lee. Bragg also informed Davis that he would resign his command unless the president removed Longstreet and other malcontents from the army. The following day, as reports filtered in about the miscues of the Wauhatchie expedition, Bragg telegraphed Davis, charging that "disobedience of orders & slowness of movements" on the part of Longstreet led to the failures in Lookout Valley and repeating his threat to resign. Davis responded by declaring that he supported Bragg but was disinclined to relieve anyone from command, including the commanding general. Disappointed with the loss of Brown's Ferry, however, President Davis suggested transferring Longstreet to East Tennessee, which Bragg readily accepted.[63]

Like others before him, Longstreet had failed to establish a cordial relationship with Bragg. Clearly in Longstreet's case he never even tried to strike an amicable relationship with his new commander. The preconceived notions that he brought with him to the West came from his contemporaries, many of whom spoke negatively of Bragg to begin with. Citing "Longstreet's inactivity and lack of ability," Bragg called him "greatly overrated" and acquiesced in Davis's plan to transfer him to East Tennessee to "see what he could do on his own resources."[64]

As the First Corps prepared to advance against Ambrose Burnside's force in East Tennessee, veterans of Longstreet's command might have noticed a deterioration of morale since their arrival in the West. The bitter animosity prevalent in the army's senior ranks had filtered down to the common soldier. As Jenkins and Law jockeyed to gain permanent command of Hood's Division, the two ambitious brigadiers used the rank and file as pawns in a power struggle that reduced the effectiveness of Longstreet's corps. This bitter rivalry caused a paralysis in the command structure, contributed to the loss of Lookout Valley, and reversed the roles of besieger and besieged at Chattanooga. Yet the defeats of late October caused the most significant deterioration of morale, as the siege on Chattanooga had already begun a downward spiral of the army's fighting spirit. A captain in the 5th South Carolina expressed his hope that the precariousness of the situation in the army's high command would not hamper the Confederate effort. "I believe we have the men to go anywhere if they are only properly led," he wrote, "and I hope every thing may be managed right with us."[65] Longstreet had also erred at Lookout Mountain, failing to assess the Federal threat in his area and costing the Confederates the upper hand at Chattanooga. The news that the First Corps would be transferred to East Tennessee on a semi-independent campaign restored the spirits of Longstreet's troops. No longer tied to Bragg's army, for which they held a thinly veiled disdain, the men from the Army of Northern Virginia looked forward to a new campaign that they hoped would bring them another victory and offer them better conditions than the misery around Chattanooga.

5

"NO MEN WHO ARE DETERMINED TO SUCCEED CAN FAIL"

KNOXVILLE, NOVEMBER 1863

RAGG'S EFFORTS TO STARVE THE ARMY OF THE CUMBERLAND into submission had miscarried. After the engagement at Wauhatchie, Hooker's troops fortified their position in Lookout Valley while Longstreet's men withdrew up the western slope of the mountain. Colonel Alexander's artillery, which had failed to shell Chattanooga effectively throughout October, was similarly ineffective against the reopened Union supply line into the city. From Lookout Mountain the long range and steep angle prevented the gunners from striking the Valley Road or Brown's Ferry. In addition, the artillery could not easily move into the valley from their positions because of the steep trails down the western slope. An infantry assault on the Union lines also proved impractical, for General Jenkins reported that more than 20,000 Federals had entrenched themselves along the Dry Valley Road facing east toward Lookout Mountain. Moreover, Federal artillery stationed at Moccasin Point dominated the lone road around the northern face of the mountain, making a Confederate advance against the supply line impossible.[1]

While the Federals fortified their position in Chattanooga and along the valley, the Southerners struggled with the hardships of the siege, particularly the poor rations and scanty supplies. Heavy rains on October 30 exacerbated their difficulties. One Texan complained, "We have been in the mud for over a month in an almost continuous rain, and are not allowed to send to Richmond for blankets and overcoats, which many of us have there, because it will not be thought of until the hospitals are filled with pneumonia and pleurisy."[2]

Despite the bleak outlook for the Confederates, on the thirty-first Bragg ordered Longstreet to reconnoiter Lookout Valley to ascertain the possibility for another assault against the Federals. He also instructed Breckinridge and Lt. Gen. William J. Hardee, who had recently rejoined the Army of Tennessee to command Polk's Corps, to accompany Longstreet. The three generals made their way to the crest of Lookout Mountain to examine the Confederate's strategic possibilities. Longstreet reported that an attack would be unfeasible. The only road around the north face of Lookout Mountain was exposed to Federal artillery, while the only other way down the mountain involved a fifty-mile detour to the south via Johnson's Crook. The trails down the western face could only be used by infantry, leaving the men exposed to enemy fire without artillery support. The three agreed that an attack on Lookout Valley was out of the question. As Jenkins reported to Longstreet earlier that day, "I think from the movements of the enemy in the valley that the status of both armies has changed."[3]

It remains unclear why Bragg sent the three officers to reconnoiter Lookout Valley if he already intended to move in the opposite direction, toward East Tennessee. Since October 25 he had complained to Davis that operations toward Lookout Valley proved difficult due to "constant rains and bad roads." Bragg proposed that a division of his army could be detached and sent to operate against the Union force under Ambrose Burnside to ensure his "discomfiture." On the twenty-ninth Davis informed Bragg that he agreed with not moving toward the Bridgeport area since reports intimated that the Federals intended to turn the Confederate left flank. Instead he complimented Bragg for earlier sending (on the seventeenth) two infantry divisions under Maj. Gen. Carter L. Stevenson to extend the army's right flank toward Knoxville in eastern Tennessee and possibly cooperate with Maj. Gen. Sam Jones, operating in southwestern Virginia with a force of about 10,000 men. On the twenty-third Stevenson's soldiers had skirmished with a Union force near Loudon, Tennessee, about thirty miles southwest of Knoxville, capturing nearly 500 prisoners and forcing the Federals to retreat toward Knoxville. Davis suggested to Bragg that if the situation in Chattanooga did not improve, he could send Longstreet to East Tennessee "to recover the country and reestablish communications with Virginia." This proposal had been influenced by Lee, who had persistently called for the return of Longstreet's men. The president suggested that Bragg could send Longstreet and his two divisions to drive Burnside from the Knoxville

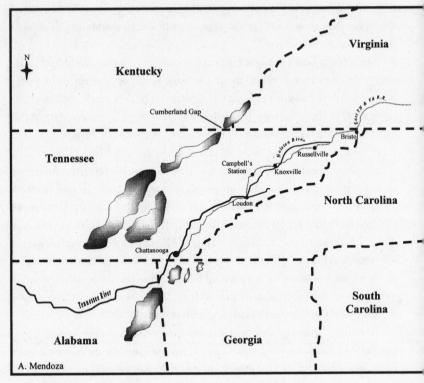

MAP 4. *The Region of the First Corps' Campaigns, 1863*

region. Bragg did not deliberate too long; the following day he wrote Davis that detaching the First Corps from the Army of Tennessee "would be great relief to me."[4]

As Bragg and Davis deliberated strategy, Longstreet learned that he would be transferred to East Tennessee. On November 3, two days after the general first heard the rumors that he would move toward Knoxville, Bragg held a conference with his leading lieutenants to discuss strategy. Longstreet recalled that he was unaware of Bragg's final decision until he arrived at the commanding general's council of war. At the meeting the First Corps commander offered his strategic views. Longstreet proposed that the Army of Tennessee withdraw behind Chickamauga Creek while a force of 20,000 advanced toward East Tennessee to strike Burnside. After eliminating the Federal threat on their right flank, the detachment could then return to the Army of Tennessee to operate against the enemy at Chattanooga by maneuvering toward the enemy's left or rear.[5]

But Longstreet's account of this council of war does not coincide with

Hardee's version. Writing the following spring, Hardee recalled that Longstreet proposed an advance on Stevenson, Alabama, and a move toward Middle Tennessee. He recalled that Bragg opposed this plan because of the lack of subsistence toward Alabama. Only after Bragg's rebuke did Longstreet propose a movement toward East Tennessee. Hardee also failed to remember any proposal to concentrate south of Chickamauga Creek. "It is but just to say, however, that if a proposition of that character had been made, it would not, in my opinion, have been approved by General Bragg," Hardee wrote.[6]

Hardee's version of events is contradicted by a letter Longstreet wrote to General Buckner just two days after the conference with Bragg:

> When I heard the report around camp that I was to go into East Tennessee . . . I thought it possible that we might accomplish something by encouraging his own move, and proposed the following plan, viz, to withdraw from our present lines, and the forces now in East Tennessee. . . . The move, as I proposed it, would have left this army in a strong position and safe, and would have made sure the capture of Burnside; that is, the army here could spare 20,000 if it were in the position that I proposed better than it can spare 12,000 occupying the lines that it now does. . . . Under present arrangements, however, the lines are to be held as they now are, and the detachment is to be, say, 12,000. We thus expose both to failure and really take no chance to ourselves of great results.[7]

Longstreet maintained that Hardee was the only person in the war council to favor his plan. "I don't think that is a bad idea of Longstreet's," Hardee reportedly said before Bragg dismissed the proposal and directed Longstreet to prepare for operations in East Tennessee. Months later Buckner wrote Longstreet that in light of the subsequent events at Chattanooga, his November 5 letter, which pointed out the weaknesses in Bragg's plan, was a "vindication of your judgment." Although no contemporary evidence explains the disparate accounts, it is likely that Hardee overlooked some details of the November 3 meeting. Longstreet's letter, written two days after the event, lends credence to his own version.[8]

Regardless of the conflicting accounts, Bragg ordered Longstreet to move into East Tennessee with the divisions of Hood and McLaws and the artillery battalions of Alexander and Maj. Austin Leyden. Since Joseph Wheeler's Cavalry Corps had operated in the region prior to the Chickamauga campaign, it was ordered to accompany the First Corps as it advanced toward Knoxville. Bragg informed Longstreet that the success of the plan depended on the First Corps's rapid movement. "Your object should be to drive Burnside out of East Tennessee first, or better, to capture or destroy him," he wrote. While Longstreet moved northeast, Bragg anticipated the return to Missionary Ridge of the divisions of Stevenson and Maj. Gen. Benjamin F. Cheatham, which had been operating with Stevenson since October 27.[9]

The basic premise of the expedition to East Tennessee appears sensible considering the few options open to Bragg in early November. First, he realized that a frontal assault on the Federal fortifications at Chattanooga would prove disastrous. Hence he planned to starve the Army of the Cumberland out of its defenses following Chickamauga. Second, Bragg refused to retreat southward toward Atlanta because it would devastate his army's already low morale and unleash another round of criticism against his generalship. Withdrawing after victory would only lend credence to the political factions in Richmond that claimed Chickamauga was strategically barren and called for his removal. Finally, a move toward the west and the Federal forces now in Lookout Valley remained impractical because of the terrain around Lookout Mountain and the strong position of Hooker's 20,000 troops, entrenched along the Dry Valley Road. Even if successful against the Federals in the valley, the Army of Tennessee would have had to move westward toward Bridgeport and face the advance of Sherman's 20,000 men rushing to reinforce Grant at Chattanooga. Moreover, the impoverished region in eastern Alabama would be unable to supply Bragg's army even if he succeeded because his line of communications, the Western and Atlantic Railroad, would be exposed to the Federals.[10]

Bragg's options had thus narrowed to just one: moving against Knoxville. The operation enjoyed advantages over advancing north or west. First, the Army of Tennessee would not have to worry about maintaining its line of supply since the East Tennessee and Georgia Railroad connected to the Western and Atlantic near Chattanooga and made its way to the northeast. The Confederates could have detailed a strong enough guard to keep the railroad open despite the presence of Federal cavalry. Moreover, from Knoxville the East Tennessee and Virginia Railroad could supply the army with provisions from southwestern Virginia and provide Bragg with reinforcements in the form of Sam Jones's 10,000 Rebel troops if necessary. Thus, from a base in East Tennessee, the Southerners could strike against Grant's rear or advance into Kentucky through the Cumberland Gap, forcing the Federals to abandon their fortifications at Chattanooga and fight on ground more favorable to the Confederates.[11]

Yet an advance into East Tennessee would place the Confederates in a harsh region destitute of subsistence during the coming winter but would not compel Grant to leave Chattanooga since his supply lines remained secure via the Tennessee River and the Bridgeport rail line. Moreover, the Rebels would be operating in a hostile area with a predominantly Unionist civilian population. Finally, some members of Bragg's army felt that sending Longstreet's corps into East Tennessee was coming too late to accomplish much.[12]

Bragg's decision to detach the First Corps in the face of a numerically superior enemy force remains one of the most controversial decisions of the Chattanooga campaign. Historians have generally criticized the general for dividing his army in such a situation. Most maintain that Bragg was motivated chiefly by a desire to rid his army of a perpetual malcontent rather than rational thought or sound strategic judgment.[13]

Thus while the proposal to send a force into East Tennessee appeared to have merit, Bragg's decision to assign Longstreet remains curious since the First Corps faced a number of disadvantages that would hurt its opportunity to succeed against Burnside. Historian Thomas Lawrence Connelly persuasively argues that Bragg could have chosen another commander for the East Tennessee campaign. Stevenson's 11,000 troops and two cavalry brigades, for instance, had been operating successfully in the region since late October. More familiar with the region, Stevenson thus had a significant advantage over Longstreet. On the eve of his campaign, Longstreet confessed to Buckner that he possessed no maps and knew nothing of the region. In addition, the Army of Northern Virginia troops had arrived without wagons or horses. Bragg himself cited the First Corps's lack of transportation as a reason for not pursuing the Federals following Chickamauga. If those reasons were not enough to recommend another force and commander, then the logistics of transferring the First Corps from its position on Lookout Mountain should have been. Since Longstreet held the left of the Confederate line around Chattanooga, his troops would find it more difficult to march to the railroad, more than ten miles east of the army's position on Missionary Ridge, than Breckinridge or Hardee, who were stationed at the center and right of Army of Tennessee.[14]

After the war Bragg attempted to shift the responsibility of assigning Longstreet to East Tennessee to Davis, asserting that he yielded his "convictions to the President's policy, and sent Longstreet instead of Breckinridge," whom Bragg later claimed was his "choice" to "capture Burnside at Knoxville." While Davis certainly did suggest Longstreet as a possible choice for the assignment, Davis wrote on October 25, several days before

Bragg informed him of the First Corps commander's tactical errors at Brown's Ferry and Wauhatchie. Bragg already had intimated Longstreet's insubordination and disobedience of orders to the president. Thus one wonders why the commander of the Army of Tennessee would assign a mission that relied on alacrity and diligence to a subordinate he blamed for the failure of his siege at Chattanooga. But Bragg's comments to General Liddell shortly after Wauhatchie about ridding himself of Longstreet and seeing what the general "could do on his own" suggest that personal motive had overridden practical military sense in making this decision.[15]

This decision can be further questioned considering the state of turmoil existing in the First Corps during the first week of November. The main problem stemmed from the rivalry between Micah Jenkins and Evander Law over the command of Hood's Division. This tense situation led Longstreet to discuss the matter with Davis as early as the president's visit to the Army of Tennessee. After the military tribunal on October 9, Longstreet informed Davis of his preference for Jenkins, but the president refused "to assign a commander." The battle at Wauhatchie exacerbated the situation, for Jenkins blamed Law for the fiasco. In his official report Longstreet complained of a lack of cooperation between the two men and cited the "jealousy between the two brigades" as a central reason for his failure to regain Lookout Valley.[16]

Although Longstreet considered arresting Law, he did not file formal charges. Instead he relieved Jerome Robertson for "want of hearty cooperation" in the attack at Wauhatchie. General Robertson, who led the Texas Brigade in support of Law, had retreated in a disorderly fashion during the engagement on the twenty-ninth. This action perturbed Longstreet and led him to believe that the Texans had abandoned their position at Jenkins's expense. On November 1 he informed army headquarters of Robertson's removal. Bragg complied with Longstreet's request, relieving Robertson of command and convening a board of inquiry to examine the case. As the brigadier prepared to defend himself against all charges, the board adjourned as the army prepared to move. Command relations in the First Corps thus remained rife with dissent and recrimination. Robertson's arrest triggered dissent from some of Longstreet's other brigadiers. "I have been relieved from my command at the request of the Lt. General," Robertson wrote Brig. Gen. Henry Lewis Benning on November 4. "I have some things to talk to you that are interesting to *us all.*" Robertson's letter suggests a congregation of disgruntled lieutenants who condemned Longstreet's action. Bragg reviewed the case against Robertson and restored him to active duty on November 8. The commander of the Texas Brigade would rejoin the First Corps en route to Knoxville.[17]

Maj. Gen. Lafayette McLaws was a West Point classmate of James Longstreet. Resolute and dependable early in the war, McLaws later chafed under Longstreet's command and left the First Corps in the worst of circumstances in 1864.
LIBRARY OF CONGRESS
(LC-B813-6773A)

The volatility of the First Corps was not isolated to Hood's Division. Lafayette McLaws, the other division commander, also had a falling out with his superior. Longstreet and McLaws were longtime friends and West Point classmates who had fought together from the Seven Days to Gettysburg before their journey to the western theater. McLaws had served admirably at Antietam and Fredericksburg but faltered under Lee's direct command at Chancellorsville. In the army's subsequent reorganization, he had been passed over for promotion in favor of A. P. Hill and Richard S. Ewell. Citing favoritism toward the Virginians, McLaws sought a transfer from the Army of Northern Virginia. The First Corps's senior division commander, he had been ill the previous winter, and Lee asked Longstreet to ascertain McLaws's ability to actively campaign during the summer of 1863. Receiving assurances from his subordinate and friend, Longstreet retained McLaws but promised Lee to keep an eye on him. "I thus became responsible for anything that was not entirely satisfactory in your command from that day," Longstreet later told McLaws.[18]

At Gettysburg Longstreet's reluctance to follow Lee's orders, as well as his command decisions on the battle's second day, infuriated McLaws. In a letter to his wife, he blamed Longstreet for the failure in Pennsylvania, writing: "I think the whole attack was unnecessary and the whole plan of battle a very bad one. General Longstreet is to be blamed for not reconnoitering the ground and for persisting in ordering the assault when his errors were discussed. During the engagement he was excited giving contradictory orders to every one, and was exceedingly [overbearing]. I consider him a humbug: a man of small capacity, very obstinate, not at all chivalrous, exceedingly conceited, and totally selfish. If I can it is my intention to get away from his command." McLaws's subsequent conduct in the West suggests that resentment had not abated. Upon his arrival at Chickamauga, the general received orders to pursue the Federals toward Chattanooga, but he faltered, claiming that his command would suffer heavy losses and requesting more ambulances. For the next several weeks, McLaws remained uncooperative, prompting Longstreet to report his recalcitrance to Bragg in mid-October. Bragg apparently convinced him to give his division commander one more chance. Although Longstreet suggested to McLaws that "he should brush up and be more prompt and active," relations between the two men portended trouble for the First Corps in the upcoming campaign.[19]

Bragg certainly knew of the internal strife that tore at the First Corps. Official correspondence kept him informed of the feud between Law and Jenkins as well as Longstreet's complaints about McLaws's intransigence. These problems should have intimated to Bragg that ordering the First Corps to East Tennessee did not bode well. The operation, which depended on swiftness and a close cooperation between Bragg and Longstreet, should not have been entrusted to a commander facing numerous external and internal obstacles. But Bragg had other motives than military expediency in sending Longstreet to East Tennessee. Perhaps he simply wanted to rid himself of troublemaker. Or as McLaws pointed out, "Gen. Bragg because of Longstreet's conduct in reference to Brown's Ferry, had reason to be disgusted with him and in my private opinion that was the reason he sent him to Knoxville."[20]

While Bragg might have yielded to personal animosity in ordering Longstreet to East Tennessee, his orders maintained that the First Corps would not be considered an independent command. The general clearly outlined his objective, "to drive Burnside out of East Tennessee first, or better, to capture or destroy him," but he remained vague as to whether Longstreet's detachment would be permanent. Longstreet thus understood that he still remained under Bragg's command. Bragg also tried to relieve him of his trepidation in advancing into an unfamiliar region, telling Longstreet that Wheeler's cavalry would join him in the expedition.[21] His insistence on a quick movement into East Tennessee was overly optimistic since the dilapidated conditions of Southern railroads had prevented all of Longstreet's men from arriving in North Georgia in time for Chickamauga. For Bragg to expect an improvement in the Confederacy's transportation system six weeks later seems absurd.

The communication breakdown between Bragg and Longstreet is evident in the correspondence between the men. After receiving Bragg's orders regarding East Tennessee, Longstreet responded with questions about the operation, thus suggesting that Bragg failed to inform him of all particulars for the campaign. Longstreet asked if Stevenson's men would be under his command or would at least be ordered to cooperate with him. He also requested information as to the enemy's dispositions in East Tennessee. The following day Bragg responded that Stevenson's Division would return to Chattanooga upon being relieved by the First Corps. This brief note also provided Longstreet a rudimentary intelligence report about the enemy in East Tennessee, referring to the Federal fortifications at Knoxville as "imperfect." He also promised him a guide for the region. Longstreet then expressed his doubts that he could maintain railroad communications with the Army of Tennessee with his two divisions. On the sixth Bragg responded that Longstreet should not worry about the railroads and that his primary focus should remain regaining possession of East Tennessee for the Confederacy.[22]

As Bragg became frustrated with Longstreet's queries, he failed to understand the perspective of his corps commander. In the past month Longstreet had witnessed the removal of his former colleague from the Army of Northern Virginia, D. H. Hill, and the transfer or demotion of other generals who had voiced their displeasure with Bragg's leadership. His close friend, Simon Buckner, had lost his departmental command and now served as a corps commander under Bragg, despite his bitter protests. Polk, the former ringleader of the anti-Bragg cabal, had also left the army. Longstreet had voiced his own displeasure at serving under Bragg and certainly recognized his precarious position in the eyes of the Davis administration. While leaving Bragg's command might appeal to Longstreet, he knew the risks involved in East Tennessee. To add to his difficulties, Longstreet, who arrived in the West audaciously predicting success, had had his confidence shaken by the events of late October. He had erred at Lookout Mountain and for the first time had begun to exhibit signs of doubt and insecurity. The general not only had misgivings about his new mission but also doubted that Bragg believed in him. "We thus expose both to failure and really take no chance to ourselves of great results," he confessed.[23]

Other officers in the Army of Tennessee shared Longstreet's doubts regarding the East Tennessee operation. "It was folly for Bragg to do this," wrote General Liddell. "But Bragg was headstrong and too often unreasonable." Colonel Alexander concurred, arguing that such a move should have been attempted weeks earlier, when the Federals remained in a weakened state in Chattanooga. "Immediately after the battle of Chickamauga it could have been safely attempted," he argued, "& sufficient force could have been spared to make the task sure & easy." Even Bragg's chief of staff, George Brent, questioned his commander's decision.[24]

Despite all the misgivings, the advance elements of Longstreet's corps arrived at Tyner's Station, eight miles east of Chattanooga, on November 5. As Bragg had directed a rapid movement to East Tennessee, the First Corps high command arrived at the railroad depot expecting transportation ready to move the 12,000 men toward Knoxville. To their disappointment, Longstreet and his lieutenants found the conditions of the railroad deplorable. They also found no food or other supplies appropriated for the campaign. Longstreet informed Brent of these problems and requested that army headquarters assist them, lest the mission be compromised for "want of transportation." An accident on the road exacerbated the delay and forced the First Corps troops to remain at Tyner's Station for two days without rations or winter clothing. All of these delays frustrated Longstreet's men. McLaws's soldiers finally managed to secure several cars, while Hood's Division marched toward Cleveland, Tennessee, thirty miles northeast of Chattanooga, in search of rolling stock.[25]

Longstreet's troops departed with elated spirits regarding their new mission, regardless of the heavy rains and thick mud that slowed their march. The veterans of the Army of Northern Virginia probably believed that a move toward East Tennessee would bring them better rations and place them a step closer to returning to Lee's army. In fact several soldiers already had regretted leaving the Old Dominion for the West. Col. Asbury Coward of the 5th South Carolina remembered that when word spread that they would march toward Sweetwater, his men became excited. "Few knew what the country was, but the name was attractively suggestive of good things to eat and drink," he noted. Pvt. James H. Hendrick, 1st Texas Infantry, expressed relief in leaving Chattanooga. A South Carolinian told his wife that while the marching proved arduous, it was better than remaining idle. General Jenkins also expressed optimism in a letter to his wife: "We are going perhaps where battles will be fought, but we will be better provided [for] I think."[26]

But this initial optimism soon gave way to the hardships of the campaign as the long delays, lack of provisions, and cold weather dampened the soldiers' spirits. "We had only expected to remain at Tyner's Station a day or two, but we were kept there until the afternoon of the 10th," reported Colonel Alexander. "My recollections of the place are only those of the struggle we had to get enough to eat, for no preparations had been made for any such delay." The march to Cleveland also caused hardships for Longstreet's officers, who had to march with the men under their command due to their horses having been sent ahead earlier. Despite the difficulties, the Confederates reached Cleveland on the eighth and ninth and boarded trains for Sweetwater, about fifty miles northeast of Chattanooga. By the eleventh the bulk of the First Corps had reached the town.[27]

Longstreet preceded his men and arrived at Sweetwater on the ninth. To his dismay, he failed to find the rations, supply wagons, and draft animals that he had requested. The First Corps's quartermaster, Maj. Raphael Moses, complained that the men had been marching for several days without meat and that foraging was fruitless in an otherwise exhausted region. Bragg responded by promising seventy wagons to the First Corps, even though only thirty-five eventually arrived in Sweetwater. Despite Bragg's efforts, Longstreet's troops still struggled with a shortage of wagons and draft animals, Capt. Frank Potts, the corps's assistant quartermaster, reported.[28]

The lack of support from the Army of Tennessee prompted Longstreet to write Bragg on the eleventh. The general groused that his troops could have traveled the fifty miles to Sweetwater in half the time if adequate rail transportation had been procured. "Instead of being prepared to make a campaign, I find myself not more than half prepared to subsist," he wrote. Infuriated with Longstreet's messages, Bragg responded on the twelfth: "Your several dispatches of to-day astonish me. . . . Transportation in abundance was on the road and subject to your orders. I regret it has not been energetically used. The means being furnished, you were expected to handle your own troops, and I cannot understand your constant applications for me to furnish them." This letter was misleading. In his orders of November 4, Bragg told Longstreet that "every preparation is ordered to advance you as fast as possible." In no subsequent message did he indicate that Longstreet had authority over transportation. On the sixth Bragg informed his subaltern that he would assign others the task of keeping the railroads moving so that Longstreet could concentrate on the campaign, stressing the urgency of the movement. Even his assurance that the countryside the First Corps would march through could provide ample sustenance was contradicted by the reports of Longstreet's quartermasters.[29]

In his postwar memoirs Longstreet suggests that Bragg assigned him the task of clearing East Tennessee with hopes of seeing him fail. Even during the campaign, he implied that Bragg failed to cooperate effectively by not providing supplies to his corps. Longstreet recalled that Stevenson received orders not to have supplies available at Sweetwater. While these recriminations cannot be proved, Bragg bears responsibility for not responding to the plight of the First Corps. His written orders of November 4 outlined the instructions for Longstreet's command and focused on the alacrity of the movement as the latter's main responsibility. When Longstreet brought the deficiencies of the operation to his notice, Bragg should have acted promptly since transportation and sustenance were under his control as departmental commander. Yet the commander's actions confirmed Longstreet's worst fears. On November 11 Bragg complained to the War Department that he had not heard from Longstreet since his departure from the Army of Tennessee. "Longstreet ought to be over the Tennessee," he wrote General Cooper in Richmond, "but I hear nothing from him." Despite the extensive correspondence from Longstreet during the past several days, Bragg lied to authorities in Richmond, suggesting that Longstreet remained uncooperative. Why he did so remains unclear, unless he sought to contribute to Longstreet's failure.[30]

While Longstreet may have suspected that Bragg's lack of cooperation stemmed from his own criticism of the general, he attempted to accomplish his mission. The delay in moving toward Knoxville enabled him to amass additional intelligence on the enemy. Instead of just 15,000 men under Burnside, Wheeler reported that Longstreet faced more than 28,000 Federals on an eighty-mile perimeter from Loudon to Rogersville, Tennessee. Wary of facing a numerically stronger foe, Longstreet requested reinforcements. The First Corps numbered about 12,000 men, and including Wheeler's cavalry corps, Longstreet led a force of about 17,000 effectives. They faced Burnside's IX Corps and XXIII Corps, which indeed numbered about 28,000 men, more than half stationed at Knoxville. Yet the Army of Tennessee could not spare additional men. Longstreet mistakenly believed that Bragg ignored his pleas for more men because of personal animosity. Instead Bragg knew as early as November 8 that Sherman had reached the Chattanooga vicinity, in effect increasing Grant's forces to more than 60,000 soldiers. If the general sent additional men to Longstreet, he risked crippling his own defenses. Nevertheless, his missives, which expressed disappointment with Longstreet's progress, prompted the First Corps to action. On the twelfth Longstreet issued orders for an advance to Loudon the next morning.[31]

With Wheeler's cavalry providing a diversion toward Marysville, fifteen miles east of Loudon, the First Corps advanced in two columns on the morning of November 13. Lying astride the East Tennessee and Georgia Railroad, Loudon seemed the only site for crossing the Tennessee River. The Confederates had to maintain close ties to the railroad since they had no other means to transport the pontoon bridges provided by Bragg's quartermasters. The Federals had a detachment of 5,000 troops on the south side of the river to delay the advancing Rebel columns and to destroy the bridge across the Tennessee. Grant asked Burnside to "hold Longstreet in check" by "skirmishing and falling back," drawing him farther away from the Army of Tennessee, until Grant could "force the enemy back from here [Chattanooga] and place a force between Longstreet and Bragg." If successful, Grant's plan would place Longstreet between Burnside and the Federals in Chattanooga, thereby cutting the First Corps's supply line. Accordingly, Union troops under Brig. Gen. Julius White offered only slight resistance as they retreated, enabling Longstreet's men to establish a bridgehead across the Tennessee.[32]

The First Corps reached Loudon on the fourteenth and prepared to cross the river that day. When Longstreet ordered Colonel Alexander to find a suitable point for the crossing, the artillery chief chose Huff's Ferry, two miles below the town. Longstreet instructed Alexander to lead the crossing while Jenkins pushed the Federals through Loudon. By the morning of the fifteenth, the Confederates marched across the Tennessee River, encountering no resistance. The Federals began their methodical retrograde movement toward Knoxville, marching along the rail line to Lenoir's Station, about nine miles northeast of Loudon. Burnside left his headquarters at Knoxville and headed toward Lenoir's Station to personally lead his troops, consisting of elements from the IX Corps and a division of the XXIII Corps, numbering about 8,000 men. The last thing Burnside wanted was to give Longstreet a reason to return to Chattanooga. Unaware of the Federals' strategy, Longstreet ordered Jenkins to lead the advance guard toward Lenoir's Station in pursuit, hoping to draw the Federals into a fight. McLaws received instructions to march on the Kingston Road, which led to Knoxville, running north and parallel to the railroad. Longstreet thus hoped that McLaws could catch Burnside and attack his flank as he retreated.[33]

The Confederate column struggled through thick mud as it pursued the Federals toward Lenoir's Station. Jenkins's men made contact with the rear guard on the afternoon of the fifteenth and gained possession of the two commanding hills southeast of the station before darkness prevented further action. The Confederates encamped for the night, and Longstreet ordered an assault for early the next day. During the night he ordered scouts

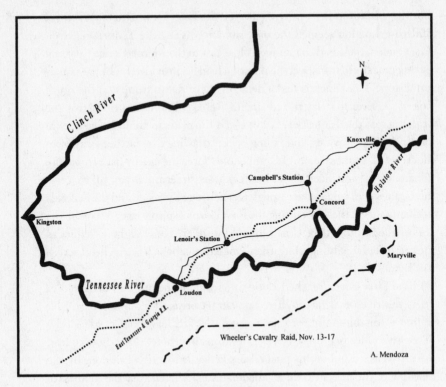

MAP 5. *The Race to Campbell's Station, November 1863*

to find a road leading to the Federal rear. While the guides searched for such a route, soldiers from the 8th Georgia could hear a commotion in the Federal camps. To Longstreet's chagrin, the guides failed to find a suitable road, and Jenkins's men marched into Lenoir's only to discover that the Federals were gone. Regimental leaders struggled to keep their men from breaking ranks to plunder the abandoned camp. After a brief delay, Longstreet sent Jenkins marching toward Campbell's Station in another attempt to capture the Yankees.[34]

Longstreet hoped to intercept Burnside before he could reach his fortifications in Knoxville. Seizing control of Campbell's Station, the junction of the Kingston and Concord roads, was crucial to this. Burnside's line of march followed the East Tennessee and Georgia Railroad until it diverged to Concord. From there, the Concord Road led north two miles to Campbell's Station, about eleven miles from Lenoir's Station. From the intersection of the Kingston and Concord roads, a single route led to Knoxville, about fifteen miles to the east. While Jenkins followed Burnside's force along the railroad, McLaws moved north along the Hotchkiss Valley Road to Eaton

Crossroad and then east along the Kingston Road, parallel to Jenkins's line of march, a distance of about nine and a half miles. If McLaws could seize the intersection, the Confederates could trap Burnside, and the East Tennessee campaign would come to a quick and successful conclusion. Longstreet allocated half of the artillery to each of the two divisions, traveling about three to five miles apart. He also ordered Col. John Hart's 6th Georgia Cavalry, which had been reconnoitering on the Kingston-Loudon Road, to assist McLaws in seizing the crossroads. Jenkins's men slogged along the muddy roads and returned fire from Burnside's rear guard, while McLaws's men marched virtually unimpeded toward Campbell's Station.[35]

But the Federal advance guard, under Col. John F. Hartranft, reached the crossroads first shortly after 11:00 A.M. on the sixteenth, about fifteen minutes before the Confederates. Hart's cavalry arrived at the station and engaged the Federal horsemen before they found themselves in front of Burnside's retreating infantry and withdrew without offering further opposition. "We allowed them to pass without molestation," wrote Pvt. J. W. Minnich of the 6th Georgia Cavalry, "and they politely and proudly disdainful of our small number ignored us completely." Hart's cavalry watched while the Federals "marched past—unharmed—and went into line of battle across the road about three-fourths of a mile above the station."[36]

Without further resistance from the Confederate cavalry, Hartranft turned his two brigades west on the Kingston Road to engage McLaws and buy the main Federal column some time. He issued orders to his small cavalry detachment to charge the Confederates at first sight and drive away any Rebel pickets from the crossroads. This bold tactic worked, and McLaws halted about a mile west of Campbell's Station. Within the hour Burnside's main force arrived at the junction and deployed to face Longstreet's corps, making a stand at Campbell's Station while Capt. Orlando M. Poe of the Corps of Engineers strengthened the Knoxville defenses. As the Federals maneuvered into position, Longstreet rode out to meet McLaws. He instructed McLaws to position his three brigades north of the Kingston Road behind a wooded area west of the station and to wait for Jenkins to get into position before launching an attack. Longstreet planned for the latter's three brigades (under Bratton, Anderson, and Law) to strike the Federal left, which stood east of the Concord Road facing west. Burnside deployed the First Division, IX Corps north of the intersection, facing McLaws to the west, while the Second Division lay south of the junction opposite Jenkins. The XXIII Corps marched on in support of Burnside's baggage train to Knoxville.[37]

Campbell's Station consisted of only a few houses clustered around the intersection of the Kingston and Concord roads. An open area about a mile wide lay between thick woods southwest and northeast of the station. Jenkins, on the Confederate right, stood behind the tree line west of the Concord Road. Longstreet ordered him to move Law's and George Anderson's brigades against the Federal left, with Bratton's Brigade in support. After Jenkins began his attack, McLaws was to launch an assault against the Federal front. Longstreet planned for McLaws to hold Burnside's force in place while Jenkins's men maneuvered toward and attacked the enemy's flank. He also ordered Alexander's guns, deployed behind Jenkins, to shell the Federals. If the plan succeeded, the First Corps still could capture Burnside and gain possession of East Tennessee rapidly, thus placing Grant in a predicament at Chattanooga. But the maneuver demanded pinpoint timing and close cooperation between two divisions that had been operating at cross-purposes for the past month.[38]

Around 3:00 P.M. Alexander's guns opened fire on the Federal line opposite Concord Road. While the artillery kept Burnside's forces occupied, Jenkins's division marched toward the Federal lines. The brigades of Bratton, Anderson, and Law marched from left to right; Benning's and Robertson's brigades remained in reserve. Anderson and Law advanced along a semicircular arc to Burnside's left flank, with the intent that Anderson's left-hand regiments would march even with the enemy lines while Law's Brigade swept into the Union left rear. Opposite the Kingston Road, McLaws waited for Jenkins's assault to develop before advancing toward the Federal right as a diversion. But Longstreet's attack soon appeared in danger of stalling because Alexander's guns failed to provide adequate support. Almost all of the shells fired either burst prematurely or failed to burst at all. One 20-pounder Parrott gun exploded, nearly wounding Longstreet, who happened to be standing nearby. In his official report Alexander complained that his artillery units experienced the same problems as at Chattanooga because the "ammunition was procured from the depots of the Army of Tennessee."[39]

As Alexander struggled to shell the enemy lines, the Federals encountered no such difficulties. Union artillery punished the Rebel infantry during the advance toward Concord Road. Before Anderson's and Law's brigades could reach their positions astride the Federal left, however, Jenkins noticed that the Federals had begun to withdraw from their original line. Unknown to the Confederates, Burnside had reconnoitered the terrain and determined that the high ground to his left seemed like an ideal site for a flanking maneuver. He accordingly ordered his units to retreat to a predetermined second line about a quarter mile behind his original position and closer to the Federal artillery. By ordering a withdrawal, Burnside disrupted the timing of the Confederate assault. Meanwhile, across the Kingston Road McLaws began to launch his attack. Longstreet ordered him to halt upon realizing that the Federals had pulled back.[40]

Although the first flanking movement miscarried, there was enough time to launch a second attack. Jenkins ordered Law and Anderson to continue with the original plan and strike the Federal left in its new position. Jenkins reported that the difficult terrain around Campbell's Station hampered rapid movement, but he persisted in attempting to hit Burnside's flank before darkness ended operations. While McLaws advanced against the Union right, the Confederates south of the Kingston Road struggled. Jenkins discovered that Law's Brigade had shifted too far to his left and now impeded Anderson. With darkness approaching, he ordered Law to launch the flanking assault on his own. But Law complained that his brigade had marched so far to the left that it had "gotten out of its line of attack." The Confederates lost time while Law repositioned his unit, and impending darkness ended the possibility for a final assault by Jenkins. During the night, Burnside withdrew to the safety of Knoxville, his rear guard skirmishing with Rebel pickets until dawn. A Confederate officer observed that the retreat, which was marked by "burning wagons, dead horses, [and] dead Yankees," hampered Longstreet's ability to pursue. Both sides agreed that the fighting at Campbell's Station proved to be a minor engagement. The Federals suffered about 300 casualties, and the Confederates about 200.[41]

The failure to destroy Burnside's forces at Campbell's Station triggered more feuding within the First Corps. Jenkins blamed Law for allowing the Federals to escape. Law, the senior brigadier on the field, was responsible for the flanking maneuver around the Union left. In his report Jenkins fumed at what he perceived to be a lost opportunity. Law protested that his "regiment of direction"—the regiment on the far left of his brigade—had moved too close to Anderson's Brigade. Jenkins rejected this explanation, insisting that Law should have immediately corrected the error during the battle. As he had after the engagement at Wauhatchie, Longstreet concurred with Jenkins's negative assessment of the Alabaman, attributing the loss at Campbell's Station to "some mismanagement by General Law."[42]

Other officers also blamed Law for the lost opportunity. Colonel Coward of the 5th South Carolina simply could not figure out how the general's experienced troops could falter in such a critical moment. In his postwar memoirs Col. G. Moxley Sorrel suggests that Law had mismanaged his brigades because of the general's want of cooperation. More accurately, Sorrel

pinpointed the real problem afflicting the First Corps during the Knoxville campaign, the jealousy between Jenkins and Law. "Ah! Would that we
could have had Hood again at the head of the division," he lamented.[43]

While some First Corps officers cited Law's failure to carry out his
flanking movement as the primary reason for Burnside's escape, rumors
surfaced once more that Law purposely blundered his assignment to embarrass Jenkins. In his postwar memoirs Longstreet indirectly accuses Law
of such a diabolical motive by quoting an unnamed staff officer's memorandum: "I know at the time it was currently reported that General Law said
he might have made the attack successfully, but that Jenkins would have
reaped the credit of it, and hence he delayed until the enemy got out of the
way." Colonel Alexander repeated the accusation, stating that he had heard
that "some of Law's company officers wrote letters supporting" the charge
that he deliberately failed to carry out his orders to prevent Jenkins from
receiving credit. Even though Alexander did not see any evidence, he suggested that Law purposely led his brigade "where the enemy could & did
discover the movement," thus causing them to withdraw to their anterior
line.[44] These postwar charges cannot be substantiated, but the recriminations suggest that the First Corps high command remained divided by
jealousy.

Law later responded with his own version of events. Writing for the
Philadelphia Weekly News after the war, he blamed the failure of the flanking maneuver on Jenkins, whom he claimed gave him an order to wait for
the rest of the division before launching his assault. Law believed that this
delay "was fatal to the success of the movement" because "by the time
the rest of the division came up the opportunity had passed and we advanced into the valley to find nothing in front of us." Moreover, he questioned Longstreet's decision to hold McLaws's Division while the flanking
maneuver developed, arguing that it should have been used to launch a
frontal assault while Jenkins maneuvered against the Federal left. Had he
been pressed, Burnside could not have withdrawn his men to their second
line, Law reasoned, and the Rebels' flanking movement would have hit the
enemy with full force.[45] Law noted that most successful flanking movements during the Civil War began with a frontal assault to hold the enemy
in place while a second force struck the enemy's flank or rear, resulting in
the defender's rout. Longstreet used such a flanking movement at Second
Manassas. But at Campbell's Station, he may have intended to reverse the
procedure, using his flanking force to hold the enemy in place and then
launching a frontal assault—a tactic that could be equally devastating. Or

perhaps Longstreet attempted to seize the Knoxville Road to cut the Federals' sole line of retreat.

McLaws offered yet another version of the events at Campbell's Station. In a personal letter to Bragg, he maintains that on the night of November 15, he received orders to bivouac and await instructions for an early morning march the next day. While preparing for the advance, McLaws states that one of his couriers, "who was acquainted with the country," informed him of a fork in the road leading directly to Campbell's Station and the vital road junction. Realizing the opportunity to strike Burnside a serious blow, he sent a message to Longstreet informing him of this and requesting permission to march that night; no reply came from the commanding general. McLaws's Division stood ready to move at daylight, but to his chagrin he did not receive marching orders until about 8:00 A.M. McLaws asserts that Longstreet lost an opportunity to defeat Burnside by not allowing him to march during the night of the fifteenth. Moreover, he criticizes the corps commander for delaying his advance on the sixteenth. McLaws's account must be analyzed carefully, however, for he wrote it after leaving the First Corps under difficult circumstances.[46]

In the race to Knoxville, Longstreet repeatedly failed to rout the numerically inferior Federals in part because the weather and the muddy roads exacerbated his command's supply problems. Unaware that Grant counted on the First Corps to march from the Army of Tennessee at Chattanooga, Longstreet unwittingly complied with his old friend's design by pushing Burnside. In Tennessee Burnside was not the same blundering commander who had launched a series of frontal assaults at Fredericksburg a year earlier. Instead, he followed Grant's directives and conducted an expert retrograde movement toward Knoxville. Burnside simply outgeneraled Longstreet. At Knoxville the Federals numbered more than 14,000 men, with more troops available in East Tennessee. After failing to destroy a part of Burnside's force in the race to Knoxville, Longstreet now faced a stronger foe behind excellent fortifications. His objective to recover East Tennessee and to rejoin the Army of Tennessee quickly now seemed doubtful. The operation that Bragg had conceived as a lightning operation now appeared to require additional time that the Confederates could not spare.

Longstreet had realized the difficulty of accomplishing the mission before he left Chattanooga in early November. Based on personal past history, he should not have expected Bragg's unconditional confidence and support. Although it is doubtful that the general deliberately sabotaged the East Tennessee operation because of his enmity for Longstreet, Bragg's bitterness in his official dispatches suggests that he ignored the First Corps commander's pleas for reinforcements and additional equipment. Consequently the advance on Knoxville took longer than expected and gave Burnside an opportunity to prepare for an attack. Nevertheless, Longstreet could have defeated the Federals at Lenoir's and Campbell's Stations but failed. Sorrel tried to explain this by blaming the poor condition of the roads. Burnside, however, had to retreat on those same roads and with a heavy baggage train that slowed his progress. On the march to Campbell's Station, Longstreet ordered McLaws and Jenkins to take separate routes to cut off the Federal advance guard. Whereas he directed Jenkins to march at double time while pursuing the Union rear guard, he failed to issue the same orders to McLaws, whose dilatory march along the Kingston Road enabled the Federals to arrive at Campbell's first and hold the vital road junction. Had Longstreet not ordered Wheeler toward Maryville, the cavalry might have changed the course of the campaign.[47]

The two problems that plagued the First Corps became Longstreet's lack of self-confidence and a want of harmony between his senior officers. The events of the previous month had caused Longstreet to doubt his ability as a commander. When Bragg failed to heed his messages about poor transportation, lack of sustenance, and the need for reinforcements, Longstreet probably imagined the worst. He worried that the mission was destined to fail—most likely at his expense—and he advanced cautiously against Burnside's forces in East Tennessee, frequently complaining to army headquarters and thereby increasing his commander's resentment. The nature of the operation also required Longstreet to work offensively, a situation he found unsettling. While the Confederates marched to confront Burnside, the Union general avoided a decisive battle in the field. Instead he conducted a skillful retreat to Knoxville and thus drew the First Corps farther away from Chattanooga. To Longstreet's credit, however, he did not panic and order a hasty assault against the Federal defenses. Operating in unfamiliar terrain and without his commander's support, Longstreet probably fared as well as could be expected in his advance into East Tennessee. Moreover, while Burnside enjoyed the confidence and cooperation of his men, the First Corps was not now the same disciplined unit that had fought in the Virginia theater under Lee. Petty jealousies and internal strife reduced the effectiveness of Longstreet's command.

Longstreet ordered his troops to bivouac on the night of the sixteenth before marching on Knoxville early the next day. His exhausted troops encamped for the night, the previous month's hardships having taken their toll. Although both commanding generals considered the battle at Campbell's Station a minor engagement, the horrors of war remained clearly evident to the men of the First Corps. During the night, while serving on picket duty, a Confederate artilleryman and a staff officer found a wounded Rebel cannoneer who lay screaming in agony. Although most of his face had been shot off and his body was torn by shrapnel, the mangled man somehow asked his comrades to ease his suffering. Despite the risk of tending to a wounded man so close to enemy lines, the artillerymen cared for their fallen comrade, administering an opiate to relieve the pain during the last moments of his life. Other men just lay on the ground trying to forget the terrors of the previous battle. In one incident that day, a Federal shell landed in the center of the 5th South Carolina Regiment as the men advanced toward the enemy, tearing off the arm of Pvt. Robert McKnight. The severed arm flew through the air and struck the head of Pvt. Lorraine Swann, killing him instantly. Lt. J. D. McConnell remembered that portions of Swann's brain had splattered on his coat.[48]

Other soldiers worried more about their next meal than the events of the campaign. After failing to capture Burnside's force, Lt. R. T. Coles of the 4th Alabama Infantry remembered that his regiment bivouacked on the night of the sixteenth "exhausted and ravenously hungry." He and Lt. William Turner had the unpleasant duty of distributing a ration of potatoes to the officers and men of the regiment. After a careful tally, Coles and Turner determined that each man "was entitled to two potatoes." The intense hunger of the two lieutenants led them to gamble for their combined lot. They agreed to draw straws for the four potatoes. "It nearly broke my heart when Turner proved to be the winner," Coles recalled. Col. John Bratton wrote his wife that the pursuit of the Federals had drained the men in his brigade, who on top of that did not have enough to eat. The struggle to obtain rations during the march to Knoxville proved so daunting that Raphael Moses had to resort to monumental measures to transport sustenance forward to the troops from his station at Sweetwater. When a railroad engineer refused to travel farther up the rail line, Moses had to "take forcible possession" of the engine and carry the foodstuffs to the men in the field.[49]

But the most important cause of demoralization in the First Corps was Longstreet's repeated failure to defeat the Federals. The eastern troops, who had journeyed west brimming with confidence, were now grumbling over lost opportunities and blaming them on Longstreet. After Chickamauga, his troops had given him the moniker "the Bull of the Woods." They now had a new nickname for their commander, "Peter the Slow." "Without doubt we had several opportunities of capturing this detachment of Burnside's army," wrote an Alabama soldier. "But our generals seem to be deficient in strategy or military ability of any kind." The optimism that had sustained the soldiers upon leaving Bragg's army gave way to demoralization and frustration as victory eluded the proud eastern troops. A Confederate cavalryman observed that Longstreet's move into East Tennessee "only netted disappointment to all engaged in it . . . and raised a bitter feeling in the army against him."[50] The declining morale stemming from the failure to score a decisive victory since Chickamauga was exacerbated by the ongoing food shortage.

Despite the disappointment of Campbell's Station, Longstreet issued orders for the First Corps to pursue the Federals the following day. At daylight on the seventeenth, McLaws led the advance guard toward Knoxville, skirmishing with enemy cavalry along the Kingston Road. The Rebels closed to within a thousand yards of Union pickets on the northwest side of the city. Finding the Federals in strongly fortified positions, Longstreet ordered his men to bivouac while he spent the rest of the day reconnoitering the area's terrain. But the Southerners stood before Knoxville fortified with confiscated Federal supplies. While pursuing Burnside from Campbell's Station, the Confederates had captured hundreds of wagons loaded with food, tools, and supplies, including a pontoon bridge, and they intended to use it all. Longstreet ordered McLaws's Division to anchor the right flank on the Holston River, while Jenkins received instructions to move to the left, thereby establishing an arc around Knoxville. On the eighteenth Kershaw's Brigade engaged the Union works on the western side of the city and suffered 140 casualties before withdrawing. Realizing that his force was not strong enough to launch additional assaults against an entrenched foe, Longstreet probed the enemy's defenses for weaknesses. Wheeler had rejoined the command on the eighteenth and received orders to patrol northeast of Knoxville, along the Tazewell Road, in case Burnside decided to retreat in that direction. The First Corps besieged the city's garrison as Longstreet planned further action.[51]

Knoxville lay on the north bank of the Holston River. The city occupied a square-mile plateau that rises about 150 feet above the river. From east to west, First, Second, and Third creeks flow in a southerly direction into the Holston. At the time First Creek separated Knoxville from East Knoxville, Mabry's Hill, and Temperance Hill. To the west Second Creek flowed along the western edge of the plateau and separated the city from College Hill, the site of East Tennessee University (later the University of Tennessee). About twelve hundred yards west of Second Creek, a second plateau rises above the river along Third Creek. South of the Holston, a series of hills rising about 300 feet above the river overlooked the city. The

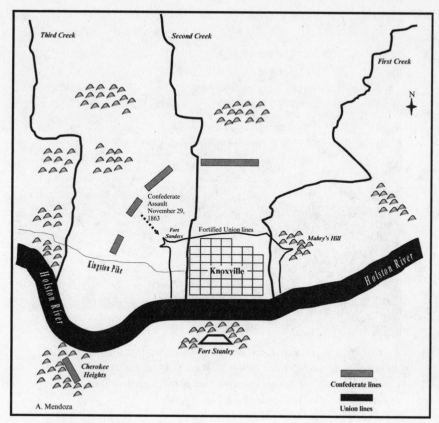

MAP 6. *Knoxville, 1863*

Union lines, prepared by Captain Poe, Burnside's chief engineer, ran in a semicircular arc, with the flanks anchored on the Holston. Beginning with a line of entrenchments, the Federals fortified their position by building dams on First and Second Creek, thus creating formidable obstacles to a frontal assault. Years later Poe noted that the failure of "Longstreet's renowned infantry . . . to carry it by assault demonstrated that there were no very serious defects" in the fortifications.[52]

For a few days Longstreet and his lieutenants reconnoitered the Knoxville lines, his men heavily skirmishing with the Union defenders, and soon focused on Fort Loudon, which the Federals had renamed Fort Sanders in honor of a fallen Union officer. The stronghold, which stood on a nearly two-hundred-foot hill north of the Kingston Road and slightly northwest of College Hill, dominated the Union position on the western side of the city. Originally built by the Confederates months earlier, Fort Sanders had

*Fort Sanders, Knoxville, Tennessee. The Federal bastion was
an imposing obstacle for Longstreet's forces. Note the tree stumps
surrounding the fort. Union engineers wrapped telegraph wire
around these to further hinder the attacking Rebels.*
LIBRARY OF CONGRESS (LC-DIG-CWPB-03507)

a trapezoidal shape with salients on the northwest and the southwest cor-
ners, while the eastern side was kept open in order to ferry troops into and
out of the fort. The other three sides of the bastion had twelve-foot-high
earthen walls whose parapets were topped with rawhide-wrapped cotton
bales, which extended the height to nearly fifteen feet. A water-filled ditch,
approximately ten feet wide and six to eight feet deep, surrounded the
fort and reached the wall's edge. Poe wrapped telegraph wire around tree
stumps encircling the citadel to present an even more formidable obstacle
to any attackers. Although Burnside had more than 14,000 men defending
Knoxville, only approximately 450 troops and a dozen cannon guarded
the fort.[53]

On the twentieth Longstreet informed Bragg that Burnside's position
was more formidable than Grant's at Chattanooga. "It seems to be a question of starvation with the enemy, or to re-enforce," he wrote. To expedite
the operation, he requested reinforcements from the Army of Tennessee.

That same day Bragg was telling the authorities in Richmond that Longstreet had failed to keep him informed about his operations near Knoxville despite repeated inquiries, also stating that he was "very much embarrassed" by this insolence.[54] On the twenty-first Longstreet repeated his request for reinforcements, stating that his "force is hardly strong" enough to take the enemy's "works by assault." Annoyed with the failure of the First Corps to strike at Burnside, the general instructed Longstreet to watch his flank and rear for Federal troops and promised to send him an additional 11,000 men. More importantly, Bragg told him that he was sending his chief engineer, Brig. Gen. Danville Leadbetter, with specific instructions.[55]

While waiting for Bragg's response, Longstreet searched for a way to defeat Burnside. At first he considered starving the Federals out of the Knoxville defenses, but reports indicated that Burnside had eight days' half-rations of bread and fifteen days' rations of beef and pork in addition to forage for the animals. Moreover, East Tennessee Unionists provided the garrison with food by floating supplies across the Holston under cover of darkness. On the twenty-first Longstreet asked McLaws if he felt confident about launching a night assault on Fort Sanders. Probably remembering the results of the disastrous night attack at Wauhatchie, the general and his brigadiers doubted the practicality of the proposal. Consequently Longstreet postponed the assault.[56]

The following day Maj. John Fairfax of Longstreet's staff reported that he found a hill on the south bank of the Holston, opposite the mouth of Third Creek, that might prove an ideal site from which to bombard the Federal lines. Longstreet ordered Alexander to ferry his guns across the river and prepare to enfilade Burnside's works. Even though Alexander doubted the practicability of the operation, the Confederates ferried Law's and Robertson's brigades also to support the batteries. For the next day and a half, Alexander's gunners hauled the heavy guns up the steep hills, known as Cherokee Heights, finally reaching the top on the twenty-fifth. Although the heights overlooked the city, the 2,400-yard range proved too far. The only other hill that commanded the Yankee fortifications stood farther east and was occupied by the Union garrison at Fort Stanley. To ascertain the strength of the enemy entrenchments, Longstreet ordered Law to make a demonstration with his brigade. Law launched an attack, but the Yankees forced his Alabamans to withdraw after suffering about fifty casualties. That day news of reinforcements from Bragg and the arrival of General Leadbetter induced Longstreet to postpone another artillery barrage.[57]

Prior to the arrival of Bragg's chief engineer, Longstreet appeared in-

Knoxville, Tennessee, from the south bank of the Holston River. East Tennessee University (now the University of Tennessee) is seen in the distance.
LIBRARY OF CONGRESS
(LC-B811-3674)

decisive. Leadbetter, a native of Maine and an 1836 West Point graduate, had supervised the construction of Fort Sanders months earlier, and his expertise seemed to settle the general. The Rebel engineer also conveyed the message that Bragg expected the First Corps to attack Burnside quickly. On the morning of the twenty-sixth, Longstreet led Leadbetter on a reconnaissance of the Federal works. After several hours of observation, the engineer declared that Fort Sanders was too formidable to attack and instead suggested an assault on the Federal position along Mabry's Hill. Later that afternoon Longstreet ordered Alexander to return his guns to the north side of the Holston. "I was never so disgusted in all my life," declared the colonel. Nevertheless, the Rebel gunners transported their artillery on their makeshift rafts to support the new assault. "Fortunately it was down Hill this time," Alexander later wrote.[58]

On the morning of the twenty-seventh, Longstreet and Leadbetter led a second reconnaissance around the Federal lines, this time accompanied by Longstreet's principal lieutenants, including Brig. Gen. Bushrod R. Johnson, who had just arrived with two brigades (the other commanded by Brig. Gen. Archibald Gracie) as Bragg's promised reinforcement. Upon closer scrutiny the officers pronounced that Mabry's Hill was too formidable and rejected Leadbetter's plan to assault the extreme right of the Union defenses. They made their way to the opposite end of the fortifications and inspected Fort Sanders once more. During this examination, Longstreet noticed a Yankee soldier walking across the ditch, which was reported to be more than five feet deep. Determined that they had been misled by faulty intelligence, he renewed his plan to assault Fort Sanders the next day, reasoning that if a Federal soldier could walk across the ditch, so could his infantry. But unknown to Longstreet, the Yankees had used planks just below the water's edge to walk across the deep-water ditch surrounding the fort.[59]

Rumors began to circulate that the Federals had advanced against Bragg at Chattanooga. Longstreet was unaware that on the twenty-fourth, Grant's army had attacked the Confederate left on Lookout Mountain. The next day Thomas's troops routed the Rebel positions on Missionary Ridge and forced Bragg to order a retreat. But the Confederates at Knoxville continued to reconnoiter the terrain, under pressure to finish Burnside quickly. Once again Longstreet ordered Alexander's guns to cross the Holston a third time and prepare to support his attack on Fort Sanders. A disgusted Alexander later wrote, "There was never a more complete fiasco than the attempt to find a favorable point for attack." Despite this criticism, Longstreet's deliberate survey of the Federal defenses suggests that he sought to find the weakest point for his assault. His belief in the defensive and his aversion to frontal attacks suggests that he did not want to sacrifice his men in a careless assault. If he took his time in front of Knoxville, it reflects his knowledge that Burnside's men had skillfully fortified their position.[60]

Longstreet ordered McLaws and Jenkins to lead the assault on Fort Sanders at daybreak on November 28. Under cover of Alexander's guns, the infantry would charge the Union picket lines. After an additional artillery barrage, the column would charge the fort itself and seize it. The comedy of errors that plagued First Corps operations around Knoxville continued on the twenty-eighth, the tenth day of the siege. This time the weather refused to cooperate as rain and fog prevented Alexander's guns from supporting the infantry. Longstreet postponed his morning assault to the afternoon and issued orders for McLaws to stand ready. McLaws was reluctant to attack at all that day because of the weather, but Longstreet persisted and personally visited his senior division commander to relate his plans. After the general left, McLaws met with his brigade commanders to discuss the assault. The battle-hardened veterans of the First Corps doubted the feasibility of the midafternoon offensive and asked Longstreet to delay the assault until the next morning. The commander acquiesced and postponed the attack one more day.[61]

The delay in attacking Fort Sanders convinced Longstreet to alter his original strategy. He abandoned the preparatory artillery barrage to preserve the element of surprise, instead ordering McLaws's troops to seize the Federal rifle pits in the predawn hours and station sharpshooters to support the charging infantry. According to the plan, two assault columns would silently converge on the northwest salient of Fort Sanders, make the attack, and capture the fort. Alexander complained that the plan's "features were crazy enough to have come out of Bedlam." After conserving precious ammunition for days, the colonel expressed disbelief that the role of his artillery would be relegated to firing signal guns to launch the morning assault.[62]

McLaws met with his brigade commanders to finalize the preparations for the next morning's assault. He and his lieutenants also discussed the need for ladders or fascines—bundles of sticks—to use in crossing the ditch. Reports indicated, however, that the ditch would not present an obstacle. Even so, the experienced generals doubted their commander's plans. The lack of support from his lieutenants probably induced Longstreet to write McLaws and ask for his cooperation in seeing the attack go smoothly. "Please urge your officers the importance of making the assault with a determination to succeed," Longstreet pleaded. "If the assault is made in that spirit, I shall feel no doubt of its success." McLaws responded by urging Longstreet to reconsider the attack the following morning in light of rumors that Bragg had been defeated and that his army had retreated into northern Georgia. He asked his commander what could be gained by attacking Burnside at Knoxville if the reports proved accurate. "And therefore I advised that the assault be not made [*sic*] but that we relinquish the siege of Knoxville at once & put our force in motion towards Virginia."[63]

While McLaws had earned the reputation of being a cautious and deliberate commander, his repeated complaints convinced Longstreet that his senior division leader held no confidence in his plans. Yet the events of the previous two months compelled Longstreet to urge McLaws again to support the attack on Fort Sanders:

> *Your letter is received. I am not at all confident that Genl. Bragg has had a serious battle at Chattanooga but there is a report that he has fallen back to Tunnel Hill. Under this report, I am entirely convinced that our only safety is in making the assault upon the enemy's positions tomorrow at daylight, and it is more important that I should have the entire support and cooperation of the officers in this connection. I do hope and trust that I may have your entire support and all the force that you may be possessed of in the execution of my*

views. It is a great mistake to suppose that there is any safety for us in
going to Virginia if Genl. Bragg has been defeated for we leave him
at the mercy of his victors. And with his army destroyed, our own had
better be also for we will be not only destroyed but disgraced. There
is neither safety nor honor in any other course than the one that I
have already chosen and advised. . . . The assault must be made at
the time appointed and must be made with a determination that will
insure success.[64]

Longstreet's missive apparently had little effect on the division commander. A few hours later Colonel Sorrel bluntly informed McLaws that the "brunt of the assault is not a time for discouraging reports."[65]

Even though the general later became the most vocal of Longstreet's critics, the planned assault on Fort Sanders had other detractors. Jenkins rode to McLaws's headquarters sometime in the afternoon of the twenty-eighth, concerned about the next day's assault based on new intelligence about the ditch's depth. He asked McLaws if his men carried fascines to cross the moat, but "he said he knew nothing of such things, and they would trust to luck in getting around or over." After leaving McLaws, Jenkins met Alexander and asked him to accompany him to First Corps headquarters to urge that Longstreet order McLaws to provide ladders to the storming party. The colonel demurred, feeling "unusually tired," probably from ferrying his artillery back and forth across the river the previous five days. Instead the Confederate artilleryman told Jenkins that he concurred and that he could relay this opinion to Longstreet. The general expressed his doubts in a letter to Longstreet, who responded by imploring Jenkins to avoid talk of defeat. "If we go in with the idea that we shall fail, we will be sure to do so," he wrote. "But no men who are determined to succeed can fail. Let me urge you not to entertain such feelings for a moment. Do not let any one fail, or any thing."[66]

Shortly before midnight, two of McLaws's brigades raced across the open field from their entrenchments and seized the Federal rifle pits. The Yankees fired a volley and withdrew to Fort Sanders, warning their comrades of the impending assault. The First Corps's surprise attack would prove to be no surprise at all.[67]

About 4:00 A.M. on the morning of November 29, Alexander's guns fired three successive shots to signal the beginning of the assault on Fort Sanders. The brigades of Benjamin Humphreys, Goode Bryan, and William Wofford marched toward the Federal bastion. The front lines tripped over the telegraph wires, causing the trailing troops to falter. Recovering

ASSAULT ON FORT SANDERS.

The assault on Fort Sanders, November 29, 1863, as depicted in this illustration by Kurz and Allison. Hundreds of Confederate soldiers became casualties of this ill-fated attack.
LIBRARY OF CONGRESS (LC-USZC4-1730)

from this first obstacle, hundreds of Rebels plunged into the ditch and struggled to climb up the fort's walls. The rain of the previous days had coated the walls of Fort Sanders with a sheet of ice, making them nearly impossible to scale. Nevertheless, the Confederates tried to boost each other over the wall on their backs and shoulders while the defenders tossed lighted artillery shells over the parapet and into the masses of attackers floundering in the water below. A few color bearers somehow managed to scale the bastion walls only to be shot down or captured by the Federals. Without the means to cross the ditch or climb the walls effectively, the attackers faced certain failure. After thirty minutes of carnage, the Rebels began to withdraw. Alexander's guns provided the troops with cover as they climbed out of the ditch and made their way back to the rifle pits, all the while under Federal fire.[68]

The First Corps veterans attacked Fort Sanders despite the strength of the Federal defenses and the doubts of their commanding officers. A South Carolinian doubted the practicality of making the assault. "It is doomed to failure," he wrote. "If they ever get into the ditch, they will be like rats in a cage trap." The men nevertheless charged the fort, despite the long odds. The deep ditch and the slippery walls proved insurmountable for the Confederate troops. A Georgia soldier complained that the walls were "one continual slope, without any place to stand upon or get a foot hold to climb up by." John Calvin Reed of the 8th Georgia later recalled seeing his comrades in a "close packed huddle" in the ditch. At that point, he remembered, "I became sure that we were not going to take the fort." A few agile soldiers managed to use their bayonets to climb the slick walls, only to be shot or pushed back down by the Yankee defenders. Once it became obvious that Sanders could not be taken, Longstreet's tenacious veterans reluctantly withdrew. In less than an hour, the First Corps suffered more than eight hundred casualties, while the Federals lost only about a dozen men. One Union soldier observed that the Confederate dead "presented the most horrible sight that I ever witnessed."[69]

Longstreet accompanied the brigades of Bushrod Johnson the morning of the attack. As they marched toward Fort Sanders in support, Capt. James M. Goggin of McLaws's staff approached the corps commander and reported the failure of the assault. Longstreet halted Johnson's brigades and issued orders for the assaulting columns to withdraw. In his postwar memoirs Longstreet seemed oblivious to the reasons why the attack failed. Disregarding the ditch, the icy walls, and the Federal defenders, he insisted that the attack failed because he prematurely ordered the withdrawal of his troops. An hour after the assault, Longstreet received a telegram from President Davis that confirmed the earlier rumors of Bragg's defeat. The president instructed the First Corps to rejoin the Army of Tennessee in northern Georgia.[70]

Regardless of Longstreet's postwar views, the disaster at Fort Sanders resulted from many reasons unrelated to an ill-timed withdrawal. For almost a month he had pursued Burnside toward Knoxville. Unknown to Longstreet, his futile attempts to capture or destroy the Federal command in East Tennessee aided Grant's strategy at Chattanooga, depriving Bragg of needed troops while Union forces grew increasingly stronger. After probing the Knoxville defenses, Longstreet delayed an attack on Burnside because of the imposing fortifications. He hesitated for more than ten days and repeatedly changed his plans, citing the need to probe for a weakness or complaining about the poor weather conditions. His decision to attack Fort Sanders, despite the rumors of Bragg's retreat from Chattanooga, reveals his poor judgment. Regardless of his postwar claims, the assault on the Federal bastion appeared destined to fail. As in his operations in Lookout Valley, Longstreet once again conducted poor reconnaissance and developed a faulty strategy.

The Knoxville campaign showed Longstreet at his worst. The failure at Lookout Valley initiated a steady erosion of confidence in his junior officers and—more importantly—in himself. Upon leaving Bragg's army, Longstreet doubted the feasibility of his mission to drive Burnside from East Tennessee. Matters worsened when Bragg failed to render the logistical support he had promised. Feeling apprehensive that he had been sent on a doomed mission, Longstreet acted uncertainly throughout his campaign. Moreover, the weather did not cooperate with the advance toward Knoxville. For days his troops slogged through rain and muddy roads as Burnside conducted an effective retrograde movement toward the city. Finally, the First Corps suffered from internal strife, which indirectly led to Burnside's escape from Campbell's Station. The antipathy of Longstreet's lieutenants only created a further deterioration of his confidence in them and himself. For various reasons McLaws and Law did not support Longstreet, and their enmity must have been apparent to him. Robertson's arrest for disobedience of orders rankled some of the other brigade commanders. All of these factors contributed to Longstreet's poor performance at Knoxville.

The fact that Longstreet did not display his usual confidence is evident in the hesitation he demonstrated in the attack on Fort Sanders. He recognized that the Federal defenses were too formidable for a frontal assault and delayed the attack on successive days. If possessed of his usual self-assurance, Longstreet probably would have canceled the plan altogether. Instead, perhaps in light of Bragg's criticisms regarding his failure to follow orders at Chickamauga and Lookout Valley, Longstreet overcompensated and deferred to Leadbetter despite his better judgment. "I will go to my grave believing that Leadbetter devised it [the attack] & imposed it upon Longstreet," Alexander later wrote, "& he afterward preferred to accept the responsibility rather than plead that he had let himself be so taken in." The artillery chief blamed himself for not voicing his opinion on the night of the twenty-eighth. "I was then too young and modest to say a word of objection," he concluded in a postwar letter.[71]

Despite Bragg's postwar accusations that Longstreet purposely sought failure because of his longstanding friendship with Grant, the corps commander simply demonstrated poor judgment and a lack of self-confidence.[72] Longstreet's insistence on launching the assault on Fort Sanders by urging his men forward with the determination to succeed likely harkened back to his service during the Mexican-American War. At Churubusco his regiment faced a similar obstacle in the Mexican tete de pont. The successful attack on an apparently impregnable stronghold had profoundly impressed the young Longstreet. Seventeen years later, facing the Federal bastion at

Knoxville, the older general desperately sought a victory that would trium-phantly conclude his campaign. At Fort Sanders, however, the Confederate attackers suffered a decisive repulse. Like Lee at Gettysburg, Longstreet failed to understand that the troops he commanded at Knoxville could not overcome formidable odds with élan and dash. His gambit bordered more on desperation than on sound strategic judgment.[73]

An additional factor influencing Longstreet's frontal assault was the lack of viable options. Historian Albert Castel has argued that during a cam-paign, commanders have limited alternatives: they can fight on the defen-sive, find a weak point in the enemy's lines and attempt to break through, choose to attack on a broad front, or attempt the most popular tactic, a flanking maneuver. Clearly the strong Federal defenses eliminated the first two options, while a flanking movement requires, in part, the enemy's co-operation. And since Burnside would not emerge out of his strong fortifi-cations to fight the Confederates on open ground, Longstreet, facing enor-mous pressure to perform, felt compelled to attack. It was an error he would not live down.[74]

Following the failed assault on Fort Sanders, Longstreet immediately arranged to return to Bragg's army, ordering his wagon trains to the rear in preparation for the anticipated move. Under a flag of truce, the Confeder-ates collected their dead and wounded while organizing their withdrawal. Later that evening a message from Bragg, dated November 26, notified Longstreet that the Army of Tennessee had fallen back to Dalton, Georgia, and that the First Corps could either rejoin him there or retire to Virginia. Finally, Longstreet recognized the impracticality of marching through the mountains to join Bragg, especially if he could not hold his position at Dal-ton. Moreover, the corps commander realized the difficulty of marching to Virginia without Bragg's logistical support. He also knew that if his forces remained at or near Knoxville, Grant would have to detach a part of his army to clear East Tennessee. Longstreet therefore decided to maintain his position in front of Burnside to relieve the pressure on Bragg by forcing Grant to send reinforcements. He countermanded his earlier instructions and ordered his cavalry, under Maj. Gen. William T. Martin, to warn him of any Federal advance through Cumberland Gap. (Martin had assumed command of Longstreet's cavalry when Bragg ordered Wheeler to return to Missionary Ridge on November 24 to protect the Confederate rear at Chattanooga.)[75]

On the evening of the twenty-ninth, Longstreet held a council of war to discuss the options. His lieutenants concurred that rejoining Bragg's army was impractical. In addition to the logistical difficulties involved in reaching northern Georgia, the generals decided that withdrawing on the same roads they had marched on to Knoxville would demoralize their men. McLaws also pointed out that if they abandoned East Tennessee to the Federals, the Confederacy would lose the support of loyal Confederates who would have to coexist with the large Unionist population. Longstreet and his subordinates therefore decided to remain in the region, but they would shift their base of operations closer to Virginia. While these senior officers deliberated, on December 1 Martin's cavalry captured a dispatch from Grant to Burnside notifying him of coming reinforcements. But Grant had arranged for a copy of this message to be captured in hopes of speeding the First Corps' withdrawal from Knoxville, unaware that Longstreet had issued orders to move along the East Tennessee and Virginia Railroad toward southwestern Virginia. At nightfall on December 4, the artillery and infantry—with Jenkins in the lead and McLaws in the rear—followed the wagon trains, with Martin's cavalry screening the move. To delay a Federal pursuit, Longstreet's artillerymen fashioned some "Quaker guns"—logs painted to resemble cannon.[76]

The battered and weary First Corps veterans marched toward Virginia in a cold, driving rain. By this time many of the men lacked shoes and most had no winter clothing. The trek through East Tennessee proved so tough on shoe leather that many wagon drivers gave their shoes to the foot soldiers. Other Rebels simply confiscated footwear from unfortunate prisoners. One Union soldier accepted his fate stoically, "When a man is captured, his shoes are captured too." Nevertheless, during their retreat from Knoxville, "The men suffered frightfully," wrote Francis Dawson, an officer on Longstreet's staff. An Alabama private remembered that most of the soldiers were "ragged and a considerable number barefooted." "It is no exaggeration," Dawson maintained, that "they left the bloody tracks of their feet on the sharp stones of the road." The troops resorted to wrapping rawhide around their bare feet. A South Carolina soldier recalled that "hundreds would gather at the slaughter pen daily and cut from the warm beef hides strips large enough to make into moccasins." Conditions were so miserable that Longstreet detailed groups of soldiers to make shoes for his corps, "so that it came about that the hides passed rapidly from the beeves to the feet of the soldiers in the form of comfortable shoes." To ensure a rapid march, the general ordered his division commanders to call roll at every halt and to order the arrest of those who failed to appear.[77]

The corps's draft animals also suffered from a lack of shoes. Without a line of supply to Bragg's army, soldiers had to resort to fishing dead animals from the Holston River and collecting horseshoes and nails from the

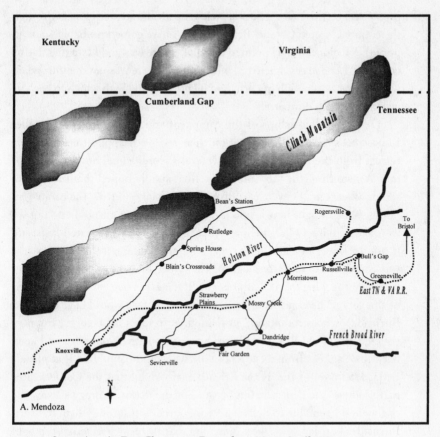

MAP 7. *Operations in East Tennessee, December 1863 to April 1864*

carcasses. Alexander reported that at least a half dozen animals floated by
each day during operations south of the river. "Our little ferry boat enabled
us to easily get the shoes off every one as it went by," he recalled. The Confederates also scoured the roads for dead Federal animals, detailing crews
to confiscate their shoes. The plight of the underfed draft animals became
acute during the march. Teamsters used double and triple teams to pull the
artillery and caissons through the muddy roads. Infantrymen jeered when
they passed Rebel cannoneers prodding a dozen horses hitched to a single
gun: "Here comes the cavalry, but what's that gun tied to the tail for?"[78]

The plight of the rank and file forced officers to relax Longstreet's strict
discipline and allow the men to forage the countryside. The First Corps
soon marched along a well-lit road as soldiers tore down fences and burned
the rails and posts to keep warm. Soldiers scavenged the countryside for
food to supplement their lean rations. "Our rations of bread have been

pretty slim on this march, but we picked up an abundance of meat through the country," noted Colonel Bratton. "I . . . have gained probably 20 or 30 pounds." Colonel Sorrel pointed out that "there was good foraging in this country." Longstreet concurred, noting how "there was never a time when we did not have enough of corn, and plenty of wood with which to keep us warm and parch our corn."[79]

Despite the hardships of the campaign and the failure at Knoxville, Longstreet's men did not dwell on their recent disappointments. Their retreat from the city restored the veterans' confidence. Some, like Captain Winsmith of the 5th South Carolina, simply hoped that the corps's senior officers might even learn from their mistakes during the campaign. "Bragg's men might be whipped," asserted one Georgia soldier, "but we were far from it." Others believed that they could have defeated Burnside if not for Bragg's defeat. A Georgia soldier maintained that "Longstreet was compelled to raise the siege of Knoxville" because of the Federal columns approaching from Chattanooga. "If it had not been for the operations of this force," he continued, "my opinion is that we would have captured Burnside's whole command." A lieutenant in the 53rd Georgia Infantry concurred: "If old Bragg had keep his position at Chattanooga and keep back the Yankees from us at Knoxville we would hav[e] had that place." D. H. Hamilton of the Texas Brigade maintained that the Confederates had "routed" the Federals, but because of the defeat of Bragg's army, the enemy had been able to detach a strong force thus forcing them to "turn Burnsides [*sic*] loose." Others lamented that Burnside elected not to fight the First Corps at Knoxville. "We expected to have a fight (and I think Longstreet rather wished it so)," wrote Colonel Bratton, "but our friends in Knoxville did not stir out of their holes as we passed around them."[80]

Years later a soldier in Kershaw's Brigade argued that the rank and file maintained their confidence in Longstreet despite the setbacks of the Knoxville campaign. "As difficulties and dangers gathered around their old chieftain, they clung to him, if possible, with greater tenacity and a more determined zeal," Augustus Dickert wrote. Thus the soldiers endured the hardships of the march with buoyant spirits. In all likelihood the men of the First Corps appeared optimistic because they thought that they were headed back to Lee's army in Virginia. Once away from Knoxville, the troops sang "Carry Me Back to Ole Virginny" with great enthusiasm.[81] Longstreet's men did not know that their return to Lee would be delayed until the following spring.

6

"I LONG FOR SOME RELIEF FROM THIS CONSTANT TOIL AND ANXIETY"

LEADERSHIP CONFLICT IN THE FIRST CORPS, 1863-64

THE DEFEAT AT KNOXVILLE CAME FIVE DAYS AFTER BRAGG LOST Chattanooga. Yet the First Corps remained in East Tennessee during the winter of 1863–64. The Confederate presence in the region hampered Union operations in that theater since the Federals dared not advance against the Army of Tennessee in North Georgia until they removed the threat to their rear. While the Union high command worried about Longstreet's presence in East Tennessee, the discontent among the First Corps's senior officers further hampered military operations and continued to distract the commanding general. The lost opportunities of the Knoxville campaign impelled Longstreet to take action against his brooding lieutenants. His patience exhausted, Longstreet would soon move against McLaws, Law, and Robertson. The difficulties with his subordinates also brought the ire of his old adversary, Braxton Bragg, who used his new position as the president's military advisor (following his resignation from the Army of Tennessee) to influence Davis's opinion of Longstreet. Consequently, Davis failed to give the general the latitude and support necessary to deal with his subordinates and eliminate the discord in his command. If Longstreet thought battling the Federals was taxing, he had no idea how difficult the struggle to command would be with his recalcitrant lieutenants. It was a trying winter for James Longstreet.

As the First Corps marched from Knoxville on December 4, 1863, its presence troubled Grant at Chattanooga. After routing Bragg's Army of Tennessee at Missionary Ridge on November 25–26, the Federals pursued the retreating Rebels to Dalton, Georgia, about twenty-five miles to the south. Grant severed Longstreet's rail link to Georgia and prepared to aid Burnside, whom the authorities in Washington had reported to be in dire straits. But he could not ignore Longstreet in East Tennessee if he advanced against Bragg in North Georgia, nor could he discount a Confederate invasion of Kentucky via Cumberland Gap. Lacking reliable intelligence, Grant assumed that Longstreet possessed a strong force that could be reinforced from Virginia, again threaten Knoxville, or move against the Federal supply lines from Nashville. As soon as his forces secured Chattanooga, Grant ordered Sherman to reinforce Burnside.[1]

The events of the previous month notwithstanding, Grant respected Longstreet's generalship. He later credited his victory at Chattanooga to Jefferson Davis, arguing that the Confederate president, by ordering Longstreet to Knoxville, reduced Bragg's army in the face of a numerically superior foe and made the assault on Missionary Ridge easier. Grant pointed out that if the Confederates had taken the city, they could have moved against East Tennessee, thereby making Chattanooga "the last battle fought for the preservation for the Union." He later commented that Davis's strategic blunder at Chattanooga served as one of the "several occasions during the war" that the Confederate president "came to the relief of the Union army by means of his *superior military genius.*"[2]

Two divisions from the Union's Army of the Tennessee and a corps from the Army of the Cumberland marched to Knoxville on November 30. Longstreet remained in the vicinity until December 4, when the two Federal columns, numbering approximately 20,000 men, approached the city. He ordered Brig. Gen. John Crawford Vaughn, commanding a force at Loudon, to delay Sherman's advance. Vaughn skirmished with the Federals' advance guard south of the Tennessee River before he withdrew, burning bridges and destroying supplies. Despite these delaying actions, Sherman would reach Knoxville in a few days. Longstreet decided to move north toward Virginia and meet a second Federal column, under Brig. Gen. John G. Foster, marching south from Cumberland Gap to link up with Sherman. Joining Longstreet's force on December 5 was Maj. Gen. Robert Ransom, commander of the District of Southwestern Virginia and Tennessee, with an additional 2,000 men.[3]

The Union high command assumed Longstreet would march northeast to Bristol to be closer to the Confederate supply depots in southwestern Virginia. After Sherman's force arrived in Knoxville on December 6, Grant issued orders for them to pursue the First Corps the following day. Sherman expected to find a beleaguered Federal force struggling to overcome the effects of Longstreet's siege, but to his surprise Burnside greeted him with a fine turkey dinner and full trimmings. Years later Sherman noted the resentment he felt for hurrying to reach Burnside with his battle-weary troops. "I had seen nothing of this kind in my field service, and could not help exclaiming that I thought 'they were starving,'" he wrote. The general nevertheless asked Burnside if he should advance against Longstreet, but Burnside objected. Rather than use Sherman's footsore soldiers, Burnside directed Maj. Gen. John Parke to use the Army of the Ohio's IX and XXIII Corps and Brig. Gen. James Shackelford's cavalry to pursue the Rebels.[4]

While the Federals deliberated the Confederate threat, Longstreet's command marched to Rutledge, about thirty miles northeast of Knoxville, in anticipation of a Federal advance from Cumberland Gap. With no immediate threat looming, Longstreet ordered his men to scour the area for subsistence. By December 8 the First Corps resumed its march toward Rogersville, thirty miles farther up the Holston River valley, passing through Bean's Station. The general again halted the corps and ordered his men to collect supplies. "The accounts that we got of the resources of the country were favorable, and we halted and put our trains out getting provisions," he reported. Although the First Corps found ample sustenance during the first days of its march in northeastern Tennessee, Longstreet knew that the onset of winter and the approaching Federal columns would ravage the countryside of all food stores. To offset this possibility, he reduced his troops to half-rations. While at Rogersville, Longstreet received a telegram from President Davis giving him discretionary power over all forces in the East Tennessee region.[5]

The president's missive encouraged Longstreet, who had struggled during the early days of his retreat up the Holston Valley with the uncertainty of his position as commander of the First Corps. Following the attack on Fort Sanders, he had received messages from Bragg instructing him to depend on his "own resources" and to return Martin's cavalry to the Army of Tennessee at its new headquarters in Dalton. Longstreet complied, sending Martin back on December 8. But now with Davis's discretionary order, he countermanded this action and retained the cavalry. Martin's horsemen received reinforcements from the cavalry brigades of Brig. Gen. William E. "Grumble" Jones and Col. Henry L. Giltner, both of which had previously served under Ransom's command in southwestern Virginia. After being granted an independent command, Longstreet bolstered his force to nearly 19,000 men. In addition to the 12,000 men in his two divisions (McLaws's and Jenkins's), he gathered the brigades of Johnson and Gracie from Buckner's Division and the brigades of Brig. Gens. Gabriel C. Wharton and Alfred E. Jackson from Ransom's Division. Vaughn's mounted brigade also made its way to Longstreet's command after its delaying action at Loudon. The Confederate force thus stood ready to meet any potential threat.[6]

The combination of the president's directive and the reinforcements from East Tennessee seemed to restore Longstreet's confidence. Although he had intended to strike at Foster's column approaching from the north, the Federals eluded him and reached Knoxville via a roundabout march farther to the west. Upon reaching the Union garrison, Foster relieved Burnside from command on December 11. Foster also assumed that Longstreet intended to retreat into Virginia and so decided to remain in Knoxville while a force under Parke pursued the Rebels. The changes in Federal command did not interest Longstreet, who intended to erase the debacle of the Fort Sanders assault by striking at the enemy. By the twelfth Parke had advanced as far as Rutledge and lingered about a two-day march from Longstreet's rear. Meanwhile, Shackelford's cavalry reached Bean's Station, about eight miles ahead of the main Federal infantry, and probed the Confederate rear guard, meeting stiff resistance from Martin's and Jones's cavalry.[7]

By the thirteenth Longstreet felt that Parke's force had come too close and decided to turn and strike. Martin's cavalry reported that the Federal units were scattered; Shackelford's cavalry and one infantry brigade held Bean's Station, while the main body lay between Rutledge and Blain's Crossroads. Bolstered by the information, Longstreet focused on the force at Bean's Station by trapping Shackelford's cavalry and the lone infantry brigade. The Federals advanced against the Confederates, their left flank protected by Clinch Mountain and their right by the Holston River. Clinch Mountain could only be crossed by a few gaps, and the Holston remained in mid-winter flood. Longstreet decided to use the terrain to his own advantage by ordering Martin's cavalry to ride south of the Holston, cross the river near Morristown, and move on Bean's Station from the south while Grumble's cavalry pushed north of Clinch Mountain to prevent "the enemy's escape by Bean's Station Gap." The infantry would march simultaneously down the narrow Holston Valley toward the Union force, thereby placing the Federals between a double-pincer movement. With no escape available, Longstreet hoped that his infantry could crush the Federals at Bean's Station and then advance against Parke's infantry at Rutledge. If successful, the Rebels could again threaten Knoxville, thereby preoccupying Grant.[8]

Longstreet issued orders for his columns to advance quietly, hoping to use the element of surprise. While the Confederates prepared to move, Shackelford learned from prisoners of Longstreet's plan to cut him off from the garrison at Knoxville. That evening he wrote Parke and requested that the infantry protect the fords on the Holston. The next morning Shackelford ordered his troops to prepare for a possible assault by blocking the roads from Rogersville and Morristown. The Federal troops took positions around Bean's Station, an old stagecoach stop between Clinch Mountain and the Holston River. A large three-story brick tavern dominated the small village, which contained a blacksmith shop and several other buildings. As Longstreet's troops approached, Shackelford's men converted the tavern, reportedly one of the finest inns between New Orleans and Baltimore prior to the war, into a stronghold by cutting portholes in the upper stories to use as perches for sharpshooters. The Federals had little time to prepare, however, for Bushrod Johnson's advance guard approached the town on the afternoon of the fourteenth.[9]

At dawn on the fourteenth, Johnson led the vanguard of Longstreet's force, followed closely by Gracie's Brigade and McLaws's and Jenkins's divisions. The cavalry also advanced—Jones riding north of Clinch Mountain, while Martin moved south of the Holston. The Confederates struggled on the muddy roads and through the bitter cold as they made their way back down the Holston Valley. The privations that hampered Longstreet's command during the previous month continued, and a number of barefoot soldiers failed to keep up with their comrades on the march to Bean's Station.[10]

The lead elements of Johnson's column clashed with Shackelford's men about three miles east of town on the Rogersville Road at about 2:00 P.M. Johnson ordered Parker's Virginia Battery, from Alexander's artillery, forward to drive the Federals back. The Virginia artillerymen complied, firing a barrage that forced Shackelford's skirmishers into Bean's Station. With Parker's guns laying down supporting fire, Johnson advanced into the town, some of his men taking cover in an abandoned stable about fifty yards east of the tavern.[11]

While Johnson pressed the Federals in his front, Longstreet ordered McLaws's lead brigade, Kershaw's, to move toward the right astride Clinch Mountain to flank the Union left. Coming under heavy fire from the Federal artillery in the town, Kershaw's men took cover behind a bluff. "The greater portion of the brigade was here huddled together in [a] jam, to avoid the shells flying overhead," wrote Augustus Dickert of the 3rd South Carolina. While Kershaw stalled under the Federal artillery barrage, Longstreet ordered Johnson to press his assault on the center, but Yankee sharpshooters firing from the hotel pinned down the Southerners. Johnson then ordered Parker's artillery to fire on the tavern, which suffered heavy damage from shelling. Near sundown, the Confederate gunners ceased firing, and Johnson's men charged into the tavern only to discover that the sharpshooters had fled through the rear of the building and out of Bean's Station. Darkness halted Longstreet's assault. Johnson's and Gracie's men suffered the brunt of the casualties, losing 30 killed and 180 wounded; the rest of Longstreet's units lost a total of 68 killed and wounded. Osmun Latrobe, Longstreet's inspector general, called the engagement at Bean's Station "the briskest little fight of the war."[12]

Longstreet halted for the night, not realizing that the trap he envisioned for Shackelford had miscarried. Jones's cavalry arrived at Bean's Station Gap as planned and drove off the Federals holding the mountain pass, seizing dozens of wagons. But instead of holding the gap and capturing the retreating Yankees, the Rebel horsemen withdrew north of Clinch Mountain to feast on the captured stores. Meanwhile, Martin's cavalry, riding south of the Holston, encountered an enemy brigade at the ford near Morristown. Rather than forcing his way across or finding another crossing, Martin waited for artillery support to arrive, thus losing precious time. Longstreet did not hear from him until the night of the fourteenth; Martin would not cross the river until the following morning. But by then it was too late, for the Federal brigade had withdrawn. Realizing that he was outnumbered, Shackelford retreated toward Rutledge and bivouacked about six miles northeast of town. His men entrenched in anticipation of an enemy assault the following morning. Except for some brief skirmishing, both sides encamped for the night.[13]

At daybreak on the fifteenth, Longstreet moved into Bean's Station only to find an abandoned camp. He ordered Jenkins, who was not engaged the previous day, to lead a pursuit of the Federals, directing Martin's cavalry to cross the Holston and provide support. Jenkins marched three miles to the southwest with about 2,500 men before encountering resistance. Halting his men, Jenkins reconnoitered the field of battle and saw a chance to sweep around the Union right, then met with Longstreet at midmorning. After conferring with his division commander, Longstreet decided to launch a flank attack on the Union right with the South Carolinian's force. He ordered Jenkins to get his men into position but to wait for Law's Brigade, which had been guarding wagon trains eight miles to the rear, to bolster the Confederate assault. Law, however, did not arrive until 2:30 P.M., and the opportunity to sweep around the enemy right passed after the Federals reinforced their position. Shortly before sunset, Jenkins reported that he feared a Union assault and requested additional troops. Longstreet ordered McLaws forward. Despite the danger of an impending assault on Jenkins, McLaws complained that his men had not been fed but sent the brigade as ordered. Apparently, Jenkins mistook a shift of troops in response to Martin's late arrival as a sign that Federals intended to attack. Once more, darkness prevented further action, and the Confederates went into bivouac.[14]

The following morning Longstreet continued to press the retreating Federals. Although the narrow valley prevented a flanking maneuver, the general believed that he could inflict heavy damage on the Yankees as they withdrew toward Knoxville. Yet McLaws's protest that his men had not received their bread rations the previous evening portended additional difficulties for the First Corps as other brigadiers followed his cue. When Longstreet rode to the front to direct the impending assault, he met with Law, who also complained that his troops had not been fed. Robertson also harped about the condition of his men. When ordered to advance, he refused, stating, "there are but three days' rations on hand, and God knows where more are to come from." The commander of the Texas Brigade claimed that he "had no confidence in the campaign" but would obey orders, though "under protest." Once more, internal dissent paralyzed the First Corps. Even though Martin's cavalry skirmished with the Federals until the evening of December 16, the listlessness of Longstreet's lieutenants halted his advance. The general ordered Jenkins, who had marched as far as Rutledge, to halt and return to camp. "There seemed so strong a desire for rest rather than to destroy the enemy, that I was obliged to abandon the pursuit," he later reported.[15]

Longstreet fumed at what he perceived to be another lost opportunity. In his official report he criticized Law for arriving late to support Jenkins. As he had done at Campbell's Station, Longstreet claimed that Law's lethargy had caused his plans to miscarry. "This was the second time during the campaign when the enemy was completely in our power, and we allowed him to escape us," he wrote. Since Law left no official after-action report, it is difficult to recreate exactly what happened. Longstreet's report, written two weeks afterward, suggests that his difficulties with Law continued to hinder operations. Yet the commander did not charge Law with disobedience of orders or conduct unbecoming an officer for his performance in the campaign.[16]

On December 17 Longstreet abandoned his pursuit of Shackelford. Maj. Gen. Gordon Granger arrived at Blain's Crossroads with his corps that day, bolstering the Federal force to about 26,000 men. Outnumbered, exhausted, and with his supplies running low, Longstreet chose prudence rather than persistence. A heavy snowstorm also discouraged him from continuing the campaign. The Confederates soon withdrew from their advanced position to go into winter quarters. On the nineteenth the First Corps began crossing the icy Holston River. Three days later the bulk of Longstreet's command arrived near the East Tennessee and Virginia Railroad. Jenkins and Johnson encamped at Morristown, with Martin's cavalry south of their position. McLaws went into winter quarters at Russellville, while Jones's cavalry and Ransom's infantry were posted at Rogersville, north of the Holston. By Christmas the men had built their "shelters for the winter," and the Knoxville campaign came to an end.[17]

Not knowing how long they would stay in East Tennessee, the veterans initially camped in tents before the cold weather and the ample supplies of wood in the surrounding region persuaded them to build cabins. The eastern troops found sufficient forage in East Tennessee as they scoured the countryside during in the last weeks of December 1863. Colonel Sorrel described the veterans at this time as "happy and cheerful." Perhaps, Longstreet's troops may have seemed buoyant to Sorrel because of their heavy consumption of spirits that the East Tennessee region provided. "There were some [moonshine] stills in the neighborhood," recalled another of Longstreet's staff officers, "and there was active demand for all the liquor these could supply." The troops did not suffer on Christmas Day. "Bright and cheerful fires burned before every tent, over which hung a turkey, a chicken, or a choice slice of Tennessee pork," recalled a soldier in Kershaw's Brigade. The winter had just begun, however, and Longstreet's men would ultimately suffer from a lack of supplies.[18]

Since the First Corps "did not succeed in bringing the enemy to battle," Longstreet regarded the engagements near Bean's Station a failure. Despite capturing dozens of wagons with much needed supplies, he had desired to achieve a "full and glorious victory," not a "fruitless one." Yet Bean's Station suggests that Longstreet had regained some of the confidence that had eluded him at Chattanooga and Knoxville. The general had designed a sound strategy to defeat Shackelford's isolated cavalry—the pincer movement could have been disastrous for the Union forces. One soldier who escaped this trap later wrote that "Longstreet's plan had been well conceived, and if it had been carried out, it is not seen how the Federal cavalry . . . could have escaped." But as Alexander observed, "Longstreet's plan miscarried in some way—as plans are always liable to do." Although the general issued precise orders, the western cavalrymen, notorious for their lack of discipline, failed to carry out his directives and allowed Shackelford to hold off Johnson while the Federals retreated toward Rutledge.[19]

In addition to the failure of his cavalry, Longstreet also had to deal with the continued lack of cooperation from Law, McLaws, and Robertson. In his report of Bean's Station, McLaws attempted to shift the blame onto Longstreet, stating that the commanding general had ordered him to reinforce Jenkins on the fifteenth only if his brigades "had been supplied with rations." Considering the general aggressiveness of the operation, it is doubtful that Longstreet allowed McLaws that latitude in ordering his brigades to the front. Most likely McLaws refused to follow his commander's orders because of the failures of the previous campaign. To cite his troops' lack of rations as a reason to delay an attack reflected poorly on his men. The Federals also suffered during the campaign, but they continued to fight.[20]

McLaws explained his deportment in a postwar letter. He pointed out that as the First Corps marched northeast through Bean's Station after the attack on Fort Sanders, he noticed that the former stagecoach stop contained "a good supply of provisions." The general also noticed that it held an ample supply of wheat and corn, and the Confederates could have used the town's mills to grind the grain. "If we were going to make a halt at all, this would be a good place," McLaws reportedly informed Longstreet. Longstreet dismissed this report, however, and continued to march up the Holston Valley. To McLaws's vexation, the Confederates "suddenly marched back" to attack Shackelford at Bean's Station, thereby losing several hundred men to take a "place we had left unoccupied a few days previous." He was furious that Longstreet had dismissed his counsel yet again. "This vacillating conduct, his failure to do those things which should be done at the right time created a great dissatisfaction," McLaws later wrote.[21] Thus when ordered to move, he grumbled that his men had not received their rations.

Longstreet, however, had ceased to be the indecisive and hesitant general of the march to Knoxville. Free from Bragg's authority and no longer feeling ostracized from Richmond, he seemed to have regained his composure after the debacle at Fort Sanders. Within a day of receiving Martin's report on Shackelford's isolated position, Longstreet acted with the decisiveness and aggressiveness that characterized his previous campaigns in Virginia. His principle subordinates reported him at the front, directing units and checking troop dispositions.[22] He planned a tactically sound assault on a numerically inferior force, issued specific orders, modified his plans in response to new developments, and went to the front to personally oversee his battle dispositions. Yet the complexity and timing of the double envelopment allowed little room for error. The use of three columns marching on separate roads depended on cooperation and discipline, two qualities that the First Corps had lacked during the entire East Tennessee campaign. While Longstreet cannot be held solely accountable for the lack of harmony in his command, as the commanding officer he bears the greatest responsibility and the bulk of the blame. The farther away the First Corps marched from Chattanooga, the more it came to mirror Bragg's dysfunctional army.

L ONGSTREET'S GENERALSHIP DID NOT CAUSE HIS PLAN TO FAIL. The First Corps's rank and file had called him "Peter the Slow," but now that moniker seemed inaccurate. If Longstreet heard the Rebel soldiers' derisive comments, he probably ignored them since troop morale usually reflects the momentum of a campaign. The First Corps had suffered successive failures since Chickamauga, and that was all that mattered. Longstreet was aware that McLaws, Law, and Robertson had criticized his conduct of the Knoxville campaign. He also believed that their lack of confidence in him directly affected their combat performance. McLaws, who considered himself "the next in command" of the corps, had been the most outspoken of the group, giving Longstreet his views and brooding when the commanding general disagreed. Aware that McLaws had sought a transfer since that summer and weary of his persistent remonstrances, on December 17 Longstreet relieved his longtime friend and West Point classmate of command and ordered him to Augusta, Georgia. When McLaws requested to know the reasons why, Sorrel informed him that he had exhibited a "want of confidence" in Longstreet's plans and that the commanding general feared these feelings would "extend more or less to the troops" under his command. On the eighteenth McLaws left his division in the temporary charge of Kershaw.[23]

Despite relieving McLaws from command, Longstreet did not immediately prefer charges. "General McLaws was not arrested when he was relieved from duty," Longstreet informed Adj. Gen. Samuel Cooper on December 20, hoping McLaws could be employed in another position for the Confederacy. "If such is the case," he told Cooper, "I have no desire that he should be kept from that service or that his usefulness should be impaired in any way by a trial." Longstreet's purpose in relieving McLaws could be traced to his experience in Bragg's army. Months earlier he had witnessed Bragg relieve his friend, Daniel Harvey Hill, from command in the Army of Tennessee for his want of confidence in the commanding general. Bragg neither filed charges nor arrested Hill, rather removing a lieutenant whom he believed "had greatly demoralized the troops he commanded" with his complaints. In late December 1863 Longstreet probably felt the same way about McLaws. He did not want to arrest his old friend, whom he had considered a loyal lieutenant just two months earlier. Yet McLaws's constant criticism could not be ignored.[24]

Years later Longstreet gave another explanation for why he sought to replace McLaws, writing that the Georgian's "health was bad and on that account, I relieved him from duty." But to Longstreet's surprise, he received orders from Richmond to put down specific charges. Upon receiving the War Department's directive, Longstreet recalled sensing that he lacked the government's support. "I knew as well as you," he later told McLaws, "that Mr. Davis would be pleased to have you make charges against me and that Gen. Bragg would be more than pleased to join you." In his memoirs Longstreet argued that he "had no desire to put charges against" McLaws and should have "failed to do so even under the direction of the authorities." Nevertheless, in what he later called an "unguarded moment," the general complied with Davis's wishes and notified the War Department that charges against McLaws would be "forwarded in a few days."[25]

Longstreet, however, underestimated McLaws's reaction. Sometime before leaving the First Corps for Georgia, the general went to Longstreet and demanded the reasons for his removal. "On my asking his reasons for the order he stated that I had not cooperated cordially with him & he was afraid that my influence would extend to the troops," McLaws later wrote. "That one of us must go," that "he could not & therefore I could." This explanation did not appease McLaws. "I demanded that charges should be preferred," he recalled. "I would not retire on his direction."[26]

Pressed by Richmond to present formal charges, Longstreet complied on December 30. He charged McLaws with "neglect of duty" during the assault on Fort Sanders with three specifications. The first specification claimed that McLaws did not provide sharpshooters and failed to give the assault columns "the protection of fire . . . during their advance and attack." The second charged McLaws with failing to "organize a select body of men to lead in the assault as is customary in such attacks" and allowing his units to advance without "definite and specific instructions." Finally, the third specification asserted that McLaws made his attack on a part of the fort considered "impassable" and that he failed "to provide any of his assaulting columns with ladders or other means of crossing the ditch and entering the enemy's works." Nowhere did he mention McLaws's performance at either Lenoir's Station or Bean's Station.[27]

If Longstreet was ambivalent about pressing charges against McLaws, there is no evidence that he felt the same when ordering the arrest of General Robertson on December 18. Longstreet had complained about the Texas Brigade commander's comportment since Chattanooga. After the failed assault on Wauhatchie, he had relieved him of command but was displeased when Bragg restored Robertson to duty since, according to Longstreet, the disgruntled brigade commander seemed to "exercise an injurious influence" over his troops. Even before the Battle of Bean's Station, the general had demonstrated antipathy about serving in East Tennessee. On December 10 Robertson wrote to General Hood and proposed that the entire brigade receive furloughs to Texas to rest and recruit additional men. Two days later he submitted his scheme to the state's representatives in the Confederate Congress.[28]

There is nothing in contemporary records to indicate that Longstreet was aware that Robertson was attempting to circumvent the chain of command in order to take his unit from the First Corps while campaigning in East Tennessee. Yet there is no doubt that the general quickly moved against his subordinate. Specifically, Longstreet charged Robertson with "conduct highly prejudicial to good order and military discipline" for failing to follow orders at Bean's Station. General Jenkins reported that when he issued orders to advance, Robertson complained about the lack of food, the mail, and the destitute condition of his men to his regimental commanders. Robertson essentially lacked confidence in the campaign and insisted on only receiving written orders, declaring that he would follow them "under protest." Jenkins believed that the general's actions were intended to "discourage" and "weaken" his regimental commanders' confidence in the assault.[29]

Considering his earlier deportment with Bragg, there was a certain sense of irony surrounding the Robertson case. Most of the grievances Robertson cited were analogous to the complaints Longstreet levied at Bragg at Chickamauga and Chattanooga. Certainly Robertson was a favorite among his men, who called him "Aunt Polly" for his devoted concern for their welfare. Yet considering the dissent that plagued the First Corps in the Jenkins-Law imbroglio, Longstreet felt compelled to support Jenkins and maintain the morale of the men under his command. The First Corps commander also blamed Bragg for the discontent in his corps. If Bragg had upheld Robertson's initial arrest in November, the general probably reasoned, he could have replaced the brigade commander and launched his campaign against Knoxville with a harmonious First Corps. Instead Longstreet viewed Bragg's interference as another design to impair his advance into East Tennessee. By the time of Bean's Station, Longstreet, frustrated with the recent setbacks, again relieved Robertson of command. On December 23 he ordered Robertson to Bristol to await trial; Brig. Gen. John Gregg would command the Texas Brigade in his place.[30]

When Longstreet filed charges against McLaws and Robertson, the disharmony in the First Corps's senior ranks weighed on him, causing his despondency to return. In the same message informing the War Department about his subordinates' removals, Longstreet requested to be relieved from command. He emphasized that he was not attempting to shift the blame to McLaws or anyone else for the failure of the recent campaigns. "It is fair to infer that the fault is entirely with me, and I desire, therefore, that some other commander be tried." But Longstreet was frustrated, for in his view he had done everything possible to destroy the Federal forces at Bean's Station only to see them escape due to a want of cooperation in his command. Perhaps he wanted the War Department to express confidence in his ability when he promised to cooperate with his eventual replacement. Longstreet learned, however, that Richmond would not sympathize with his plight. General Cooper informed Longstreet that he had no authority to "relieve officers of his command from duty and send them beyond the limits of his command." The adjutant general directed Longstreet to recall McLaws and prepare for trial.[31]

Government officials considered Longstreet's resignation but delayed making a decision until they could find a suitable successor. Cooper informed Lee of Longstreet's request and inquired if he would consider exchanging Ewell, in command of the Army of Northern Virginia's Second Corps, for Longstreet. But Lee was bothered by this resignation request and offered a definite assessment of Longstreet's attributes: "I do not know the reasons that have induced him to take this step, but hope that they are not such as to make it necessary. I do not know any one to take his place in either position. I do not think it advantageous that he and Lieutenant-General Ewell should exchange corps, believing that each corps would be more effective as at present organized. I cannot, therefore, recommend their exchange." Regardless of the setbacks in the West, Lee continued to hold Longstreet in high regard, describing him as indispensable and maintaining that he should remain in command in East Tennessee.[32]

While Longstreet struggled with Richmond, McLaws went on the offensive to refute the charges against him. Within days of his removal, McLaws copied documents from Longstreet's headquarters and wrote his brigade commanders to gather testimonials for his defense. On December 18 he wrote General Benning and asked him to "take an interest in my affairs." McLaws told his fellow Georgian, "[t]hat I have differed from Genl.

Longstreet in his military measures, there can be no doubt." But he denied that his "command has been influenced" by these differences, stating that Longstreet's assertions remained "totally without foundation." Being less than completely honest, McLaws confessed that whenever he had heard "dissatisfaction" among the troops, he had done everything in his power to "encourage" his men. McLaws gathered and mailed all pertinent material directly to Richmond, less it be "suppressed at Longstreet's headquarters." But before he left his division, approximately five hundred of the men gathered around their commander's headquarters, hoping to hear him speak. McLaws refused to address his troops since "it was not proper for me to make remarks upon the campaign" since it would "destroy confidence in the leaders."[33]

McLaws wrote General Cooper on December 29 and included a copy of his Knoxville report as well as copies of the order relieving him. Despite his critical carping of the previous two months, the general insisted that it did not influence his performance in battle: "I have differed in opinion with General Longstreet concerning many things, but that this difference influenced my own conduct or that of the troops under my command I utterly deny."[34]

McLaws also wrote his friends, family, and colleagues to elicit their assistance against what he perceived to be a breach of his military record and personal honor. He corresponded extensively with his wife, Emily, informing her of every detail of the case. McLaws enlisted the assistance of his brother William to lobby the authorities in Richmond for their support. The division commander also informed allies within the First Corps to continue to campaign on his behalf in the court of public opinion. Dr. Joseph Ganahl, a surgeon in Longstreet's corps, received McLaws's recognition. "Doctor G has already silenced several slanders, and had done me considerable benefit by correcting false impressions made by Longstreet's emissaries," McLaws informed his wife. "You have in your own experience no doubt, noticed how a community is prejudiced with very little effort when there is no one present to represent the other side."[35]

On January 21, 1864, the Adjutant and Inspector General's Office ordered McLaws's court-martial to convene on February 3 at Russellville, Tennessee. The office appointed the court members in its Special Orders No. 21: Maj. Gens. Simon B. Buckner and Charles W. Field, and Brig. Gens. George T. Anderson, John Gregg, Benjamin G. Humphreys, James L. Kempner, and Francis T. Nicholls. Maj. Garnett Andrews, assistant adjutant general, served as judge advocate. The orders also directed that a

Pres. Jefferson Davis failed to fully trust Longstreet due to the general's association with anti-administration officers and politicians.
LIBRARY OF CONGRESS
(LC-BH82-2417)

second trial take place, this one for General Robertson. McLaws, who went to Georgia after his removal, hurried back to East Tennessee.³⁶

Robertson's trial began first. The court experienced early delays in convening. On February 3 the court lost the list of witnesses and had to wait until Jenkins could "send up the names again." After continued delays, the court finally met on the twelfth. Witnesses described Robertson's erratic conduct at Bean's Station and provided testimony of how the brigadier general complained of the campaign's hardships and delayed advancing his brigade until the fighting had ended. Robertson's trial concluded that same day. Four days later, on the sixteenth, Longstreet ordered the brigadier "to go to Richmond to await sentencing." There is no official record of the verdict on the case, but Robertson later wrote that the court acquitted him of "improper motives" but disapproved of his management of the Texas Brigade and recommended a reprimand that would entail being relieved of command. Cpl. J. B. Polley of the 4th Texas Infantry provided a different account of the trial. According to Polley, the Texas Brigade's official historian, Robertson was found guilty, but Davis and Cooper declared the charges "frivolous and utterly insufficient to justify" and overturned the court's decision later that spring.[37]

Despite the discrepancies between the two versions, Robertson would not return to the First Corps. Sometime after receiving word of the trial's outcome, the general requested and received a transfer to the Lone Star State. Robertson's removal was not well received by the Texans. According to Pvt. A. B. Hood of the 5th Texas, there was a "great dissatisfaction" in the Texas Brigade because of Robertson's arrest. Even though Hood confessed to be "ignorant of the charges," Robertson's trial had "gained the sympathy of every man in his command." In fact Secretary of War James Seddon received petitions signed by some of the company commanders of the 4th and 5th Texas as well as the 3rd Arkansas, lamenting the loss of Robertson and urging the War Department to reinstate him.[38]

But not every member of the Texas Brigade approved of Robertson's style of leadership. Maj. C. M. Winkler of the 4th Texas viewed the Robertson case from a slightly different perspective. Winkler recognized the brigade commander's faithful regard for his men, but he believed that the general's disobedience of orders was insubordinate and deserved punishment. The previous year Pvt. Rufus K. Felder of the 5th Texas criticized Robertson for "thinking more of enjoyment & promotion than he did of his company." When Robertson was promoted to colonel of the 5th Texas, Felder questioned the Confederate government's assessment of officers. Regardless, on April 9 Robertson bid farewell to his old brigade. The following month he received instructions to report to Maj. Gen. John B. Magruder, the commander of the District of Texas. By June the secretary of war ordered him to assume command of the Lone Star State's reserve forces, with the task of recruiting soldiers for the Confederacy. In March 1865 Robertson received orders to report to Magruder for active field command, but by the time preparations were made, the eastern armies were surrendering and the Civil War was coming to a close.[39]

McLaws's trail was scheduled to convene the day after Robertson's concluded. On the thirteenth, before the court could hear witness testimony, Longstreet ordered its adjournment, informing Buckner that he needed the members of the court and certain witnesses for action against the enemy. Originally proposed as a two-week postponement, Major Andrews informed McLaws later on the thirteenth that the court had adjourned indefinitely until summoned again by Buckner. Longstreet's directive was legitimate, for his forces moved against Knoxville the next day and maneuvered to Strawberry Plains before the War Department's refusal to send reinforcements aborted the advance a week later. On the fourteenth, as the First Corps resumed active operations, Longstreet ordered McLaws to travel to Abingdon, Virginia, until further notice. The wait of the last six weeks had weighed on McLaws. "I am tired of this delay [and] this uncertainty and wish something positive, something definite to occur," he wrote his wife.[40]

The accused general attempted to vindicate himself at the expense of Longstreet's reputation. McLaws began drawing up charges of his own against Longstreet, developing a new theory as to why he was relieved from command. To a female friend he explained that Longstreet's vendetta against him could be traced to the siege at Chattanooga, when McLaws refused to join the anti-Bragg cabal in its attempts to oust the Army of Tennessee commander. The Georgian claimed that he objected to Longstreet's "conspiracy" and voiced his support for Bragg. He later realized that his outspoken support of the general had earned him Longstreet's disapproval. "Gen. L. has never forgiven my not joining that clique the object of which was to place him in command of the Army of East [sic] Tennessee," McLaws wrote. The disgruntled general also pointed out the failure at Knoxville and suggested that it contributed to Bragg's defeat at Chattanooga. McLaws concluded that Longstreet "has nothing to recommend him as a commander but the possession of a certain Bullheadedness, it is mortifying when one feels that he is allowed to tyranise [sic], as he is doing."[41]

While McLaws continued to correspond with friends and Confederate officials, he found in the War Department a very important ally in his campaign for vindication. After a short retirement following his resignation from the Army of Tennessee in December 1863, Braxton Bragg accepted Jefferson Davis's appointment to serve as the president's military advisor. In February 1864 McLaws enlisted the help of his brother Abram Huguenin ("Hu") to ask Bragg for advice in refuting Longstreet's charges. To their relief, they found in the general a willing accomplice. Hu told his brother that Bragg believed Longstreet's resentment of the McLaws-Bragg friendship had led to his crusade to oust his senior division commander. Bragg also warned General McLaws to be on "guard as Buckner was a most perfect Jesuit & totally unreliable" as president of the court.[42]

Reassured now that he had an ally in the War Department, McLaws began to correspond with Bragg, providing him with a synopsis of his case and soliciting counsel. McLaws believed that the charges against him appeared "to have been an after thought." Bragg responded by offering advice on how to bring about Longstreet's downfall. Calling the case "so extraordinary and involved so much calculated to destroy the integrity of the service," he promised "to use the information" in the War Department. Bragg encouraged McLaws to go on the offensive and pledged to provide evidence "ample to convict [Longstreet] of disobedience of orders, neglect of duty and want of cordial co-operation and support, which resulted in all the disasters after Chickamauga." The letter, which also declared support for General Law, suggests that the president's military advisor sought to gain revenge for Longstreet's role in composing the petition requesting his removal.[43]

Bragg's correspondence influenced McLaws's views. After reading these missives, McLaws changed his theory as to why Longstreet relieved him from command. Rather than believe he was merely a scapegoat for a failed assault, the Georgian now endorsed Bragg's more sinister plot, which maintained that Longstreet delayed his march to Knoxville and sabotaged the campaign in order to see Bragg fail at Chattanooga.[44] McLaws also recounted how Bragg told him that Longstreet was $30,000 short when he resigned as paymaster from the U.S. Army and concluding, "there must have been *Collusion*" between Longstreet and Grant at Chattanooga.[45]

As McLaws gathered testimonials and support for his upcoming trial, further delays hampered the court. Longstreet continued to grant leaves of absence to subpoenaed witnesses while his troops remained in winter's quarters. "He kept me for months without trial, although a court was ordered [he] would give a member of the court a leave then another," McLaws later wrote. The general complained to the judge advocate that Longstreet seemed to be manipulating the court: "Leaves of absence are being granted so profusely that I must request that you notify Genl. Longstreet that . . . witnesses are required." The War Department acted on McLaws's complaints. On March 12 Buckner received a telegram from Cooper informing him that the "court was ordered for this office and Genl. Longstreet has no control over it." The adjutant general instructed him to order the return of the absent members of the court and to proceed "without regard to hours." Buckner informed Cooper that Longstreet had cooperated with the court and that some of the leaves of absence "were of the most urgent character." He maintained, "It is proper for me to say that every facility has been rendered the court, and no interference has been designed with its proceedings." Cooper's message was a day late anyway, for McLaws's trial had commenced on March 11 at Midway, Tennessee.[46]

For three days the court listened to witnesses describing the assault on Fort Sanders before adjourning until the sixteenth and resuming for three more days. The charges against McLaws had a poor foundation. Although he failed to exhibit confidence in Longstreet's plans, the general had carried out his orders—the attack on Fort Sanders was simply ill-conceived. Even witnesses for the prosecution seemed to side with McLaws. One of Longstreet's strongest supporters, E. P. Alexander (who had received promotion to brigadier general earlier that spring), testified that Confederate reconnaissance believed the ditch in the northwestern corner of the enemy works was not a significant obstacle. According to McLaws, Longstreet "*himself* testified that he did not expect me to have ladders" to cross the ditch. Other witnesses offered similar testimony in regards to the other specifications. The court ultimately found McLaws innocent of the first two charges—that he failed to advance his sharpshooters on the night of the twenty-eighth and that he did not organize a select body of troops to assault Fort Sanders. On the third specification the court found the division commander guilty of failing to provide ladders for his men to cross the ditch and recommended a sixty-day suspension for McLaws. Such a light sentence for a grievous offense suggested a vindication for the Georgian.[47]

The War Department printed the results of the trial on May 4. The "Findings and Sentence of the Court," however, displeased Adjutant General Cooper, who reprimanded the court for its "guilty" verdict on the third specification. He admonished its members for "irregularities . . . fatal to the record," including the frequent adjournments and the leaves of absence granted to key participants. Cooper believed that the decision was "not sustained by the evidence" and declared that the "proceedings, finding, and sentence of the court are disapproved." Even though the adjutant general had the final word on McLaws's restoration to command, behind the scenes Bragg had lobbied for his friend's reinstatement. On May 7 Special Orders No. 107 declared that McLaws immediately rejoin his command.[48]

As McLaws traveled from Georgia to Richmond to return to his post (the First Corps by then had returned to the Army of Northern Virginia), he prepared several drafts of a speech he intended to give the troops upon his arrival. In each version he chronicled the events from his removal in late December, through the trial, and to his return to his division. But the general's return to the First Corps would not receive the acclaim he assumed would be forthcoming. During a layover in Richmond, McLaws met with Davis, who told him that "there was a bitter feeling in the corps" regarding his return. With the First Corps now reattached to the Army of Northern Virginia, General Lee intervened and suggested that McLaws "be put on duty elsewhere." Despite McLaws's protests to the contrary, Richmond assigned the Georgian to the Department of South Carolina, Georgia, and Florida. He would not return to his former division.[49]

HE MCLAWS AND ROBERTSON TRIALS WERE NOT THE ONLY PER-
sonal conflicts plaguing the First Corps during the winter and spring
of 1864. The rivalry between Jenkins and Law had hampered Longstreet's command since the Chattanooga campaign. According to an officer in the Alabama Brigade, Law was "disappointed in his aspirations" to
command Hood's Division and "did not care whether he aided Longstreet
or Jenkins in anything." Longstreet already held a low opinion of Law and
blamed him for the losses at Wauhatchie, Campbell's Station, and Bean's
Station, despite never filing formal charges. The commanding general's
criticisms, coupled with the hostility from Jenkins, were too great for Law,
whose sense of personal honor obliged him to take action. Thus in a letter
dated December 17, 1863, he resigned. Law outlined his service in the First
Corps, pointing out how he led Hood's Division while wounds incapacitated its former commander. Acknowledging that Jenkins outranked him
by "six or seven weeks," Law complained that the South Carolinian was
not identified with Hood's Division, and his appointment to command was
"in opposition to the expressed wishes of the officers." Frustrated for not
receiving a promotion for his service, he described the situation as an "injustice." Nevertheless, the tone of the document remained amicable, and
Law assured Longstreet that he did not turn in his resignation "in a spirit of
resentment." Rather he claimed that without being commander of Hood's
Division, he could no longer serve with "enthusiasm."[50]

On December 19 Law submitted his resignation to Longstreet and requested to personally take the document to the War Department in order
to seek service in the cavalry. After months of conflict, Longstreet must
have been relieved to be rid of a troublesome subordinate. He agreed to
Law's unusual request and "cheerfully granted" him a leave of absence. In
Richmond, Law visited Hood while the latter convalesced at the home of
Gen. G. W. Smith. Hood implored him to reconsider resigning, convincing
his former subordinate to allow him to hold the letter until Law decided to
present it to Seddon. What Hood hoped to accomplish remains unknown.
He and Law ultimately met with the secretary of war, but the letter never
reached the War Department. Apparently, by the time the two generals visited Seddon's office, the Alabaman had changed his mind. Since he did not
officially tender his resignation, Law assumed that he remained on a leave
of absence and in command of the Alabama Brigade.[51]

While Law traveled to Richmond, the regimental officers of his brigade
submitted a petition requesting transfer from the First Corps. On December 20 Col. William F. Perry, commanding the brigade in Law's absence,
forwarded the document to Jenkins, the division commander. The Ala-

bamans specifically requested transfer to Alabama or Georgia to replenish their ranks, which had been depleted by the recent campaigns. This request probably infuriated Longstreet, who had dealt with problems from Hood's old division since Chattanooga. In his endorsement of the transfer, Longstreet requested that the regimental commanders furnish a testimonial stating that Law had nothing to do with their action. Coming on the heels of the general's resignation, Longstreet suspected that the officers of the brigade colluded with their commander to leave for "less arduous service." Nevertheless, on December 26 all but one of the Alabamans submitted a statement that they had wanted a transfer for several months, maintaining that their request had nothing to do with Jenkins commanding the division. They insisted that Law had no knowledge of their intentions or their petition. The lone exception, Col. Alexander A. Lowther of the 15th Alabama, did not sign the explanatory letter with his brother officers, noting separately that he only signed the original petition for transfer because he was told that Law wanted the petition forwarded to the First Corps headquarters.[52]

Lowther's statement convinced Longstreet that Law had maneuvered along mutinous lines by encouraging the Alabamans to leave the First Corps. On January 7, 1864, he endorsed the petition, forwarding it to Richmond with the assertion that Law had deceived him when requesting a leave of absence to submit his resignation. The corps commander instead claimed that the general's real motive was to go to the Confederate capital to transfer his brigade from the First Corps by lobbying the authorities to grant his officers' petition. Law remained in Richmond until March 1. When he returned to East Tennessee, Longstreet had him arrested for "conduct highly prejudicial to good order and military discipline" and charged him with obtaining a leave of absence "under false pretenses," describing Law's real motive as "aiding the petition and returning to the brigade as its commander." An infuriated Longstreet claimed that Law maneuvered to "create discontent amongst his troops, by encouraging them to hope for more pleasant service" in Alabama or Georgia.[53]

Apparently Longstreet was unaware that Law never turned in his letter of resignation to the War Department. For all he knew, the general submitted the document, but it had yet to be read by General Cooper. To the corps commander's discomfiture, Cooper informed him that Law's resignation had never reached the War Department in an official capacity, stating that the document "was presented by a friend of General Law unofficially to the Secretary of War, and never came through the regular channel as an official paper." This latest revelation further enraged Longstreet. On April 8 he added a second charge, of "conduct unbecoming an officer and a gentleman," against Law. He now claimed that when Law obtained his leave of absence in December 1863, he promised to take his letter of resignation to the War Department and deliver it in person. When the document failed to appear with the proper authorities, Longstreet reasoned, Law committed a grave offense—robbing the War Department of official government property. Law soon obtained the counsel of two former lawyers, Brig. Gen. Benjamin Humphreys and Col. William C. Oates.[54]

After the arrest and trials of Robertson and McLaws, the War Department refused to consider another court-martial of a senior First Corps officer. On April 26 Longstreet asked Cooper if he had received the charges against Law. The adjutant general responded the following day, emphasizing that the charges "are not entertained" and ordered him to allow Law to resume his command. At this point, as the First Corps returned to the Army of Northern Virginia in late April, Lee learned of the dissension in Longstreet's command. After receiving the War Department's rejection of charges against Law, Longstreet asked for his commander's support. He informed Lee that he believed the First Corps's failures at Lookout Mountain and Campbell's Station were due to Law's want of cooperation. He also stated that Law's maneuvering to obtain his brigade's transfer through deception demonstrated behavior of a "very grave character." If Law returned to the First Corps unscathed, Longstreet argued, it would diminish his own authority over the troops. He thereby gave Lee an ultimatum: if Law returned, he would resign.[55]

Lee concurred with Longstreet's assessment. "I examined the charges against General Law," Lee wrote Cooper on April 30, "and find them of a very grave character." The general urged Cooper to convene a court-martial to try Law, whose actions apparently displeased Lee. "There have been instances of officers obtaining indulgences on not the true grounds, which I think discreditable and prejudicial to military discipline, and should be stopped," Lee informed Cooper. If a court could not be convened, he stated, Law should be relieved of command until an investigation into the charges could be conducted. On May 5 Cooper forwarded Longstreet's charges against Law and Lee's letter to Davis, who did not appreciate Longstreet's persistent efforts to arrest Law. The president, however, directed Secretary Seddon to inform Lee of all the specifics surrounding Law's case. He then reprimanded Longstreet for alleging that Law's performance at Lookout Valley and Campbell's Station contributed to the First Corps's failures in both engagements. "If General Law misbehaved at Lookout Mountain or elsewhere in the face of the enemy," Davis declared, "charges should have been preferred, not injurious statements made in a letter to prejudice his case in a different transaction."[56]

While Longstreet struggled with the War Department, Law countered his commander's every move. he had secured influential political allies in his campaign against Longstreet, including even the president. In October 1863, when Davis visited the Army of Tennessee, he had recommended Law to lead Hood's Division, but Longstreet refused, insisting that Jenkins receive the promotion instead. Six months later Longstreet's conflict with Generals Robertson and McLaws probably influenced Davis to support Law. Moreover, the president still resented Longstreet's behavior at his military conference and his deportment toward Bragg. During the Knoxville campaign, Bragg had misleadingly complained of Longstreet's failure to communicate with army headquarters and painted a negative image of the corps commander with Davis.[57]

In addition to securing Davis's support, Law had easily managed to gain Bragg's assistance. Sometime in late February 1864, Law visited with Bragg to discuss his problems with Longstreet. The president's military advisor, who had just counseled McLaws on Longstreet's blame for the loss of Chattanooga, was willing to cooperate with Law to bring about the First Corps commander's downfall. He wrote McLaws on March 1 and informed him of Law's situation, suggesting that the two generals forge an alliance to censure Longstreet. On April 29, while under arrest, Law wrote McLaws to discuss the latter's pending court decision and their mutual hatred for Longstreet. Through the use of his informants in the War Department, Law first notified McLaws of the court's impending decision. After this, he got down to the task at hand—organizing an offensive to discredit Longstreet and file countercharges against their commander. Law suggested a two-prong offensive: If McLaws could cover the Knoxville campaign and the corps commander's transgressions against Fort Sanders, Law could concentrate on bringing charges against Longstreet for filing a false report at Lookout Valley and for his apathy in pursuing the Federals to Knoxville in mid-November 1863. He felt confident about their chances of success. "I don't think either of us have anything to fear, if we will act promptly and energetically," Law wrote. "Longstreet's most certainly on the wane both in and out of the army."[58]

Ultimately Law and McLaws did not file charges against Longstreet. About a week after Law wrote McLaws, Richmond became preoccupied with countering the latest Federal offensive. On May 5, 1864, Ulysses S. Grant, the new general in chief of the Union armies, launched a massive advance against Richmond coinciding with Union offensives against other

Confederate strongholds. Grant's attempt to maneuver against Lee's left flank near the Rapidan River resulted in the Battle of the Wilderness on May 5-6. During the second day of combat, Generals Longstreet and Jenkins were shot—the latter fatally—while reconnoitering their lines. Filing charges would have appeared inappropriate considering the gravity of Longstreet's wounds. Like his comrade McLaws, Law would ultimately leave the First Corps. The Alabaman returned to Lee's army in May but only served a month before he received a wound at the Battle of Cold Harbor on June 3. Even while he recovered in South Carolina, Law carried a bitter grudge against Longstreet. When the two generals returned to duty later that year, Law refused to serve under Longstreet. Receiving Lee's condemnation for his deportment, the Alabaman requested to be reassigned. He left the Army of Northern Virginia for the Confederate cavalry, serving under Joseph E. Johnston during the Bentonville campaign in 1865.[59]

THE INTERNAL PROBLEMS OF THE FIRST CORPS HIGH COMMAND frustrated Longstreet. He traced these difficulties to Chattanooga and his criticism of Bragg. Evidently, Longstreet's strained relationship with McLaws worsened after the division commander allied himself with the Army of Tennessee commander. But Longstreet remained unaware of McLaws's hostility toward him since the Gettysburg campaign. As a result their relationship quickly degenerated during operations around Chattanooga. The corps commander also blamed the rivalry between Jenkins and Law as a primary factor that debilitated his command. Longstreet believed that the jealousy between the two men had led to a breakdown in the command structure. Accordingly, in December 1863 he decided to restructure his fractious division and restore his corps as an efficient combat unit. After Law left for Richmond to turn in his resignation, Longstreet wrote the War Department and requested that Maj. Gen. Robert Ransom, who had joined the First Corps following the siege of Knoxville, be appointed to command Hood's Division. Longstreet cited the jealousy between Jenkins and Law as to the reason why he wanted Ransom. If the authorities did not approve of Ransom, he reasoned, perhaps Maj. Gen. William Henry Chase Whiting, presently serving in Wilmington, North Carolina, could be appointed instead. To replace McLaws, he suggested Brig. Gen. Joseph Kershaw.[60]

It is not clear why Longstreet suggested that Ransom lead Hood's old division if he had been supporting Jenkins all this time. While admitting that the division had been "much impaired" by the infighting, he perhaps grew frustrated with Jenkins as well. As a Jenkins biographer has noted, the

South Carolinian had no reason to be jealous of Law—he was the senior officer and held command. Yet to be involved in such petty bickering did not reflect well on his reputation or aid the effectiveness of the division. It is possible that Longstreet grew weary of constantly defending his protégé and sought some sort of relief from the constant friction. He confessed, however, that it would be difficult to restore the "division with its former pride and prestige." In the case of Whiting, Longstreet's motives are easier to discern. In his letter Longstreet suggests that his old friend, D. H. Hill, who was without an active field command since Bragg replaced him, could potentially take Whiting's place at Wilmington. Finally, it is also feasible that he merely offered Ransom and Whiting as possible replacements as a conciliatory gesture to Richmond.[61]

Apparently, Longstreet's request to appoint Ransom did not impress the president. Davis endorsed the general's letter to the War Department with a critical sentence admonishing him for failing to foresee the problem resulting from the Jenkins-Law rivalry. "If General Jenkins were assigned to another command, the difficulty, long since anticipated, might be overcome," Davis wrote. Seemingly surprised by the president's critical comment, General Cooper ordered the sentence deleted from the telegraph response to Longstreet. The War Department simply informed him that neither Ransom nor Whiting could be assigned to command Hood's Division.[62]

But Richmond had other plans for Longstreet's corps. On February 12, 1864, Davis ordered Maj. Gen. Charles Field, a native of Kentucky and a West Point graduate, to command Hood's Division. Recognizing the implications of his prior request, Longstreet tried to explain to the War Department that he did not hold Jenkins responsible for the inefficiency of the division. If his earlier letters discussing the Jenkins-Law rivalry created a false impression of the former, they had been misconstrued. Rather Longstreet held Law and Robertson responsible for the internal strife. In his view Law should have accepted Jenkins's appointment as his superior officer and followed orders. Since the two generals had left the First Corps, Longstreet argued, the division had been restored to its proficient character. The corps commander's pleas notwithstanding, the government remained adamant that Field assume command.[63]

Frustrated with the War Department's lack of support, Longstreet maneuvered to give Jenkins a division command. He probably recalled the loyalty of Joe Johnston after the Battle of Seven Pines and sought to support Jenkins in the same manner. Even though he had suggested an alternative commander for Hood's Division, the War Department's intransigence only convinced Longstreet to rally behind Jenkins. Soon after he heard of Field's appointment, the general ordered Buckner, whose small division (two brigades) remained on temporary service with the First Corps, to assume command of Hood's Division. With Buckner's position vacant, Longstreet assigned Field to the open slot. Longstreet reasoned that if Buckner received a transfer to another department, he could then assign Jenkins to the helm of Hood's Division, the position he originally wanted for his protégé. Lee himself had first suggested that Buckner could command Hood's Division. Longstreet thus reasoned that he was following Lee's earlier recommendation when he offered Buckner as a possible replacement for Jenkins. But Cooper immediately counteracted this scheme. On March 4 the adjutant general directed Longstreet to assign Field to replace Jenkins. But Longstreet was adamant. He telegraphed Richmond and asked if Field could instead take McLaws's Division. A frustrated Cooper sent a terse telegram instructing Longstreet to assign Field to the "division to which he was assigned."[64]

If Longstreet seemed indignant with Field's appointment, he felt he had probable cause. In his view Davis and the War Department had failed to give him the necessary support to lead effectively in what was essentially an independent command, thwarting his every move. Longstreet must have assumed the worst when his old adversary, Bragg, was appointed as the president's military advisor. Yet his suspicions had a basis in fact. In late February, when Longstreet wrote Cooper that the Federals had advanced toward his position in East Tennessee, Bragg endorsed the telegram before forwarding it to the president, writing that the dispatch and its "antecedents, evince a want of information and unsteadiness of purpose not calculated to inspire confidence." While Bragg informed Davis of Longstreet's deficiencies as a commander, he worked with McLaws to bring about the general's downfall. His messages and letters to Law and McLaws urging them to file charges against Longstreet suggests that during his tenure as the Davis's military advisor, Bragg did everything in his power to further lower the president's opinion of the First Corps commander.[65]

Simple obstinacy in accepting the War Department's policies did not dictate Longstreet's reluctance to accept Field.[66] He had other reasons to question an outsider being transferred into his command. After all, the regimental officers of the Alabama Brigade had cited Jenkins's lack of service with the division as their reason to support Law instead. By that same logic, some of Jenkins's men questioned the appointment of Field. A South Carolinian wrote, "General Field was a very gallant officer and worthy man but he compared unfavorably with Jenkins' [*sic*] superb military tact and talent, whose promotion to the command of [Hood's] Division would have been but a just acknowledgment to his past important services." Field had received a serious wound during the Second Battle of Manassas that kept him from active field duty for about a year. During his recovery, he served as superintendent of the Bureau of Conscription at Richmond. Accordingly, Longstreet asked the War Department to explain why Field received the assignment to Hood's Division. His query elicited a firm response from Cooper. The adjutant general lectured Longstreet on military protocol and declared that his conduct in questioning the president's military appointments "is considered highly insubordinate and demands rebuke." Despite Longstreet's ambivalence, Field took command of Hood's Division while Jenkins resumed command of his brigade.[67] By the time the First Corps returned to the Army of Northern Virginia, it would have two new commanders, Generals Field and Kershaw, leading the divisions that had left to reinforce Bragg in the fall of 1863.

While serving in the Virginia theater, Longstreet did not experience major difficulties with his subordinates.[68] Yet during the months on detached service, the First Corps struggled through three court-martials and friction with the War Department. Although the arrests of McLaws, Robertson, and Law gave the impression that Longstreet carried out a vendetta against his lieutenants, the fact remains that each general failed to cooperate effectively with their commanding officer. The malcontents criticized Longstreet's plans and objected to his strategy for reasons other than his generalship. While a military leader may accept the council and alternate views of his subordinates, the fashion in which McLaws, Robertson, and Law voiced their dissent threatened to destroy the integrity of the corps. Each of them, when directed to advance against the enemy during the campaign at Bean's Station, refused to follow orders. Longstreet regarded their actions as insubordinate and believed that in future engagements, these officers could threaten the lives of their comrades if they disregarded orders again.

It is important to note, however, that in the case of McLaws, Longstreet did not originally prefer charges, instead simply wanting him transferred. Longstreet was disenchanted with McLaws's lack of aggressiveness following Chickamauga and thought that the general could best serve the Confederacy elsewhere. As late as October 1863, Longstreet regarded McLaws as a close confidant, sharing with him ideas on strategy and promotion. He even wrote him a complimentary letter in which he states, "I do not wish that there should be any secrets between us so far as I am concerned." In contrast, McLaws had held Longstreet in contempt since Gettysburg and longed to get away from his authority. After arriving in northern Georgia, McLaws grew distant from his commander and even breached military protocol by circumventing Longstreet when requesting a leave of absence during the siege of Chattanooga. When detached to Knoxville, McLaws continued to display an antipathy toward Longstreet that prompted the corps commander to urge his cooperation.[69]

By the time of Bean's Station, Longstreet had had enough of McLaws's intransigence and wanted him relieved from further duty with his corps, even citing McLaws's poor health as a reason for removal. When the War Department informed him that he could not relieve an officer and order him beyond his command boundaries, Longstreet had to prefer charges. But the general's lack of enthusiasm for a court-martial was evident in the weak charges he levied against McLaws. Although McLaws initially claimed that Longstreet sought to shift the blame for the Fort Sanders debacle onto him, the fact remains that before he filed charges, the corps commander claimed full responsibility for the campaign's failures. Nevertheless, when the division commander received word that Longstreet wanted to relieve him for want of confidence, he struck back out of personal honor. Ultimately, the court found McLaws innocent of all but one charge and levied a punishment so light that it vindicated him. Even Longstreet was relieved when the War Department overturned the court's decision.[70]

In the case of McLaws, Longstreet was only following Bragg's precedent, having successfully removed D. H. Hill from command for want of cooperation at Chickamauga. Despite Hill's attempts to obtain a court trial, the authorities in Richmond refused to acquiesce to his demands since no charges had been filed against him. Longstreet probably thought his similar troubles with McLaws could be dealt with in the same way. The First Corps commander failed, however, to consider that unlike Bragg, he did not have the president's support. When he informed the War Department that he had relieved McLaws, General Cooper demanded that Longstreet prefer charges. By the time the court reached a decision, McLaws's campaign to discredit Longstreet had succeeded in further diminishing the corps commander's prestige.[71]

In Law's case, Longstreet was justified in preparing charges against his subordinate but erred in failing to contain his own anger and irritation. When the general resigned in late December, Longstreet thought all would be well. But when the regimental officers of Law's Brigade turned in a petition for a transfer out of the First Corps, he became suspicious of a conspiracy and furious at Law for his role in an alleged plot. When Law returned to East Tennessee, Longstreet ordered his arrest. Weary of Longstreet's earlier problems with McLaws and Robertson, the War Department refused to entertain charges against Law. Even though Lee found the allegations to be of a serious character and deserving of an investigation, the government dismissed any action against Law. Longstreet failed to consider how the authorities would perceive this latest action, and his anger was not easily restrained. He continued to demonstrate poor judgment by lashing out against the Alabama Brigade.[72]

The War Department did not help assuage the acrimony in the First Corps. The actions of Cooper and Davis probably reflected the feelings of the military advisor to the president, Braxton Bragg. The general brought a strong antipathy toward Longstreet, whom he blamed for the loss of Lookout Valley and, by extension, Chattanooga and his command of the Army of Tennessee. Bragg forwarded official dispatches to the War Department suggesting that Longstreet seemed to lack confidence. His actions in Richmond continued his steady stream of deceitful messages to the president that had begun during the Knoxville campaign portraying the First Corps commander as a troublesome malcontent. In addition, lacking the basis for removing Longstreet for his performance at Chattanooga, Bragg sought to use the disgruntled McLaws and Law to help him oust the general from command.[73]

The difficulties with his subordinates and the War Department intensified the distress Longstreet already felt. He acknowledged his failures in East Tennessee and worried about his strained relationship with Richmond. Realizing that he had lost political influence in the War Department, he resorted to asking Lee for assistance. In some ways Longstreet's tarnished reputation within the Confederate high command perhaps explains Joe Johnston's hesitance to join forces with the First Corps commander. The western department commander was well informed of Longstreet's problems with Bragg following Chickamauga. Accordingly, after assuming command of the Army of Tennessee in December 1863, Johnston might have been cautious about uniting with his one-time protégé, who had polarized key figures in Richmond by that time. Moreover, fearing that Davis wished he would fail in his field command, Johnston was apprehensive that any suggestions he might make regarding command arrangements might evoke an immediate rejection from the president.[74]

All of this weighed on Longstreet, and he revealed the depths of his depression in a private letter to D. H. Hill. Significantly he pointed out the War Department's ambivalence in the spring of 1864. "I have no doubts of the intentions of the authorities towards me," Longstreet confessed. "The only obstacle is a good, or rather plausible reason" to be relieved from command. The general realized that his objections to the policies of Bragg and Davis had returned to haunt him, and he became depressed, waiting for what he felt to be his inevitable dismissal from the First Corps. Unlike Hill, who still protested his removal from Bragg's army, Longstreet welcomed the opportunity for early retirement. "I long for some relief from this constant toil and anxiety," he wrote. "When it [removal from command] comes without any fault of my own, and when it cannot be said that I abandoned my post, it will be hailed with delight." In a closing statement Longstreet reveals the change to his persona. "You have often spoken of my excess of confidence," he confessed to Hill, "and . . . you will be quite relieved when you learn that all confidence is gone."[75]

While Longstreet struggled with the discipline of his senior officers, he had erred in allowing his frustration and anger to overrule his good sense and judgment. As his struggle with Law reached a climax in April 1864, Longstreet decided to punish the Alabama Brigade by transferring it to Buckner's Division before returning to the Army of Northern Virginia. Even though Lee countermanded this action, it indicates the depths of Longstreet's aggravation. That same frustration influenced his impolitic behavior toward the authorities in Richmond. Longstreet blundered in resisting the War Department's appointments and questioning Davis's policies. Ultimately, the president decided to keep Longstreet in command in the "interests of the service," but he disliked the general's past conduct in the Bragg controversy.[76]

During all of this, the common soldiers remained largely unaware of the complexity of events in the high command, observing the unfolding drama only on superficial terms.[77] Even though the men knew that their generals had been arrested, other difficulties preoccupied their day-to-day activities. The daily necessities of food, shelter, and clothing remained foremost in their minds. The winter of 1863–64 proved to be one of the harshest in memory, and the soldiers of the First Corps struggled to overcome deficiencies in shoes and winter clothing. Moreover, they soon depleted the foraging areas that had provided ample sustenance in December 1863 and January 1864. After the siege of Knoxville, the eastern veterans came to believe themselves headed back to Lee's army, only to stop midway and encamp in an unfriendly region whose population was divided in their sympathies. Nevertheless, Longstreet's troops continued to skirmish with Federal units, and the First Corps continued to be a formidable presence in East Tennessee.

7

"BITTER COLD, EVERYTHING FROZEN"

THE FIRST CORPS IN EAST TENNESSEE, WINTER 1863-64

URING THE WINTER OF 1863–64, THE PROBLEMS WITHIN THE First Corps's high command had a minimal effect on the hardships of the common soldiers. The rank and file instead focused on the struggle to find sustenance in an area where the citizens were bitterly divided in their loyalty to the Union or Confederacy. Despite the conflict with his lieutenants and the War Department, Longstreet continued to tend to his daily duties of supplying his army and planning strategy. Struggling to overcome deficiencies in transportation, clothing, and food, his soldiers longed to return to the Army of Northern Virginia. In April 1864 the War Department fulfilled their wishes with orders to return to Lee's army, delighting both the officers and the men and bringing their seven-month sojourn in Georgia and Tennessee to an end.

Since the assault on Fort Sanders, Longstreet had retreated up the Holston River valley, focusing on the Federals in Knoxville to his front and at Cumberland Gap to his right. When the First Corps and its supporting contingent went into winter quarters, most of the soldiers had no direct knowledge of East Tennessee. The regiments came from South Carolina, Georgia, Texas, Arkansas, and Mississippi, and most of the soldiers were not familiar with the region where they would spend the next five months. The Confederates occupied Tennessee's Great Valley, an area about twenty-five miles wide and forty miles long located twenty miles northeast of Knoxville. The Great Smokey Mountains border the valley on the south, while the Clinch Mountains bound the north. The valley itself is a fertile region between the Holston and French Broad rivers, tributaries of the Tennessee River, which surge through the mountain ranges. Longstreet established his headquarters in Russellville, along the East Tennessee and Virginia Railroad running south of the Holston, while the cavalry set up a defensive perimeter about twenty-five miles long extending from Rutledge on the north to Dandridge on the south. From Russellville the First Corps controlled the railroad from that point east, thus maintaining a vital supply link with the Confederate capital. With the rivers anchoring the flanks, Longstreet had established a strong defensive position that forced any Federal advance directly through the Holston Valley.[1]

Stationed at Russellville and Morristown, five miles apart, the divisions of McLaws and Jenkins straddled the railroad. Constructed in the 1850s, the East Tennessee and Virginia Railroad ran northeast from Knoxville to Russellville, then southeast to Greeneville before it continued northeast again all the way to Bristol on the Tennessee-Virginia border. Travel was especially difficult for the Confederates during the winter months. The turnpikes and roads used to transport goods and livestock in the antebellum years only allowed slow and difficult movement for armies operating in the region. East Tennessee lacked macadamized roads, and only one such route, which ran from Morristown to the Cumberland Gap, could be found in the area. The heavy rains of the recent months had turned roadbeds into quagmires, and the onset of winter cold had frozen the muddy ruts. Wagons thus easily broke down on the rough roads in the hilly terrain.[2]

The First Corps arrived in the Great Valley with preconceived notions of the land and people living there. While stationed in Chattanooga, Col. John Bratton of Jenkins's Brigade had described Tennesseans as "deplorable." He compared them to Virginians, claiming that the citizens of the Old Dominion were "superior to this western population." Bratton might have been biased since many people in East Tennessee held strong Unionist sentiments in contrast to other parts of the state. Jefferson and Greene counties, where McLaws's and Jenkins's commands bivouacked, were solidly pro-Union. In 1861 the majority of voters there had rejected secession. But divided allegiances marked the constituencies north and south of the two counties. By 1862 Maj. Gen. Edmund Kirby Smith, commanding the Department of East Tennessee, reported that he struggled to arrest Unionist leaders and protect Confederate sympathizers. He received the War Department's approval to declare martial law but still found it difficult to maintain order in the divided region. Later that year his successor, Maj.

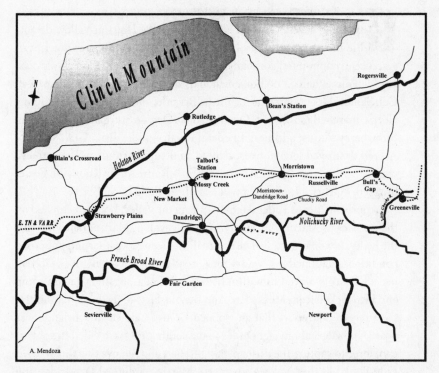

MAP 8. *The Great Valley, East Tennessee*

Gen. Sam Jones, reported that the valley still remained under Unionist influence as he attempted to enforce conscription. By 1863 Richmond had declared East Tennessee a hostile region.[3]

In addition to the Unionist population in this rough country, Longstreet also faced a strong Federal presence to the southwest. After the Battle of Bean's Station, Union troops returned to Knoxville and secured the outlying areas, establishing a large arms-and-supplies depot about fifteen miles northeast at Strawberry Plains.[4]

Grant visited Knoxville on December 31 to determine why Foster's Army of the Ohio had failed to expel Longstreet from East Tennessee. To his chagrin, he found Foster's army suffering from a want of clothing and shoes. Nevertheless, the general continued to feel a "particular anxiety" over Longstreet's presence in the region and ordered Foster to advance against the Confederates yet again. Three weeks later he received a telegram from Foster, who declared, "It is absolutely necessary that the army have rest."[5] Longstreet thus remained a threat on Grant's left flank, maneuvering a mere twenty-five miles from the depot at Strawberry Plains.

RANT'S DESIRE TO PUSH LONGSTREET OUT OF EAST TENNESSEE prodded several Federal advances into the Holston Valley, despite the inclement weather. In late December Brig. Gen. Samuel Sturgis, recently appointed commander of the Army of the Ohio's cavalry, assembled more than 6,000 horsemen in the first attempt against Longstreet. Col. Samuel Mott, commanding the 1st Brigade, 2nd Division, XXIII Army Corps, marched in support. On Christmas Day, as Sturgis advanced from Strawberry Plains, additional Federal cavalry under Brig. Gen. William Averell destroyed locomotives, depots, and supply stores in Longstreet's rear along the East Tennessee and Virginia Railroad. At Knoxville Foster bragged, "General Longstreet will feel a little timid now."[6]

Apprising him of Federal movements in the valley, Longstreet relied on the services of Martin's three divisions of cavalry.[7] Martin, believing that the Federals would not advance due to the inclement weather and poor road conditions, stationed his cavalry on a broad front. On the night of December 28, Sturgis moved to within fifteen miles of Longstreet's main camp and bivouacked from Mossy Creek to the outskirts of Talbot's Station. He soon received a report that an isolated Confederate cavalry brigade was near Dandridge, about eight miles to the south. Sturgis decided to split his own force to capture the unsuspecting Rebels and remove this threat to his right flank. As the Yankees advanced, Martin reinforced Dandridge and ordered an assault on the remaining Federal units near Talbot's Station. Advancing from the east along the East Tennessee and Virginia Railroad, Martin's dismounted cavalrymen launched their assault on the morning of the twenty-ninth, driving back the Union pickets. By 9:00 A.M. they had overwhelmed the Union soldiers, who immediately sent couriers to recall Sturgis. By early afternoon the Federal column returned to support their comrades, turning the tide of battle as they struck the Confederate left. By 4:30 P.M. the Confederate attack had stalled. Facing a numerically superior force, Martin ordered his men to withdraw toward Morristown. The engagement at Mossy Creek cost Sturgis 109 casualties, while Martin's horsemen suffered about 300.[8]

The Confederate loss in the engagement at Mossy Creek rankled Longstreet. As a result of the battle, Martin's cavalry had to retreat closer to the First Corps's infantry units, narrowing the distance between Longstreet and the Federals. The proximity of the opposing armies enabled the Union high command to determine that they needed to move closer to the foraging area near Dandridge, for they also needed additional subsistence since steamboats from Chattanooga could not reach Knoxville because of icy river conditions. Thus by early January 1864 both sides realized that they needed to gain control of the area along the French Broad River. On January 14 Maj. Gen. John Parke, taking over for Foster, who remained ill in Knoxville, ordered another offensive toward Dandridge with three cavalry divisions, led by Sturgis, and three infantry divisions, commanded by Maj. Gen. Gordon Granger. That day Longstreet received Martin's report of the Federal advance and immediately ordered his troops to march toward Dandridge too.[9]

Unsure if the move toward Dandridge indicated a feint against his left flank, Longstreet ordered the divisions of McLaws (now temporarily commanded by Brig. Gen. William T. Wofford) and Ransom to advance along the railroad toward Mossy Creek, while the divisions of Jenkins and Bushrod Johnson marched toward Dandridge. He also directed Alexander's artillery to join Johnson. As the infantry marched toward their objectives, Martin's cavalry received orders to move toward Dandridge along a parallel route on the Chucky Road. Longstreet rode with Martin as the Confederates slogged on the frozen roads. In his memoirs the general recalled that the "bitter freeze of two weeks had made the rough angles of mud as firm and sharp as so many freshly-quarried rock." The conditions were so difficult that he ordered all the shoeless men to remain behind as camp guards. By midafternoon of the fifteenth, Longstreet had sixty-one regiments of infantry, twenty pieces of artillery, and eighteen regiments of cavalry slowly advancing toward Dandridge.[10]

Although the Confederates marched as rapidly as possible, Sturgis's horsemen beat them to the town, arriving on the night of the fifteenth. Receiving reports of Martin's cavalry approaching from the northeast, Sturgis planned a double envelopment of the Rebel force the next day. He ordered his main units to march on the Dandridge–Morristown Road while the remainder of his force advanced toward Martin on Chucky Road. The next day the Union commander put his plan into motion, ordering his brigades to proceed on separate paths toward the Confederate cavalry. Although his strategy was sound in theory, Sturgis did not figure on Longstreet's infantry marching southwest on the Morristown Road. Five miles outside of Dandridge, the Federal cavalry, under Col. Israel Garrard, suddenly encountered Jenkins's column, leading the advance guard of Longstreet's infantry. Stunned and overwhelmed by the Rebels, Garrard immediately ordered a withdrawal toward Dandridge. By nightfall the Rebels had "pushed the enemy back nearer the town." Meanwhile on the Chucky Road, Sturgis also encountered stiff resistance from Martin's units. Unable to dislodge them, he too retired toward Dandridge.[11]

During the night, Sturgis, bolstered by the arrival of Parke and addi-

tional infantry, set up a defensive perimeter around the town and prepared
for the impending Confederate attack. Meanwhile, Longstreet and his
lieutenants made plans for an assault the next day. The general ordered a
flanking maneuver against the Federal left while Martin's cavalry occupied
their front. Unaware of the strength of the enemy, Longstreet instructed the
assault to begin around noon so darkness could allow for a concealed withdrawal if necessary. At noon on January 17, the Confederates advanced and
clashed with the Federals just outside of Dandridge; by dusk they were in
command of the battlefield. That evening Parke held a council of war. Rumors circulated that Longstreet had received reinforcements from Virginia,
and Parke's subordinates worried about being trapped far from their base.
With the Union commanders split over their next course of action, Parke
decided to withdraw during the night. The Federals built large campfires
to trick the Confederates and cover their retreat. By 11:00 P.M. the Union
troops began marching toward Strawberry Plains. The next morning
Longstreet's men entered the town only to find it abandoned. The general
did not pursue the retreating Union force because of the poor condition of
his troops and horses. The Confederates had suffered 150 casualties in the
battle, about half of the Federal losses.[12]

Despite the distraction of arresting some of his key lieutenants, Longstreet had competently handled the minor affair at Dandridge. He used
Martin's cavalry units for reconnaissance, and when notified of an impending advance against the town, he reacted quickly, sending a large force to
meet the Federals. Once engaged, Longstreet continued to act more aggres-
sively than in October and November 1863, personally leading his men and
making troop dispositions during battle. Even though failing to capture
the Union army, Longstreet succeeded in pushing the enemy out of the
contested foraging area in Jefferson County. He only displayed hesitance in
ordering his attack to begin at midday on the seventeenth. Yet the general
faced several obstacles that day that warranted caution. First, his units operated in unfamiliar territory away from their base at Morristown. He did
not know the strength of the opposing force nor how soon reinforcements
could be brought up. His troops also had to fight in miserable weather conditions with inadequate shoes and clothing. Since the new year, the weather
in East Tennessee had hovered near zero degrees. Even though the tem-
perature had warmed slightly by the third week of January, conditions were
still difficult. Finally, Longstreet could not chase the retreating Federals on
the eighteenth because, as he explained in his official report: "Our infantry
was not in condition to pursue, half of our men without shoes. Our cavalry

almost as badly off for want of clothing." The First Corps had won a minor victory that boosted morale and captured a "few arms and equipment." Yet the strategic situation remained as before; Longstreet's force was in an isolated, backwater theater under threat of a large Federal force nearby.[13]

Following Dandridge, the Federals moved south of the French Broad, while Longstreet withdrew to the Russellville-Morristown area. Even though the First Corps returned to its winter base, the commanding general left Johnson's Division and Martin's cavalry in the vicinity of Dandridge to protect his foragers. The Federals continued to disrupt Confederate foraging in the area, however, capturing several wagons and inflicting about a hundred casualties in various raids. On the twenty-fifth Longstreet ordered Martin to cross the river and advance toward Sevierville, about fifteen miles west of Dandridge. The Rebel horsemen rode south of the French Broad on the twenty-sixth and encountered Sturgis's cavalry that day, driving them back before darkness ended the fighting. The next morning the Federals assumed the offensive and attacked at Fair Garden, where the Rebel horsemen had concentrated their forces. By late afternoon Sturgis had forced Martin to withdraw. The Union cavalry pursued the next day, capturing and killing additional Rebels before Johnson's brigades began to cross the river in support of Martin. As a result of the engagement, the Confederates suffered more than two hundred casualties, while the Federals lost about half that number. Both sides withdrew to their previous positions.[14]

The fighting at Fair Garden disconcerted Longstreet. He depended on the French Broad Valley for sustenance, and the Federal presence in the area threatened his army's forage supply. He held Martin responsible for the situation. Earlier on New Year's Eve, Longstreet had informed him that he regretted the "many desertions" in the cavalry and encouraged the general to "repress" any feelings of discontent he could sense with his troops. Apparently Martin's conduct did not mollify Longstreet in mid-January, for the corps commander continued to press him "to please let us know if the enemy is advancing."[15] The engagement at Fair Garden further injured Martin's standing with Longstreet, who pleaded with Cooper to send a replacement and also requested additional cavalry reinforcements from Wheeler's corps in North Georgia.[16] Longstreet hoped to make the western horsemen into effective fighting units, not mere pickets or raiders. In late January he boasted that the cavalry had "learned more of its duties since I came here than in all its previous service." Yet Martin disliked the general and chafed at serving under him. Tired of the constant prodding, Martin soon allied himself with McLaws. "If in any way by correspondence I can serve you," he wrote McLaws while the general awaited trial, "I will do so with great pleasure." Martin's actions thus suggest another fractured command relationship between Longstreet and one of his subordinates.[17]

But the conduct of the cavalry was not the only predicament for the First Corps during January. Since withdrawing from Knoxville, Longstreet's forces had engaged the Federals four times, inflicting more than 900 casualties while suffering approximately 1,200. The Confederates had successfully repelled each Federal advance, but they had been pushed farther back while the enemy continued to threaten their foraging areas. For this reason, Longstreet wrote Lee on January 10 to discuss the strategic situation in East Tennessee. He described his position as precarious. "I am just strong enough to tempt the enemy to concentrate against me," Longstreet wrote, "and either destroy me or drive me back as far as he chooses." Despite his earlier assertions concerning the importance of operations in the West, the general concluded that Richmond now functioned as the main theater of operations, and if Lee so ordered, the First Corps could return to the Army of Northern Virginia by early March. But rather than remain in Virginia, Longstreet proposed an advance against Washington. Once again he supported his notion of the strategic offensive maneuver combined with the tactical defense. He also seemed resigned to the notion of not reuniting with Johnston, admitting to Lee that Johnston could not aid him in East Tennessee. For his part, Johnston balked at the idea, complaining that his army was not strong enough to venture beyond its position in North Georgia and rejecting any proposals for joint operations.[18]

Lee responded on the January 16, applauding Longstreet for seeking a "way to reach the enemy." He hesitated, however, to use Virginia as a base from which to launch an invasion due to the "exhausted" nature of the region. The Army of Northern Virginia commander instead seemed optimistic of a Kentucky invasion if the logistics could be worked out. When Longstreet received Lee's letter a few weeks later, he replied that a Kentucky invasion seemed like an ideal opportunity to strike at the North. On February 3 Lee informed Davis of the situation in East Tennessee and proposed two movements. First, he suggested that Longstreet receive reinforcements so he could march into Kentucky and threaten Grant's line of communications. Second, if Davis did not find a Kentucky invasion feasible, the president could transfer Longstreet back to Virginia for an advance against Washington to produce "sufficient apprehension." Davis objected to both proposals. On the twentieth he instead transferred most of Martin's cavalry to Joe Johnston's Army of Tennessee. Upon assuming command of the western army in December 1863, Johnston had requested all available troops in preparation for the spring campaigns. When Longstreet objected to the transfer of Martin's cavalry by alerting the War Department that he would have to withdraw closer to Virginia to maintain a line of supply, Davis replied that he could not retire too far beyond Morristown in case of a Federal advance through the Cumberland Gap.[19]

Despite his ambivalence about Martin's abilities, Longstreet lamented the transfer of the cavalry, whose absence would further impede operations against the Federals. Longstreet now was left with two cavalry brigades, commanded by Cols. Arthur A. Russell and George G. Dibrell, to serve as the eyes of his command. Even without an effective cavalry force, the First Corps marched against Knoxville in early February, advancing as far as Strawberry Plains. Longstreet, however, refused to attack the enemy post when he recognized the "strength of the Federal fortifications was greatly improved since the last siege." He requested reinforcements to resume operations against the city, but the authorities in Richmond determined that Confederate forces were already spread too thin and rejected the proposal. Longstreet had figured that if he could threaten Knoxville, he could force Grant to send a part of Sherman's army back toward East Tennessee and thus delay any Federal advance in North Georgia. When the War Department rejected his proposals, the general moved his headquarters from New Market to Morristown on February 22 and issued orders for his infantry to withdraw from Strawberry Plains and the rich foraging area near Dandridge. Upon reaching their new base, his troops entrenched and awaited a possible Federal advance. Within a few days Longstreet again moved his headquarters to Greeneville, less than five miles east of his main force at Bull's Gap. Longstreet's corps established a defensive perimeter that used Bull's Gap as its axis, running from the Holston River on the north to the Nolichucky River on the south.[20]

As he prepared to fall back from Morristown, Longstreet wrote Lee and again suggested a bold invasion of the North. After outlining the difficulties of his position in East Tennessee, he proposed a movement that would incorporate his January 10 plan to mount his infantry. The general suggested that he could move his command, on mules and horses, across the Cumberland Mountains and into Kentucky, then seize the railroad between Louisville and Nashville and compel the Federals to fall back, thereby freeing Johnston's army to advance into Tennessee. To emphasize the gravity of the strategic situation facing the Confederacy, Longstreet told Lee, "We have no time to spare."[21]

Although Lee met with Davis in Richmond to discuss strategy during the last week of February, Longstreet's proposal was probably ignored because a Federal cavalry raid near the capital interrupted the conference and prompted Lee to return to his army. A few days later Lee received another letter from Longstreet repeating his earlier plan, though with a few modifications. This time he suggested that Lee join him with part of his army and advance into Kentucky, while Johnston's contingent marched toward Richmond. Longstreet admitted that his proposal would take "great exertions" but believed that it would yield "great results." Once more his plan failed to interest Lee, who kindly reminded Longstreet of the impracticality of providing horses for the First Corps and supplying the animals with sufficient forage. Lee instead proposed that Longstreet combine with Johnston to advance into Middle Tennessee, "where provisions and forage can be had." Since he was not familiar with the terrain of the region, Lee asked Longstreet to study the situation and communicate with Johnston.[22]

Longstreet had already been in contact with Johnston prior to Lee's instructions, discussing with his former commander Richmond's proposal for a move into Middle Tennessee. But Johnston hesitated to advance because of his army's perceived weaknesses. Since the reunion that Longstreet had longed for since the fall of 1863 failed to materialize, he now sought to return to Lee. His problems with the War Department over the arrest of the three generals influenced Longstreet to travel to Lee's headquarters at Orange Court House, Virginia, to promote his proposal. He arrived there around March 10 with an even bolder invasion plan than the one previously offered. Longstreet suggested that Beauregard advance from South Carolina toward Abingdon, Virginia, where his troops would join the First Corps and march into central Kentucky. Meanwhile, Johnston's army could advance across Alabama and Tennessee into Kentucky, where the two forces would strike at the enemy in northern Tennessee. According to Longstreet, Lee approved of the Kentucky invasion and asked him to present it to Davis. "I objected that the mere fact of its coming from me would be enough to cause its rejection," Longstreet remembered, "and asked, if he approved, that he would take it and submit it as his own." On the twelfth both men traveled to Richmond to meet with the president, the secretary of war, and Bragg. Acknowledging Johnston's hesitance to invade Kentucky, Davis rejected the plan and reiterated his earlier proposal for the Army of Tennessee to move north from its base in Dalton toward Nashville. Sensing a good deal of tension from some of the attendees, Longstreet was relieved when the president adjourned the meeting and promised to consider all proposals.[23]

Leaving Richmond for Petersburg, where his wife resided, Longstreet continued to lobby for his plan. In a March 15 letter to Davis, the general

reiterated many of his earlier points, suggesting that his troops, in conjunc-
tion with Beauregard, could advance into Kentucky and ultimately link up
with Johnston's army, after which the combined force could strike "a blow
at the enemy" in Tennessee. That day Longstreet informed Beauregard
that the president still had not rejected his proposal, but he feared a delay
in making a decision would be unfortunate for the Confederacy; he also
wrote Lee and Johnston urging them to support his plan. But Longstreet
did not have to wait long for Davis's decision. The president responded on
the twenty-first, providing a clear, but stiff, summary explaining why he
rejected the scheme. Davis cited the paucity of horses in the Confederacy to
mount Longstreet's men, a lack of forage in the area, and the poor condition
of the Southern railways as reasons why he could not approve the Kentucky
invasion. He also feared weakening other areas of the Confederacy for a
strategy he considered impractical.[24]

Longstreet's letter to Davis had failed to clarify the ultimate intention
of his proposal, a demonstration to end the war. In a March 27 letter to
Brig. Gen. Thomas Jordan, Beauregard's chief of staff, the First Corps
commander declared that the move into Kentucky was a "political move"
designed to demoralize the war-weary North: "The enemy will be more or
less demoralized and disheartened by the great loss of territory which he
will sustain, and he will find great difficulty in getting men enough to operate with before the elections in the fall, when in all probability Lincoln will
be defeated and peace will follow in the spring. . . . It would be a powerful
argument against Lincoln and against the war. Lincoln's re-election seems
to depend upon the result of our efforts during the present year." Aware
of the limited forage in East Tennessee and worried about the feasibility
of the Confederacy winning a drawn-out military struggle, he felt that the
War Department should strike at the morale of the North to evoke peace
negotiations despite the inherent risks.[25]

Longstreet's proposals for an invasion of Kentucky are significant,
suggesting that his confidence had returned, his letter to D. H. Hill notwithstanding. He desired a strategic offensive into enemy territory, where
his force would wait for the Federals to attack at a place offering favorable
ground. Longstreet's idea of using his command as a large raiding force had
some merit. If mounted, the Confederates could avoid a numerically stronger force and maneuver around the enemy's rear until they could compel the
Federals to withdraw from their present positions. Moreover, the general's
experiences in East Tennessee influenced his views on using mounts. For
weeks he had advocated that Martin's men fight as mounted infantry. While
the icy roads and lack of shoes limited the infantry, the cavalry had ma-

neuvered easily over the poor roads of the region. Longstreet thus argued that if he could provide mounts for his corps, "the greater rapidity of our movements" would enable his troops to collaborate with the Confederacy's other armies. To ease the War Department's burden of providing mounts, he directed his regimental commanders to order the troops to furnish their own mounts for a general movement.[26]

More importantly, this plan relied on the combined forces to restore Southern hopes and dishearten the North. Longstreet determined that the Confederate high command's present policy of concentrating forces defensively would lead to defeat since the Union would always be able to raise additional manpower and ultimately "close the chapter" on the South's bid for independence. He thus hoped that by maneuvering an army in the North, the Confederates could affect the fall elections of 1864. The general accurately described the political situation in the Union when he pointed out the need to defeat Lincoln in the polls. "If he is reelected," Longstreet warned, "the war must continue, and I see no way of defeating his re-election except by military success." His pleas for altering present strategy did not signify that he had lost hope. Rather, Longstreet recognized that the only way the South could counter the North's industrial and economic might would be through waging a war against Northern public opinion.[27]

Yet for all its merits, the proposal proved impractical. Even though Lee was piqued by the prospect of another invasion in early January, Longstreet's unreasonable logistical requests caused his plan to unravel. As Steven E. Woodworth, a scholar of the Confederate high command, points out, Longstreet "might as well have suggested putting his infantrymen on the backs of war elephants." While the general had correctly gauged the political situation in the North, he failed to accurately analyze the South's resources in 1864. The War Department could not possibly supply enough horses and mules for Longstreet's men that spring. In addition, the food shortages throughout the South weakened many of the mounts at hand, especially those in East Tennessee.[28] Longstreet's plan thus seems quixotic at best. If anything, it demonstrated that he wanted to get out of East Tennessee.

AFTER THE MILITARY CONFERENCE IN RICHMOND, LONGSTREET returned to First Corps headquarters on March 18. Although he had participated in discussions of grand strategy for over three months and ordered his regimental commanders to have their troops to procure horses, the junior officers and rank and file remained mostly unaware of grand strategy. The First Corps veterans instead concerned themselves more with the day-to-day challenges of acquiring food, keeping warm, and remaining healthy than contemplating what new campaign might arise. These concerns did not mean that the troops would not speculate as to the high command's intentions or even start rumors as to where the army was headed, what it sought to accomplish, or what type of force they would face. But overall such discussions consisted of conjecture based on limited information. A Georgia soldier, for instance, confessed that he could not tell "much that is reliable" from his officers about the army's strategy. A private in Wofford's Brigade concurred, informing his father that there seemed "to be some important movement on foot, the nature of which I am unable to find out."[29]

Often the men resorted to asking their families to follow the newspapers in order to find out the latest information about the army's maneuvers. Since the onset of the war, journalists had attached themselves to the armies and provided information to the civilian population. A member of the 10th Georgia acknowledged this fact when he informed his wife, "For the positions of the fighting I refer you to the papers." In some cases Southern newspapers employed volunteer soldier-journalists, usually using pseudonyms, to report the news of the army. The First Corps proved no exception, having "Personne," a contributor to the *Charleston Courier,* writing detailed articles of the campaigns in East Tennessee. The *Houston Tri-Weekly Telegraph* proclaimed that "Personne" was "perhaps the ablest and most reliable of all newspapers correspondents." This soldier-journalist was such a prominent figure that Capt. John Christopher Winsmith of the 5th South Carolina urged his mother to read the *Courier* for the army's activities.[30]

Few topics inspired more curiosity than Longstreet's directive to acquire horses. "We are all ordered to furnish ourselves with horses in 90 days," wrote Pvt. John Barry. "I think the whole corps is to be mounted."[31] The notion that the general intended to use his troops as mounted infantry had circulated within the First Corps for weeks. Captain Winsmith was not sure whether the report was genuine or a scheme intended to deceive the Yankees. Another soldier admitted that he could only speculate that Longstreet intended to advance into Kentucky on horseback. These rumors on campaigns and grand strategy often came to an inglorious end without additional information. A few weeks after Barry wrote his father imploring him to provide a horse because he "would not like to be left out" of the impending campaign, the Georgian concluded that "the idea of our being mounted seems to have died out as I heard nothing said about it now."

Ultimately, Barry joined others in the conclusion that the general's strategy "is not known to us privates."[32]

While Longstreet's veterans attempted to grapple with future army movements, the central concern for most of them remained the procurement of food. The primary responsibility for feeding the army fell upon Maj. Raphael Moses, Longstreet's chief commissary officer. A native of South Carolina and a former lawyer, Moses had accomplished great feats for the First Corps in the West. He had cajoled, wrangled, and once even commandeered a train to feed Longstreet's army since its march to Knoxville. W. R. Houghton, a sergeant in Benning's Brigade, attested to the major's dedication and efficiency by relating a story of how the commissary officer spent a night grinding corn to provide the men with breakfast the following morning. Industrious in his methods, Moses sometimes engaged in blackmail to procure sustenance for the First Corps. When citizens of East Tennessee refused to hand over bacon to the Confederate Army, he confiscated their sheep. Upon the seizure of their farm animals, the Tennesseans tendered the coveted meat. Despite his irregular methods, the major was proud to have acquired the much-needed bacon.[33]

Apparently Moses initially did not have many problems acquiring food, for East Tennessee held ample sustenance when the First Corps arrived in December 1863. In his memoirs Longstreet describes overflowing forage wagons and land where "cattle, sheep, and swine, poultry, vegetables, maple-sugar, honey, were all abundant for immediate wants of the troops." While the general's memory might have been tempered by decades of nostalgia and romantic wistfulness, contemporary evidence suggests that his men suffered no shortage of food during December 1863 and January 1864. A private in the 4th Texas wrote his wife describing the "first-rate chicken pie" and "genuine coffee" he enjoyed the day after Christmas. The abundance of food described by Private West represented something new to the men of the First Corps. Since leaving Bragg's army in early November, they had struggled with short rations and deficient sustenance. But upon arriving in the Holston Valley, Longstreet's soldiers enjoyed a generous diet. "We are now living very well," proclaimed William Montgomery of the 3rd Georgia Battalion, "but I assure you it is quite a late thing." A South Carolinian also claimed that he and his comrades "are getting plenty to eat now"—so much in fact that he complained that the "boys look fat and sorry."[34]

Yet by late January and early February, the effects of the harsh Tennessee winter, combined with the presence of two large armies foraging and fighting in the same area, took a toll on the valley and its food supplies.

Exacerbated by the presence of Unionist and Confederate guerrillas who harassed military and civilian targets, the effects of war soon ravaged the region. Even army mounts and civilian livestock suffered from insufficient foodstuffs. Unable to provide feed for their horses and cattle, Tennessee farmers watched their animals die. In the month of February 1864, more than 10,000 Federal mounts died from lack of feed and forage in East Tennessee. The following month E. P. Alexander informed his wife, "We have used up all the forage here & our animals are partly starving."[35]

Near Greeneville, Longstreet's veterans recognized the depletion of the region and the effect it had on the army. By that time they had to rely on a diet of cornbread and bacon. "We had little to eat," remembered Capt. W. J. McLeod of the 6th South Carolina. "More than once we were rationed an ear corn . . . one ear to the man." The small allotments of food did not satisfy the soldiers, forcing many like Private Montgomery to eat three days' rations in one sitting. Others like Sergeant Houghton confessed that they "would have stolen bread from a baby, if there had been bread and a baby to be found."[36]

The Confederates foraged and scavenged the East Tennessee countryside to supplement their meager diets. Hungry soldiers often liberated the needed sustenance from local farmers. A veteran of Kershaw's Brigade offered a unique perspective into the methodology of a forager: "The brotherhood of 'foragers' was a peculiar institute, and some men take as naturally to it as the duck to water. They have an eye to business, as well as pleasure, and the life of a 'forager' becomes almost an art. They have a peculiar talent, developed by long practice of nosing out, hunting up, and running to quarry anything in the way of 'eatables or drinkables.' . . . These foragers had the instinct (or acquired it) and the gifts of a 'knight on the road' of worming out of the good house-wife little dainties, cold meats, and stale bread." Both Union and Confederate troops were notorious for pilfering civilian food wherever their armies marched, and the actions of many of these soldiers prompted local citizens to file complaints with regimental officers. But these officers, who suffered alongside their men for want of food, often looked the other way or cooperated with the foragers. D. H. Hamilton, a sergeant in the 1st Texas, recalled how one officer, upon finding out that soldiers under his command had stolen a hog from a local farmer, joined the banquet. "Boys when you get a good thing count me in and I will hold you harmless," the captain told the enlisted men.[37]

Nevertheless, the men did not live comfortably that winter in Tennessee. A Georgia soldier complained, "our rations of meat is nothing," considering that "I can put one days allowance of meat in my mouth at one time." Even though it seemed as if they appropriated every bit of available food from civilians, this was often still not enough. Clearly some soldiers objected to the practice of liberating the civilian population of their wares, but most rationalized their actions in light of their present circumstances. "I am as yet guilty of no misdemeanor," confessed another Georgia private. "But being a soldier I may sometimes be compelled to hook better things now and then, such as a coop of chickens for instance." Yet the guilt of scrounging for food caused some to doubt their actions. One South Carolinian feared that they "lived mostly by foraging," and it often led "some of the boys into rather bad habits for the time." Other veterans noted how the extensive foraging was an affront to an already hostile civilian population. In April 1864 Longstreet's headquarters received a petition from the citizens of Sullivan County, located about forty miles to the northeast, to spare them from the army's "depredations" and to enforce action against illegal impressments. "Our army is getting to be as much dreaded as the low down thieving Yankees," observed one Confederate.[38]

While foraging gave Longstreet's veterans quick and sometimes easy access to food in East Tennessee, the Rebels also used other methods to deliver the same results. Some men simply wrote home and asked their families to send food asking them to help supplement their meager rations with anything they could spare.[39] Yet despite the soldiers' requests, receiving food from home proved an uncertain venture, considering the unreliable mail service and their isolated position in East Tennessee. If any did receive additional provisions from home, these items probably did little to relieve his hunger. Some of Longstreet's soldiers simply found purchasing food from merchants and vendors a more efficient way of supplementing their scant rations. Known as sutlers, these civilian peddlers had followed Union and Confederate armies since the onset of war. In East Tennessee they preyed on Longstreet's hungry Rebels and made significant profits, sometimes in the range of 1,000 percent. Since some commands forbade sutlers from their camps, soldiers often walked several miles to buy their wares. Andrew Boyd complained to his father that he had to walk about five miles to get dinner, only to be charged two dollars for a meal of beef and bread. A Georgia sharpshooter also complained that he had paid two and a half dollars for a turkey. Since most Confederate enlisted men earned eleven dollars a month, spending almost 20 percent of one's monthly pay on a single meal was frustrating, if not disheartening. Yet most of Longstreet's men got off lightly when compared to prices in other parts of East Tennessee. In Knoxville, for instance, wartime inflation caused prices to skyrocket. By February 1864 flour cost twenty dollars a barrel, and butter one dollar a pound. The cost of other amenities such as coffee and sugar had increased to one dollar a pound for the former and seventy cents a pound for the latter. Faced with such daunting prices, some veterans later recalled how they looked forward to skirmishing with the enemy, for doing so might lead to capturing some vital supplies.[40]

The particularly harsh winter exacerbated the effect of short rations on Longstreet's men, who were nearly unanimous in describing the bitter winter that beset the First Corps. Orlando T. Hanks of the Texas Brigade recalled the winter of 1863-64 as "bitter cold, everything frozen," claiming to have seen icicles "almost as large as an ordinary man" during his stay in East Tennessee. Andrew McBride of the 10th Georgia described how he and his comrades had been "under shot and shell, fire and bullets by day and under snow and sleet, frost and rain by night." Despite having camped in the snow at Fredericksburg, Virginia, the previous winter, a South Carolinian thought the East Tennessee winter proved worse. A. C. Sims of the 1st Texas recalled how he and his comrades had to keep moving all night to prevent "freezing to death," while one of Alexander's cannoneers described New Year's as "the coldest day I ever experienced." A few weeks later another cold wave hit the region, dropping temperatures to below freezing and dumping more than a foot of snow on the camps. The weather did not abate, lasting several weeks and further frustrating the troops. One veteran believed it "was the hardest winter that we had ever experienced." "It rained, sleeted, and snowed so much," he maintained, that their campfires remained in constant peril of being extinguished. Moxley Sorrel observed that the cold inspired "some of the grandest campfires ever seen." Even the commanding general kept abreast of the weather, noting that the "thermostat . . . averaged between 0 and 20 [degrees]" during the first week of January.[41]

While the First Corps veterans struggled with the weather, other soldiers tried to make the best of things, even joking about the cold. John Evans of the 53rd Georgia Regiment wrote his wife: "Mollie, we have had some very cold weather here. Snow has lay on the ground for a week or ten days at a time. If you had come along where I was lying you would have thought it was a pile of snow. I have often read of soldiers lying in the snow country and seeking warmth under snow. I doubted it very much until I experienced it and I find it to be true. I was warm while I was under the snow, but when I woke up in the morning and raised my head the snow dropped in my bosom [and] it was very cold." A South Carolinian noted that the cold weather sometimes brought out the playful side of men. "We had plenty [of] snow balling in the army, and it is a fine sight to observe one regiment attack another with snow balls," Captain Winsmith wrote. "Sometimes they have hard fought battles, and prisoners and camps are taken. I saw some of our Brigade rout a Cavalry Regt passing their camps." The cold weather persisted, and as late as mid-March, veterans still complained of snow.[42]

Once Longstreet determined to set camp, his troops quickly built winter quarters to combat the elements. Robert T. Coles of the 4th Alabama recalled that "we proceeded to erect shelters and make ourselves as comfortable under the circumstances." Without delay, the soldiers commenced "chopping logs and splitting boards for cabins" despite a shortage of proper tools. The men scoured the countryside for building materials, using logs, stones, and planks to construct their shelters. Since these elaborate shanties would serve as their temporary homes, soldiers used impressive engineering skills. One veteran provided his wife a vivid description of his lodgings: "We have built a good cabin to spend the winter in. It is built fourteen by twelve feet, lies east and west, the chimney in the east end of the house. The house is eight logs high[,] covered with planks[,] some pointing to the south. . . . I suppose we have as good a place to winter as any set in camps or the best I have seen." Private Montgomery of the 3rd Georgia Sharpshooters spent three days working on his cabin. Adding a chimney to his lodge on the third and final day, Montgomery proudly described how he finished his work by "sitting by a good fire enjoying the fruits of my labor." With the possibility of remaining in camp for several months, these veterans made their quarters as comfortable as possible. By Christmas the encampment "looked like a little city," recalled one South Carolinian.[43]

The First Corps troops needed to procure warm quarters because of the poor condition of their clothing. Even though some soldiers arrived in the West with new uniforms, they failed to bring their winter coats and extra baggage since they assumed their transfer to Bragg's army would be brief. By the time winter set in, the threadbare clothing of Johnny Reb proved inadequate. Conditions were so bad that Private Montgomery thought it was "enough to make tears come from the most hardened soul." Thomas J. Goree complained of the high cost of clothes. Instead of purchasing new attire, he resigned himself to "patching up and turning" his old coats for the winter. The shortage of appropriate clothing in East Tennessee and the high prices for clothing throughout the Confederacy prompted some Rebels to write home and request additional apparel. The pleas from the Confederate troops, in turn, rallied Southerners to come to their aid. In Columbus, Georgia, the Ladies Soldiers' Friend Society organized a clothing drive and advertised in their local newspaper for clothing and blankets.

The Confederate quartermaster there, Col. F. W. Dillard, also contributed to the cause by appealing to citizens to donate old shoes and cowhides to the soldiers in East Tennessee. In some cases, however, soldiers remained wary of receiving too many articles of clothing from home lest they alienate some of the comrades. After receiving a supply of clothes from his sister, a Georgia private asked her not to send him any more until she heard from him again.[44]

While Longstreet's corps desperately needed additional shirts, pants, and coats for the winter months, the need for new shoes dominated the soldiers' thoughts. Since the march from Knoxville, these veterans had suffered from insufficient or nonexistent footwear. As early as December 13, 1863, Longstreet had notified Adjutant General Cooper about his men's need for boots, asserting that half of his command did not own a pair of shoes. The plight of the First Corps reflected problems in the rest of the Confederacy as leading generals wrote to Richmond to complain of a lack of adequate footwear. Regardless, Rebel soldiers throughout the South continued to suffer without shoes during the winter.[45]

Without shoes, the cold weather limited the troops' capacity to maneuver effectively. Col. John Bratton observed that using "Barefooted men on half rations" could only lead to a disastrous winter campaign. Consequently the veterans of the First Corps, at the urging of their commander, devised various methods to provide their own foot cover. Longstreet ordered details to cut moccasins from beef hides, producing as many as a hundred pairs of shoes per day. To the men who had to wear them, these "Longstreet's Moccasins," as D. H. Hamilton of the Texas Brigade referred to them, "fits like the skin." "Once they were put on they 'stayed put,'" recalled the Texan. Sgt. W. R. Houghton of the 2nd Georgia thought the moccasins "were better than nothing, for a time." Without adequate footwear, some soldiers directed their ire toward the authorities in Richmond, claiming that the government had forgotten about the rank and file. Nevertheless, the men endured the harsh conditions until the Quartermasters Department finally furnished Longstreet's command with the requisite footwear in February 1864. An additional 1,500 pairs of shoes came from the citizens of South Carolina and provided much needed relief for the veterans.[46]

Facing such harsh conditions, First Corps soldiers began deserting in greater numbers by 1864. The motivation for these men is difficult to gauge, but the carnage of war, the inclement weather, and the shortage of food certainly contributed to a general sense of despondency in the ranks. Moreover, the presence of Union forces in North Georgia influenced many soldiers from that state to leave for home as the local citizens' morale plummeted. Some Georgia troops expressed a desire to serve in Johnston's army since "we will be much nearer to home than we are at present." Others simply had had enough of the disappointments during the winter of 1863–64 and chose to leave the ranks, regardless of the risks. One Georgia soldier maintained that if he could only go home, he would be the "happiest mortal that Ever lived." A soldier in the 8th Georgia seemed to pinpoint why these men wanted out: "We have seen the worst part of this war since we came to Tenn."[47]

The desertion of Confederate troops was a complex problem, constantly pitting the advocates of self-interest against those who believed that it was better to fight on for the sake of honor and country. Similarly, Confederate officials continually struggled to devise methods to combat desertion, ranging from harsh punishments to amnesty. Longstreet, like the War Department, addressed the problem inconsistently. The commanding general had initially responded to the increasing desertion rates while in East Tennessee by punishing those who were caught. If captured, soldiers found guilty of deserting their units could suffer a harsh sentence, even death. A South Carolinian noted, "There is a great many men deserting from hear [sic]; they are shooting them every week." Such strict measures met with approval from those who remained. Some soldiers, like Sergeant Houghton, welcomed the stiff punishment since a "deserter was not supposed to have much more rights than a snake." Others, like Lt. Launcelot Minor Blackford, a military court clerk assigned to Longstreet's corps, approved of the stern penalties because they curbed further desertion and supported the war effort. In February 1864 Blackford informed his mother that his court had sentenced four or five men to death for desertion. "Desertion must be put down if it costs the life of every tenth or fifth man in the army," he wrote.[48]

While the harsh punishment for potential deserters could serve as a strong deterrent, in some cases the public scorn of being labeled a shirker persuaded most to remain in the service. Clearly the need to motivate the men was evident when the women of Columbus, recognizing the extreme hardships of the soldiers in East Tennessee, wrote a letter of inspiration just before Christmas imploring their loved ones to persevere. "The country may become demoralized," they wrote, "but the women and the army will ever be undismayed and undaunted." The women pleaded for their men to continue the gallant fight and to refrain from worrying about their families at home. The letter was signed by 126 ladies of Columbus, many of whom had relatives serving with the 17th Georgia Regiment.[49]

As the ranks continued to be depleted by absentees, Longstreet adopted a more lenient policy of granting furloughs to raise morale and discourage the men from deserting. The general also attempted to augment his corps' strength by granting furloughs first to men who promised to bring in additional recruits.[50] Allowing soldiers brief passes to visit family and friends at home provided the men a brief respite from the hardships of war. The policy was not lost on the rank and file as the troops noticed "a great many men going home on furloughs; some for one cause and some for another." Yet despite the lenient attitude, the high command tried to exclude Georgia and Texas troops from the liberal furlough policy because they feared that a temporary leave might become permanent. In the case of Georgia, government officials recognized that the presence of Sherman's army in the state had created additional fears among the civilians that could spark waves of desertion as soldiers left their units to return home to protect their families and loved ones. Consequently some of the Georgia soldiers under Longstreet's command failed to get a leave of absence, while their compatriots from South Carolina, Mississippi, and Alabama went home for brief stays. As for Texas, the loss of Vicksburg in July 1863 greatly demoralized Texans, signifying an added threat to the Lone Star State as Federal armies cut off the Trans-Mississippi from the rest of the Confederacy. Afterward rank-and-file Texans felt farther away from their homes, and desertion increased among them as many feared a Yankee occupation of their native state. Texas soldiers complained that they were being unfairly treated because their homes were west of the Mississippi and officials refused to grant lengthy furloughs. Jeremiah Caldwell of the 4th Texas protested that he and his comrades had "no privileges whatever" regarding temporary leaves. For their part, some Georgians failed to notice that they had been singled out. A soldier in the 10th Georgia "was much elated" with the thought that he would get a furlough, but a meeting with one of Longstreet's staff officers convinced him that his "hope was ill founded . . . for not only did I learn that I would not get my furlough, but I also learned that I would march in the direction of the enemy instead of home in the morning." Despite the unsympathetic treatment of selected units, soldiers noted the positive effects of Longstreet's policies by the early spring. "We have more men present for duty than we have had for some time past," wrote John Evans of the 53rd Georgia.[51]

The commanding general did not ignore the dissatisfaction of his men. In a private letter to Maj. Gen. J. E. B. Stuart, Longstreet acknowledged that his "troops grumble a little . . . at these hardships, but they are in fine spirits as to their military condition." In fact he attempted to raise the corps's morale by attending to the added needs and concerns necessary to earn the respect and admiration of his troops. Longstreet paid particular attention to inspecting the hospitals and visiting the sick and wounded under his command. The infirm soldiers particularly received his additional care and concern. In December, when his troops captured a Federal wagon train carrying a large supply of coffee at Bean's Station, Longstreet placed it under guard and distributed several hundred pounds for the sick and wounded. Conscientious acts like these assured the general that he could maintain the favor of his men.[52]

While some recognition may be given to Longstreet for motivating his men and reducing demoralization, the real credit lies with the First Corps's veterans. The men who had fought valiantly at Antietam and Gettysburg saw their stay in East Tennessee as another trial they had to endure. "Our campaign has indeed been a severe one—enough to tax the energies and fortitude of the sternest soldiers and the men who have not flinched through all its varied scenes deserves their country's gratitude," observed Captain Winsmith. Even the distraction of the arrests and trials of three generals did not demoralize the men. Concerned about such a reaction, though, the War Department ordered Col. Archer Anderson to inspect the soldiers of the First Corps to determine their morale. In April Anderson found "no dissensions" among the officers of Longstreet's command and that the general possessed "the confidence and affection of his officers and men." Despite this cursory examination of the corps, his description was accurate. One Georgian declared that "upon the whole," the soldiers in East Tennessee "are not entirely devoted to brooding, melancholy, and gloomy retrospects." Another soldier seemed in awe of the corps's ability to withstand the hardships of East Tennessee. "If anyone had told me before the war that men could have borne for month after month . . . what we have," wrote an Alabama captain, "I would have thought it all talk. And I recollect when we first came into the service we grumbled at fare that we would now think the greatest luxuries." On February 17 the Confederate Congress acknowledged the sacrifices of these men when it rewarded a "Resolution of Thanks to Lieutenant General Longstreet and the Officers and Men of His Command" for the "bravery, fortitude and energy" they had displayed in their campaigns.[53]

Despite the hardships of camp life in East Tennessee, the soldiers passed the time writing letters to friends and family during their idle moments. They notified their correspondents of their health, the weather, and sometimes offered descriptions of skirmishes with the enemy. The letters served as a vital link to the outside world, and the veterans of the First Corps highly prized the communication. One Georgia soldier informed his wife that anytime he received one of her letters, he would "read and read it, through" a number of times. While the isolation of Longstreet's command sometimes limited the availability of writing supplies, the soldiers went through significant efforts to maintain contact with home. In addition to using confiscated stationary from Federal soldiers, some veterans simply sacrificed their pay to buy the requisite paper.[54]

The Confederates in East Tennessee placed a strong emphasis on the importance of mail call, yet the poor condition of the Southern railways and the isolated position of the army often led to irregular service Longstreet's soldiers frequently complained that they had not received letters from home in months. One man in the 4th Alabama complained that the mail service in East Tennessee "is very irregular and very unsatisfactory," while Sergeant Houghton of the 2nd Georgia noted that he saw "no mail for three months." Private West of the Texas Brigade complained that he had only received three letters since the Gettysburg campaign. "I fear that many which would have been very precious to me, which would have come as rays of sunshine to a storm-beaten traveler, have been lost by the wayside or been perused by strangers," he despaired, "but nevertheless, you must continue to send them, for if I get one in ten, it will only be prized the more." Regardless of its inconsistency, mail call provided the men with an outlet from the hardships of the campaign.[55]

While the letters home discussed a variety of topics, the difficulty of living in a hostile region became a frequent theme. The Unionists provided a constant challenge to Longstreet's corps as foragers, pickets, and supply trains often had to endure the threat of "bushwhackers." Guerrillas burned bridges, tore down telegraph lines, and plundered supplies from both sides with impunity. Colonel Sorrel described the Unionist sympathizers as a people "without pity or compassion—generosity and sympathy were strangers to them." But he failed to recognize that a majority of the region opposed secession, despite the rest of the state's overwhelming support for the Confederacy. East Tennessee Unionists had refused to accept Confederate occupation, resisted conscription and war taxes, and continually harassed Rebel troops. Soldiers noticed that foraging became an increasingly risky venture, often requiring large groups of men in order to deter ambush. "It was a rough country with a tough set of people, men and women, and we had to fight all of them," opined D. H. Hamilton of the Texas Brigade, with only slight exaggeration. Brigadier General Alexander wrote that "society is in a horrible condition & hardly a week passes" without a murder being committed. Clearly the dual hazards of fighting regular troops and irregular guerrillas frustrated the Confederates.[56]

The volatility of the region threatened the soldiers in Longstreet's command, forcing them to take the offensive against the perpetrators. In one instance soldiers from the Texas Brigade attempted to capture some guerrillas during a nighttime excursion. The Texans surrounded the farm of a reported bushwhacker and broke into the house, only to find him hiding under a bed with a loaded gun. His wife intervened, not to save his life but rather to "take him from under the bed and out of the house, and to leave her no nasty mess to clean up." Even though other men attempted to pursue and capture Unionist guerrillas, their quarry usually eluded capture by taking refuge in the mountains.[57]

A few First Corps veterans actually managed to forge friendships with some citizens of East Tennessee during their winter stay. These Confederate sympathizers attempted to make life more bearable for the Rebel soldiers by opening their homes and sharing their food. While the men gratefully acknowledged this friendly treatment, they paid particular attention to the members of the opposite sex. A group of South Carolina soldiers encamped near a home "where a bevy of pretty young girls lived" and partook in friendly snowball fights with the ladies. Others seemed to enjoy such company too, writing about their experiences socializing with the fairer sex. Andrew McBride of Bryan's Brigade wrote that on Christmas Day he and his comrades "dined with some very pretty girls." As a result of a favorable impression, McBride and his comrades soon looked forward to another dinner party, "where it is expected that the night will be filled with music." Lieutenant Coles of the 4th Alabama happily recorded that two "sprightly girls" from a "family of good Southern people, an exception in that section," often gave them access to their extensive library for reading material.[58]

Yet despite the hospitality shown by several East Tennesseans, some Confederates remained critical of the local residents. Members of Parker's Virginia Battery complained that the local ladies did not appreciate the visiting Virginians, as evinced in a derisive song they sang about the eastern soldiers: "I would not marry a Virginia boy, They are so small, And they never grow tall." John Evans, a soldier in the 53rd Georgia Regiment, also did not care for the attention of the women of East Tennessee, declaring that the "ladys in this country is very homely," an opinion he formed after attending several parties during his stay in the Great Valley. The attention of the opposite sex notwithstanding, some soldiers regretted withdrawing toward Virginia in the spring of 1864 and leaving behind those Confederate sympathizers who had made their stay easier. "It is the best society I have met in Tennessee," declared Franklin Gaillard, a soldier in Kershaw's Brigade, "and we all regret leaving friends we have made to the tender mercies of the Tories and the Yankees."[59]

Socializing with civilians was a very welcomed diversion for some very bored soldiers. The weather and the conditions of the roads prevented major campaigning, and with the exception of minor skirmishes, both sides filled the hours with mundane duties. Some soldiers complained that they had "no drilling to do, no guard duty to do. Nothing but to cook and a plenty time to do it in." One Georgian wrote that he was so bored, he resorted to washing his own clothes and accomplishing "quite a job of it." Years later a South Carolinian recalled that he and his comrades "had nothing to do but rest up" after skirmishing with the enemy.[60]

To combat the boredom, Longstreet's men engaged in a variety of activities typical for Civil War soldiers, the most popular being drinking and gambling. The soldiers of Kershaw's Brigade recalled that they "were bent on having a good time in East Tennessee." After foraging during the day, they would fight roosters, "regiment against regiment," in the evenings. Since no alcohol was found within the camp, soldiers had to forage the countryside in search of whiskey or other spirits. Officers and enlisted men went to great lengths to acquire the necessary drinks to pass the time. One of Longstreet's staff officers, Col. Walter Fairfax, even ordered a detail of men to march to the home of Andrew Johnson in Greeneville in search of alcohol, simply because the Tennessee politician had a reputation for enjoying a drink or two.[61]

Another vice prevalent in the First Corps was tobacco. Soldiers found that the depleted conditions in East Tennessee prevented them from acquiring a good smoke or a good chew. W. R. Houghton complained: "Plug tobacco could not be had, and 'stingy green' the unpressed leaf raised in the surrounding country, was all we had, and very scarce. We could hear of the men who would leave the fire and go behind a tree to take a chew, being fearful they would be asked to divide." Capt. Charles Blackford concurred with Houghton's assessment of the quality of East Tennessee tobacco, having chewing tobacco sent from home for personal use and for bartering with the locals. The native Virginian pointed out that his tobacco had "regular purchasing power" and that he could acquire "one gallon of sorghum molasses, a turkey, three chickens or three dozens eggs" for one "plug" of his Old Dominion tobacco. To his amazement, "everybody here uses tobacco—men, women, girls and boys all smoke, chew or dip snuff or all three." The significance of tobacco was not lost on Lt. Richard Lewis of

Jenkins's Brigade, who determined that it could lead to a bustling business for an enterprising Confederate. Lewis maintained that tobacco ruled the "articles of this country." According to the South Carolinian, a gentleman had to carry "a pretty heavy pocket of tobacco, for the first thing they [Tennesseans] wished to know after he is introduced: 'Have you got a *chaw of tobacco.*'"[62]

Yet not every soldier in Longstreet's corps focused on the vices prevalent among the ranks. During the winter of 1863–64, the religious fervor found in the Great Revivals that followed the Gettysburg campaign continued in the encampments in East Tennessee. The clergy faced a significant challenge saving souls, considering the debauchery prevalent in a winter camp, but they prevailed in fortifying the confidence of many in the rank and file. "It took a devoted man to be patient in constant hearing of profanity, ribaldry, and general deviltry of camp life," noted a South Carolina soldier. George Butler, the chaplain for the 3rd Arkansas, seemed shocked with the soldiers' behavior when he wrote: "Sister Emma, you have no idea how much wickedness is carried on in the army. A great many of our soldiers curse and swear, lie and steal as if they had no consciouses [*sic*]." To combat the lewdness in camp, President Davis reminded the soldiers of the importance of acknowledging God and offering up their humility in the face of the enemy. On April 8, 1864, he declared a day of "humiliation, fasting, and prayer" and ordered the suspension of all military activity so as to pray for an "honorable peace" and a "free government." The Confederate soldiers in East Tennessee complied with the president's order and celebrated the sermons in camp.[63]

Clearly the three months in the Great Valley had tested the character of the First Corps veterans. After a string of battlefield failures, from Chattanooga to Knoxville, the soldiers endured another series of trials: shortages of food and clothing coupled with the unpredictability of living in a hostile region. They could have been overwhelmed with demoralization and desertion. Yet the majority of the men remained strong in the face of adversity, looking forward to another spring campaign and the end of the war. Although the soldiers grumbled and complained while stationed in East Tennessee, their protests were similar to the usual gripes associated with the idleness and hardships of camp life. The veterans of the First Corps wanted to achieve a victory over the enemy, something that had eluded them for a long time. If that success came in a more enjoyable setting, away from the harsh weather and the destitute surroundings, so much the better.

THE OPPORTUNITY TO ENGAGE THE ENEMY HAD BEEN LIMITED since late February, when Longstreet wrote Lee about his proposals to march on Kentucky. For a month the general had canvassed the Confederate military and civil leadership to mount his men for an invasion of the North. His lobbying efforts even took him to the Confederate capital to meet with Davis and Bragg. Longstreet returned to East Tennessee on March 18, 1864, to await the president's response. But before he learned of the president's decision, Longstreet discovered that the Federals were advancing on his position near Bull's Gap. On the nineteenth he informed General Cooper that three Union corps marched in his direction. That day the War Department ordered the remaining cavalry under Longstreet's command, led by Colonel Dibrell, to rejoin Johnston's army. Even without his cavalry, Longstreet ordered his troops out to meet the enemy. By the twenty-second, however, he reported that the Federals had withdrawn to their defenses at Knoxville. The commanding general ordered his soldiers to retire to Bristol the following day, citing the lack of cavalry to provide reconnaissance.[64]

Longstreet and his command were on alert for a week, scrutinizing Federal movements to ascertain where the next strike would appear. On March 31 he determined that the enemy had begun to withdraw from East Tennessee and was heading toward Virginia. Longstreet immediately wrote Lee and informed him of these developments. He contacted Lee once more on April 2 and confirmed his earlier report. The general had acquiesced to Longstreet's presence in East Tennessee because he believed that the initial Federal threat might be toward Johnston's army in North Georgia. Moreover, President Davis still held the notion of uniting Longstreet with Johnston for a strike toward Middle Tennessee. But the latest reports led Lee to believe that the next Union offensive would take place in Virginia now that Grant had taken the field with George Meade's Army of the Potomac near the Rapidan River line. On April 12 he informed Davis that he needed to recall Longstreet's corps in light of this information. Even before he received Lee's message, the president had already begun to fulfill his request. On April 7 the War Department ordered Longstreet to "move as rapidly as possible by rail" to rejoin the Army of Northern Virginia. Delayed by problems with the railroads, Longstreet began to move toward Virginia on the eleventh, shipping the staff and horses ahead of the infantry and artillery. The men did not lament their departure. One Alabama soldier recalled leaving East Tennessee "without any regrets at parting" as they made their way "triumphantly rejoicing, back to old battle-torn Virginia and 'Mars'

Robert." Another veteran noted that the enthusiasm for returning to the
Old Dominion stemmed from the fact that the troops could never forget the
hardships of the East Tennessee campaign. Sergeant Houghton concurred,
writing that "the E. Tn campaign was the hardest we ever had." Yet John
Bratton of Jenkins's Brigade spoke for almost every soldier when he wrote,
"nobody objects to leaving this country."[65]

From Bristol the First Corps made its way through Lynchburg, Virginia,
and Charlottesville before arriving at Mechanicsville, approximately five
miles west of Gordonsville and the Army of Northern Virginia's camps, on
the twenty-second. The trip had taken ten days, and the soldiers returned
to Lee's army in good health and high spirits despite a train derailment that
cost two men their lives and injured several dozen others. Upon arriving
in Virginia, morale increased in the First Corps. Even the slightest things
buoyed a soldier's spirits. The men at last had returned to General Lee, and
the enthusiasm nearly overwhelmed them. As historian Lisa Laskin has
argued, the soldiers of the Army of Northern Virginia viewed themselves
as the Confederacy's last hope, remaining committed to the war and maintaining a sense of pride in their commanders. Thus as the First Corps arrived, memories of the easterners' impressive battlefield record lifted their
spirits. Major Goree described a wonderful sense of delight upon returning to Virginia. "We will soon be on our old tramping grounds fighting
old acquaintances," wrote Sgt. P. T. Vaughn. The trials and tribulations of
the last six months were forgotten as the officers and men celebrated their
return and displayed an enthusiasm for a new campaign.[66]

Lee's veterans reciprocated this enthusiasm. Soon after Longstreet's
soldiers returned to the Army of Northern Virginia, Col. Walter Taylor of
Lee's staff described it as "a reunion of a family." Other soldiers also demonstrated joy at Longstreet's return for the upcoming spring campaigns. On
April 29 Lee ordered a review of the First Corps to welcome the returning
veterans and to inspect his troops. Even though the campaign in the West
had left Longstreet's men dirty and ragged, they made every effort to ready
themselves for General Lee. A South Carolinian noted that "everything
possible that could add to our looks and appearances was done to make
an acceptable display before our commander in chief." The First Corps
marched in double columns on a large field in full view of Lee, his officers,
and civilian spectators. This display moved Lee, and tears rolled down
his cheeks during the procession. The soldiers shared their commander's
sentiments, one officer referring to the review as "a military sacrament, in
which we pledged anew our lives."[67]

The First Corps's two divisions, now under the command of Gener-

A postwar photograph of James Longstreet, the highly controversial Confederate commander whose Lost Cause demonization eclipsed his wartime reputation.
LIBRARY OF CONGRESS
(LC-B813-2014)

als Field and Kershaw, took position on Lee's rear left, five miles behind the corps of Lt. Gens. A. P. Hill and R. S. Ewell. Their return augmented Lee's army to about 65,000 men to face Grant's 100,000 troops. The celebration did not last very long, for on May 4 reports reached Lee that the Federals had begun to advance across the Rapidan River toward the Confederate right flank. Receiving orders to move forward, Longstreet directed his corps toward the Wilderness, an area of thick scrub brush and trees near Chancellorsville. Even though his troops did not arrive on the field until the second day of battle, they prevented the collapse of Hill's Third Corps. While inspecting his lines later that afternoon, Longstreet and his staff were mistaken for Federal cavalry and shot by their own troops. Longstreet suffered wounds to his throat and right shoulder, while General Jenkins and two other staff officers died as a result of the errant volley. General Field assumed temporary command of the corps and led one final assault before darkness ended the fighting. The Battle of the Wilderness had cost the Federals more than 17,000 casualties and the Confederates more than 8,000.[68]

Despite the hardships and adversity of the previous seven months, the men of the First Corps returned to Lee's army ready to prove themselves once more. They had longed to win a decisive battle against the enemy, and while the Wilderness failed to produce a decisive victory, the First Corps felt proud to have contributed to the repulse of Grant's army. The inconclusive skirmishes against the Federals during the previous winter months did nothing to abate the fighting spirit of the Longstreet's veterans. Most of them withstood the weather, the scarcity of food, and the turmoil between their commander and his key lieutenants in good order. Even though they expressed a strong desire to return to Lee's army, their sentiments did not reflect a negative view of Longstreet. Rather, they and the rest of the Confederacy revered Lee as the general who would most likely lead them to victory.[69]

Moreover, the men felt that they had contributed to the war effort based on their victory at Chickamauga. Chattanooga, Knoxville, and East Tennessee notwithstanding, the First Corps veterans had not lost their fighting spirit. Neither had their commanding general. At the Wilderness, distance prevented Longstreet from taking part in the first day's battle, but once he arrived, he acted decisively and demonstrated why Lee had called him his "Old Warhorse."

CONCLUSION

ESPITE THE CONTRIBUTIONS OF THE EASTERN TROOPS TO THE
Confederate victory at Chickamauga, several historians have maintained that the detachment of James Longstreet and the First Corps
to the West proved a resounding failure. They have cited the general's ambition and his brooding nature as reasons why the results of the transfer
fell short of expectations. Attempting to analyze Longstreet's actions and
reactions to events in the western theater reveals a series of longstanding
grievances and animosities that placed him at a disadvantage from the time
he arrived in North Georgia. Clearly Longstreet contributed to these quarrels and obstacles. Yet the challenges facing the general and his men should
be taken into account when assessing their contribution to the Confederate
war effort in the West.

A year prior to arriving at Ringgold Station, Longstreet fell out of favor
with President Davis and the War Department when he reportedly criticized the president's close friend, Gen. Albert Sidney Johnston, and allied
himself with influential politicians who railed against the Davis administration. Before the Civil War Longstreet had a lengthy history of being
open and friendly to those with the power to help him. Seeking to be a
soldier since he was a young boy, Longstreet concentrated on achieving
that goal in his early years by using his family's political connections to secure an appointment to the U.S. Military Academy. Following his service in
the Mexican-American War, the young officer married the daughter of his
commanding officer, Col. John Garland, and employed his father-in-law's
influence to secure plumb assignments in the peacetime army. After joining
the Confederate Army, Longstreet continued his practice of using influential friends and politicians to secure advancement. When he remained
loyal to his initial commander, Joseph E. Johnston, who quarreled with
Davis throughout the war, Longstreet's relationship with the president deteriorated. Davis also disapproved of the general's alliance with Louis T.
Wigfall, a political opponent and critic of the administration's policies.[1]

The practice of writing influential politicians and seeking assistance
in military matters was not uncommon during the Civil War. Prominent

generals such as Ulysses S. Grant, William T. Sherman, Pierre G. T. Beauregard, John Bell Hood, and even Thomas J. "Stonewall" Jackson, among others, all had influential politicians who assuaged hurt feelings, served as benefactors, or helped shape military careers. Thus when Longstreet communicated with Wigfall and Johnston, he acted no worse than his contemporaries. Yet he failed to consider the consequences his political maneuvering would have on his standing with the Davis administration.[2]

Despite Longstreet's intrusion into the realm of politics and lobbying, the War Department ordered him to reinforce the Army of Tennessee and serve under its troubled commander, Gen. Braxton Bragg. After Chickamauga he became disillusioned with Bragg after the general's failure to pursue the defeated Federals immediately following the battle. Longstreet later joined the army's dissatisfied senior generals in criticizing the commanding general. The president may have considered Longstreet one of Lee's chief lieutenants, but he resented his role in the anti-Bragg cabal. While the episode remains a poor chapter in Longstreet's military career, Davis should be criticized for not stepping in earlier and removing Bragg, who had clearly lost the confidence of his men prior to the arrival of the First Corps.

Accordingly Longstreet had to struggle with the embarrassment of receiving the president's rebuke for petitioning to remove Bragg. By late October 1863 he was the lone remaining general among those who had campaigned for Bragg's resignation to remain with the Army of Tennessee, and his strained relationship with the commanding general made communication between the two difficult. Davis's insistence during his meeting with the army's leading officers that Longstreet provide a frank assessment of Bragg in his commander's presence had created a tense situation that made a cordial working relationship between the two generals impossible.

Adding to the complexity of Longstreet's problems at Chattanooga was the internal friction within his own corps. Upon his detachment to the West, Longstreet gained the transfer of Brig. Gen. Micah Jenkins and actively sought to promote him to command one of his divisions. Yet Jenkins's preexisting rivalry with Brig. Gen. Evander Law, who also aspired to obtain the divisional command, hindered the ability of the First Corps to function as a capable fighting unit as soldiers and officers divided in their loyalty to the two brigadiers. But the Law-Jenkins rivalry was not the only problem facing Longstreet. Maj. Gen. Lafayette McLaws, his other division commander, had grown weary of his commanding general and longed to leave the First Corps. Following Chickamauga, McLaws demonstrated an antipathy for "Old Pete" that affected his command. That a third lieutenant showed displeasure with Longstreet was thus no surprise as Brig. Gen.

Jerome Robertson, the commander of the Texas Brigade, challenged the general's authority.

Finally the First Corps's detachment to East Tennessee created additional obstacles that hindered its ability to function as an effective fighting unit. After the disastrous attack on Fort Sanders at Knoxville, Longstreet marched his force to the northeast and continued to spar with Federal units in the region. Another lost opportunity to rout a strong Union force exasperated the general and forced him to rid his command of a few recalcitrant subordinates. While his efforts to remove uncooperative generals might have appeared as an attempt to shift the blame for the mishandled operations about Knoxville, in Longstreet's view he was merely trying to restore order to his corps.

By the time the general preferred charges against his lieutenants, his prestige and political influence with the authorities in Richmond had been greatly diminished. In fact Longstreet's old nemesis, Bragg, had assumed the role of President Davis's military advisor after his resignation from active field command following the debacle at Missionary Ridge. Bragg's presence in the War Department proved to be Longstreet's final challenge in independent command. In his new capacity Bragg advised the dismissed subordinates to take action against Longstreet while offering the War Department a negative portrayal of the First Corps chieftain. Longstreet did not help his own cause by resisting the president's preferences in regard to Law's arrest and Hood's permanent replacement. Yet his actions suggest that he had grown frustrated with the administration's lack of support. After all, he had witnessed Bragg remove his own troublesome subordinates with the president's complete approval. Longstreet thus believed that the War Department should at least provide him the benefit of the doubt in regards to promoting a general to command one of his divisions. The angst he felt is evident in how the general sought to unfairly punish the men of Law's Alabama Brigade, whom he believed had conspired with their commanding general to transfer out of the First Corps.[3]

While Longstreet struggled to restore discipline and harmony among his senior officers, the rank and file maintained their discipline and morale amid adversity. Although the First Corps did experience a number of desertions during its stay in East Tennessee, these predominantly came from Georgia and Alabama units and did not reflect a general dissatisfaction with Longstreet's leadership. Instead the number of desertions appears comparable to other Confederate departments during the winter of 1863–64. The soldiers' dedication to their cause was evident even before their arrival in northern Georgia when some participated in the destruction of a pro-Unionist newspaper office in North Carolina. The troops who traveled to reinforce Bragg demonstrated an intense loyalty to the Confederacy that helped maintain their esprit de corps in East Tennessee. Even though the junior officers and rank and file grumbled about their hardships in that Unionist region and the lost opportunities of the latest campaign, their letters and journals indicate no outright indignation against their commanding general. In all probability the animosity of East Tennessee's Unionist population galvanized the First Corps.[4]

During their seven-month sojourn in the West, the First Corps veterans complained of a variety of factors: the weather, the lack of food, and sometimes the neglect from the authorities in Richmond. The men even longed to rejoin Robert E. Lee's army in Virginia. But their desire to return to the Old Dominion did not necessarily reflect a lack of confidence in Longstreet, but rather their belief that under Lee's leadership they could regain the support of Richmond and experience battlefield success once more. Their letters and diaries are replete with complaints, though again no outright indignation toward their commanding general. Longstreet's men grumbled to be sure, but their grousing principally stemmed from the momentum of the campaign and hardships associated with marching and fighting during a harsh winter.

In analyzing Longstreet's campaigns in Georgia and Tennessee, some of the general's most glaring failings as a military commander came at Chattanooga and Knoxville. Yet to understand Longstreet's shortcomings as a general, it is necessary to appreciate the complexity of the events surrounding his service in the West. When he became embroiled in the preexisting cabal to oust Bragg, he did so partly out of a distorted sense of duty to the Confederacy. After Chickamauga the Army of Tennessee's senior officers, who had campaigned for over a year to remove Bragg from command, probably filled Longstreet with notions that the fate of the nation rested in his hands lest he fail to offer them his support. Motivated by a sincere and somewhat accurate belief that Bragg could no longer serve as the Army of Tennessee's commander, as well as the possibility of promotion, Longstreet joined the generals' cause.

Longstreet's participation was shameful, but it must be noted that the tension between Bragg and his principle lieutenants had festered long before the First Corps arrived. In a way Longstreet became a pawn in the intrigue. Furthermore, Davis placed his generals in an unwinnable situation when he held his conference with the army's high command during the siege of Chattanooga. The officers could either tell the president what he wanted to hear and forsake their sense of honor, or they could remain honest and criticize Bragg, thereby risking Davis's antagonism. Clearly whichever path they chose held serious consequences. The fact that Longstreet was the sole survivor of Davis's military tribunal is testament to his military reputation and prestige.

Nevertheless, his denouncement of Bragg served as the catalyst for the distrust and resentment that would hamper Longstreet's remaining months in the West. Following Davis's conference, Bragg and Longstreet failed to work in unison toward defeating the Federals in Chattanooga. But it is unfair to blame the lack of communication between the two men solely on Longstreet's stubbornness and petulant nature. Instead he grew apprehensive that Bragg sought his removal after witnessing the purge of the general's detractors in October 1863. For the remainder of his service with the Army of Tennessee, Longstreet's actions and strategic errors demonstrated a lack of self-reliance and a hesitance not generally evident in his other campaigns. By the spring of 1864, the corps commander even confessed that he lacked his old confidence because he feared that the administration sought his removal.

Longstreet's most glaring strategic errors in the West, his failure at Lookout Valley and his assault on Knoxville, suggest that poor judgment and extrinsic factors, not negligence caused by his brooding and sulking as historians have generally emphasized, led to the defeats. In the case of Lookout Valley, he commanded his corps as he had in Virginia, delegating authority and leaving the details of day-to-day affairs to his subordinates. As a corps commander, it is understandable why Longstreet remained focused on the larger picture rather than immersing himself in the particulars of operations and deployments at the regimental and brigade level. But this backfired at Brown's Ferry when the rivalry between Jenkins and Law led to a shifting of troops away from the pivotal sector on the eve of an enemy assault. Longstreet simply failed to correctly gauge the Federal threat to Lookout Valley. There is no excuse for his miscalculation. Nevertheless, the preceding weeks had shaken Longstreet's nerve and convinced him that anything Bragg proposed must be wrong. The aftereffects of the presidential military conference and the birth of his son also contributed to the distractions leading to his poor judgment. Moreover, Bragg made the First Corps responsible for an area equal in size to the rest of his line around Chattanooga but with fewer men than the rest of the Army of Tennessee. Clearly Longstreet failed, but to cite petulance and sinister motives is ignoring the contemporary evidence that suggests that he tried—albeit unsuccessfully—to remain vigilant.[5]

As for the Knoxville campaign, Bragg's desire to see what Longstreet "could do on his own resources" led to a slow start that hampered the easterners' departure from the Chattanooga area.[6] Without adequate food and transportation, the First Corps moved slowly toward the enemy while Bragg wrote misleading messages to Richmond complaining of Longstreet's intransigence and lack of cooperation. By the time the Confederates reached Knoxville, the delays of the previous weeks had allowed the Federals to enhance the city's defenses. Once Longstreet was forced to undertake a siege operation, he began working at cross-purposes with Bragg's plan to strike the enemy a quick blow and return to Chattanooga. Longstreet's strength was in working with the strategy he favored best, the strategic offensive followed by the tactical defense. Yet throughout his service in the West, he was forced to fight on the tactical offensive on almost every occasion. In the assault on Fort Sanders, his fear and frustration influenced the decision to order an attack he deemed doubtful to succeed. Pressed by Bragg's chief engineer, dealing with disgruntled subordinates, and wary of his troops' declining morale, Longstreet was left with little choice but to do something against the Knoxville defenders. If he vacillated, it would suggest that he was uncooperative with Bragg's directives; if he retreated, it would lead to further carping from his senior officers. After his experiences at Chattanooga, Longstreet dared not risk another failure. In order to convince himself and others about the chances of success against Fort Sanders, Longstreet then argued that men who were properly motivated could overcome any obstacle. But the Federals at Knoxville were not the Mexicans at Churubusco. That the attack failed surprised no one.

Certainly Longstreet had additional personal weaknesses that affected his ability to command, and in Tennessee several of these came to the forefront. First, he had always spoken freely and bluntly, as was his custom. But in service to the Confederacy, the general should have avoided the political discourse that later afflicted his command in the West. Even though he felt that he spoke honestly and in the best interest of the service, military protocol dictated that he should not have criticized his commanding general nor questioned the administration's policies. Moreover, his comments about Davis's appointments also reflected poorly on Longstreet and influenced how the authorities in Richmond viewed the corps commander while he served in East Tennessee and experienced his own problems with internal dissent. It is ironic that Longstreet's struggle to command his own corps was strikingly similar to Bragg's difficulties with his own lieutenants during the latter's tenure with the Army of Tennessee. When Longstreet complained of a lack of support from the War Department, it is understandable why Davis failed to offer him the same treatment as he had other departmental commanders. That Bragg remained at the president's side also proved debilitating to Longstreet's authority. To his credit, however, the First Corps commander did not openly criticize Bragg during the remaining months of his service in the West, despite the latter's attempt to portray him as a malcontent during the Knoxville and East Tennessee campaigns.

Longstreet's inability to harness his anger and frustration in dealing with his lieutenants marked another weakness. Unlike Lee, who consistently employed a guarded approach in dealing with subordinates, Longstreet could be distant, even cold to those whom he felt had offended him. Although an experienced field commander with years of military service under his belt, he failed to adequately gauge his division and brigade leaders and inspire them to work in harmony. As a result he spent most of his time squabbling with them and with the War Department. To be sure, Longstreet was not the only Confederate general to have trouble with his subordinates. Other contemporaries, including Stonewall Jackson and Bragg, shared his difficulties with uncooperative lieutenants. Even his onetime mentor, Joseph E. Johnston, struggled with dissatisfied subalterns during the Atlanta campaign. In Johnston's case the criticism and political maneuvering of one of his disgruntled generals contributed to his removal from command. Yet Longstreet's stubbornness and sense of honor overrode his good judgment as his personnel problems led him to appear petty and vindictive. If Longstreet lashed out against his lieutenants, perhaps it stemmed from his need to sustain his command. His struggles to rein in his generals and his quarrel with the War Department over the appointment of commanders reduced his influence in Richmond. For this, Longstreet ultimately bears responsibility.[7]

The general's performance in the West has been used by his critics as proof of his shortcomings as a commander and a strategist. But closer examination of his service with Bragg's army reveals him to be a general who understood the war in its totality. Longstreet grasped the fact that if the Confederacy were to win, it needed to concentrate forces and strike against the North itself. Along with other influential Confederates, Longstreet realized that the War Department had neglected the vast region west of the Appalachians and that its attention needed to be diverted away from the Virginia theater. His grasp of strategy continued into the spring of 1864 when he proposed an invasion of Kentucky to draw the Federals from Johnston's front in northern Georgia. Even though Longstreet failed to take into account his plan's logistical problems, it does not detract from the fact that he recognized the situation facing the Confederacy during the last eighteen months of the war.

As a tactician Longstreet contributed to the Army of Tennessee's lone victory in the West. Despite his late arrival on the battlefield and after only a few hours of preparation, he organized his wing and arranged his units into an attack column that pierced the Federal line. He continued to lead his men for the rest of the day, making dispositions where appropriate and shifting his troops as the situation demanded. As a recent student of the campaign notes, "James Longstreet's actions at Chickamauga showed this able tactician at his best."[8]

Longstreet's service in the western theater also demonstrated his ability to effectively manage a large command. While campaigning in East Tennessee, he actively sought the procurement of food and supplies to his army, writing to the War Department for the necessary materials to campaign in that hostile region. That he knew of the suffering of his soldiers is evident in how he visited the hospitals and offered his men confiscated wares to ease their suffering. From his service in the frontier army and his experience under Lee, Longstreet recognized the importance of feeding and supplying troops to maintain morale.[9]

As far as assessing the Knoxville and East Tennessee campaigns, it is a more complex task than simply deeming them a military failure. Certainly the First Corps did not snare Ambrose Burnside nor divert troops from Johnston's front as Davis hoped during the winter of 1863–64. And the months spent in winter quarters were marked by only minor battles and skirmishes. But to lay the blame solely on Longstreet's shoulders is undeserved. Davis proposed the detachment of the First Corps to Knoxville in part to remove the last remaining dissenting element from the Army of Tennessee. Bragg had already purged his command of all other suspected detractors. Thus to the president, it was more important to sustain Bragg than to consider the possibility that the senior generals were right and that a new commander was needed for the army. To be sure, Longstreet approved of his transfer since he found it awkward to continue working with Bragg after the embarrassing round-robin conference. Yet he did not perceive the difficulties his command would experience.

Once detached from Bragg's army, the campaign faced several problems beyond Longstreet's control. First, contrary to prior intelligence reports, Longstreet's 17,000 men would not be adequate to ensure the capture of Burnside's army and the retaking of Knoxville, a heavily fortified city protected by more than one hundred guns.[10] Moreover, his force suffered from transportation difficulties and a lack of supplies as soon as the expedition got underway. For this Bragg, as departmental commander, bears some responsibility. In September 1863 he had rejected Longstreet's proposal to move around the Federal left at Chattanooga due to a lack of adequate transportation. That Bragg did not recognize the First Corps's difficulties a month later reflects poorly on his ability and suggests that personal motives overrode strategy in detaching Longstreet. Finally, for a mission that depended on alacrity, the War Department failed to consider that in order to succeed, Longstreet needed to engage Burnside in open battle. Davis's and Bragg's strategy to detach the First Corps played perfectly into the Federals' plans, for General Grant ordered Burnside to conduct a retrograde movement into the Knoxville defenses to try to draw Longstreet away from Chattanooga while he concentrated his army for a final assault against the Rebel siege lines.

While Longstreet's command remained in East Tennessee for several months without significant accomplishments, the stalemate of the campaign reflected a general state of affairs on the Union-Confederate front lines from northern Georgia to Virginia. Longstreet merely followed the directives of the War Department, which ordered his force to remain in the region and prevent a Union advance into southwestern Virginia. Despite his repeated attempts to strike at the Federals in East Tennessee, Richmond did not provide the adequate reinforcements necessary to ensure success. Longstreet may be criticized for the disastrous attack on the Knoxville defenses, but his conduct following the siege was commendable. He regained his aggressiveness and developed well-conceived plans to strike at Union forces northeast of Knoxville. If his subordinates failed to carry out their orders, that should not detract from the general's skills as a tactician.

That the Chattanooga and East Tennessee campaigns had no detrimental effect on Longstreet's reputation was reflected in how the veterans of the Army of Northern Virginia welcomed the return of the general and the First Corps in April 1864. As Col. Walter H. Taylor, Lee's adjutant, wrote to his wife: "Old Pete Longstreet is with us and all seems propitious." Longstreet and his men responded by helping repulse the Federal advance at the Battle of the Wilderness on May 5–6. Despite suffering a serious wound while arranging his troops during the battle's second day, Longstreet succeeded in relaying the particulars of his assault and his objectives to his subordinates.[11]

In time, however, the enemies he made during his service in the western theater would become instrumental members of the Southern Historical Society and ardent supporters of the Lost Cause interpretation, criticizing Longstreet's conduct during the war.[12] When he responded to his former comrades, Longstreet attacked his critics and provided several historical inaccuracies that further diminished his influence with his former troops and contributed to the creation of the myth that he had cost the Confederacy the war because of his performance at Gettysburg. Lost in the maelstrom over the Gettysburg controversy was Longstreet's performance in the western theater. And even after the defeats, retreats, desertions, and insubordination of a few lieutenants, Longstreet found the will to keep going.

FIRST CORPS, ARMY OF NORTHERN VIRGINIA

Longstreet's Corps
Lt. Gen. James Longstreet

McLaws's Division
Maj. Gen. Lafayette McLaws

KERSHAW'S BRIGADE
Brig. Gen. Joseph Kershaw
2nd South Carolina, Lt. Col. Franklin Gaillard
3rd South Carolina, Col. James D. Nance
7th South Carolina: Lt. Col. Elbert Bland,
    Maj. J. S. Hard, Capt. E. J. Goggins
8th South Carolina, Col. John W. Henagan
15th South Carolina, Col. Joseph F. Gist
3rd South Carolina Battalion, Capt. Joshua M. Townsend

HUMPHREYS'S BRIGADE
Brig. Gen. Benjamin G. Humphreys
13th Mississippi, Lt. Col. Kennon McElroy
17th Mississippi, Lt. Col. John C. Fiser
18th Mississippi, Capt. W. F. Hubbard
21st Mississippi, Lt. Col. D. N. Moody

WOFFORD'S BRIGADE
Brig. Gen. William Wofford
16th Georgia, Col. Henry P. Thomas
18th Georgia, Col. Z. S. Ruff
24th Georgia, Col. Robert McMillan
3rd Georgia Battalion Sharpshooters, Lt. Col. N. L. Hutchins
Cobb's (Georgia) Legion, Lt. Col. Luther Glenn
Phillips (Georgia) Legion, Lt. Col. E. S. Barclay

BRYAN'S BRIGADE

Brig. Gen. Goode Bryan
10th Georgia, Col. John B. Weems
50th Georgia, Col. Peter McGlashan
51st Georgia, Col. Edward Ball
53rd Georgia, James P. Simms

Hood's Division
Maj. Gen. John B. Hood

JENKINS'S BRIGADE

Brig. Gen. Micah Jenkins
1st South Carolina, Col. Franklin Kilpatrick
2nd South Carolina Rifles, Col. Thomas Thompson
5th South Carolina, Col. Asbury Coward
6th South Carolina, Col. John Bratton
Hampton Legion, Col. Martin Gary
Palmetto Sharpshooters, Col. Joseph Walker

ROBERTSON'S BRIGADE

Brig. Gen. Jerome Robertson
Col. Van H. Manning
3rd Arkansas, Col. Van H. Manning
1st Texas, Capt. R. J. Harding
4th Texas: Lt. Col. John P. Bane, Capt. R. H. Bassett
5th Texas: Maj. J. C. Rogers, Capt. J. S. Cleveland, Capt. T. T. Clay

LAW'S BRIGADE

Brig. Gen. Evander M. Law
Col. James Sheffield
4th Alabama, Col. Pinckney D. Bowles
15th Alabama, Col. W. C. Oates
44th Alabama, Col. William F. Perry
47th Alabama, Maj. James M. Campbell
48th Alabama, Lt. Col. William M. Hardwick

ANDERSON'S BRIGADE

Brig. Gen. George T. Anderson
7th Georgia, Col. W. W. White
8th Georgia, Col. John R. Towers
9th Georgia, Col. Benjamin Beck
11th Georgia, Col. F. H. Little
59th Georgia, Col. Jack Brown

BENNING'S BRIGADE

Brig. Gen. Henry L. Benning

2nd Georgia: Lt. Col. William S. Shepherd, Maj. W. W. Charlton

15th Georgia: Col. Dudley M. Dubose, Maj. P. J. Shannon

17th Georgia, Lt. Col. Charles W. Matthews

20th Georgia, Col. J. D. Waddell

ARTILLERY BATTALION

Lt. Col. Edward Porter Alexander

Fickling's (South Carolina) Battery, Capt. William Fickling

Jordan's (Virginia) Battery, Capt. Tyler Jordan

Moody's (Louisiana) Battery, Capt. George Moody

Parker's (Virginia) Battery, Capt. William Parker

Taylor's (Virginia) Battery, Capt. Osmond B. Taylor

Woolfolk's (Virginia) Battery, Capt. Pichegru Woolfolk

NOTES

Abbreviations

B&L   Clarence C. Buel and Robert U. Johnson, eds., *Battles and Leaders of the Civil War*, 4 vols. (New York: 1884–88; reprint, Edison, N.J.: Castle, 1994).

CAH   Center for American History, University of Texas, Austin

DU   Rare Book, Manuscript, and Special Collections Library, Duke University, Durham, N.C.

GL   Gilder Lehrman Collection, New York Historical Society, New York

HL   Department of Manuscripts, Huntington Library, San Marino, Calif.

HU   Frederick M. Dearborn Collection, Houghton Library, Harvard University, Cambridge, Mass.

JD   Jefferson Davis, *Jefferson Davis, Constitutionalist: His Letters, Papers, and Speeches*, 10 vols., ed. Dunbar Rowland (Jackson: Mississippi Department of Archives and History, 1923).

LC   Manuscripts Division, Library of Congress, Washington, D.C.

LSU   Special Collections, Hill Memorial Library, Louisiana State University, Baton Rouge

LV   Library of Virginia, Richmond

MC   Eleanor S. Brockenbrough Library, Museum of the Confederacy, Richmond, Va.

NA   Confederate Records Division, National Archives, Washington, D.C.

NC   Division of Archives and History, North Carolina State Department of Cultural Resources, Raleigh

NYPL   Manuscripts and Archives Division, New York Public Library

OR   *The War of the Rebellion: A Compilation of the Official Records of Union and Confederate Armies*, 128 vols. (Washington, D.C.: Government Printing Office, 1880–91).

SCDAH   South Carolina Department of Archives and History, Columbia

SCL   South Caroliniana Library, University of South Carolina, Columbia

SCRC   Harold B. Simpson Confederate Research Center, Hill College, Hillsboro, Tex.

SHC   Southern Historical Collection, University of North Carolina, Chapel Hill

TU   Tulane University, Department of Manuscripts, New Orleans

VHS   Virginia Historical Society, Richmond

WR   Western Reserve Historical Society, Cleveland, Ohio

Preface

1. Piston, *Lee's Tarnished Lieutenant*, 174–85.
2. Jeffry D. Wert, "James Longstreet and the Lost Cause," in Gary Gallagher, ed., *The Myth of the Lost Cause and Civil War History* (Bloomington: University of Indiana Press, 2000), 127–43.
3. Eckenrode and Conrad, *James Longstreet*, 168–213, 214–68; Sanger and Hay, *James Longstreet*, 156–99, 200–255; W. Thomas, *"Pete" Longstreet*, 117–70, 171–211, 297–315. For discussions on Gettysburg, see the bibliographic essay in Gallagher, *Third Day at Gettysburg*, 203–206; and Carol Reardon, *Pickett's Charge in History and Memory* (Chapel Hill: University of North Carolina Press), 205–13.
4. Wert, *General James Longstreet*, 15, 242–97, 298–377.

Chapter 1

1. J. Longstreet, *Manassas to Appomattox*, 437. See also Freeman, *R. E. Lee*, 3:167; Freeman, *Lee's Lieutenants*, 3:224; and Wert, *General James Longstreet*, 303.
2. Wert, *General James Longstreet*, 301; James Longstreet to Louis T. Wigfall, May 13, 1863, Wigfall Papers, LC.
3. Wert, *General James Longstreet*, 22.
4. J. Longstreet, *Manassas to Appomattox*, 15. See also Wert, *General James Longstreet*, 23–32; Piston, "Lee's Tarnished Lieutenant" (PhD diss.), 11–15; and Morrison, *"Best School in the World,"* 88–89. For criticism of Longstreet's academic background, see the works of Robert K. Krick, Judith Lee Hallock, H. J. Eckenrode, Bryan Conrad, and Steven E. Woodworth.
5. Wert, *General James Longstreet*, 33–44; Piston, *Lee's Tarnished Lieutenant*, 5–6. For background, see Eisenhower, *So Far from God;* and Winders, *Mr. Polk's Army.*
6. Eisenhower, *So Far from God*, 324–25; Wert, *General James Longstreet*, 43–44.
7. H. D. Longstreet, *Lee and Longstreet at High Tide*, 214; Eisenhower, *So Far from God*, 325–26; Wert, *General James Longstreet*, 44.
8. James Longstreet to Lafayette McLaws, Nov. 28, 1863, McLaws Papers, DU.
9. Wert, *General James Longstreet*, 45–46; Eisenhower, *So Far from God*, 328–42. These events are also chronicled in Johnson, *Winfield Scott*, 204–207.
10. Symonds, *Joseph E. Johnston*, 67–71.
11. Wert, *General James Longstreet*, 34–35; J. Longstreet, *Manassas to Appomattox*, 18; William Garrett Piston, "Petticoats, Promotions, and Military Assignments: Favoritism and the Antebellum Career of James Longstreet," in DiNardo and Nofi, *James Longstreet*, 53–70.
12. Piston, "Lee's Tarnished Lieutenant," 109–12; Wert, *General James Longstreet*, 52; James Longstreet to A. B. Moore, Feb. 15, 1861, *OR*, ser. 4, 1:182 (all *OR* references are to series 1 unless otherwise indicated; whenever a volume consists of two or more parts, the part number will follow the volume number in parentheses).
13. William D. Longstreet to Jefferson Davis, Feb. 22, 1861, noted in Crist and

Dix, *Papers of Jefferson Davis,* 7:58; J. L. M. Curry to Leroy P. Walker, June 25, 1861, *OR,* 1:400. For a description of Davis's involvement in the minutiae of commissions, see W. C. Davis, *Jefferson Davis,* 339-44; and Cooper, *Jefferson Davis, American,* 332-33, 424-29, 520-21.

14. Wert, *General James Longstreet,* 53; Piston, *Lee's Tarnished Lieutenant,* 11-12; Weigley, *A Great Civil War,* 1-28.

15. Wert, *General James Longstreet,* 52-53; Piston, "Lee's Tarnished Lieutenant," 111; Thomas J. Goree to Sarah W. K. Goree, June 23, 1861, in Cutrer, *Longstreet's Aide,* 19.

16. J. Longstreet, *Manassas to Appomattox,* 30. For additional detail on Longstreet's commission and resignation, see Wert, *General James Longstreet,* 54.

17. J. L. M Curry to L. P. Walker, June 25, 1861, *OR,* ser. 4, 1:400; Thomas J. Goree to Sarah W. K. Goree, June 23, 1861, in Cutrer, *Longstreet's Aide,* 19; Piston, "Lee's Tarnished Lieutenant," 125.

18. See Coffman, *The Old Army,* 48-49, 60-61; and Skelton, *American Profession of Arms,* 181-220, 282-304.

19. McWhiney and Jamieson, *Attack and Die,* 153-60; Piston, *Lee's Tarnished Lieutenant,* 5-7.

20. Piston, "Lee's Tarnished Lieutenant," 124-26; Wert, *General James Longstreet,* 58-67.

21. Wert, *General James Longstreet,* 67-77. For detailed studies of the campaign, see W. C. Davis, *Battle at Bull Run;* and Rafuse, *A Single Grand Victory.*

22. DiNardo, "Southern by the Grace of God," 1011-32; Wert, *General James Longstreet,* 67-71; Piston, "Lee's Tarnished Lieutenant," 126.

23. W. C. Davis, *Jefferson Davis,* 359-61; Symonds, *Joseph E. Johnston,* 126-28; Woodworth, *Davis and Lee at War,* 53-58; McMurry, "Enemy at Richmond," 5-31; Richard M. McMurry, "Joseph E. Johnston in Virginia," in Woodworth, *Leadership and Command,* 1-13; Newton, *Joseph E. Johnston,* 5-9; Cooper, *Jefferson Davis, American,* 363-64.

24. Wert, *General James Longstreet,* 80-90; Piston, *Lee's Tarnished Lieutenant,* 16; W. C. Davis, *Jefferson Davis,* 365; Woodworth, *Davis and Lee at War,* 62-67; *OR,* 5:885-86; Thomas J. Goree to Sarah W. K. Goree, Sept. 28, 1861, in Cutrer, *Longstreet's Aide,* 46.

25. Woodworth, *Davis and Lee at War,* 82; Cate, *Lucius Q. C. Lamar,* 85; Woodworth, *Davis and Lee at War,* 82. See also Piston, "Lee's Tarnished Lieutenant," 142-43.

26. King, *Louis T. Wigfall,* 133-35; Symonds, *Joseph E. Johnston,* 178-79; W. C. Davis, *Jefferson Davis,* 445-46.

27. J. Longstreet, *Manassas to Appomattox,* 65-66; Wert, *General James Longstreet,* 102-110; *OR,* 12(3):832; Newton, *Joseph E. Johnston,* 48-58; Woodworth, *Davis and Lee at War,* 113-17.

28. Alexander, *Fighting for the Confederacy,* 81; Sears, *To the Gates of Richmond,* 120-24; Woodworth, *Davis and Lee at War,* 140-43; Wert, *General James Longstreet,* 121-25; Symonds, *Joseph E. Johnston,* 165-74.

29. *OR,* 11(1):933-35, 942, 11(3):580, 939-40; Wert, *General James Longstreet,*

121-25; G. W. Smith, *Battle of Seven Pines*, 65; Symonds, *Joseph E. Johnston*, 172-75; Sears, *To the Gates of Richmond*, 120-24.

30. J. E. Johnston to G. W. Smith, June 28, 1862, in Gustavus W. Smith, "Two Days of Battle at Seven Pines," in *B&L*, 2:243; *OR*, 11(1):936, 939; Symonds, *Joseph E. Johnston*, 169-70, 173-74. See also Freeman, *Lee's Lieutenants*, 1:256-63; J. Longstreet, *Manassas to Appomattox*, 92; J. E. Johnston, *Narrative of Military Operations*, 133; and Eckenrode and Conrad, *James Longstreet*, 53-55.

31. Robert K. Krick, "'If Longstreet . . . Says So, It Is Most Likely Not True': James Longstreet and the Second Day at Gettysburg," in Krick, *The Smoothbore Volley*, 63-67; Hallock, *Longstreet in the West*, 36-37, 75; DiNardo and Nofi, *James Longstreet*, 36; A. Cash Koeniger, "Prejudices and Partialities: The Garnett Controversy Revisited," in *The Shenandoah Valley Campaign of 1862*, ed. Gary Gallagher (Chapel Hill: University of North Carolina Press, 2003), 219-33; Stacy D. Allen, "If He Had Less Rank: Lewis Wallace," in Woodworth, *Grant's Lieutenants*, 63-89.

32. E. Thomas, *Robert E. Lee*, 225; Freeman, *Lee's Lieutenants*, 1:262-63; Carol Reardon, "From 'King of Spades' to 'First Captain of the Confederacy': R. E. Lee's First Six Weeks with the Army of Northern Virginia," in Gallagher, *Lee the Soldier*, 312-13; Connelly, *Marble Man*, 16-17.

33. *OR*, 11(2):492; J. Longstreet, *Manassas to Appomattox*, 112-13; Piston, *Lee's Tarnished Lieutenant*, 20; Wert, *General James Longstreet*, 133-52.

34. Longstreet's role is detailed in Wert, *General James Longstreet*, 153-79; James Longstreet, "Our March against Pope," in *B&L*, 2:514-15, 522; and J. Longstreet, *Manassas to Appomattox*, 159.

35. Woodworth, *Davis and Lee at War*, 186-87; Sears, *Landscape Turned Red*. Longstreet's role is covered in J. Longstreet, *Manassas to Appomattox*, 263; James Longstreet, "Invasion of Maryland," in *B&L*, 2:672; and Wert, *General James Longstreet*, 181.

36. Owen, *In Camp and Battle with the Washington Artillery*, 157. Similar versions of this incident appear in Sorrel, *Recollections*, 116; J. Longstreet, *Manassas to Appomattox*, 262; and Wert, *General James Longstreet*, 200.

37. James Longstreet to Joseph E. Johnston, Oct. 6, 1862, J. Longstreet Papers, DU.

38. Piston, *Lee's Tarnished Lieutenant*, 26-27; Wert, *General James Longstreet*, 206-207; DiNardo and Nofi, *James Longstreet*, 32.

39. James Longstreet to Louis T. Wigfall, Nov. 7, 1862, Wigfall Papers, LC; Piston, "Petticoats, Promotions, and Military Assignments," 53-70; Connelly and Jones, *Politics of Command*, 49-86. According to Wigfall's biographer, the Texan's feud with Davis was not public knowledge as late as the summer of 1863. King, *Louis T. Wigfall*, 184.

40. "A Quarrel and Its Ending: Why Jefferson Davis and General Longstreet Fell Out," *New York Times*, June 4, 1893; W. C. Davis, *Jefferson Davis*, 270, 374-78; Woodworth, *Jefferson Davis and His Generals*, 46-50.

41. Piston, "Lee's Tarnished Lieutenant," 185; W. C. Davis, *Union that Shaped the Confederacy*.

42. Longstreet's role in the campaign is analyzed in Wert, *General James Longstreet*, 215–23. For general studies of Fredericksburg, see Sutherland, *Fredericksburg and Chancellorsville;* and Rable, *Fredericksburg! Fredericksburg!*

43. Woodworth, *Jefferson Davis and His Generals*, 185–88; Symonds, *Joseph E. Johnston*, 187–88; Glatthaar, *Partners in Command*, 95–133.

44. James Seddon to Louis T. Wigfall, n.d., in Wright, *A Southern Girl in '61*, 104. See also Louis T. Wigfall to Joseph E. Johnston, Feb. 27, 1863, Wigfall Family Papers, CAH; Symonds, *Joseph E. Johnston*, 221–25; and Connelly and Jones, *Politics of Command*, 49, 53, 65, 69, 70.

45. James Longstreet to Louis T. Wigfall, Feb. 4, 1863, Wigfall Papers, LC; Freeman, *Lee's Lieutenants*, 3:40.

46. Woodworth, *Jefferson Davis and His Generals*, 212. As for historians who argue that Longstreet sought to obtain an independent command, see Eckenrode and Conrad, *James Longstreet*, 215–20; Hallock, *Longstreet in the West;* Woodworth, *Davis and Lee at War*, 218–19, 224; Freeman, *Lee's Lieutenants*, 3:222; and Downey, *Storming of the Gateway*, 21. For those who cite Longstreet's "restless ambition" and the fact that he was overshadowed by Lee and Jackson as reasons he sought a transfer west, see Wert, *General James Longstreet*, 206–207; Piston, *Lee's Tarnished Lieutenant*, 40–41; Woodworth, *Davis and Lee at War*, 218; Sanger and Hay, *James Longstreet*, 196–97; and Eckenrode and Conrad, *James Longstreet*, 160–61, 164, 219. For a study of politics in the Union high command, see Goss, *The War within the Union High Command*, xvi–xvii, 109–22, 133–35, 192–211. The concept of ambition and politics in the Confederate Trans-Mississippi is analyzed in Prushankin, *Crisis in Confederate Command*, 2–3, 77–78, 194–95. Other generals, including Ulysses S. Grant, William T. Sherman, P. G. T. Beauregard, and John Bell Hood, employed the assistance of politically connected friends during the war. See B. D. Simpson, *Ulysses S. Grant*, 78–80, 246–47, 254–55; Marszalek, *Sherman*, 147–48, 182, 185–86, 374; Williams, *P. G. T. Beauregard*, 73–74, 96–97, 172–73; and McMurry, *John Bell Hood*, 118–21.

47. Wills, *War Hits Home*, 108–10, 111–13; Cormier, *Siege of Suffolk*, 12–19; *OR*, 18:1034; Wert, *General James Longstreet*, 232–36, 240.

48. J. Longstreet, *Manassas to Appomattox*, 326–27, 331; Wert, *General James Longstreet*, 239–41; Piston, *Lee's Tarnished Lieutenant*, 42–43; Connelly and Jones, *Politics of Command*, 80–87, 122–23, 130–33.

49. See James Longstreet, "The Mistakes of Gettysburg," and "Lee in Pennsylvania," in McClure, *Annals of the War*, 619–34, 416–17; and J. Longstreet, *Manassas to Appomattox*, 331.

50. Longstreet to Wigfall, May 13, 1863.

51. Wert, *General James Longstreet*, 245–46.

52. Sears, *Gettysburg;* Coddington, *Gettysburg Campaign;* Woodworth, *Davis and Lee at War*, 230–34.

53. R. E. Lee to Jefferson Davis, July 31, 1863, in Freeman, *Lee's Dispatches*, 110–12; *OR*, 29(2):640–41; H. D. Longstreet, *Lee and Longstreet at High Tide*, 63–65; James Longstreet to Louis T. Wigfall, Aug. 2, Aug. 18, 1863, Wigfall Papers, LC; J. Longstreet, *Manassas to Appomattox*, 434.

54. R. E. Lee to James Longstreet, Aug. 31, 1863, in Dowdey and Manarin, *Wartime Papers of R. E. Lee,* 594–96; E. Thomas, *Robert E. Lee,* 309–10.

55. Wert, *General James Longstreet,* 301.

56. *OR,* 29(2):699.

57. Woodworth, *Davis and Lee at War,* 255–56.

58. Ibid., 255–57; *OR,* 29(2):700–701, 702, 706, 711–12; Wert, *General James Longstreet,* 302–303; J. Longstreet, *Manassas to Appomattox,* 436.

59. Wert, *General James Longstreet,* 301. See also Longstreet to Wigfall, May 13, 1863.

60. Hallock, *Braxton Bragg,* 26, 36–37, 40–41.

Chapter 2

1. For detailed analysis of these movements, see Cozzens, *This Terrible Sound,* 33, 34, 48, 57–59; Woodworth, *Six Armies in Tennessee,* 19–46; and Connelly, *Autumn of Glory,* 172–73.

2. *OR,* 29(2):726; Pickenpaugh, *Rescue by Rail,* 28–29; Wert, *General James Longstreet,* 303. For details on Longstreet's travels via his circuitous route, see W. G. Robertson, "Rails to the River of Death," 55.

3. Woodworth, *While God Is Marching On,* 214–15, 273; Laine and Penny, *Law's Alabama Brigade,* 137; Lee, *Recollections and Letters,* 105–106. Lee's complete proclamation appears in Woodworth, *While God Is Marching On,* 273.

4. Wilkinson and Woodworth, *Scythe of Fire,* 265–66; Faust, "Christian Soldiers," 72; Woodworth, *While God Is Marching On,* chap. 11.

5. *OR,* 29(2):746; W. H. Taylor, *General Lee,* 223. Hood was still recovering from an arm wound suffered at Gettysburg, but he decided to rejoin the First Corps nonetheless. See Hood, *Advance and Retreat,* 61.

6. Sorrel, *Recollections,* 189; Alexander, *Fighting for the Confederacy,* 286; Pickenpaugh, *Rescue by Rail,* 28–29.

7. Pickenpaugh, *Rescue by Rail,* 34; Black, *Railroads of the Confederacy,* 184–91; Coward, *The South Carolinians,* 83; Laine and Penny, *Law's Alabama Brigade,* 141; Wert, *General James Longstreet,* 305. The quote is also found in Pickenpaugh, *Rescue by Rail,* 35.

8. Dickert, *Kershaw's Brigade,* 263; Polley, *Hood's Texas Brigade,* 199.

9. Pickenpaugh, *Rescue by Rail,* 35; Rufus K. Felder to Dear Mother, Oct. 12, 1863, Rufus K. Felder Papers, 5th Texas Infantry File, SCRC; Mixson, *Reminiscences of a Private,* 42–44; Dawson, *Reminiscences,* 100, 106–107; Sorrel, *Recollections,* 191; Oates, *War between the Union and the Confederacy,* 253.

10. Wert, *General James Longstreet,* 305; Alexander, *Fighting for the Confederacy,* 286; Laine and Penny, *Law's Alabama Brigade,* 142; Pickenpaugh, *Rescue by Rail,* 36; Lafayette McLaws to Dear Wife, Sept. 19, 1863, McLaws Papers, SHC.

11. J. Longstreet, *Manassas to Appomattox,* 436; *OR,* 21(2):713–14; James Longstreet to Louis T. Wigfall, Sept. 12, 1863, Wigfall Papers, LC.

12. Connelly and Jones, *Politics of Command,* chap. 3; King, *Louis T. Wigfall,* 166. See also Wert, *General James Longstreet,* 304–305.

13. *OR*, 27(2):1052; Yates, "Governor Vance and the Peace Movement," 1–25; Freeman, *Lee's Lieutenants*, 3:219.

14. *OR*, 51(2):770; G. B. McKinney, *Zeb Vance*, 185–89; *Raleigh Weekly Standard*, Oct. 2, 1863. See also Tucker, *Zeb Vance*, 352–53.

15. *OR*, 29(2):710, 51(2):763–65.

16. *Raleigh Weekly Standard*, Oct. 2, 1863; *OR*, 51(2):765, 768; G. B. McKinney, *Zeb Vance*, 187.

17. *OR*, 51(2):770.

18. Ibid., 778; Dameron, *Benning's Brigade*, 2:87–88; Pickenpaugh, *Rescue by Rail*, 40–41.

19. Sorrel, *Recollections*, 221; Power, *Lee's Miserables*, 11.

20. Pickenpaugh, *Rescue by Rail*, 42; Laine and Penny, *Law's Alabama Brigade*, 142; Cozzens, *This Terrible Sound*, 110–11, 119–20. Hood's Division included Robertson's Texas Brigade (1,300 strong), Law's Alabama Brigade (2,000 strong), and Benning's Georgia Brigade (1,200 strong).

21. *OR*, 30(2):287–88; Sorrel, *Recollections*, 192–93; Wert, *General James Longstreet*, 306.

22. Sorrel, *Recollections*, 192–93; J. Longstreet, *Manassas to Appomattox*, 438.

23. Connelly, *Autumn of Glory*, 193; Cozzens, *This Terrible Sound*, 89–92, 120; Hallock, *Braxton Bragg*, 65; *OR*, 30(4):657.

24. *OR*, 30(2):287; McMurry, *John Bell Hood*, 76–77.

25. Woodworth, *Six Armies in Tennessee*, 103; Wert, *General James Longstreet*, 308.

26. J. Longstreet, *Manassas to Appomattox*, 439; Sorrel, *Recollections*, 193.

27. *OR*, 30(2):33, 363; Woodworth, *Six Armies in Tennessee*, 102–103; Connelly, *Autumn of Glory*, 208–209; Cozzens, *This Terrible Sound*, 316; J. Longstreet, *Manassas to Appomattox*, 439.

28. J. Longstreet, *Manassas to Appomattox*, 440; James R. Furqueron, "The Bull of the Woods: James Longstreet and the Confederate Left at Chickamauga," in DiNardo and Nofi, *James Longstreet*, 113–14.

29. Elliott, *Soldier of Tennessee*, 130; J. Longstreet, *Manassas to Appomattox*, 440–41; Furqueron, "Bull of the Woods," 113–14; Cozzens, *This Terrible Sound*, 316.

30. Hood, *Advance and Retreat*, 63; Laine and Penny, *Law's Alabama Brigade*, 158; Woodworth, *Six Armies in Tennessee*, 105–106, 112; James Longstreet to Edward Porter Alexander, June 17, 1869, Alexander Papers, SHC; Cozzens, *This Terrible Sound*, 316.

31. Longstreet to Alexander, June 17, 1869.

32. Stocker, *From Huntsville to Appomattox*, 133; Coward, *The South Carolinians*, 84.

33. *OR*, 30(2):289–90, 357–59; J. Longstreet, *Manassas to Appomattox*, 440.

34. Bridges, *Lee's Maverick General*, 209. For further details on the Polk-Hill episode, see Cozzens, *This Terrible Sound*, 302–303, 305–309; Woodworth, *Six Armies in Tennessee*, 103–104; Woodworth, *Jefferson Davis and His Generals*, 235–36; Connelly, *Autumn of Glory*, 211–16; and Parks, *General Leonidas Polk*, 333–35.

35. Cozzens, *This Terrible Sound,* 310; Woodworth, *Six Armies in Tennessee,* 106, 107–108; Hallock, *Braxton Bragg,* 73–74; Tucker, *Chickamauga,* 228–33.

36. *OR,* 30(2):288, 363–64. Bragg biographer Judith Lee Hallock argues that even had Polk's attack gone forward at the designated hour, Longstreet's "delays" would have prevented it from succeeding. *Braxton Bragg,* 74.

37. *OR,* 30(2):303; Cozzens, *This Terrible Sound,* 369.

38. For details of the misunderstanding within the Union high command, see Cozzens, *This Terrible Sound,* 362–63, 365, 367; Woodworth, *Six Armies in Tennessee,* 114–16; and Tucker, *Chickamauga,* 254–59.

39. *OR,* 30(2):303, 457.

40. Ibid, 495; Cozzens, *This Terrible Sound,* 371; Woodworth, *Six Armies in Tennessee,* 120. Woodworth suggests that a wheel to the left would not have been a good idea because "there were no longer all that many of the enemy on the left to be rolled" and "would now expose Longstreet's wing to attack from the flank and rear by the unbroken Union formations to the north."

41. *OR,* 30(2):342; Tucker, *Chickamauga,* 288–89; Cozzens, *This Terrible Sound,* 394–96.

42. *OR,* 30(2):288; Furqueron, "Bull of the Woods," 123; Wert, *General James Longstreet,* 313.

43. Cozzens, *This Terrible Sound,* 374; J. Longstreet, *Manassas to Appomattox,* 448; Sorrel, *Recollections,* 203–204; Furqueron, "Bull of the Woods," 124; *OR,* 30(2):518.

44. *OR,* 30(2):458; Skoch and Perkins, *Lone Star Confederate,* 98; Polley, *Hood's Texas Brigade,* 209; Hood, *Advance and Retreat,* 63–64; *OR,* 30(2):288.

45. *OR,* 30(2):288, 503; Benjamin Humphreys, "A History of the Sunflower Guards," Claiborne Papers, SHC.

46. *OR,* 30(2):504, 510.

47. J. Longstreet, *Manassas to Appomattox,* 449–50; Lamers, *Edge of Glory,* 354–55.

48. *OR,* 30(2):357; J. Longstreet, *Manassas to Appomattox,* 450–51; Owen, *In Camp and Battle with the Washington Artillery,* 281–82.

49. Cozzens, *This Terrible Sound,* 454–55; Woodworth, *Six Armies in Tennessee,* 122; Wert, *General James Longstreet,* 316.

50. J. Longstreet, *Manassas to Appomattox,* 452. Longstreet's account, written more than forty years after the battle, must be analyzed for accuracy. In his official report he claims that Bragg informed him that the right wing's troops "had been beaten back so badly that they could be of no service to me." *OR,* 30(2):289.

51. Wert, *General James Longstreet,* 317; Woodworth, *Six Armies in Tennessee,* 126–27; J. Longstreet, *Manassas to Appomattox,* 452.

52. *OR,* 30(2):289, 305; Furqueron, "Bull of the Woods," 140–47. Hindman had been wounded at noon but continued to lead his troops until the evening, when he relinquished command to Brig. Gen. Patton Anderson.

53. *OR,* 30(2):289, 359; Elliott, *Soldier of Tennessee,* 133; Wert, *General James Longstreet,* 317–18; Woodworth, *Six Armies in Tennessee,* 127–28; Cozzens, *This Terrible Sound,* 502–509.

54. Sorrel, *Recollections,* 201; Elliott, *Soldier of Tennessee,* 134; Cozzens, *This Terrible Sound,* 496-97.

55. Piston, *Lee's Tarnished Lieutenant,* 71; Wert, *General James Longstreet,* 319-21 (Breckinridge quote, 320); *OR,* 30(2):290; Chesnut, *Diary from Dixie,* 307.

56. J. Longstreet, *Manassas to Appomattox,* 455-56; James Longstreet to Braxton Bragg, Sept. 20, 1863 (6:15 P.M.), and James Longstreet to Braxton Bragg, Sept. 21, 1863 (6:40 A.M.), Bragg Papers, WR; *OR,* 30(4):682; Connelly, *Autumn of Glory,* 229-30; Cozzens, *This Terrible Sound,* 513. In a postwar letter to D. H. Hill, Longstreet explained that he did not notify Bragg of the victory on the Confederate left because he felt that the loud cheers emanating from the Rebel soldiers should have sufficed. James Longstreet to D. H. Hill, July [?], 1884, in Daniel Harvey Hill, "Chickamauga—The Great Battle of the West," in *B&L,* 3:659.

57. Liddell, *Liddell's Record,* 147; Braxton Bragg to Samuel Cooper, Sept. 21, 1863, Bragg Papers, DU.

58. *OR,* 30(2):37, 289, 30(4):705; Braxton Bragg to James Seddon (copy for the president), Sept. 24, 1863, Bragg Papers, DU. See also Sorrel, *Recollections,* 196-97. Bragg's official report, written three months after the battle and following a bitter dispute with Longstreet, must be analyzed carefully. In a telegram to the secretary of war, Bragg states that the army's movements remained "much retarded by limited field transportation & the breaks on the road."

59. Connelly, *Autumn of Glory,* 230-31; Hallock, *Braxton Bragg,* 84-85; Woodworth, *Jefferson Davis and His Generals,* 238. For analysis of the senior officers' criticisms of Bragg, see Parks, *General Leonidas Polk,* 341; Bridges, *Lee's Maverick General,* 226-27; Symonds, *Stonewall of the West,* 152-53; Hill, "Chickamauga," 662; and J. Longstreet, *Manassas to Appomattox,* 464. "The corps was ready to march or fight at dawn in the morning, with thinned rank, it is true, but with buoyant and exultant spirits," Hill recalled. See *OR,* 30(2):45. Found in General Polk's possession after his death in July 1864, Hill's report after Chickamauga was forwarded to the War Department in August 1864.

60. McLaws, "After Chickamauga," 50; Dawson, *Reminiscences,* 100-101.

61. James Longstreet to Louis T. Wigfall, Sept. 12, 1863, Wigfall Papers, LC; Sorrel, *Recollections,* 193; Connelly, *Autumn of Glory,* 230.

62. Connelly, *Autumn of Glory,* 224, 226-28; Eckenrode and Conrad, *James Longstreet,* 234-35; Woodworth, *Six Armies in Tennessee,* 122, 126-27; Cozzens, *This Terrible Sound,* 455.

Chapter 3

1. Woodworth, *Six Armies in Tennessee,* 132, 135-36.

2. *OR,* 30(2):23; Hallock, *Braxton Bragg,* 82-85; Woodworth, *Six Armies in Tennessee,* 132-35; Wert, *General James Longstreet,* 319.

3. Connelly, *Autumn of Glory,* 231-33; *OR,* 30(2):53; Wert, *General James Longstreet,* 319 (Forrest quote); Connelly, *Autumn of Glory,* 230-34. For Forrest's notes to Polk on the Federal retreat from Chattanooga, see Nathan Bedford Forrest to Braxton Bragg, Sept. 21, 1863, Polk Papers, LC. Thomas L. Connelly is critical of Bragg's

failure to implement a new strategy, describing the Army of Tennessee's high command as "paralyzed."

4. *OR*, 30(2):54; Cozzens, *This Terrible Sound*, 529. Bragg's letter to Davis quoted in Bridges, *Lee's Maverick General*, 227-28.

5. *OR*, 30(2):47, 55-56; Parks, *General Leonidas Polk*, 334-35; Bridges, *Lee's Maverick General*, 229-30; Chesnut, *Diary from Dixie*, 307.

6. McWhiney, *Braxton Bragg*, 252-60; Hay, "Bragg and the Southern Confederacy," 279; Woodworth, *Jefferson Davis and His Generals*, 106-107; Sword, *Mountains Touched with Fire*, 20.

7. McWhiney, *Braxton Bragg*, 1, 23-24, 52, 89, 90, 118, 141, 154, 178, 213-24; *OR*, 7:258, 10(2):371.

8. McWhiney, *Braxton Bragg*, 240.

9. McDonough, *War in Kentucky*, 26; McWhiney, *Braxton Bragg*, 154, 265.

10. For detailed information on Bragg's 1862 invasion of Kentucky, see Hess, *Banners to the Breeze*, 20-24, 28-29, 30-31; McDonough, *War in Kentucky*, chaps. 1-2; McWhiney, *Braxton Bragg*, 281-82; and Woodworth, *Jefferson Davis and His Generals*, 130-31.

11. *OR*, 16(2):1109-1112, 1119-22. For details on the command responsibilities during the Kentucky campaign, see McWhiney, *Braxton Bragg*, 320.

12. McDonough, *War in Kentucky*, 310-14; Hess, *Banners to the Breeze*, 113-14; Woodworth, *Jefferson Davis and His Generals*, 162; Steven E. Woodworth, "Davis, Polk, and the End of Kentucky Neutrality," in Woodworth, *No Band of Brothers*, 12-18.

13. Steven E. Woodworth, "Soldier with a Blunted Sword: Braxton Bragg and His Lieutenants in the Chickamauga Campaign," in ibid., 70-72.

14. Symonds, *Joseph E. Johnston*, 187-94, 195; Woodworth, *Jefferson Davis and His Generals*, 173-74, 176-80; W. C. Davis, *Jefferson Davis*, 476, 491; Glatthaar, *Partners in Command*, 120-22.

15. See McWhiney, *Braxton Bragg*, 374-75; W. C. Davis, *Breckinridge*, 354.

16. *OR*, 20(1):699, 701; McWhiney, *Braxton Bragg*, 375-78; Cozzens, *No Better Place to Die*, 209-213. What Bragg intended to accomplish with his letter is unknown. Perhaps he sought sympathy or maybe he wanted to identify his detractors, whom he believed numbered only a few. See Cozzens, *No Better Place to Die*, 209.

17. *OR*, 23(2): 613-14. Although he declared his confidence in Bragg, Davis maintained that if the general lacked the support of his men, Johnston could assume control of the army. In reality Davis doubted Bragg's ability after the losses in Kentucky and Murfreesboro, and he considered appointing Lt. Gen. James Longstreet in his place, an idea the president ultimately rejected because he did not want to "rob Lee of one of his chief lieutenants and thereby cripple his only successful army." W. C. Davis, *Jefferson Davis*, 492-93.

18. Joseph E. Johnston to Louis T. Wigfall, Mar. 4, 1863, Wigfall Papers, LC; Symonds, *Joseph E. Johnston*, 198-201; Braxton Bragg to William Whann Mackall, Feb. 14, 1863, in Mackall, *A Son's Recollections*, 195; *OR*, 23(2):624; Woodworth, *Jefferson Davis and His Generals*, 198.

19. Braxton Bragg to Jefferson Davis, May 22, 1863, Bragg Papers, DU. For de-

tails on the Tullahoma campaign, see Steven E. Woodworth, "Braxton Bragg and the Tullahoma Campaign," in Woodworth, *Art of Command,* 157–78.

20. Hallock, *Braxton Bragg,* 26, 36–37, 40–41; Woodworth, "Soldier with a Blunted Sword," 71–80.

21. For further study of the grievances of each general toward Bragg, see Neal and Kremm, *Lion of the South,* 107–108, 164–66; Stickles, *Simon Bolivar Buckner,* 224–25; Connelly and Jones, *Politics of Command,* 68–70; and *OR,* 23(2):962.

22. Woodworth, "Soldier with a Blunted Sword," 70–80; Cozzens, *This Terrible Sound,* 57; Connelly, *Autumn of Glory,* 172–73; Woodworth, *Jefferson Davis and His Generals,* 228–38.

23. Cozzens, *This Terrible Sound,* 531; Hallock, *Braxton Bragg,* 89–91; Woodworth, *Jefferson Davis and His Generals,* 238–39; Bridges, *Lee's Maverick General,* 234.

24. *OR,* 30(2):67; John Euclid Magee Diary, Sept. 26, 1863, DU; J. Longstreet, *Manassas to Appomattox,* 464; Parks, *General Leonidas Polk,* 342.

25. *OR,* 30(4):705–706, 52(2):549.

26. Wert, *General James Longstreet,* 326; *OR,* 30(4):708; Parks, *General Leonidas Polk,* 343; Bridges, *Lee's Maverick General,* 234. Bridges argues that Hill's desire to oust Bragg was not motivated by his desire to see command of the Army of Tennessee go to Longstreet: "In all likelihood his [Hill's] preference for Bragg's replacement was his former commander, Johnston."

27. See Connelly, *Autumn of Glory,* 237–38; Woodworth, *Jefferson Davis and His Generals,* 239; Hallock, *Braxton Bragg,* passim; Cozzens, *This Terrible Sound,* 531; Connelly and Jones, *Politics of Command,* 69; Freeman, *R. E. Lee,* 3:167; and Freeman, *Lee's Lieutenants,* 3:221–22.

28. McLaws, "After Chickamauga," 59.

29. W. W. Mackall to Wife, Oct. 10, 1863, in Mackall, *A Son's Recollections,* 183; *OR,* 30(4):742.

30. *OR,* 30(2):56, 57; James Longstreet to John C. Brown, Apr. 14, 1888, J. Longstreet Papers, DU; Cozzens, *This Terrible Sound,* 529–32; Wert, *General James Longstreet,* 326–27. See also Woodworth, *Jefferson Davis and His Generals,* 238.

31. Generals to Jefferson Davis, Oct. 4, 1863, Daniel Harvey Hill Papers, LV; *OR,* 30(2):65–66; Cozzens, *This Terrible Sound,* 531–32; Connelly, *Autumn of Glory,* 238–40; John C. Brown to James Longstreet, Apr. 14, 1888, J. Longstreet Papers, DU. Although Breckinridge was present at the October 4 meeting at which the generals drafted the petition to President Davis, he later refused to sign the document because he was waiting for a court of inquiry with Bragg regarding his conduct at the Battle of Stones River. See W. C. Davis, *Breckinridge,* 381–82.

32. J. Longstreet, *Manassas to Appomattox,* 465; D. H. Hill to Jefferson Davis, Oct. 30, 1886, in *JD,* 9:498–500; Archer Anderson, "Memorandum of Archer Anderson," Oct. 16, 1863, Anderson Collection, MC. In his postwar letter to the former Confederate president, Hill writes: "Now I had nothing to do with the Petition to the President of the Confederate States for the removal of Gen. Bragg, save that I signed it willingly. Gen. Polk got it [the letter] up and it was written by Gen. Buckner. I did not canvass for it or discuss it. I honestly believed that the fruits of victory were lost

through the fault of Bragg and therefore signed the Petition readily." At the time W. W. Mackall, Bragg's chief of staff, informed his wife that "Buckner was one of the first to sign the petition." See W. W. Mackall to Wife, Oct. 5, 1863, in Mackall, *A Son's Recollections,* 180–81.

33. Mackall to Wife, Oct. 5, 1863; *OR,* 30(4):728.

34. *OR,* 30(2):55; 52(2):533; Woodworth, *Jefferson Davis and His Generals,* 240.

35. *OR,* 52(2):534, 535.

36. Jefferson Davis to Braxton Bragg, Oct. 3, 1863, Polk Papers, LC; *OR,* 30(2):68–69; Parks, *General Leonidas Polk,* 350–53; Jefferson Davis to John C. Breckinridge, Oct. [8], 1863, Jefferson Davis Papers, Jefferson Davis Association, Rice University, Houston, Tex. (Cohasso Inc. Catalog, Oct. 11, 1977, photocopy); "President Davis's Visit to Gen. Bragg—Address," in *JD,* 6:57–58; W. C. Davis, *Jefferson Davis,* 519; Woodward, *Mary Chesnut's Civil War,* 482–83; Woodworth, *Jefferson Davis and His Generals,* 241. See also McDonough, *Chattanooga,* 35.

37. Connelly, *Autumn of Glory,* 241; W. C. Davis, *Jefferson Davis,* 492–93, 519, 550; Woodworth, *Jefferson Davis and His Generals,* 241; Cozzens, *This Terrible Sound,* 531–32.

38. James Longstreet to Frank A. Burr, Nov. 25, 1883, Longstreet Papers, HU; James Longstreet to E. P. Alexander, Aug. 26, 1902, Alexander Papers, SHC; J. Longstreet, *Manassas to Appomattox,* 465.

39. Jefferson Davis to Braxton Bragg, June 29, 1872, in *JD,* 7:321; W. C. Davis, *Jefferson Davis,* 521; *OR,* 30(4):746–47. See also Connelly, *Autumn of Glory,* 245. William J. Cooper writes, "The decision to retain Bragg as commanding general of the Army of Tennessee was disastrous." *Jefferson Davis, American,* 457.

40. Stickles, *Simon Bolivar Buckner,* 336; W. C. Davis, *Jefferson Davis,* 521; Wert, *General James Longstreet,* 328; J. Longstreet, *Manassas to Appomattox,* 466–67, 468. Longstreet also claims that Davis offered him command of the army that day, but he declined. Longstreet wrote his memoirs more than forty years after these events took place, and his memory apparently failed him in this instance.

41. Buckner quoted in M. B. Morton, "Last Surviving Confederate General," *Confederate Veteran,* 17 (Feb. 1909): 83; Woodward, *Mary Chesnut's Civil War,* 482. Buckner's memory of events more than forty years after the fact must be analyzed carefully.

42. Sorrel, *Recollections,* 201; George W. Brent Journal, Oct. 11, 1863, Bragg Papers, WR; Archer Anderson to My Dear Father, Oct. 13, 1863, Anderson Collection, MC; Bragg quoted in Liddell, *Liddell's Record,* 152; *OR,* 30(2):148; James Longstreet to D. H. Hill, Oct. 18, 1863, Longstreet Letters, GL.

43. Alexander, *Fighting for the Confederacy,* 308; Davis quoted in *Richmond Dispatch,* Oct. 24, 1863, Jefferson Davis Papers, Jefferson Davis Association (photocopy; first quote); Davis quoted in *Memphis [Atlanta] Appeal,* Oct. 14, 1863, in Crist and Dix, *Papers of Jefferson Davis,* 10:24 (second quote); Magee Diary, Oct. 10, 13, 14, 1863, DU; W. W. Mackall to Wife, Oct. 12, 1863, in Mackall, *A Son's Recollections,* 184–85; Brent Journal, Oct. 14, 1863, Bragg Papers, WR; Cozzens, *Shipwreck*

of Their Hopes, 28; John P. Maloney to W. D. Langlois, Oct. 19, 1863, John Percy Maloney Papers, 1st Texas Infantry File, SCRC.

44. *OR,* 30(4):744. See also Christopher Winsmith to My Dear Kate, Oct. 21, 1863, Winsmith Letters, MC.

45. On Bragg's purge and reorganization of his army, see Connelly, *Autumn of Glory,* 246-51; Woodworth, *Jefferson Davis and His Generals,* 244-45; and Hallock, *Braxton Bragg,* 99-102, 104-105. For Davis's view of Longstreet, see W. C. Davis, *Jefferson Davis,* 550.

46. Liddell, *Liddell's Record,* 154; *OR,* 31(3):604; Wills, *Confederacy's Greatest Cavalryman,* 142-49; Brent Journal, Oct. 30, 1863, Bragg Papers, WR.

47. W. W. Mackall to Wife, Oct. 10, 1863, in Mackall, *A Son's Recollections,* 183-84.

48. W. W. Mackall to Wife, Sept. 29, 1863, in ibid., 178-79.

49. *OR,* 30(4):187.

50. Hallock, *Braxton Bragg,* 104-106, 118-19; Stickles, *Simon B. Buckner,* 237-39; Losson, *Tennessee's Forgotten Warriors,* 116-18; Connelly, *Autumn of Glory,* 250-52; Cozzens, *Shipwreck of Their Hopes,* 2-7, 34, 38, 47; McDonough, *Chattanooga,* 48-54.

51. Wert, *General James Longstreet,* 317-21; McLaws, "After Chickamauga," 56; James Longstreet to Louis T. Wigfall, Sept. 12, 1863, Wigfall Papers, LC. It is worth noting that McLaws's account, written years after he and Longstreet had their falling out, must be analyzed carefully.

52. *OR,* 29(2):749, 52(2):549; Wert, *General James Longstreet,* 329.

53. Hallock, *Braxton Bragg,* 107. Hallock's study of James Longstreet in the West is highly critical of the general, assigning him the prime responsibility for Bragg's troubles with his subordinates. She argues that "Bragg's most serious and far-reaching troubles would revolve around him [Longstreet]. Longstreet had stopped at nothing in his efforts to dislodge Bragg. His subversive tactics on his own behalf, and his refusal to carry out properly the responsibilities of a subordinate, boded ill for the future of the Army of Tennessee, and for the Confederate States of America." Hallock, *Longstreet in the West,* 53.

54. Hill's biographer takes this stance. See Bridges, *Lee's Maverick General,* 234.

55. W. C. Davis, *Jefferson Davis,* 550; Jefferson Davis to Braxton Bragg, Nov. 1, 1863, in *JD,* 6:73. Historians have been critical of Longstreet's role in signing his name to a petition designed to remove his commanding officer, suggesting that he served as the catalyst for the dysfunctional state of Bragg's army. Yet the problems in the Army of Tennessee continued long after Longstreet and Bragg each left it. When Lt. Gen. John Bell Hood wrote critical letters to the authorities in Richmond criticizing his commanding general, Joseph E. Johnston, during the Atlanta campaign of 1864, the problems in the high command continued. In Johnston's case the information Hood provided led to that general's removal in July 1864. While historians have been critical of Hood's actions, Longstreet's negative reputation as an ambitious officer continues to overshadow his one-time subordinate. See Symonds, *Joseph E.*

Johnston, 323-25; McMurry, *John Bell Hood,* 119; and Connelly, *Autumn of Glory,* 417. Some scholars have even praised Hood for his actions. See Stephen Davis, "A Reappraisal of the Generalship of John Bell Hood in the Battles for Atlanta," in Theodore P. Savas and David Woodbury, eds., *The Campaign for Atlanta* (Campbell, Calif.: Savas-Woodbury Press, 1994), 62, 67-71.

56. Jefferson Davis to Braxton Bragg, June 29, 1872, in *JD,* 7:321; Christopher Winsmith to My Dear Father, Oct. 4, 1863, Winsmith Letters, MC; Charles Blackford to Dear Wife, Oct. 3, 25, 1863, in Blackford, *Letters from Lee's Army,* 210-11, 224; Alexander, *Fighting for the Confederacy,* 307. For evidence of desertion and low morale in the Army of Tennessee, see Cozzens, *Shipwreck of Their Hopes,* 28-29, 31-32.

Chapter 4

1. H. C. Kendrick to Dear Parents, Jan. 6, 1863, Kendrick Papers, SHC; McPherson, *For Cause and Comrades,* 159; Wiley, *Life of Johnny Reb,* 340; Gary Gallagher, "Lee's Army Has Not Lost Any of its Prestige: The Impact of Gettysburg on the Army of Northern Virginia and the Confederate Home Front," in Gallagher, *Third Day at Gettysburg,* 8; Sword, *Southern Invincibility,* 213; Polley, *Hood's Texas Brigade,* 205-206. See also Christopher Winsmith to Dear Mother, Sept. 21, 1863, Winsmith Letters, MC. Col. Walter Herron Taylor, Lee's adjutant, confirmed the positive state of morale, writing, "This is a good old army—no despondency here." Walter Taylor to Dear Bettie, Aug. 8, 1863, in Tower and Belmont, *Lee's Adjutant,* 67.

2. Lafayette McLaws to Wife, Aug. 14, 1863, McLaws Papers, SHC; Sorrel, *Recollections,* 195; Daniel, *Soldiering in the Army of Tennessee,* 20; Daniel Harvey Hill, "Chickamauga—Great Battle in the West," in *B&L,* 3:640; Hood, *Advance and Retreat,* 62. Longstreet's correspondence with Lee suggests that he believed the First Corps could have defeated the Union's western army and promptly returned to Virginia.

3. *OR,* 29(2):714; Piston, *Lee's Tarnished Lieutenant,* 67-68; Hood, *Advance and Retreat,* 63; Sword, *Southern Invincibility,* 215.

4. Sword, *Southern Invincibility,* 215; Baumgartner and Strayer, *Echoes of Battle,* 62; Cater, *As it Was,* 158-59.

5. Andrews, *South Reports the Civil War,* 356-57.

6. Charles Blackford to Dear Wife, Oct. 11, 1863, in Blackford, *Letters from Lee's Army,* 214. For additional officers' accounts, see Oates, *War between the Union and the Confederacy,* 265; Benjamin Humphreys, "History of the Sunflower Guards," Claiborne Papers, SHC; and Sorrel, *Recollections,* 196.

7. Benjamin Abbott to Green Haygood, Sept. 26, 1863, in Lane, *"Dear Mother,"* 275; Mixson, *Reminiscences of a Private,* 44; Andrew McBride to Dear Fannie, Sept. 29, 1863, McBride Papers, DU; John West to Dear Brother, Oct. 13, 1863, in West, *Texan in Search of a Fight,* 114; Polley, *Hood's Texas Brigade,* 212. See also Winkler, *Confederate Capital,* 146. In contrast to the eastern troops, Larry Daniel maintains that a significant number of veterans in the Army of Tennessee continued to support Bragg. *Soldiering in the Army of Tennessee,* 136-37.

8. Cozzens, *Shipwreck of Their Hopes,* 14-17.

9. Ibid.; Sword, *Mountains Touched with Fire,* 83–87; Woodworth, *Six Armies in Tennessee,* 12–13.

10. Woodworth, *Six Armies in Tennessee,* 144–45; Sword, *Mountains Touched with Fire,* 84–85; Cozzens, *Shipwreck of Their Hopes,* 18–19; Connelly, *Autumn of Glory,* 232.

11. Woodworth, *Six Armies in Tennessee,* 135, 141; Cozzens, *Shipwreck of Their Hopes,* 19–20; McDonough, *Chattanooga,* 24–25.

12. Wert, *General James Longstreet,* 330; Cozzens, *Shipwreck of Their Hopes,* 20; Woodworth, *Six Armies in Tennessee,* 141, 156; Connelly, *Autumn of Glory,* 255–57.

13. John C. West to My Precious Wife, Sept. 24, 1863, in West, *Texan in Search of a Fight,* 108; J. K. Munnerlyn to [?], n.d., Munnerlyn Letters, SHC; Abbott to Haygood, Sept. 26, 1863, in Lane, *"Dear Mother,"* 274; James Crowder to Dear Mother, Sept. 29, 1863, in Mathis, *Land of the Living,* 76. The First Corps had not brought cold-weather clothing since they believed they would return to Virginia before winter. See H. B. Simpson, *Hood's Texas Brigade,* 337.

14. *(Houston, Tex.) Tri-Weekly Telegraph,* Nov. 6, 1863; John B. Evans to Mollie, Sept. 28, 1863, Evans Papers, DU; [?] to Dear Father, Oct. 14, 1963, in *(Houston, Tex.) Tri-Weekly Telegraph,* Nov. 15, 1863; Robert Boyd to Dear Friend, Sept. 30, 1863, Boyd Papers, DU; John Bratton to Dear Bettie, Sept. 28, 1863, Bratton Confederate Letters, SCDAH; Paul Turner Vaughn Diary, Sept. 30, 1863, Vaughn Diary and Letters, SHC. See also the letter of Maj. Clinton M. Winkler, 4th Texas Infantry, in Baumgartner and Strayer, *Echoes of Battle,* 125–26.

15. Cozzens, *Shipwreck of Their Hopes,* 33, 34; Alexander, *Fighting for the Confederacy,* 304, 305; [?] to Dear Pa, Sept. 25, 1863 [Headquarters, Alexander's Battalion, Near Ringgold, Ga.], Confederate Archives, DU; Sword, *Mountains Touched with Fire,* 94.

16. McDonough, *Chattanooga,* 47; Cozzens, *Shipwreck of Their Hopes,* 9.

17. *OR,* 30(4):713. See also Sword, *Mountains Touched with Fire,* 108–109; and Cozzens, *Shipwreck of Their Hopes,* 30.

18. Watkins, *"Co. Aytch,"* 100; John Blackford to Wife, Oct. 1, 1863, in Blackford, *Letters from Lee's Army,* 209; John Bratton to Dear Wife, Oct. 1, 1863, Bratton Confederate Letters, SCDAH; Vaughn Diary, Oct. 14, 1863, Vaughn Diary and Letters, SHC; William Montgomery to Wife, Oct. 24, 1863, in Montgomery, *Georgia Sharpshooter,* 92; Lafayette McLaws to Dear Wife, Oct. 14, 1863, McLaws Papers, SHC. See also Polley, *Hood's Texas Brigade,* 214. Polley later writes that the eastern soldiers were "not accustomed to an unvarying diet of corn meal and lean beef" in Tennessee, and thus "bowel complaints prevailed to an alarming extent."

19. John Barry to Dear Sister, Nov. 4, 1863, Barry Papers, SHC; Alexander, *Fighting for the Confederacy,* 301; Mixson, *Reminiscences of a Private,* 44; Christopher Winsmith to Dear Kate, Oct. 19, 1863, Winsmith Letters, MC; John C. West to Dear Wife, Oct. 9, 1863, in West, *Texan in Search of a Fight,* 120. Maj. C. M. Winkler of Hood's Texas Brigade describes Chattanooga as an "exhausted, mountainous, poor country." *Confederate Capital,* 147.

20. For weather conditions, see Osmun Latrobe Diary, Oct. 1–31, 1863, Latrobe Diary and Letters, VHS; Charles E. Leverich Diary, Oct. 1–31, 1863, LSU; McLaws

to Dear Wife, Oct. 14, 1863; George W. Brent Journal, Oct. 1–31, 1863, Bragg Papers, WR; and Cozzens, *Shipwreck of Their Hopes*, 30. Capt. John C. Winsmith of the 5th South Carolina pointed out how the heavy rains inhibited Longstreet's men from receiving full rations from the commissary. See Christopher Winsmith to My Dear Mother, Oct. 15, 1863, Winsmith Letters, MC.

21. Wilkinson and Woodworth, *Scythe of Fire*, 272; Weitz, *A Higher Duty*, 71–72, 171–82; Weitz, *More Damning than Slaughter*, 213–17; Cozzens, *Shipwreck of Their Hopes*, 28–29; *OR*, 31(3):869–70; Richard H. Brooks to Dear Wife, Oct. 19, 1863, in Holland, *Keep All My Letters*, 109. According to Freeman, Longstreet was aware of the threat of desertion from his Georgia troops prior to leaving for the West and attempted to prepare for such actions. *Lee's Lieutenants*, 3:223.

22. W. W. Mackall to Wife, Oct. 12, 1863, in Mackall, *A Son's Recollections*, 185; John Bratton to Dear Wife, Oct. 10, 1863, Bratton Confederate Letters, SCDAH. See also Cooper, *Jefferson Davis, American*, 456.

23. Thomas J. Goree to Dearest Mother, Nov. 11, 1861, in Cutrer, *Longstreet's Aide*, 53; R. E. Lee to Jefferson Davis, July 11, 1862, in Freeman, *Lee's Dispatches*, 33–35; Baldwin, *Struck Eagle*, 208–10, 212–66; Swisher, *Prince of Edisto*, 101–102; Swanson and Johnson, "Conflict in East Tennessee," 101–110.

24. James Longstreet to Lafayette McLaws, Oct. 18, 1863, McLaws Papers, SHC; J. Longstreet, *Manassas to Appomattox*, 467. McLaws wrote an endorsement on this letter alleging that "Longstreet wanted to get rid of Hood who was equally as uncooperative as Longstreet and equally blind to his own demerits & was more a politician." McLaws's comments must be analyzed carefully considering that he wrote them after a bitter dispute with Longstreet. McMurry argues that Hood returned to his division prior to Chickamauga to prevent an outsider (Jenkins) from assuming command. *John Bell Hood*, 76.

25. Polley, *Hood's Texas Brigade*, 213; Laine and Penny, *Law's Alabama Brigade*, xiv–xvii, 178, 179, 186–202, 208–222; Swanson and Johnson, "Conflict in East Tennessee," 101–104. Baldwin argues that Law resented Jenkins's authority as senior faculty member at Kings College, and "relations between the two men eventually became quite bitter." *Struck Eagle*, 16. Jenkins's biographer refutes the existence of a prewar rivalry. See Swisher, *Prince of Edisto*, 100.

26. *OR*, 18:326; Laine and Penny, *Law's Alabama Brigade*, xv, 57–59, 120–21; *OR*, 27(2):358.

27. Coward, *The South Carolinians*, 83; Swisher, *Prince of Edisto*, 102; Laine and Penny, *Law's Alabama Brigade*, 178. See also H. B. Simpson, *Hood's Texas Brigade*, 331–32; and Polley, *Hood's Texas Brigade*, 213–14. For a detailed analysis of First Corps soldiers refusing to defer to appointed officers, see Brooks, "Social and Cultural Dynamics of Soldiering," 535–72.

28. Woodworth, *Six Armies in Tennessee*, 129–49; Cozzens, *Shipwreck of Their Hopes*, 1–7; Sword, *Mountains Touched with Fire*, 46–54.

29. James Longstreet to Osmun Latrobe, May 28 ,1886, Latrobe Diary and Letters, VHS; Wert, *General James Longstreet*, 331.

30. Woodworth, *Six Armies in Tennessee*, 153–54.

31. Cozzens, *Shipwreck of Their Hopes*, 42.

32. *OR*, 31(1):224; Law, "Lookout Valley," Carman Papers, NYPL; Coles, *From Huntsville to Appomattox*, 140; Vaughn Diary, Oct. 11, 1863, Vaughn Diary and Letters, SHC; Evander M. Law, "From Chickamauga to Chattanooga," *Philadelphia Weekly Press*, July 11, 1888.

33. *OR*, 31(1):216, 52(2):549; Brent Journal, Oct. 26, 1863, and George Brent to James Longstreet, Oct. 25, 1863, Bragg Papers, WR.

34. Law, "Lookout Valley"; Laine and Penny, *Law's Alabama Brigade*, 182; Baldwin, *Struck Eagle*, 224. Law argues that he "considered it of the first importance to the safety of this force and the continuance of the blockade of the roads, that a sufficient number of troops should be placed at my disposal, to picket the river front of the valley." See also Law, "From Chickamauga to Chattanooga."

35. Longacre, *Soldier to the Last*, 118–19, 120–27; Dyer, *From Shiloh to San Juan*, 99–108; Cozzens, *Shipwreck of Their Hopes*, 19–20, 33–34. Kelly's cavalry division comprised two brigades under Cols. William B. Wade and J. Warren Grigsby.

36. *OR*, 52(2):552, 31(3):606–607; George Brent to James Longstreet, Oct. 30, 1863, and J. B. Burtwell to J. P. Jones [inspector general, Army of Tennessee], "Report of information received from Colonel Grigsby, Commanding Cavalry," Nov. 3, 1863, Bragg Papers, WR. Conducted by the inspector of cavalry for the Army of Tennessee, Maj. J. B. Burtwell, the investigation did not include Longstreet's version of events. See also Connelly, *Autumn of Glory*, 256.

37. *OR*, 31(1):92–94, 97, 52(2):550–51; Cozzens, *This Terrible Sound*, 72. Sorrel wrote Jenkins, "Colonel Grigsby, commanding the cavalry near Trenton, has been ordered, *in case he is driven back*, to occupy the mountain passes in the mountain and to hold them" (emphasis added). Hooker reported slight resistance from Confederate pickets on the twenty-eighth.

38. Connelly, *Autumn of Glory*, 268–69; Dyer, *From Shiloh to San Juan*, 111.

39. Longstreet had nine brigades under his command, while the corps of Hardee and Breckinridge had a total of twenty-nine brigades. See *OR*, 30(2):11–20, 31(1):223.

40. Laine and Penny suggest that Jenkins's recall of these three regiments, "though not serious on its face, . . . is the sort of irritant one might inflict upon a subordinate in the hope of driving him away." *Law's Alabama Brigade*, 182. Jenkins's recent biographers argue otherwise. Swisher maintains that the general was following specific instructions. *Prince of Edisto*, 107. Baldwin suggests that it was Longstreet who ordered the return of the three regiments. *Struck Eagle*, 225.

41. James Longstreet to Lafayette McLaws, Oct. 14, 1863, McLaws Papers, SHC; *OR*, 31(1):220–23. See also Wert, *General James Longstreet*, 334–35; Connelly, *Autumn of Glory*, 255–57; and Sword, *Mountains Touched with Fire*, 124–25.

42. J. Longstreet, *Manassas to Appomattox*, 468. According to Longstreet's postwar recollection, he "suggested a change of base to Rome, Georgia, a march of the army to the railway bridge of the Tennessee River at Bridgeport, and the crossing of the river as an easy move, one that would cut the enemy's rearward line, interrupt his supply train, put us between his army at Chattanooga and the reinforcements moving to join him, and force him to precipitate battle or retreat." See also Wert, *General James Longstreet*, 334–35; and Sword, *Mountains Touched with Fire*, 123–24.

43. For proponents of this view, see Cozzens, *Shipwreck of Their Hopes*, 57; Connelly, *Autumn of Glory*, 256-66; Woodworth, *Jefferson Davis and His Generals*, 248; Woodworth, *Six Armies in Tennessee*, 156-57; Hallock, *Braxton Bragg*, 121-26; and Hallock, *Longstreet in the West*, 23-24, 41-53.

44. Cozzens, *Shipwreck of Their Hopes*, 53-57.

45. Oates, *War between the Union and Confederacy*, 273; Law, "Lookout Valley."

46. *OR*, 31(1):82-85, 86-87, 224-26; Sword, *Mountains Touched with Fire*, 119-20; Cozzens, *Shipwreck of Their Hopes*, 61-65.

47. Oates, *War between the Union and the Confederacy*, 275-77; Sword, *Mountains Touched with Fire*, 120-21; Cozzens, *Shipwreck of Their Hopes*, 63-65.

48. Law, "Lookout Mountain"; Sword, *Mountains Touched with Fire*, 121.

49. Liddell, *Liddell's Record*, 155-56.

50. *OR*, 31(1):221, 222 (two letters, no time given).

51. George W. Brent to James Longstreet, Oct. 27, 1863 (11:00 P.M.), Bragg Papers, WR; *OR*, 31(1):217; J. Longstreet, *Manassas to Appomattox*, 474; Brent Journal, Oct. 28, 1863, Bragg Papers, WR; Woodworth, *Six Armies in Tennessee*, 162-63; J. Longstreet, *Manassas to Appomattox*, 474-75. Brent recorded that "Gen. Bragg visited Lookout Mountain. He found that his orders of yesterday had not been executed." See also Liddell, *Liddell's Record*, 156-57; and Wert, *General James Longstreet*, 335.

52. George Brent to James Longstreet, Oct. 28, 1863, Bragg Papers, WR; Liddell, *Liddell's Record*, 157; McDonough, *Chattanooga*, 88-89; Sword, *Mountains Touched with Fire*, 128-29; Connelly, *Autumn of Glory*, 259; Cozzens, *Shipwreck of Their Hopes*, 78-79.

53. *OR*, 31(1):219; Law, "Lookout Valley."

54. J. Longstreet, *Manassas to Appomattox*, 475; George Brent to James Longstreet, Oct. 28 (6:00 P.M.), Oct. 28, 1863 (7:30 P.M.), Bragg Papers, WR; Brent Journal, Oct. 28, 1863, Bragg Papers, WR. See also Connelly, *Autumn of Glory*, 260; Cozzens, *Shipwreck of Their Hopes*, 79; and George Brent to James Longstreet, Oct. 28, 1863, Bragg Papers, WR.

55. J. Longstreet, *Manassas to Appomattox*, 476-77; *OR*, 31(1):223.

56. Micah Jenkins to G. M. Sorrel, Nov. 2, 1863 [Jenkins's Report on Lookout Valley], M. Jenkins Papers, SCL; McDonough, *Chattanooga*, 89. Although the *Official Records* cite that no record of Jenkins's report was found, all indications point to the handwritten document in the Micah Jenkins Papers at the South Caroliniana Library as being his official report on the Wauhatchie engagement. See *OR*, 31(1):219n. Some historians suggest that Longstreet sought to discredit Law. See Swanson and Johnson, "Conflict in East Tennessee," 105; and Woodworth, *Six Armies in Tennessee*, 164. Swisher is critical of Longstreet's handling of the operation. *Prince of Edisto*, 113-14. Baldwin argues that it was an "unfortunate error." *Struck Eagle*, 227.

57. *OR*, 31(1):113; Cozzens, *Shipwreck of Their Hopes*, 83-89; Laine and Penny, *Law's Alabama Brigade*, 188-89; Baldwin, *Struck Eagle*, 231-33; Christopher Winsmith to My Dear Father, Oct. 29, 1863, Winsmith Letters, MC.

58. Law, "Lookout Valley"; Jenkins to Sorrel, Nov. 2, 1863; Baldwin, *Struck Eagle*, 231–33; Laine and Penny, *Law's Alabama Brigade*, 191–93.

59. Jenkins to Sorrel, Nov. 2, 1863; *OR*, 31(1):227–28; Woodworth, *Six Armies in Tennessee*, 167.

60. Woodworth, *Six Armies in Tennessee*, 150–68; Wert, *General James Longstreet*, 336–38; Law, "Lookout Valley."

61. J. P. Thomas, *Career and Character of Micah Jenkins*, 17; *OR*, 31(1):228, 232–33; Law, "Lookout Valley"; J. Longstreet, *Manassas to Appomattox*, 477; Wert, *General James Longstreet*, 337; Baldwin, *Struck Eagle*, 234–35. Bratton's reconstruction of events suggests that Law's forces were still engaged when he received his orders to withdraw. Moreover, he thanks Law and his couriers for their conduct during the battle.

62. Wert, *General James Longstreet*, 335–37; Baldwin, *Struck Eagle*, 227.

63. Brent Journal, Oct. 30, 1863, Bragg Papers, WR; Braxton Bragg to Jefferson Davis, Oct. 29, 1863, in *JD*, 6:69–71. See also Woodworth, *Jefferson Davis and His Generals*, 248; and Connelly, *Autumn of Glory*, 262–66.

64. Bragg quoted in Liddell, *Liddell's Record*, 157.

65. Christopher Winsmith to My Dear Kate, Oct. 8, 1863, Winsmith Letters, MC.

Chapter 5

1. Micah Jenkins to G. M. Sorrel, Oct. 31, 1863, Jenkins Papers, DU. See also Connelly, *Autumn of Glory*, 261–62; and "Map of the Roads and Trails of Lookout Mountain," McLaws Papers, SHC.

2. Micah Jenkins to G. M. Sorrel, Oct. 31, 1863, Jenkins Papers, DU; John C. West to My Dear Sister, Oct. 31, 1863, in West, *Texan in Search of a Fight*, 126. See also John Euclid Magee Diary, Oct. 30, 1863, DU.

3. *OR*, 31(1):218; Jenkins to Sorrel, Oct. 31, 1863. President Davis engineered Hardee's transfer to Bragg's army to replace Leonidas Polk. See *OR*, 52(2):555; and Jefferson Davis to William J. Hardee, Oct. 30, 1863, Davis Papers, TU.

4. *OR*, 31(1):8–10, 31(4):760–61, 52(2):548, 557; Jefferson Davis to Braxton Bragg, Oct. 29, 1863, Davis Papers, TU. Bragg had detached Stevenson on October 17 with orders to "press vigorously toward Knoxville . . . press the enemy's rear and [drive] him back as far as their commands will allow."

5. *OR*, 31(1):455; James Longstreet to Simon B. Buckner, Nov. 5, 1863, Civil War Papers, TU; J. Longstreet, *Manassas to Appomattox*, 480–81.

6. *OR*, 31(1):474.

7. Longstreet to Buckner, Nov. 5, 1863.

8. Ibid.; *OR*, 52(2):560–61.

9. *OR*, 31(1):9–10, 31(3):634; Longacre, *Soldier to the Last*, 129–30.

10. Bragg's options are outlined in Woodworth, *Six Armies in Tennessee*, 174–75; Edward Carr Franks, "The Detachment of Longstreet Considered: Braxton Bragg, James Longstreet, and the Chattanooga Campaign," in Woodworth, *Leadership and Command*, 29–65; and Woodworth, *This Grand Spectacle*, 32–33.

11. Woodworth, *Six Armies in Tennessee,* 174–75; Franks, "Detachment of Longstreet Considered," 49–53.

12. Bryan, "Civil War in East Tennessee" (PhD diss.), 118–59; Groce, *Mountain Rebels,* 109–126; Alexander, *Fighting for the Confederacy,* 311.

13. Wert, *General James Longstreet,* 339; Piston, *Lee's Tarnished Lieutenant,* 76; Eckenrode and Conrad, *James Longstreet,* 250–51; Sanger and Hay, *James Longstreet,* 220; Connelly, *Autumn of Glory,* 261, 263; Connelly and Jones, *Politics of Command,* 71–72; McDonough, *Chattanooga,* 98; Cozzens, *Shipwreck of Their Hopes,* 105; Woodworth, *Jefferson Davis and His Generals,* 248; Horn, *Army of Tennessee,* 294; Sword, *Mountains Touched with Fire,* 147; Seitz, *Braxton Bragg,* 390, 406. One Bragg biographer holds alternate views on Longstreet's transfer, arguing that Bragg "probably did not injure his chances" by sending away the First Corps. See Hallock, *Braxton Bragg,* 126; and *Longstreet in the West,* 71.

14. Longstreet to Buckner, Nov. 5, 1863; *OR,* 30(2):37; Connelly, *Autumn of Glory,* 263–64; McDonough, *Chattanooga,* 100; J. Longstreet, *Manassas to Appomattox,* 461. Woodworth argues that President Davis, under pressure to return the First Corps to Lee's army, influenced Bragg's decision to send Longstreet to East Tennessee. *Six Armies in Tennessee,* 176.

15. Braxton Bragg to E. T. Sykes, Feb. 8, 1873, copy in McLaws Papers, SHC; Liddell, *Liddell's Record,* 157.

16. J. Longstreet, *Manassas to Appomattox,* 468; *OR,* 31(2):219.

17. *OR,* 31(1):466–67, 468; Jerome B. Robertson to Henry L. Benning, Nov. 4, 1863, Benning Papers, SHC; Wert, *General James Longstreet,* 337–38; J. Longstreet, *Manassas to Appomattox,* 517.

18. James Longstreet to Lafayette McLaws, July 25, 1873, McLaws Papers, SHC. For a biographical sketch of McLaws, see Oeffinger, *Soldier's General,* 1–61; and Robert K. Krick, "Longstreet Versus McLaws—and Everyone Else—at Knoxville," in Krick, *The Smoothbore Volley,* 85–98.

19. Lafayette McLaws to Dear Wife, July 7, 1863, ibid.; Dawson, *Reminiscences,* 101; James Longstreet to Braxton Bragg, Oct. 16, 1863, Longstreet Papers, HU.

20. Lafayette McLaws to [?], n.d., McLaws Papers, SHC.

21. *OR,* 31(3):634–45; Franks, "Detachment of Longstreet Considered," 46.

22. James Longstreet to Braxton Bragg, Nov. 4, 1863, Braxton Bragg to James Longstreet, Nov. 5, 1863, and Braxton Bragg to James Longstreet, Nov. 6, 1863, Bragg Papers, WR; H. B. Simpson, *Hood's Texas Brigade,* 348

23. Longstreet to Buckner, Nov. 5, 1863. Wert points to Longstreet's insecurity after the Knoxville campaign. *General James Longstreet,* 359.

24. Liddell, *Liddell's Record,* 157; Alexander, *Fighting for the Confederacy,* 311; Brent Journal, Nov. 1, 5, 1863, Bragg Papers, WR. J. B. Polley, a corporal in the Texas Brigade, later called Longstreet's detachment "suicidal." *Hood's Texas Brigade,* 221.

25. Wert, *General James Longstreet,* 340–41; Sorrel, *Recollections,* 210; *OR,* 31(3):670; Osmun Latrobe Diary, Nov. 7–8, 1863, Latrobe Diary and Letters, VHS; J. Longstreet, *Manassas to Appomattox,* 483.

26. Charles Blackford to Dear Wife, Nov. 6, 1863, in Blackford, *Letters from Lee's*

Army, 227; John Percy Maloney to W. D. Langlois, Oct. 19, 1863, John Percy Maloney Papers, 1st Texas Infantry File, SCRC; Coward, *The South Carolinians,* 93; John Bratton to Dear Wife, Nov. 3, 1863, Bratton Confederate Letters, SCDAH; James H. Hendrick to Dear Mother, Nov. 8, 1863, James H. Hendrick Papers, 1st Texas Infantry File, SCRC; Micah Jenkins to Wife, Nov. 7, 1863, Jenkins Papers, DU. By late October Col. C. V. Winkler expressed a desire to return to Virginia to fight under Lee. *Confederate Capital,* 147.

27. Alexander, *Fighting for the Confederacy,* 312; Wert, *General James Longstreet,* 341; Evander M. Law, "Burnside and Longstreet in East Tennessee," *Philadelphia Weekly Press,* July 18, 1888; J. Longstreet, *Manassas to Appomattox,* 476.

28. *OR,* 31(1):476–77, 31(3):670.

29. James Longstreet to General Bragg, Nov. 11, 1863, and Braxton Bragg to James Longstreet, Nov. 4, 6, 1863, Bragg Papers, WR; *OR,* 31(1):476–77, 31(3):634, 686, 687. Longstreet informed Bragg of the problems with transportation on the twelfth. Woodworth criticizes Longstreet's frequent messages. *Six Armies in Tennessee,* 177.

30. J. Longstreet, *Manassas to Appomattox,* 483; *OR,* 31(3):680–81; *OR,* 31(3):681; Woodworth, *Six Armies in Tennessee,* 177.

31. *OR,* 31(3):292, 671, 687; Woodworth, *Six Armies in Tennessee,* 178; Wert, *General James Longstreet,* 342.

32. *OR,* 31(1):273–74, 376–77, 456–57; J. Longstreet, *Manassas to Appomattox,* 486; Longacre, *Soldier to the Last,* 130–31; Ulysses S. Grant, "Chattanooga," in *B&L,* 3:695.

33. Alexander, *Fighting for the Confederacy,* 315–16; Law, "Burnside and Longstreet in East Tennessee"; Marvel, *Burnside,* 307–308, 312; T. A. Johnston, "Failure before Knoxville," 58–59; *OR,* 31(1):456–57, 525–26.

34. *OR,* 31(1):457–58, 525; Wilkinson and Woodworth, *Scythe of Fire,* 274.

35. J. Longstreet, *Manassas to Appomattox,* 492; Dyer, *From Shiloh to San Juan,* 113–14; Latrobe Diary, Nov. 16, 1863, Latrobe Diary and Letters, VHS; Minnich, "Pegram's Brigade at Chickamauga," TU; J. Longstreet, *Manassas to Appomattox,* 492–93; *OR,* 31(1):457–58, 480–81.

36. Minnich, "Pegram's Brigade at Chickamauga," TU.

37. Orlando Poe, "The Defense of Knoxville," in *B&L,* 3:733–34; Wert, *General James Longstreet,* 344–45; *OR,* 31(1):273–75, 457–58, 480–83, 31(3):332–33; Marvel, *Burnside,* 312–13; J. Longstreet, *Manassas to Appomattox,* 492.

38. *OR,* 31(1):457–58, 477–78, 480–81; Alexander, *Fighting for the Confederacy,* 315–16; Laine and Penny, *Law's Alabama Brigade,* 203–204; Wert, *General James Longstreet,* 344–45.

39. *OR,* 31(1):478, 525–26; Laine and Penny, *Law's Alabama Brigade,* 205; Alexander, *Fighting for the Confederacy,* 316. For Alexander's opinion toward the Army of Tennessee's artillery, see Daniel, *Cannoneers in Gray,* 106; and Klein, *Edward Porter Alexander,* 97.

40. *OR,* 31(1):483; Law, "Burnside and Longstreet in East Tennessee."

41. *OR,* 31(1):273–75, 483, 527; Christopher Winsmith to My Dear Father, Nov. 18, 1863, Winsmith Letters, MC; Wert, *General James Longstreet,* 345.

42. *OR,* 31(1):458, 528.

43. Wert, *General James Longstreet,* 345; Coward, *The South Carolinians,* 97-98; Sorrel, *Recollections,* 211-12.

44. J. Longstreet, *Manassas to Appomattox,* 494-95; Alexander, *Fighting for the Confederacy,* 317. Alexander writes favorably of both Law and Jenkins.

45. Law, "Burnside and Longstreet in East Tennessee."

46. Lafayette McLaws to Braxton Bragg, Nov. [?, 1864?], McLaws Papers, SHC. A copy of a twenty-two-page letter to Bragg is in the McLaws Papers (SHC). In his postwar account Law argues that McLaws remained inactive on the morning of the sixteenth "by General Longstreet's order . . . and though it was known by every man in the Confederate camp that General Burnside's forces were in full retreat, and although McLaws was under arms and ready to move at daylight, he did not receive the order to march on Campbell's Station until 8 o'clock A.M." Law, "Burnside and Longstreet in East Tennessee."

47. Sorrel, *Recollections,* 210.

48. Krick, *Parker's Virginia Battery,* 206; Baldwin, *Struck Eagle,* 248.

49. Stocker, *From Huntsville to Appomattox,* 149; John Bratton to My Dear Wife, Nov. 10, 1863, Bratton Confederate Letters, SCDAH; *OR,* 31(1):477. See also *OR,* 31(3):703. Longstreet reports that a railroad engineer had to be arrested for refusing to haul rations to his army.

50. Woodworth, *Six Armies in Tennessee,* 206; Turner Vaughn to [?], Jan. 21, 1864, in Vaughn, "Diary of Turner Vaughan," 600; Minnich, "Pegram's Brigade at Chickamauga," TU; Dickert, *Kershaw's Brigade,* 297.

51. *OR,* 31(1):458-59, 483-84, 31(3):707-708; Latrobe Diary, Nov. 17-18, 1863, Latrobe Diary and Letters, VHS; Edward Porter Alexander Diary, Nov. 17-18, 1863, Alexander Papers, SHC; Dickert, *Kershaw's Brigade,* 304-307; Seymour, *Divided Loyalties,* 138-45; Wert, *General James Longstreet,* 346.

52. Poe, "Defense of Knoxville," 734-36; Alexander, *Fighting for the Confederacy,* 317-25; Seymour, *Divided Loyalties,* 151-52; Marvel, *Burnside,* 315.

53. Seymour, *Divided Loyalties,* 177-83; T. A. Johnston, "Failure before Knoxville," 61-62; Edward P. Alexander, "Longstreet at Knoxville," in *B&L,* 3:749-50; Poe, "Defense of Knoxville," 734-36; Marvel, *Burnside,* 320-21; Latrobe Diary, Nov. 18-20, 1863, Latrobe Diary and Letters, VHS; Alexander Diary, Nov. 18-19, 1863, Alexander Papers, SHC.

54. *OR,* 31(3):721, 723, 52(2):562-63. Davis responded to Bragg's missive the same day, writing: "The failure of Genl. Longstreet to keep you advised of his operations is unaccountable. You had better order him to report fully the events of each day."

55. Ibid., 31(3):732 (two letters), 737.

56. Ibid., 31(1):269, 484; Poe, "Defense of Knoxville," 345; Woodworth, *Six Armies in Tennessee,* 206-207; Krick, "Longstreet Versus McLaws," 96.

57. Latrobe Diary, Nov. 25, 1863, Latrobe Diary and Letters, VHS; Laine and Penny, *Law's Alabama Brigade,* 211; James Longstreet to Colonel Alexander, Nov. 25, 1863, Alexander Papers, SHC.

58. Alexander, *Fighting for the Confederacy,* 323-24. For background on Leadbetter, see Warner, *Generals in Gray,* 176-77.

59. *OR,* 31(1):460, (3):757; Latrobe Diary, Nov. 27, 1863, Latrobe Diary and Letters, VHS; Alexander Diary, Nov. 27, 1863, Alexander Papers, SHC; Joseph Ganahl to Lafayette McLaws, Sept. 26, 1890, McLaws Papers, SHC; Lafayette McLaws to Marcus J. Wright, June 7, 1882, ibid.; Cummings, *Yankee Quaker, Confederate General,* 274; Marvel, *Burnside,* 326; Wert, *General James Longstreet,* 349.

60. Alexander, *Fighting for the Confederacy,* 325; Krick, *Parker's Virginia Battery,* 209-210; Alexander, *Military Memoirs,* 485-86. Soldiers expressed confidence in Longstreet's strategy. Days before the planned assault, Capt. John Christopher Winsmith wrote, "Longstreet's plans are doubtless good, and we must wait patiently until he sees proper to give his orders for execution." Christopher Winsmith to My Dear Mother, Nov. 22, 1863, Winsmith Letters, MC.

61. *OR,* 31(1):479, 486.

62. Wert, *General James Longstreet,* 349-50; Alexander, *Fighting for the Confederacy,* 327.

63. *OR,* 31(3):487, 491-92, 755; "Deposition of Brigadier General Goode Bryan," Feb. 11, 1864, McLaws Papers, DU.

64. James Longstreet to Lafayette McLaws, Nov. 28, 1863, McLaws Papers, SHC. A version of this letter appears in *OR,* 31(1):494.

65. *OR,* 31(3):758.

66. Ibid., 756, 757; Alexander, *Fighting for the Confederacy,* 326.

67. Marvel, *Burnside,* 325-26; Alexander, *Fighting for the Confederacy,* 327.

68. The best secondary accounts on the assault are found in Seymour, *Divided Loyalties,* 177-203; Krick, "Longstreet Versus McLaws," 96-102; T. A. Johnston, "Failure before Knoxville," 69-73; and Woodworth, *Six Armies in Tennessee,* 206-212.

69. Coward, *The South Carolinians,* 101; Lieutenant Collins to Gen. Goode Bryan, Dec. 1, 1863, McLaws Papers, SHC; Wilkinson and Woodworth, *Scythe of Fire,* 280; Goode Bryan to Lafayette McLaws, Dec. 1, 1863, McLaws Papers, SHC; *OR,* 31(1):290-92; Benjamin Humphreys, "A History of the Sunflower Guards," Claiborne Papers, SHC; T. A. Johnston, "Failure before Knoxville," 74; T. A. Johnston, "Fort Sanders Survivor's Story," 61. Marvel cites Federal casualties at eight killed and five wounded. *Burnside,* 329.

70. *OR,* 31(1):461. Many details from the participants of the attack on Fort Sanders are found in the McLaws Papers (SHC). McLaws gathered testimonials and depositions while awaiting a court-martial for his conduct in the assault. See the Depositions of Capt. W. Hartsfield and Capt. G. W. Vandergrift, Feb. 17, 1864; Joseph B. Kershaw, Feb. 19, 1864; Captain Martin, Feb. 17, 1864; Lt. Col. W. C. Holt; and Captain Fuller, Feb. 17, 1864. In addition, letters of support from Benjamin Humphreys (Dec. 1, 1863), Goode Bryan (Jan. 16, 1864), and John Allyus (Feb. 12, 1864) during the trial also include details of the attack on Fort Sanders. See also McLaws's postwar correspondence with Marcus J. Wright (June 7, 1872) and Joseph Ganahl (Sept. 26, 1890). This is just a sampling of the documents related to McLaws's court-martial.

Additional background information is found in Oeffinger, *Soldier's General*, 42–46; Krick, "Longstreet Versus McLaws," 85–116; J. Longstreet, *Manassas to Appomattox*, 507; *OR*, 31(1):461; and Latrobe Diary, Nov. 29, 1863, Latrobe Diary and Letters, VHS.

71. Alexander, *Fighting for the Confederacy*, 327; Edward Porter Alexander to William Bearley, Oct. 17, 1870, in Bearley, "Recollections of the East Tennessee Campaign," TU.

72. In a postwar letter McLaws reports that Bragg had accused Longstreet of treason. He alleges that as a U.S. paymaster before the war, Longstreet was more than $30,000 dollars short in his accounts. Longstreet therefore "did not take any steps to assault Burnside until he had drawn an additional force [Bushrod Johnson] from Bragg." Thus, when the brigades were "beyond recall," General Grant attacked Bragg and forced him to retreat. McLaws maintains that Longstreet sabotaged Bragg's mission to East Tennessee to help his antebellum friend defeat the Confederates at Chattanooga. See Braxton Bragg to E. T. Sykes, Feb. 8, 1873, and McLaws to [?], n.d., McLaws Papers, SHC.

73. J. Longstreet, *Manassas to Appomattox*, 507.

74. Albert Castel, "Mars and the Reverend Longstreet: Or, Attacking and Dying in the Civil War," in Castel, *Winning and Losing*, 126–30.

75. *OR*, 31(1):540–66, 546, 31(3):680, 681, 758, 760; Latrobe Diary, Nov. 29, 1863, Latrobe Diary and Letters, VHS; Wert, *General James Longstreet*, 354; Longacre, *Soldier to the Last*, 131–32.

76. Latrobe Diary, Nov. 29, Dec. 1–4, 1863, Latrobe Diary and Letters, VHS; "General Orders No. 9," Alexander Papers, SHC; *OR*, 31(1):461–62, 500–501, 546; Krick, *Parker's Virginia Battery*, 212.

77. Alexander, "Longstreet at Knoxville," 750; Dawson, *Reminiscences*, 110; Burton and Botsford, *Historical Sketches of the Forty-Seventh Alabama Infantry*, 19; Dickert, *Kershaw's Brigade*, 316; J. Longstreet, *Manassas to Appomattox*, 521; "First Corps Circular," Dec. 6, 1863, Alexander Papers, SHC. See also Alexander, *Fighting for the Confederacy*, 330–31. For supporting evidence of the hardships of the First Corps's men on this march, see J. Longstreet, *Manassas to Appomattox*, 526; Sorrel, *Recollections*, 209; and Wilkinson and Woodworth, *Scythe of Fire*, 280.

78. Alexander, *Fighting for the Confederacy*, 322; Sorrel, *Recollections*, 220.

79. Alexander, *Fighting for the Confederacy*, 331; Houghton and Houghton, *Two Boys*, 68–69; John Bratton to Dear Wife, Dec. 9, 1863, Bratton Confederate Letters, SCDAH; Sorrel, *Recollections*, 217; J. Longstreet, *Manassas to Appomattox*, 515.

80. Christopher Winsmith to My Dear Father, Dec. 1, 1863, and Christopher Winsmith to My Dear Mother, Dec. 11, 1863, Winsmith Letters, MC; John Barry to Dear Sister, Jan. 19, 1864, Barry Papers, SHC; Andrew Jay McBride to Dear Fannie, Dec. 14, 1863, McBride Papers, DU; John Evans to Wife, Jan. 24, 1864, Evans Papers, DU; Hamilton, "Company M, First Texas Volunteer Infantry" (unpublished manuscript); Bratton to Dear Wife, Dec. 9, 1863.

81. Dickert, *Kershaw's Brigade*, 317; Polley, *Hood's Texas Brigade*, 223. See also Coles, *From Huntsville to Appomattox*, 151; and Christopher Winsmith to My Dear Father, Dec. 9, 1863, Winsmith Letters, MC.

Chapter 6

1. B. D. Simpson, *Ulysses S. Grant,* 243; Woodworth, *Six Armies in Tennessee,* 203–205; Cozzens, *Shipwreck of Their Hopes,* 386; Castel, *Decision in the West,* 18–19.

2. Ulysses S. Grant, "Chattanooga," in *B&L,* 3:709–711.

3. *OR,* 31(1):461–62, 31(3):779, 33(2):535; Cozzens, *Shipwreck of Their Hopes,* 252–53; J. Longstreet, *Manassas to Appomattox,* 510; Wert, *General James Longstreet,* 354.

4. Sherman, *Memoirs,* 1:368; Marvel, *Burnside,* 232–33; Marszalek, *Sherman,* 246–47.

5. *OR,* 31(1):462, 463, 31(3):784; J. Longstreet, *Manassas to Appomattox,* 511.

6. *OR,* 31(1):462–63, 32(2):640–43; Lambert, *Grumble,* 59–61; Cummings, *Yankee Quaker, Confederate General,* 275–76.

7. *OR,* 31(1):463, 31(3):359, 384, 391.

8. Ibid., 415, 463; Speed, "Battle of Bean's Station," 112–18.

9. Harrison, "Battle beyond Knoxville," 21; Speed, "Battle of Bean's Station," 113–14.

10. *OR,* 31(1):463–64, 534–36.

11. Ibid.; Krick, *Parker's Virginia Battery,* 215.

12. Dickert, *Kershaw's Brigade,* 323–24; *OR,* 31(1):463–64, 494–95, 534–36, 546–47; Krick, *Parker's Virginia Battery,* 215–16; Cummings, *Yankee Quaker, Confederate General,* 276–77; Osmun Latrobe Diary, Dec. 14, 1863, Latrobe Diary and Letters, VHS.

13. *OR,* 31(1):393, 406, 463–64; Harrison, "Battle beyond Knoxville," 46; Lambert, *Grumble,* 71.

14. *OR,* 31(1):464–65, 529; Baldwin, *Struck Eagle,* 253.

15. *OR,* 31(1):464, 470, 530, 546–47.

16. Ibid., 464; Harrison, "Battle beyond Knoxville," 47; Laine and Penny, *Law's Alabama Brigade,* 215. See also J. Longstreet, *Manassas to Appomattox,* 514.

17. J. Longstreet, *Manassas to Appomattox,* 515; Latrobe Diary, Dec. 22, 1863, Latrobe Diary and Letters, VHS; *OR,* 31(1):465, 31(3):839; Lambert, *Grumble,* 73, 92. Jones's command was later moved north of Clinch Mountain.

18. Richard Lewis to Dear Mother, Dec. 31, 1863, in Lewis, *Camp Life,* 77; John C. West to My Precious Wife, Dec. 27, 1863, in West, *Texan in Search of a Fight,* 137; J. Longstreet, *Manassas to Appomattox,* 520; Coles, *From Huntsville to Appomattox,* 153; Sorrel, *Recollections,* 219; Dawson, *Reminiscences,* 110; Dickert, *Kershaw's Brigade,* 329, 330. Dickert describes a "plentitude of 'moonshine.'"

19. J. Longstreet, *Manassas to Appomattox,* 514; Speed, "Battle of Bean's Station," 116; Alexander, "Longstreet at Knoxville," 750; Dyer, *From Shiloh to San Juan,* 119–20. Wheeler's biographer argues that western cavalry had a "tendency toward depredations upon the enemy" since these men "were not trained soldiers with a military point of view; they were citizen soldiers with a frontier outlook."

20. *OR,* 31(1):495. For conditions of the Federal troops during the pursuit of Longstreet, see Allardice, "Longstreet's Nightmare," 36.

21. Lafayette McLaws to Marcus J. Wright, June 7, 1882, McLaws Papers, SHC.

22. See the reports of Micah Jenkins and Bushrod Johnson, *OR,* 31(1):529, 534.

23. McLaws to Wright, June 7, 1882; "Orders No. 27," Dec. 17, 1864, McLaws Papers, DU; *OR,* 31(1):497; G. M. Sorrel to Lafayette McLaws, Dec. 17, 1864, McLaws Papers, DU; G. M. Sorrel to Lafayette McLaws, Dec. 17, 1863, in Oeffinger, *Soldier's General,* 214; "Orders No. 168," McLaws Letters, GL.

24. James Longstreet to Samuel Cooper, Dec. 20, 1863, McLaws Papers, SHC (a copy of the letter is also found in Oeffinger, *Soldier's General,* 215); Braxton Bragg to E. T. Sykes, Feb. 8, 1873, Bragg Papers, WR; James Longstreet to Lafayette McLaws, Oct. 18, 1863, McLaws Papers, SHC.

25. James Longstreet to J. F. H. Claiborne, Apr. 6, 1880, Claiborne Papers, SHC; James Longstreet to Lafayette McLaws, July 25, 1873, McLaws Papers, SHC; J. Longstreet, *Manassas to Appomattox,* 548; *OR,* 31(1):468; Piston, *Lee's Tarnished Lieutenant,* 78.

26. Lafayette McLaws to Marcus J. Wright, June 7, 1882, McLaws Papers, SHC.

27. *OR,* 31(1):503–504; "Charges and Specifications Preferred against Maj. Genl. L. McLaws," McLaws Papers, DU. The most detailed study of McLaws's court-martial is found in Robert K. Krick, "Longstreet Versus McLaws—and Everyone Else—at Knoxville," in Krick, *The Smoothbore Volley,* 85–116.

28. J. B. Robertson to J. B. Hood, Dec. 10, 1863, and J. B. Robertson to Texas Delegation in the Confederate States Congress, n.d., in J. B. Robertson, *Touched with Valor,* 52–55.

29. *OR,* 31(1):465–66, 470; H. B. Simpson, *Hood's Texas Brigade,* 384–85; Wert, *General James Longstreet,* 360–61.

30. H. B. Simpson, *Hood's Texas Brigade,* 222; "4th and 5th Texas Petition the War Department," in J. B. Robertson, *Touched with Valor,* 57–58; Wert, *General James Longstreet,* 361. Simpson refers to Robertson as "Aunt Pollie."

31. *OR,* 31(1):468, 469.

32. Ibid., 469, 33:1075.

33. Lafayette McLaws to Henry L. Benning, Dec. 18, 1863, Benning Papers, SCH; Lafayette McLaws to Joseph Ganahl, July 23, 1894, McLaws Papers, SHC. See also Goode Bryan to Lafayette McLaws, Jan. 16, 1864, and Benjamin Humphreys to Lafayette McLaws, Feb. 16, 1864, McLaws Papers, SHC.

34. Lafayette McLaws to Samuel Cooper, Dec. 29, 1863, McLaws Papers, SHC.

35. Lafayette McLaws to My Dear Wife, Mar. 8, 1864, ibid.

36. Oeffinger, *Soldier's General,* 43; Krick, "Longstreet Versus McLaws," 104–105.

37. Osmun Latrobe to Micah Jenkins, Feb. 3, 1863, and Osmun Latrobe to Jerome B. Robertson, Feb. 16, 1864, Longstreet Order and Letter Book, CAH; "Charges and Specifications against Gen. J. B. Robertson," Andrews Papers, SHC (a copy is found in *OR,* 31(1):470); H. B. Simpson, *Hood's Texas Brigade,* 384–85; Wert, *General James Longstreet,* 361; Polley, *Hood's Texas Brigade,* 225.

38. A. B. Hood to Cousin Jennie, Feb. 14, 1864, A. B. Hood Papers, 5th Texas Infantry File, SCRC; Fourth and 5th Texas to Secretary of War, Jan. 26, 1864, and

"Third Arkansas Resolutions," n.d., in J. B. Robertson, *Touched with Valor,* 57–59; Collier, *"They'll Do to Tie To,"* 169. Collier does not mention a petition in his history of the 3rd Arkansas. For a study on how Texas volunteers viewed their officers, see Charles E. Brooks, "Popular Sovereignty in the Confederate Army: The case of Colonel John Marshall and the Fourth Texas Infantry Regiment," in Sheehan-Dean, *View from the Ground,* 199–218.

39. H. B. Simpson, *Hood's Texas Brigade,* 386–87; *OR,* 34(4):692; J. B. Robertson to Soldiers, Apr. 9, 1864, in J. B. Robertson, *Touched with Valor,* 64; Winkler, *Confederate Capital,* 151; Rufus K. Felder to Dear Mother, Mar. 3, 1862, Rufus K. Felder Papers, 5th Texas Infantry File, SCRC. See also Brooks, "Social and Cultural Dynamics of Soldiering," 565.

40. James Longstreet to Lafayette McLaws, Feb. 13, 1864, James Longstreet to Dear General [Simon Buckner], Feb. 13, 1864, and Major [Garnett Andrews] to Lafayette McLaws, Feb. 13, 1864, McLaws Papers, SHC; James Longstreet to Jefferson Davis, Mar. 16, 1864, Longstreet Papers, HU; D. C. Smith, *Campaign to Nowhere,* 175–76; Lafayette McLaws to My Dear Wife, Feb. 17, 1864, McLaws Letter Book, vol. 1, McLaws Papers, SHC.

41. Lafayette McLaws to Lizzie Ewell [Lizinka Brown Ewell], Feb. 29, 1864, Ewell Papers, LC; Krick, "Longstreet Versus McLaws," 103–104. In contrast to McLaws's bitter feelings during his trial, a year earlier the general maintained that "General Longstreet . . . has no superior as a soldier in the Southern Confederacy." See Lafayette McLaws to Miss Lizzie, Feb. 18, 1863, Ewell Papers, LC.

42. Woodworth, *Jefferson Davis and His Generals,* 256; Hallock, *Braxton Bragg,* 164; Hu McLaws to My Dear L[afayette McLaws], n.d., McLaws Papers, SHC (portions of this letter were copied in McLaws to Wife, Feb. 18, 1864, McLaws Letter Book, vol. 1, ibid.).

43. Lafayette McLaws to Dear Wife, Mar. 8, 1864, McLaws Letter Book, vol. 1, McLaws Papers, SHC; Lafayette McLaws to Braxton Bragg, Feb. 28, 1864, and Braxton Bragg to Lafayette McLaws, Mar. 4, 1864, Bragg Papers, WR. A copy of the March 4 letter, dated March 1, appears in *OR,* 52(2):633–34. McLaws also forwarded a copy of Bragg's letter to his wife. See McLaws to My Dear Wife, Mar. 8, 1864.

44. For evidence of McLaws's shifting views, see Lafayette McLaws to D. H. Hill, Jan. 25, 1864, Hill Papers, NC. In this letter McLaws concludes that "Gen. L[ongstreet] failed in his campaign, and thought to divert attention from his great want of capacity by charging me the neglect of some minor details." His later correspondence with his wife, his brother, Lizzie Ewell, Bragg, and Law argued that Longstreet singled out McLaws for the latter's earlier alliance with Bragg at Chattanooga, citing it as a likely reason for his removal from command.

45. Lafayette McLaws to [?], n.d. [postwar], McLaws Papers, SHC. In his later years Bragg maintained that Grant's success at Chattanooga could be attributed to Longstreet, who allowed the opening of the "Cracker Line." "No man (Grant) was under greater obligations to a traitor [Longstreet]," Bragg later wrote. See Braxton Bragg to E. T. Sykes, Feb. 8, 1873, Bragg Papers, WR (a copy exists in McLaws Papers, SHC).

46. Lafayette McLaws to Marcus J. Wright, June 7, 1873, McLaws Papers, SHC;

Lafayette McLaws to Garnett Andrews, Feb. 27, 1864, Andrews Papers, SHC; Samuel Cooper to Simon B. Buckner, Mar. 12, 1864, McLaws Papers, SHC; "March 16, 1864 Testimony of the Court," ibid.; Simon B. Buckner to Samuel Cooper, Mar. 12, 1864, Longstreet Order and Letter Book, CAH; Lafayette McLaws to Dear Wife, Mar. 12, 1864, McLaws Papers, SHC.

47. Lafayette McLaws to Dear Wife, Mar. 12, 1864; Lafayette McLaws to Marcus J. Wright, June 7, 1882, McLaws Papers, SHC; "Finding and Sentence of the Court," *OR*, 31(1):505; Oeffinger, *Soldier's General*, 44. For a detailed analysis of the testimonials, see the court transcripts in McLaws Papers, SHC; and Krick, "Longstreet Versus McLaws," 108-115.

48. Krick, "Longstreet Versus McLaws," 115; *OR*, 31(1):506, 36(2):955, 966.

49. Lafayette McLaws to Joseph Ganahl, July 23, 1894, McLaws Papers, SHC; Oeffinger, *Soldier's General*, 46.

50. Oates, *War between the Union and the Confederacy*, 281. See "Appendix G—Resignation of E. M. Law," in Laine and Penny, *Law's Alabama Brigade*, 371.

51. J. Longstreet, *Manassas to Appomattox*, 519; Oates, *War between the Union and the Confederacy*, 339; Laine and Penny, *Law's Alabama Brigade*, 218.

52. Laine and Penny, *Law's Alabama Brigade*, 218-19.

53. Ibid.; *OR*, 31(1):471.

54. *OR*, 31(1):471-72; Laine and Penny, *Law's Alabama Brigade*, 221.

55. *OR*, 31(1):472, 473, 475; Wert, *General James Longstreet*, 375; Piston, *Lee's Tarnished Lieutenant*, 80.

56. *OR*, 31(1):473.

57. J. Longstreet, *Manassas to Appomattox*, 467-68; Piston, *Lee's Tarnished Lieutenant*, 79; *OR*, 31(3):723. See also *OR*, 52(2):562-63.

58. *OR*, 52(2):633-34; E. M. Law to Lafayette McLaws, Apr. 29, 1864, McLaws Papers, SHC.

59. Laine and Penny, *Law's Alabama Brigade*, 224, 269-70, 283, 316-17; Wert, *General James Longstreet*, 376; Warner, *Generals in Gray*, 175.

60. *OR*, 31(3):735, 866-67; Wert, *General James Longstreet*, 373; Dickert, *Kershaw's Brigade*, 338-39. Piston believes that Longstreet wanted to prepare Kershaw for possible career advancement. *Lee's Tarnished Lieutenant*, 81.

61. Baldwin, *Struck Eagle*, 256-57; *OR*, 31(3):866-67. Joseph E. Johnston had earlier recommended Whiting for promotion to lieutenant general on December 31, 1863, so he could lead a corps in the Army of Tennessee. See *OR*, 31(3):882.

62. *OR*, 31(3):867. Longstreet was not alone in reacting against Richmond's appointments. Even Stonewall Jackson believed that commanders should have final approval in assigning subordinate commanders. See J. I. Robertson, *Stonewall Jackson*, 371.

63. *OR*, 32(2):726; Charles W. Field, "Campaign of 1864-1865—Narrative of Major General C. W. Field," *Southern Historical Society Papers* 14 (1886): 542; Laine and Penny, *Law's Alabama Brigade*, 220; Wert, *General James Longstreet*, 373-74.

64. James Longstreet to Simon Buckner, Mar. 4, 1864, Longstreet Order and Letter Book, CAH; Wert, *General James Longstreet*, 373; Freeman, *Lee's Lieutenants*, 3:311; *OR*, 32(2):567, 32(3):583.

65. *OR,* 52(2):633; Braxton Bragg to Lafayette McLaws, Mar. 1, 1864, McLaws Papers, SHC.

66. In a postwar narrative not intended for publication, Field does not mention being received poorly by the men of the First Corps. See Field, "Campaign of 1864–1865," 542.

67. Hagood, "Memoirs of the First South Carolina Regiment," SCL; *OR,* 32(2):738; Warner, *Generals in Gray,* 87; Wert, *General James Longstreet,* 374.

68. The one exception was Longstreet's feud with Maj. Gen. Ambrose Powell Hill after the Seven Days campaign. See Freeman, *Lee's Lieutenants,* 3:313; and Wert, *General James Longstreet,* 153–55.

69. Piston, *Lee's Tarnished Lieutenant,* 78; James Longstreet to Lafayette McLaws, Oct. 18, 1863, and Lafayette McLaws to Marcus J. Wright, June 7, 1882, McLaws Papers, SHC. Swisher argues that McLaws "lost his nerve" upon arriving in the West. *Prince of Edisto,* 137.

70. Longstreet to Claiborne, Apr. 6, 1880; James Longstreet to Lafayette McLaws, July 25, 1873, McLaws Papers, SHC; *OR,* 31(1):467–68; J. Longstreet, *Manassas to Appomattox,* 548.

71. *OR,* 30(2):148; James Longstreet to D. H. Hill, Oct. 18, 1863, Longstreet Letters, GL; Piston, *Lee's Tarnished Lieutenant,* 78–82.

72. *OR,* 31(1):473; Wert, *General James Longstreet,* 375; Swisher, *Prince of Edisto,* 137.

73. *OR,* 31(3):723, 52(2):633.

74. Ibid., 30(4):742; Symonds, *Joseph E. Johnston,* 249–54.

75. James Longstreet to Daniel Harvey Hill, Mar. 21, 1864, Hill Papers, LV. Wert points to Longstreet's despondency in East Tennessee. *General James Longstreet,* 359

76. Oates, *War between the Union and the Confederacy,* 339; Wert, *General James Longstreet,* 375; Laine and Penny, *Law's Alabama Brigade,* 221; *OR,* 31(1):470.

77. Hood to Cousin Jennie, Feb. 14, 1864.

Chapter 7

1. Amick, "Great Valley of East Tennessee," 35–37, 40–42; Groce, *Mountain Rebels,* 1–20; J. Longstreet, *Manassas to Appomattox,* 520–21; D. C. Smith, *Campaign to Nowhere,* 35; *OR,* 31(1):462.

2. Groce, *Mountain Rebels,* 1–4.

3. John Bratton to Dear Wife, Oct. 23, 1863, Bratton Confederate Letters, SCDAH; Groce, *Mountain Rebels,* 21–45; Noel C. Fisher, "Definition of Victory: East Tennessee Unionists in the Civil War and Reconstruction," in Sutherland, *Guerrillas, Unionists, and Violence,* 90–93, 100; Bryan, "'Tories amidst Rebels,'" 3–5, 6–7; Fisher, "'Leniency Shown Them Has Been Unavailing,'" 278–89. Groce attributes much of the animosity toward the Confederacy on Kirby Smith's policies while commander of the Department of East Tennessee. *Mountain Rebels,* 85–87.

4. D. C. Smith, *Campaign to Nowhere,* 26.

5. *OR,* 32(2):99–101, 183.

6. Ibid., 31(3):394, 504; Collins, *Averell's Salem Raid,* 23-64, 65-104, 129. General Foster appointed Sturgis to command the army's cavalry on December 12, 1863.

7. Jones, the other cavalry commander, held the extreme right flank of Longstreet's corps, beyond Clinch Mountain, and would be unavailable for any movements in the Great Valley. See Lambert, *Grumble,* 92. Lambert points out that Jones was stationed at Jonesville, Tennessee, approximately "a two days ride" from Russellville, to respond to any "force coming through the Clinch River Valley."

8. *OR,* 31(1):547-49, 649-50, 656-57, 662-64; D. C. Smith, *Campaign to Nowhere,* 50-76.

9. *OR,* 32(1):80-81, 32(2):82; D. C. Smith, *Campaign to Nowhere,* 100-101; Wert, *General James Longstreet,* 367; J. Longstreet, *Manassas to Appomattox,* 535-36.

10. *OR,* 32(2):556; D. C. Smith, *Campaign to Nowhere,* 105-106; J. Longstreet, *Manassas to Appomattox,* 526-28; Krick, *Parker's Virginia Battery,* 223.

11. D. C. Smith, *Campaign to Nowhere,* 106-107, 112; J. Longstreet, *Manassas to Appomattox,* 528; *OR,* 32(1):92-93.

12. *OR,* 32(1):79, 93-94; J. Longstreet, *Manassas to Appomattox,* 528-30; Wert, *General James Longstreet,* 367-68.

13. *OR,* 32(1):93.

14. Ibid., 32(1):94, 32(2):131-38, 147-48, 149, 150, 606, 609, 610, 611. A copy of Longstreet's report to Cooper is also found in Longstreet Order and Letter Book, CAH. A good secondary account of the engagement is found in D. C. Smith, *Campaign to Nowhere,* 143-63.

15. James Longstreet to William T. Martin, Dec. 31, 1863, and G. M. Sorrel to W. T. Martin, Jan. 15, 1864, Longstreet Order and Letter Book, CAH. On January 1 Longstreet wrote Martin to thank him for his service and reminded him not to "lose heart because the work has not yet ended as favourably as one would have it." See James Longstreet to W. T. Martin, Jan. 1, 1864.

16. *OR,* 32(1):150, 32(2):632. Longstreet had Maj. Gen. Wade Hampton in mind as early as January 19. But the War Department refused to grant Longstreet's request because he still had Brig. Gens. W. E. Jones and Ransom under his command. Jones, however, was stationed at Cumberland Gap and not quickly accessible to Longstreet's everyday needs. See Lambert, *Grumble,* 114.

17. *OR,* 32(2):597; William Martin to Lafayette McLaws, Feb. 10, 1864, McLaws Papers, SHC; Wert, *General James Longstreet,* 362.

18. *OR,* 32(2):541-42, 604, 606. In a letter to Davis, Johnston expressed doubts of reuniting with Longstreet due to the lack of transportation. Longstreet's attempt to propose a movement on Knoxville was rebuffed by the general for "want of supplies and cavalry" on January 23, 1864. Longstreet's proposal to mount his infantry probably came from his close friend, Simon B. Buckner, who had petitioned Davis to reorganize the Kentucky troops into a "State organization" and to mount them to return to their native state. See *OR,* ser. 4, 3:31-32.

19. *OR,* 32(2):568-69, 653-54, 656, 667, 760-61; James Longstreet to Jefferson Davis, Feb. 20, 1864, and Jefferson Davis to James Longstreet, Feb. 21, 1864, Davis

Papers, DU. Martin's Division, less the two brigades under Cols. Arthur A. Russell and George G. Dibrell, returned to the Army of Tennessee.

20. James Longstreet to Jefferson Davis, Mar. 16, 1864, Longstreet Papers, HL; *OR,* 32(2):790; J. Longstreet, *Manassas to Appomattox,* 541–42; Latrobe Diary, Feb. 20–26, 1864, Latrobe Diary and Letters, VHS; Sorrel, *Recollections,* 223–24.

21. *OR,* 32(2):789–90; Connelly and Jones, *Politics of Command,* 143–48; Wert, *General James Longstreet,* 368–69.

22. *OR,* 33(3):582–83, 594–95.

23. James Longstreet to Joseph E. Johnston, Mar. 3, 1864, JO 233–35, Johnston Papers, HL; J. Longstreet, *Manassas to Appomattox,* 544–45; Wert, *General James Longstreet,* 368; Piston, *Lee's Tarnished Lieutenant,* 82.

24. James Longstreet to Jefferson Davis, Mar. 15, 1864, Longstreet Papers, HU; *OR,* 32(3):627, 637–42; Connelly and Jones, *Politics of Command,* 149–52. When he wrote to Lee, Longstreet enclosed a copy of his letter to the president and implored the general to continue to support the plan because he feared Davis and Bragg would not seriously consider any proposal coming from him. "Your influence with the President, and your prestige as a great leader, will enable you to cause its adoption and successful execution," Longstreet declared.

25. *OR,* 32(3):679–80; Wert, *General James Longstreet,* 372; Piston, *Lee's Tarnished Lieutenant,* 85–86.

26. *OR,* 32(2):639; John Alexander Barry to Dear Pa, Feb. 27, 1864, Barry Papers, SHC. Barry, a private in Wofford's Brigade, wrote, "we are all ordered to furnish ourselves with horses in 90 days." In March 1864 Col. Martin Gary of the Hampton Legion succeeded in procuring horses for his men and had his unit designated as mounted infantry. His command then received a transfer from Jenkins's Brigade to move into South Carolina to obtain additional horses and men. See Baldwin, *Struck Eagle,* 261.

27. Piston, *Lee's Tarnished Lieutenant,* 82–83, 86; Wert, *General James Longstreet,* 372; *OR,* 32(3):680.

28. Woodworth, *Davis and Lee at War,* 268; Moore, *Confederate Commissary General,* 244–45; Wert, *General James Longstreet,* 371; Coward, *The South Carolinians,* 122. Connelly and Jones suggest that General Lee was equally oblivious in regards to logistical operations. *Politics of Command,* 41–43.

29. Samuel Pierce Kenney to Wife, Mar. 5, 1864, Kenney Papers, DU; Barry to Dear Pa, Feb. 27, 1864.

30. Andrew J. McBride to Dear Fannie, Jan. 25, 1864, McBride Papers, DU; John C. Winsmith to My Dear Kate, Nov. 4, 7, 1863, and Christopher Winsmith to My Dear Mother, Dec. 11, 1863, Winsmith Letters, MC; *(Houston, Tex.) Tri-Weekly Telegraph,* Nov. 6, 1863; "Personne" to [?], "Longstreet's Campaign—Correspondence of the Charleston Courier," Dec. 9, 1863, Alexander Papers, SHC; Lafayette McLaws to D. H. Hill, Jan. 25, 1864, Hill Papers, NC. For background on the role of journalists and Civil War armies, see Perry, *Bohemian Brigade;* Harris, *Blue and Gray in Black and White;* and Andrews, *South Reports the Civil War.*

31. Barry to Dear Pa, Feb. 27, 1864. See also Christopher Winsmith to My Dear

Kate, Feb. 27, 1864, Winsmith Letters, MC. Winsmith wrote, "Many are of the opinion that we are going into Kentucky, and that we will go as mounted infantry, but of course all is mere speculation thus far."

32. Christopher Winsmith to My Dear Kate, Mar. 8, 1864, Winsmith Letters, MC; Edward A. Thorne to Dear Wife, Feb. 28, 1864, Thorne Papers, DU; John Barry to Dear Sister, Mar. 7, 1864, and John Barry to Dear Sister, Mar. 21, 1864, Barry Papers, SHC. See also Richard Brooks to Dear Wife, Feb. 28, 1864, in Holland, *Keep All My Letters,* 113.

33. Houghton and Houghton, *Two Boys,* 187; Moses, "Autobiography," SHC. For a description of Moses commandeering a train near Knoxville, see *OR,* 31(1):477.

34. J. Longstreet, *Manassas to Appomattox,* 520, 542; John C. West to Wife, Dec. 25–27, 1863, in West, *Texan in Search of a Fight,* 137; Christopher Winsmith to My Dear Father, Dec. 11, 1863, and Christopher Winsmith to My Dear Mother, Dec. 20, 1863, Winsmith Letters, MC; William Montgomery to My Dear Aunt Frank, Jan. 19, 1864, in Montgomery, *Georgia Sharpshooter,* 100; Mixson, *Reminiscences of a Private,* 59; Andrew Boyd to Robert Boyd, Feb. 21, 1864, Boyd Papers, DU.

35. Bryan, "Civil War in East Tennessee," 142; E. P. Alexander to Dear Wife, Mar. 23, 1864, Alexander Papers, SHC.

36. Andrew Boyd to Robert Boyd, Mar. 17, 1864, Boyd Papers, DU; Houghton and Houghton, *Two Boys,* 68, 69; Coker, *History of Company G,* 138–39; Montgomery Diary, Mar. 19, 1864, in Montgomery, *Georgia Sharpshooter,* 45. See also Wert, *General James Longstreet,* 366. "We are not living as well as we was," Andrew Boyd revealed to his father, "this part of the country is entirely eat out."

37. Dickert, *Kershaw's Brigade,* 329–30; Hamilton, "Company M, First Texas Volunteer Infantry," 29.

38. Brooks to Dear Wife, Feb. 28, 1864; Barry to Dear Sister, Mar. 7, 1864; Coker, *History of Company G,* 138–39; *OR,* 32(3):850–51; Robert Rutledge to Father, Apr. 8, 1864, quoted in Bryan, "Civil War in East Tennessee," 136.

39. P. T. Vaughn to Dear Pa, Apr. 13, 1864, Vaughn Diary and Letters, SHC. Vaughn later received promotion to lieutenant before resigning on December 12, 1864.

40. Wiley, *Life of Johnny Reb,* 100; J. I. Robertson, *Soldiers Blue and Gray,* 72–73, 79; A. Boyd to R. Boyd, Mar. 17, 1864; William Montgomery to Aunt Frank, Jan. 20, 1864, in Montgomery, *Georgia Sharpshooter,* 104; Bryan, "Civil War in East Tennessee," 138–39; Benjamin Humphreys, "A History of the Sunflower Guards," Claiborne Papers, SHC. The high costs of meals are confirmed in Brooks to Dear Wife, Feb. 28, 1864.

41. Hanks quoted in J. D. Hood, "Yellow Rose in the Old Dominion" (M.A. thesis), 98; Andrew McBride to Dear Wife, Jan. 9, 1864, McBride Papers, DU; A. Boyd to R. Boyd, Feb. 21, 1864; Rev. A. C. Sims, "Recollections of the Civil War," A. C. Sims Papers, 1st Texas Infantry File, SCRC; Krick, *Parker's Virginia Battery,* 219; McClendon, *Recollections,* 200; Sorrel, *Recollections,* 220; James Longstreet to J. E. B. Stuart, n.d., SA 219, Stuart Papers, HL.

42. John Evans to Dear Wife, Jan. 8, 1864, Evans Papers, DU; Christopher Winsmith to Dear Janie, Apr. 5, 1864, and Christopher Winsmith to My Dear Mother,

Mar. 22 and [?], 1864 (two letters), Winsmith Letters, MC; Edward Porter Alexander to Wife, Mar. 17, 1864, Alexander Papers, SHC; R. H. Brooks to Dear Wife, Mar. 23, 1864, in Holland, *Keep All My Letters,* 116.

43. Coles, *From Huntsville to Appomattox,* 153; John C. West to My Precious Wife, Dec. 26, 1863, in West, *Texan in Search of a Fight,* 137; Evans to Dear Wife, Jan. 8, 1864; Montgomery Diary, Dec. 25, 1863, in Montgomery, *Georgia Sharp-shooter,* 38; John Barry to Dear Sister, Jan. 19, 1864, Barry Papers, SHC; Coward, *The South Carolinians,* 103. Asbury Coward of Jenkins's Brigade recorded that in building the shanties, "The only drawback was lack of tools."

44. *OR,* 31(1):481; Dickert, *Kershaw's Brigade,* 268, 302; William Montgomery to Aunt Frank, Jan. 18, 1864, in Montgomery, *Georgia Sharpshooter,* 100; Thomas J. Goree to Sarah W. K. Goree, Feb. 8, 1864, in Cutrer, *Longstreet's Aide,* 116; P. T. Vaughn to Dear Pa, Jan. 20, 1864, Vaughn Diary and Letters, SHC; Christopher Winsmith to My Dear Father, Feb. 10, 1864, Winsmith Letters, MC; E. G. Worsham to Dear James, n.d., E. L. Worsham Papers, 4th Texas Infantry File, SCRC; R. H. Brooks to Dear Wife, Apr. 1, 1864, in Holland, *Keep All My Letters,* 117; Dameron, *Benning's Brigade,* 2:102–103; John Barry to Dear Sister, Feb. 23, 1864, Barry Papers, SHC; James Kennedy to Dear Sister, Oct. 25, 1863, James H. Kennedy Papers, 1st Texas Infantry File, SCRC. According to G. M. Sorrel, the price for a coat was $350; boots, $250; trousers, $125; and a shirt, $50. *Recollections,* 232. Even the Texans received some of the shoes from the Georgia ladies. See Winkler, *Confederate Capital,* 153.

45. *OR,* 31(3):818, 1095, 1132, 32(2):559, 604, 637.

46. William Montgomery to Dear Aunt Frank, Jan. 19, 1864, in Montgomery, *Georgia Sharpshooter,* 100; Sorrel, *Recollections,* 219; John Bratton to Dear Wife, Dec. 18, 1863, Bratton Confederate Letters, SCDAH; Hamilton, "Company M, First Texas Volunteer Infantry," 27; Houghton and Houghton, *Two Boys,* 67; Vaughn to Dear Pa, Jan. 20, 1864; Wert, *General James Longstreet,* 366; *OR,* 32(3):667.

47. Kenney to Dear Wife, Mar. 5, 1864; Wert, *General James Longstreet,* 367; Wilkinson and Woodworth, *Scythe of Fire,* 282. For a detailed study on the desertion of Georgia soldiers, see Weitz, *A Higher Duty,* 72. Weitz notes, "By January 1864, East Tennessee was firmly under Union control, providing those Georgians [in Longstreet's corps] with the opportunity to slip into the Union lines."

48. A. Boyd to R. Boyd, Feb. 21, 1864; Houghton and Houghton, *Two Boys,* 76; Rubin, *Shattered Nation,* 78–79. For a discussion on the inconsistencies of dealing with desertion, see Weitz, *More Damning than Slaughter,* 63–64, 77, 81, 87–88, 94–98, 156–57, 243–44.

49. Rubin, *Shattered Nation,* 78–79; Dameron, *Benning's Brigade,* 2:103–104.

50. John Barry to Dear Sister, Oct. 17, Nov. 4, 1863, Barry Papers, SHC; Winsmith to My Dear Father, Feb. 10, 1864. For an example of the dialogue that often influenced Confederate soldiers to return home, see Richard H. Brooks to Dear Wife, Mar. 17, 23, 1864, in Holland, *Keep All My Letters,* 115–16. Brooks felt that he needed to return home to save the family farm. Pvt. John Barry believed that obtaining a leave to bring in a new recruit was difficult. He nevertheless sought the help of his family to secure a coveted furlough. "You seem to think there is a good chance for

Pa to get a recruit," he mentioned to his sister. "I hope he will succeed as I would not miss going home for anything. I think if I could get home I would mend up a little."

51. John Evans to Dear Wife, Jan. 24, 1864, Evans Papers, DU; Weitz, *A Higher Duty,* 72–73; Grear, "Texans to the Front" (PhD diss.), 140–48; Jeremiah Caddell to Dear Mother and Father, Mar. 3, 1864, Jeremiah Caddell Papers, 4th Texas Infantry File, SCRC; Andrew McBride to Dear Fannie, Feb. 9, 1864, McBride Papers, DU; John Barry to Dear Sis, Apr. 19, 1864, Barry Papers, SHC. See also Weitz, *More Damning than Slaughter,* 225–32; and Polley, *Hood's Texas Brigade,* 225.

52. James Longstreet to J. E. B. Stuart, Jan. 10, 1864, Stuart Papers, HL; John Blackford to Wife, Jan. 28, 1864, in Blackford, *Letters from Lee's Army,* 236.

53. Christopher Winsmith to My Dear Father, Dec. 17, 1863, Winsmith Letters, MC; Archer Anderson to George W. Brent, Apr. 14, 1864, Davis Papers, TU; McBride to Dear Fannie, Jan. 9, 1864; Wiley, *Life of Johnny Reb,* 148; *OR,* 31(1):549–50. See also Montgomery to Dear Aunt Frank, Jan. 19, 1864, in Montgomery, *Georgia Sharpshooter,* 100. Anderson's report must be scrutinized carefully since he concedes that he made a "limited observation" of the First Corps.

54. McBride to Dear Fannie, Jan. 9, 1864; Houghton and Houghton, *Two Boys,* 70; Barry to Dear Sister, Mar. 7, 1864. For the significance of mail in the comfort of the troops, see also Polley, *Hood's Texas Brigade,* 224.

55. Houghton and Houghton, *Two Boys,* 69; Vaughn to Dear Pa, Jan. 20, 1864; Evans to Dear Wife, Jan. 24, 1864; John C. West to Dear Wife, Jan. 9, 1864, in West, *Texan in Search of a Fight,* 138. Evans also complained, "I have not received a letter since I left Virginia."

56. Sorrel, *Recollections,* 221; Fisher, *War at Every Door,* 3–5; Hamilton, "Company M, First Texas Volunteer Infantry," 23; Alexander to Dear Wife, Mar. 23, 1864. For an example of this frustration, see Richard Lewis to Dear Mother, Dec. 11, 1863, in Lewis, *Camp Life,* 73.

57. William Fletcher, *Rebel Private, Front and Rear* (Austin: University of Texas Press, 1954), 81; H. B. Simpson, *Hood's Texas Brigade,* 368–69; Sorrel, *Recollections,* 221.

58. Groce, *Mountain Rebels,* 24–27, 46–67, 153–56; Dickert, *Kershaw's Brigade,* 326–27; Christopher Winsmith to My Dear Mother, Feb. 12, 1864, Winsmith Letters, MC; McBride to Dear Fannie, Jan. 9, 1864; Coles, *From Huntsville to Appomattox,* 154.

59. Krick, *Parker's Virginia Battery,* 221; John Evans to Dear Sister, Jan. 3, 1864, Evans Papers, DU; Franklin Gaillard to Maria Gaillard, Mar. 18, 1864, Gaillard Civil War Letters, SHC.

60. Evans to Dear Wife, Jan. 24, 1864; John Barry to Dear Pa, Feb. 27, 1864, Barry Papers, SHC; Mixson, *Reminiscences of a Private,* 59.

61. Dickert, *Kershaw's Brigade,* 327; Moses, "Autobiography," SHC.

62. Houghton and Houghton, *Two Boys,* 69; Charles Blackford to Wife, Jan. 22, 1864, in Blackford, *Letters from Lee's Army,* 235; Richard Lewis to Dear Mother, Mar. 20, 1863, in Lewis, *Camp Life,* 85. South Virginia, in particular, profited from the manufacture and sale of tobacco to the western states of the Confederacy during the war. See Siegel, *Roots of Southern Distinctiveness.*

63. Houghton and Houghton, *Two Boys,* 77; George Emery Butler to Emma Butler, Dec. 2, 1863, in Huckaby and Simpson, *Tulip Evermore,* 38; *OR,* 32(3):749; Montgomery Diary, Apr. 8, 1864, in Montgomery, *Georgia Sharpshooter,* 47. For analysis of the Great Revivals of 1863–64, see Woodworth, *While God Is Marching On,* 277–78; and Wiley, *Life of Johnny Reb,* 180–85.

64. *OR,* 32(3):654, 655, 667, 669–70; J. Longstreet, *Manassas to Appomattox,* 547.

65. *OR,* 32(3):720, 737, 33:1282, 51(2):1076; Robert E. Lee to Jefferson Davis, Mar. 25, 1864, in Freeman, *Lee's Dispatches,* 142, 144; John Bratton to Wife, Apr. 12, 1864, Bratton Confederate Letters, SCDAH; Coles, *From Huntsville to Appomattox,* 155; McClendon, *Recollections,* 201; Houghton and Houghton, *Two Boys,* 67. See also C. M. Winkler to Wife, Apr. 5, 1864, in Winkler, *Confederate Capital,* 155. For an analysis of the events surrounding the decision to reinforce Lee, see Woodworth, *Davis and Lee at War,* 268–70.

66. Latrobe Diary, Apr. 11–22, 1864, Latrobe Diary and Letters, VHS; Alexander, *Fighting for the Confederacy,* 343; Wert, *General James Longstreet,* 372; Lisa Laskin, "'The Army Is Not Near So Much Demoralized as the Country Is': Soldiers in the Army of Northern Virginia and the Confederate Home Front," in Sheehan-Dean, *View from the Ground,* 91–92, 109–111; Robert Boyd to Dear Father, Apr. 22, 1864, Boyd Papers, DU; Thomas J. Goree to Sarah W. K. Goree, Apr. 26, 1864, in Cutrer, *Longstreet's Aide,* 122; Christopher Winsmith to My Dear Father, Apr. 23, 1864, Winsmith Letters, MC; Vaughn to Dear Pa, Apr. 20, 1864; Power, *Lee's Miserables,* 11–12; John Barry to Dear Sister, Apr. 19, 1864, Barry Papers, SHC. Barry preferred Virginia to "anyplace else."

67. W. H. Taylor to James Longstreet, Apr. 26, 1864, reprinted in William Jones et al., eds., *Southern Historical Society Papers,* 52 vols. (1876–1959; reprint, Wilmington, N.C.: Broadfoot, 1990–92), 5:268; Wert, *General James Longstreet,* 376; Dickert, *Kershaw's Brigade,* 340; Power, *Lee's Miserables,* 12; Coles, *From Huntsville to Appomattox,* 158; Freeman, *R. E. Lee,* 3:266; Alexander, *Military Memoirs,* 493.

68. Rhea, *Battle of the Wilderness,* 354–66; Robert E. L. Krick, "Like a Duck on a June Bug: James Longstreet's Flank Attack, May 6, 1864," in Gallagher, *Wilderness Campaign,* 236–57.

69. For a detailed analysis of how Lee was viewed by both his men and the civilian population, see Gary Gallagher, "The Idol of His Soldiers and the Hope of His Country: Lee and the Confederate People," and "The Army of Northern Virginia in May 1864: Lee and the Crisis of High Command," both in Gallagher, *Lee and His Generals,* 3–20, 79–81.

Conclusion

1. Wert, *General James Longstreet,* 19–55; Piston, *Lee's Tarnished Lieutenant,* 1–7; Piston, "Petticoats, Promotions, and Assignments," in DiNardo and Nofi, *James Longstreet,* 53–70.

2. B. D. Simpson, *Ulysses S. Grant,* 78–80, 246–47, 254–55; Marszalek, *Sherman,*

147–48, 182, 185–86, 374; Williams, *P. G. T. Beauregard,* 73–74, 96–97, 172–73; J. I. Robertson, *Stonewall Jackson,* 318–22; McMurry, *John Bell Hood,* 118–21.

3. In his new capacity as Davis's military advisor, Bragg appeared to be carrying out a vendetta against all of his old foes, attempting to engineer their downfalls through his machinations at the War Department. See Hallock, *Braxton Bragg,* 188–95; and Castel, *Decision in the West,* 356–57.

4. Weitz, *A Higher Duty,* 72–73; Weitz, *More Damning than Slaughter,* 149–82, 225–32, 243–44.

5. James Longstreet to Lafayette McLaws, Oct. 14, 18, 1863, McLaws Papers, SHC.

6. Bragg quoted in Liddell, *Liddell's Record,* 157.

7. Symonds, *Joseph E. Johnston,* 324–29; McMurry, *Atlanta 1864,* 94–95, 137–39.

8. James R. Furqueron, "The Bull of the Woods: James Longstreet and the Confederate Left at Chickamauga," in DiNardo and Nofi, *James Longstreet,* 153. See also Piston, *Lee's Tarnished Lieutenant,* 71–72.

9. Wert, *General James Longstreet,* 366–67; *OR,* 31(1):549–50.

10. *OR,* 31(1):267.

11. Col. Walter Taylor to Wife, Apr. 24, 1864, in Tower and Belmont, *Lee's Adjutant,* 155; R. E. L. Krick, "Like a Duck on a June Bug," 236–57.

12. Bragg served as vice president, then president, of the Southern Historical Society Papers in the late 1860s. Davis later contributed articles, lauding Lee and criticizing Longstreet. See Piston, *Lee's Tarnished Lieutenant,* chaps. 6–11.

BIBLIOGRAPHY

Manuscripts and Archival Collections

Center for American History, University of Texas at Austin.

Bragg, Braxton. Letters.
Civil War Miscellany.
Longstreet, James. Order and Letter Book, 1863–65.
Wigfall Family Papers.

Confederate Records Division, National Archives, Washington, D.C.

Compiled Service Records of Confederate Generals and Staff Officers, and Non-regimental Enlisted Men, Record Group 109 (microcopy 331).
Letters Received by the Confederate Adjutant and Inspector General, 1861–65, M474, rolls 57, 124.
Letters Received by the Confederate Secretary of War, 1861–65, Record Group 109, M437.

Department of Manuscripts, Tulane University, New Orleans, La.

Association of Army of Northern Virginia Papers.
Bearley, William H. "Recollections of the East Tennessee Campaign, Battle of Campbell Station, November 16, 1863; Siege of Knoxville, November 17–December 5, 1863."
Brent, George W. Papers.
Civil War Papers, Executive Papers.
Confederate Personnel.
Davis, Jefferson. Papers.
Longstreet, James. Letter.
Minnich, J. W. "Pegram's Brigade at Chickamauga, September 18–21, 1863."
Walton, James B. Collection. Letterbook, 1863–64.
White, W. Charlton. Papers.

Division of Archives and History, North Carolina State Department of Cultural Resources, Raleigh.

Hill, Daniel Harvey. Papers.

Eleanor S. Brockenbrough Library, Museum of the Confederacy, Richmond, Va.

Anderson, Archer. Collection.
Bragg, Braxton. Collection.

Georgia Room Letter Book.
Hill, Daniel Harvey. Collection.
Longstreet, James. Order and Letter Book, 1865.
Southern Historical Society Collection.
Winsmith, Capt. John Christopher. Letters, 1859–66.

Frederick M. Dearborn Collection. Houghton Library,
Harvard University, Cambridge, Mass.

Hill, Daniel Harvey. Papers.
Longstreet, James. Papers.

Gilder Lehrman Collection. The New York Historical Society, New York.

Longstreet, James. Letters.
McLaws, Lafayette. Letters.

Harold B. Simpson Confederate Research Center, Hill College, Hillsboro, Tex.

1st Texas Infantry File.
4th Texas Infantry File.
5th Texas Infantry File.

Hill Memorial Library, Louisiana State University, Baton Rouge.

Leverich, Charles E. Diary.
Fairfax, John Walter. Papers. Film 5735, Confederate Military Manuscripts, Series
     A: Holdings of the Virginia Historical Society

Huntington Library, San Marino, Calif.

Johnston, Joseph E. Papers.
Stuart, James E. B. Papers.

Jefferson Davis Association, Rice University, Houston, Tex.

Davis, Jefferson. Papers.

Library of Congress, Washington, D.C.

Ewell, Richard Stoddert. Papers.
Johnston, Joseph E. Papers.
Longstreet, James. Papers.
Polk, Leonidas. Papers.
Wigfall, Louis T. Papers.

Library of Virginia, Richmond.

Hill, Daniel Harvey. Papers.

Manuscripts and Archives Division, New York Public Library, New York.

Law, Evander McIvor. "Lookout Valley: Memorandum of General E. M. Law." Box
     4, Ezra Ayers Carman Papers.

Rare Book, Manuscript, and Special Collections
Library, Duke University, Durham, N.C.

Boyd, Robert. Papers.
Bragg, Braxton. Papers.
Brent, George. Papers.
Confederate Archives: Army, Miscellany Officers' and Soldiers' Letters, June–
    December 1863 and January–July 1864
Davis, Jefferson. Papers.
Evans, John B. Papers.
Ewell, Benjamin Stoddard and Richard Stoddert. Papers.
Ferguson, Samuel Wragg. Memoirs.
Hill, Daniel Harvey. Papers.
Jenkins, Micah. Papers.
Johnston, Joseph E. Papers.
Kenney, Samuel P. Papers.
Law, Evander McIvor. Papers.
Longstreet, Augustus B. Papers.
Longstreet James. Letters (microfilm).
Longstreet James. Papers.
Munford-Ellis Papers.
Magee, John Euclid. Diary.
McBride, Andrew. Papers.
McLaws, Lafayette. Papers.
Thorne, Edward. Papers.

Rosenburg Library, Galveston, Tex.

Bragg, Braxton. Papers.

South Carolina Department of Archives and History, Columbia.

Bratton, Gen. John. Confederate Letters.
Hagood, James. "Memoirs of the First South Carolina Regiment of Volunteer Infan-
    try in the Confederate War."
Jenkins, John. Papers.
Law, Evander McIvor. Papers.

South Caroliniana Library, University of South Carolina, Columbia.

Hagood, James R. "Memoirs of the First South Carolina Regiment of Volunteer
    Infantry in the Confederate War."
Jenkins, John. Papers.
Jenkins, Micah. Papers.
Nance, James Drayton. Papers.

Southern Historical Collection, University of North Carolina, Chapel Hill.

Alexander, Edward Porter. Papers.
Andrews, Garnett. Papers.

Barry, John A. Papers.

Benning, Henry Lewis. Papers.

Benson, Berry. Papers.

Bragg, Braxton. Papers.

Campbell Family Papers.

Claiborne, John F. H. Papers.

Confederate Sketches.

Dabney, Charles. Papers.

Fuller, Joseph P. Papers.

Gaillard, Franklin. Civil War Letters.

Hill, Daniel Harvey. Papers.

Kendrick, H. C. Papers.

Law, Evander McIvor Papers.

Long, Armistead L. Papers.

Longstreet, James. Papers.

McLaws, Lafayette. Papers.

Minor, Philip Barbour. Letter.

Moses, Raphael. Autobiography. Collection 529.

Munnerlyn, James K. Letters.

Pendleton, William Nelson. Papers.

Polk-Brown-Ewell Papers.

Polk, Leonidas. Papers.

Tucker, Glenn. Papers.

Vaughn, Paul Turner. Diary and Letters.

Venable, Charles. Papers.

Virginia Historical Society, Richmond.

Confederate States of America, Army, Department of Northern Virginia. Special Orders.

Latrobe, Osmun. Diary and Letters, 1862–65.

Western Reserve Historical Society, Cleveland, Ohio

Bragg, Braxton. Papers, 1833–79. William P. Palmer Collection of Confederate Papers, MSS 2000 (microfilm edition).

Newspapers

Atlanta Journal
National Tribune
New Orleans Times
New York Times
Raleigh Weekly Standard
Richmond Daily Enquirer
Richmond Dispatch

Richmond Times
(Houston, Tex.) Tri-Weekly Telegraph

Published Primary Sources

Alexander, Edward P. *Fighting for the Confederacy: The Personal Recollections of General Edward Porter Alexander.* Edited by Gary Gallagher. Chapel Hill: University of North Carolina Press, 1989.

————. *Military Memoirs of a Confederate.* New York: Charles Scribner's Sons, 1907.

Anderson, Archer. "Address of Col. Archer Anderson on the Campaign and Battle of Chickamauga." *Southern Historical Society Papers* 9, no. 9 (1881): 385–417.

Austin, J. P. *The Blue and the Gray: Sketches of a Portion of the Unwritten History of the Great American Civil War, a Truthful Narrative of Adventure, with Thrilling Reminiscences of the Great Struggle on Land and Sea.* Atlanta: Franklin Printing and Publishing, 1899.

Baumgartner, Richard A., and Larry M. Strayer, eds. *Echoes of Battle: The Struggle for Chattanooga, an Illustrated Collection of Union and Confederate Narratives.* Huntington, W.Va.: Blue Acorn, 1996.

Blackford, Susan L., ed. *Letters from Lee's Army, or Memoirs of Life in and out of the Army in Virginia during the War between the States.* New York: Charles Scribner's Sons, 1947.

Buel, Clarence C., and Johnson, Robert U. *Battles and Leaders of the Civil War.* 4 vols. 1884–88. Reprint, Edison, N.J.: Castle, 1994.

Burton, Joseph Q., and Theophilus F. Botsford. *Historical Sketches of the Forty-Seventh Alabama Infantry Regiment, C.S.A.* Montgomery, Ala.: Confederate Publishing, 1909.

Carnes, W. W. "Chickamauga." *Southern Historical Society Papers* 14 (1886): 398–405.

Cater, Douglas J. *As it Was: Reminiscences of a Soldier of the Third Texas Cavalry and the Nineteenth Louisiana Infantry.* Austin: State House, 1990.

Chesnut, Mary Boykin. *A Diary from Dixie.* Edited by Ben A. Williams. Boston: Houghton Mifflin, 1949.

Coker, James L. *History of Company G, Ninth South Carolina Regiment, Infantry, and of S. C. Army.* Greenwood, S.C.: Attic, 1979.

Confederate Veteran Magazine. 40 vols. Nashville, 1893–1934.

Coward, Asbury. *The South Carolinians: Colonel Asbury Coward's Memoirs.* Edited by Natalie Jenkins Bond and Osmun Latrobe Coward. New York: Vantage, 1968.

Crist, Lynda L., and Mary S. Dix, eds. *The Papers of Jefferson Davis.* 11 vols. to date. Baton Rouge: Louisiana State University Press, 1972–.

Cutrer, Thomas W., ed. *Longstreet's Aide: The Civil War Letters of Major Thomas J. Goree.* Charlottesville: University Press of Virginia, 1995.

Davis, Jefferson. *Jefferson Davis, Constitutionalist: His Letters, Papers, and Speeches.*

10 vols. Edited by Dunbar Rowland. Jackson: Mississippi Department of Archives and History, 1923.

———. *The Rise and Fall of the Confederate Government.* Vol. 2. New York: Da Capo, 1992.

Dawson, Frances W. *Reminiscences of Confederate Service.* Charleston, S.C.: News and Courier Book Press, 1882.

Dickert, Augustus. *History of Kershaw's Brigade: With Complete Roll of Companies, Biographical Sketches, Incidents, and Anecdotes.* Dayton, Ohio: Morningside, 1973.

Dowdey, Clifford, and Louis H. Manarin., eds. *The Wartime Papers of R. E. Lee.* Boston: Little, Brown, 1965.

Earp, Charles A. "A Confederate Aide-de-Camp's Letters from the Chattanooga Area, 1863." *The Journal of East Tennessee History* 67 (1995): 106–119.

Everson, Guy R., and Edward H. Simpson. *Far, Far from Home: The Wartime Letters of Dick and Tally Simpson, 3rd South Carolina Volunteers.* New York: Oxford University Press, 1994.

Freeman, Douglass Southall, ed. *Lee's Dispatches: Unpublished Letters of General Robert E. Lee, C.S.A., to Jefferson Davis and the War Department of the Confederate States of America, 1862–65.* Baton Rouge: Louisiana State University Press, 1994.

Fremantle, James A. L. *Three Months in the Southern States: April–June 1863.* New York: J. Bradburn, 1864.

Gorgas, Josiah. *Journals of Josiah Gorgas, 1857–1878.* Edited by Sarah W. Wiggins. Tuscaloosa: University of Alabama Press, 1995.

Grant, Ulysses S. *Personal Memoirs of U. S. Grant.* New York: Da Capo, 1991.

Hood, John B. *Advance and Retreat: Personal Experiences in the United States & Confederate States Armies.* Edited by Richard Current. Bloomington: Indiana University Press, 1959.

Holland, Katherine S. *Keep All My Letters: The Civil War Letters of Richard Henry Brooks, 51st Georgia Infantry.* Macon, Ga.: Mercer University Press, 2003.

Houghton, M. B., and W. R. Houghton. *Two Boys in the Civil War and After.* Montgomery, Ala.: Paragon, 1912.

Huckaby, Elizabeth Paisley, and Ethel C. Simpson, eds. *Tulip Evermore: Emma Butler and William Paisley: Their Lives in Letters, 1857–1887.* Fayetteville: University of Arkansas Press, 1985.

Johnston, Joseph E. *Narrative of Military Operations Directed during the Late War between the States.* New York: Appleton, 1874.

Johnston, Terry A., ed. "A Fort Sanders Survivor's Story." *Columbiad* 4, no. 1 (Spring 2000): 43–65.

Jones, John B. *A Rebel War Clerk's Diary.* Edited by Earl Schenck Miers. Baton Rouge: Louisiana State University Press, 1993.

Jones, John William. *Personal Reminiscences, Anecdotes, and Letters of General Robert E. Lee.* New York: Neale, 1874.

Kean, Robert G. *Inside the Confederate Government: The Diary of Robert Garick*

Hill Kean. Edited by Edward Younger. Baton Rouge: Louisiana State University Press, 1957.

Lane, Mills, ed. *"Dear Mother, Don't Grieve about Me, If I Get Killed, I'll Only Be Dead": Letters from Georgia Soldiers in the Civil War.* Savannah: Beehive, 1977.

Laswell, Mary, ed. *Rags and Hope: The Memoirs of Val C. Giles, Four Years with Hood's Brigade, Fourth Texas Infantry, 1861–1865.* New York: Coward-McCann, 1961.

Law, Evander McIvor. "Burnside and Longstreet in East Tennessee." *Philadelphia Weekly Press,* July 18, 1888.

——. "From Chickamauga to Chattanooga." *Philadelphia Weekly Press,* July 25, 1888.

——. "The Virginia Campaign of 1862." *Philadelphia Weekly Press,* October 26– November 1, 1887.

Lee, Robert E., Jr. *Recollections and Letters of Robert E. Lee.* New York: Konecky and Konecky, 1992.

Lewis, Richard. *Camp Life of a Confederate Boy of Bratton's Brigade, Longstreet's Corps, C.S.A.: Letters Written by Lieutenant Richard Lewis of Walker's Regiment to His Mother during the War.* Charleston, S.C.: News and Courier Book Press, 1883.

Liddell, St. John R. *Liddell's Record.* Edited by Nathaniel C. Hughes. Baton Rouge: Louisiana State University Press, 1997.

Long, A. L., ed. *Memoirs of Robert E. Lee: His Military and Personal History Embracing a Large Amount of Information Hitherto Unpublished.* Edison, N.J.: Blue and Grey, 1983.

Longstreet, James. *From Manassas to Appomattox: Memoirs of the Civil War in America.* 1896. Reprint, New York: Konecky and Konecky, 1959.

Mackall, William W. *A Son's Recollections of His Father.* New York: E. P. Dutton, 1930.

Manigault, Arthur M. *A Carolinian Goes to War.* Edited by R. Lockwood Tower. Columbia: University of South Carolina Press, 1983.

Martin, W. T. "A Defence of General Bragg at Chickamauga." *Southern Historical Society Papers* 11 (1883): 201–206.

Mathis, Ray, ed. *In the Land of the Living: Wartime Letters by Confederates from the Chattahoochee Valley of Alabama and Georgia.* Troy, Ala.: Troy State University Press, 1997.

McClendon, William. *Recollections of War Times by an Old Veteran under Stonewall Jackson and Lieutenant James Longstreet.* Montgomery, Ala.: Paragon, 1909.

McClure, Alexander, ed. *The Annals of the War Written by its Leading Participants North and South Originally Published in the* Philadelphia Weekly Times. Dayton, Ohio: Morningside, 1988.

McLaws, Lafayette. "After Chickamauga." In *Addresses Delivered before the Confederate Veteran Association of Savannah, Georgia, to Which is Appended the President's Annual Report.* Savannah: Braid and Hutton Printers, 1898.

Mixson, Frank M. *Reminiscences of a Private: Company "E," 1st S.C. Volunteers, Jenkins' Brigade, Lee's Army, 1861–1865.* Columbia, S.C.: State, 1910.

Montgomery, George F., ed. *Georgia Sharpshooter: The Civil War Diary and Letters of William Rhadamanthus Montgomery.* Macon, Ga.: Mercer University Press, 1997.

Oates, William C. *The War between the Union and the Confederacy and Its Lost Opportunities, with a History of the Fifteenth Alabama and the Forty-Eight Battles in Which It was Engaged.* Dayton, Ohio: Morningside, 1985.

Oeffinger, John C., ed. *A Soldier's General: The Civil War Letters of Major General Lafayette McLaws.* Chapel Hill: University of North Carolina Press, 2002.

Owen, William Miller. *In Camp and Battle with the Washington Artillery of New Orleans.* New Orleans: Pelican, 1964.

Parker, Eddy R., ed. *Touched by Fire: Letters from Company D, Fifth Texas Infantry, Hood's Brigade, Army of Northern Virginia, 1862–1865.* Hillsboro, Tex.: Hillsboro College Press, 2000.

Polley, J. B. *Hood's Texas Brigade: Its Marches, Its Battles, Its Achievements.* New York: Neale, 1910.

Robertson, Jerome B. *Touched with Valor: Civil War Papers and Casualty Reports of Hood's Texas Brigade.* Edited by Harold B. Simpson. Hillsboro, Tex.: Hill Junior College Press, 1964.

Sherman, William T. *Memoirs of General William T. Sherman.* New York: Da Capo, 1984.

Skoch, George, and Mark W. Perkins, eds. *Lone Star Confederate: A Gallant and Good Soldier of the Fifth Texas Infantry.* College Station: Texas A&M University Press, 2000.

Smith, Gustavus W. *The Battle of Seven Pines.* Dayton, Ohio: Morningside, 1974.

Snell, William R., ed. *Myra Inman: A Diary of the Civil War in East Tennessee.* Mercer, Ga.: Mercer University Press, 2000.

Sorrel, G. Moxley. *Recollections of a Confederate Staff Officer.* New York: Konecky and Konecky, 1994.

Speed, Thomas. "Battle of Bean's Station, East Tennessee." *Southern Bivouac: A Monthly Literary and Historical Magazine* 2 (November 1883): 112–18.

Stocker, Jeffrey D., ed. *From Huntsville to Appomattox: R. T. Coles's History of 4th Regiment, Alabama Volunteer Infantry, C.S.A., the Army of Northern Virginia.* Knoxville: University of Tennessee Press, 1996.

Stout, L. H. *Reminiscences of General Braxton Bragg.* Hattiesburg: Book Farm, 1876.

Taylor, John Dykes. "History of the 48th Regiment, Alabama Infantry." *Montgomery (Ala.) Advertiser,* March 9, 1902.

Taylor, Richard. *Destruction and Reconstruction: Personal Experiences of the Late War.* New York: Da Capo, 1995.

Taylor, Walter H. *Four Years with General Lee.* Edited by James I. Robertson Jr. Bloomington: Indiana University Press, 1996.

———. *General Lee: His Campaigns in Virginia, 1861–1865, with Personal Reminiscences.* Dayton, Ohio: Morningside, 1975.

Todd, George. *First Texas Regiment.* Waco: Texian, 1964.

Tower, R. Lockwood, and John S. Belmont, eds. *Lee's Adjutant: The Wartime Letters of Colonel Walter Herron Taylor, 1862–1865.* Columbia: University of South Carolina Press, 1995.

U.S. War Department. *The War of the Rebellion: A Compilation of Official Records of Union and Confederate Armies.* 128 vols. Washington, D.C.: Government Printing Office, 1880–91.

Vaughan, Paul Turner. "Diary of Turner Vaughan, Co. 'C,' 4th Alabama Regiment, C.S.A., Commenced March 4th, 1863, and Ending February 12th, 1864." *Alabama Historical Quarterly* 18, no. 4 (Winter 1956): 573–604.

Watkins, Samuel R. *Co. Aytch: A Side Show of the Big Show.* New York: Macmillan, 1962.

West, John C. *A Texan in Search of a Fight: Being the Diary and Letters of a Private Soldier in Hood's Texas Brigade.* Introduction by Harold B. Simpson. Waco: Texian, 1969.

Winkler, A. V. *The Confederate Capital and Hood's Texas Brigade.* Austin: Eugene Von Boeckmann, 1894.

Woodward, C. Vann, ed. *Mary Chesnut's Civil War.* New Haven, Conn.: Yale University Press, 1981.

Wright, D. Giraud. *A Southern Girl in '61: The Wartime Memories of a Confederate Senator's Daughter.* New York: Doubleday, 1905.

Secondary Sources

Alexander, Joseph. "Defending Marye's Heights." *Military Historical Quarterly* 9, no. 3 (1997): 86–96.

Allardice, Bruce L. "Longstreet's Nightmare in Tennessee." *Civil War: The Magazine for the Civil War Society* 18, no. 4 (1990): 32–43.

Ambrose, Stephen. *Honor, Duty, Country: A History of West Point.* Baltimore: Johns Hopkins University Press, 1966.

Amick, H. C. "The Great Valley of East Tennessee." *Economic Geography* 10, no. 1 (January 1934): 35–52.

Andrews, J. Cutler. *The South Reports the Civil War.* Princeton: Princeton University Press, 1970.

Austerman, Wayne. "Longstreet Goes Home." *Civil War Times Illustrated* 20, no. 3 (1981): 32–33.

Baldwin, James J. *The Struck Eagle: Micah Jenkins, the Fifth South Carolina Volunteers, and the "Palmetto Sharpshooters."* Shippensburg, Pa.: Burd Street, 1996.

Bill, Alfred H. *Rehearsal for Conflict: The War with Mexico, 1846–1848.* New York: Alfred A. Knopf, 1947.

Black, Robert C., III. *The Railroads of the Confederacy.* Chapel Hill: University of North Carolina Press, 1952.

Boatner, Mark M. *The Civil War Dictionary.* New York: David M. McKay, 1959.

Bradley, Paul F. "Feuding Confederate Commanders." *America's Civil War* 10, no. 5 (November 1997): 46–53.

Bridges, Hal. *Lee's Maverick General: Daniel Harvey Hill.* New York: McGraw-Hill, 1961.

Brooks, Charles E. "The Social and Cultural Dynamics of Soldiering in Hood's Texas Brigade." *The Journal of Southern History* 67, no. 3 (August 2001): 535–72.

Brown, Ken Masterson. *Retreat from Gettysburg:* Lee, Logistics, and the Pennsylvania Campaign. Chapel Hill: University of North Carolina Press, 2005.

Bryan, Charles F., Jr. "'Tories amidst Rebels': Confederate Occupation of East Tennessee, 1861–63." *The East Tennessee Historical Society's Publications* 60 (1988): 3–22.

Cabell, Sears W. *The Bulldog: Longstreet at Gettysburg and Chickamauga, in Light of the Official Records.* Atlanta: Ruralist, 1938.

Campbell, James B. "East Tennessee during the Federal Occupation, 1863–1865." *The East Tennessee Historical Society's Publications* 19 (1947): 64–80.

Carhart, Tom. *Lost Triumph:* Lee's Real Plan at Gettysburg and Why It Failed. New York: Penguin, 2005.

Carmichael, Peter S., ed. *Audacity Personified:* The Generalship of Robert E. Lee. Baton Rouge: Louisiana State University Press, 2004.

Castel, Albert. *Decision in the West: The Atlanta Campaign of 1864.* Lawrence: University Press of Kansas, 1993.

———. *Winning and Losing in the Civil War: Essays and Stories.* Columbia: University of South Carolina Press, 1996.

Cate, Wirt Armistead. *Lucius Q. C. Lamar: Secession and Reunion.* Chapel Hill: University of North Carolina Press, 1935.

Coddington, Edwin B. *The Gettysburg Campaign: A Study in Command.* New York: Charles Scribner's Sons, 1968.

Coffman, Edward C. *The Old Army: A Portrait of the American Army in Peacetime, 1784–1898.* Oxford: Oxford University Press, 1986.

Collier, Calvin L. *"They'll Do to Die To!": The Story of the Third Regiment, Arkansas Infantry, C.S.A.* Little Rock: Pioneer, 1959.

Collins, Darrell. *General William Averell's Salem Raid:* Breaking the Knoxville Supply Line. Shippensburg, Pa.: White Mane, 1999.

Connelly, Thomas L. *Army of the Heartland: The Army of Tennessee, 1861–1862.* Baton Rouge: Louisiana State University Press, 1967.

———. *Autumn of Glory: The Army of Tennessee, 1862–1865.* Baton Rouge: Louisiana State University Press, 1973.

———. *The Marble Man: Robert E. Lee and His Image in American Society.* Baton Rouge: Louisiana State University Press, 1977.

———. "Robert E. Lee and the Western Confederacy: A Critique of Lee's Strategic Ability." *Civil War History* 15, no. 2 (June 1969): 116–32.

Connelly, Thomas Lawrence, and Archer Jones. *The Politics of Command: Factions and Ideas in Confederate Strategy.* Baton Rouge: Louisiana State University Press, 1973.

Cooper, William J. *Jefferson Davis, American.* New York: Alfred A. Knopf, 2000.

Cormier, Steven A. *The Siege of Suffolk: The Forgotten Campaign.* Lynchburg, Va.: H. E. Howard, 1989.

Coulter, E. Moulton. "The Ante-Bellum Academy Movement in Georgia." *Georgia Historical Quarterly* 5 (December 1921): 11–34.

Cozzens, Peter. *No Better Place to Die: The Battle of Stones River.* Urbana: University of Illinois Press, 1991.

———. *The Shipwreck of Their Hopes: The Battles for Chattanooga.* Urbana: University of Illinois Press, 1994.

———. *This Terrible Sound: The Battle of Chickamauga.* Urbana: University of Illinois Press, 1992.

Crowson, E. T. "Jenkins, Coward, and the Yorkville Boys." *Sandlapper Magazine* 7, no. 12 (December 1974): 32–36.

Cummings, Charles M. *Yankee Quaker, Confederate General: The Curious Career of Bushrod Rust Johnson.* Rutherford, N.J.: Fairleigh Dickinson University Press, 1971.

Dameron, J. David. *Benning's Brigade: A History and Roster of the Second, Seventeenth, and Twentieth Georgia Volunteer Regiments.* 2 vols. Westminster, Md.: Heritage, 2005.

———. *General Henry Lewis Benning: "This Was a Man"—A Biography of Georgia's Supreme Court Justice and Confederate General.* Westminster, Md.: Heritage, 2002.

Daniel, Larry J. *Cannoneers in Gray: The Field Artillery of the Army of Tennessee.* Tuscaloosa: University of Alabama Press, 1984.

———. *Soldiering in the Army of Tennessee: A Portrait in the Life of a Confederate Army.* Chapel Hill: University of North Carolina Press, 1994.

Davis, William C. *Battle at Bull Run: A History of the First Major Campaign of the Civil War.* Conshohocken, Pa.: Stackpole, 1995.

———. *Breckinridge: Statesman, Soldier, Symbol.* Baton Rouge: Louisiana State University Press, 1973.

———. *A Government of Our Own: The Making of the Confederate Government.* New York: Free Press, 1994.

———. *Jefferson Davis: The Man and His Hour.* New York: Harper Collins, 1991.

———. *The Union that Shaped the Confederacy: Alexander Stephens and Robert Toombs.* Lawrence: University Press of Kansas, 2001.

DiNardo, Richard L. "Southern by the Grace of God but Prussian by Common Sense: James Longstreet and the Exercise of Command in the U.S. Civil War." *Journal of Military History* 66, no. 4 (December 2002): 1011–32.

DiNardo, R. L., and Albert A. Nofi, eds. *James Longstreet: The Man, the Soldier, the Controversy.* Conshohocken, Pa.: Combined Publishing, 1998.

Dowdey, Clifford. *Lee.* Boston: Little, Brown, 1965.

———. *Lee's Last Campaign: The Story of Lee and His Men against Grant—1864.* Lincoln: University of Nebraska Press, 1988.

Downey, Fairfax D. *Storming of the Gateway: Chattanooga, 1863.* New York: David McKay, 1960.

Dyer, John P. *From Shiloh to San Juan: The Life of "Fightin' Joe" Wheeler.* Baton Rouge: Louisiana State University Press, 1941.

Eckenrode, James, and Bryan Conrad. *James Longstreet: Lee's War Horse.* Foreword by Gary W. Gallagher. Chapel Hill: University of North Carolina Press, 1986.

Eicher, John H., and David J. Eicher. *Civil War High Commands.* Stanford: Stanford University Press, 2001.

Eisenhower, John S. D. *Agent of Destiny: The Life and Times of General Winfield Scott.* New York: Free Press, 1997.

———. *So Far from God: The U.S. War with Mexico, 1846–1848.* New York: Random House, 1989.

Eliot, Ellsworth, Jr. *West Point in the Confederacy.* New York: G. A. Baker, 1941.

Elliott, Sam Davis. *Soldier of Tennessee: General Alexander P. Stewart and the Civil War in the West.* Baton Rouge: Louisiana State University Press, 1999.

Faeder, Gustav. "The Best of Friends and Enemies: Grant and Longstreet." *Civil War Times Illustrated* 26, no. 6 (1987): 16–24.

Faust, Drew Gilpin. "Christian Soldiers: The Meaning of Revivalism in the Confederate Army." *The Journal of Southern History* 52, no. 1 (February 1987): 63–90.

Fink, Harold S. "The East Tennessee Campaign and the Battle of Knoxville in 1863." *East Tennessee Historical Society's Publications* 29 (1957): 79–117.

Fisher, Noel C. "Definitions of Loyalty: Unionist Histories of the Civil War in East Tennessee." *Journal of East Tennessee History* 67 (1995): 58–88.

———. "'The Leniency Shown Them Has Been Unavailing': The Confederate Occupation of East Tennessee." *Civil War History* 40, no. 4 (December 1994): 275–91.

———. *War at Every Door: Partisan Politics and Guerilla Violence in East Tennessee, 1860–1869.* Chapel Hill: University of North Carolina Press, 1997.

Fitzgerald, O. P. *Judge Longstreet, a Life Sketch.* Nashville: Publishing House of the Methodist Episcopal Church, South, 1891.

Freehling, William. *Prelude to Civil War: The Nullification Controversy in South Carolina, 1816–1833.* New York: Harper and Row, 1966.

Freeman, Douglas Southall. *Lee's Lieutenants: A Study in Command.* 3 vols. New York: Charles Scribner's Sons, 1942–44.

———. *R. E. Lee: A Biography.* 4 vols. New York: Charles Scribner's Sons, 1934–35.

Gallagher, Gary W., ed. *The Fredericksburg Campaign.* Chapel Hill: University of North Carolina Press, 1995.

———. *Jubal A. Early, the Lost Cause, and Civil War History: A Persistent Legacy.* Milwaukee: Marquette University Press, 1995.

———, ed. *Leaders of the Lost Cause:* New Perspectives on the Confederate High Command. New York: Stackpole, 2002.

———, ed. *Lee and His Generals in War and Memory.* Baton Rouge: Louisiana State University Press, 1998.

———, ed. *Lee the Soldier.* Lincoln: University of Nebraska Press, 1996.

———. "Scapegoat in Victory: James Longstreet at Second Manassas." *Civil War History* 33, no. 4 (December 1988): 294–307.

——, ed. *The Second Day at Gettysburg: Essays on Confederate and Union Leadership.* Kent, Ohio: Kent State University Press, 1993.

——, ed. *The Third Day at Gettysburg and Beyond.* Chapel Hill: University of North Carolina Press, 1994.

——, ed. *The Wilderness Campaign.* Chapel Hill: University of North Carolina Press, 1997.

Glatthaar, Joseph T. *Partners in Command: The Relationships between Leaders in the Civil War.* New York: Free Press, 1994.

Goss, Thomas Joseph. *The War within the Union High Command: Politics and Generalship during the Civil War.* Lawrence: University Press of Kansas, 2003.

Gow, June I. "Chiefs of Staff in the Army of Tennessee under Braxton Bragg." *Tennessee Historical Quarterly* 27 (1968): 341-60.

——. "Military Administration in the Confederate Army of Tennessee." *Journal of Southern History* 40, no. 2 (May 1974): 183-98.

——. "The Johnston and Brent Diaries: A Problem of Authorship." *Civil War History* 14, no. 1 (March 1968): 46-50.

Grimsley, Mark. *And Keep Moving On:* The Virginia Campaign, May-June 1864. Lincoln: University of Nebraska Press, 2002.

——. "In Not So Dubious Battle: The Motivations of American Civil War Soldiers." *Journal of Military History* 62, no. 1 (January 1998): 175-88.

——. "Rear Guard at Williamsburg." *Civil War Times Illustrated* 24, no. 3 (May 1985): 10-13.

Groce, W. Todd. *Mountain Rebels: East Tennessee Confederates and the Civil War, 1860-1870.* Knoxville: University of Tennessee Press, 1999.

Hallock, Judith L. *Braxton Bragg and Confederate Defeat.* Vol. 2. Tuscaloosa: University of Alabama Press, 1991.

——. *General James Longstreet in the West: A Monumental Failure.* Fort Worth: Ryan Place, 1995.

Harris, Brayton. *Blue and Gray in Black and White: Newspapers in the Civil War.* Washington, D.C.: Brassey's, 1999.

Harrison, Lowell. "Battle beyond Knoxville: Confederates Turn and Fight at Bean's Station." *Civil War Times Illustrated* 26, no. 3 (May 1987): 16-21, 46-47.

Harsh, Joseph L. "Battlesword and Rapier: Clausewitz, Jomini, and the American Civil War." *Military Affairs* 38 (December 1976): 133.

——. *Taken at the Flood: Robert E. Lee and Confederate Strategy in the Maryland Campaign of 1862.* Kent, Ohio: Kent State University Press, 1999.

Hassler, William W. "The 'Ghost' of General Longstreet." *Georgia Historical Quarterly* 65 (1981): 22-27.

Hastings, Earl C., and David S. Hastings. *A Pitiless Rain: The Battle of Williamsburg, 1862.* Shippensburg, Pa.: White Mane, 1997.

Hattaway, Herman, and Archer Jones. *How the North Won: A Military History of the Civil War.* Urbana: University of Illinois Press, 1983.

Haughton, Andrew. *Training, Tactics, and Leadership in the Confederate Army of Tennessee.* Portland, Ore.: Frank Cass, 2000.

Hay, Thomas Robson. "The Battle of Chattanooga." *Georgia Historical Quarterly* 8 (1924): 121–41.

———. "Braxton Bragg and the Southern Confederacy." *Georgia Historical Quarterly* 9 (1925): 267–316.

———. "The Campaign and Battle of Chickamauga." *Georgia Historical Quarterly* 7 (1923): 213–50.

Hebert, Walter H. *Fighting Joe Hooker.* New York: Bobbs-Merrill, 1944.

Hess, Earl J. *Banners to the Breeze: The Kentucky Campaign, Corinth, & Stones River.* Lincoln: University of Nebraska Press, 2000.

Hirshson, Stanley. *The White Tecumseh: A Biography of William T. Sherman.* New York: John Wiley and Sons, 1997.

Holden, Walter. "Confusion on the Road to Wauhatchie." *Military History* (December 1996): 50–56.

Hoobler, James A. *Cities under the Gun: Images of Occupied Nashville and Chattanooga.* Nashville: Rutledge Hill, 1986.

Horn, Stanley. *The Army of Tennessee.* Norman: University of Oklahoma Press, 1993.

Hughes, Nathaniel Cheairs. *General William J. Hardee: Old Reliable.* Baton Rouge: Louisiana State University Press, 1965.

Hughes, Robert M., ed. "Some Letters from the Papers of J. E. Johnston." *William and Mary Quarterly* 20 (October 1931): 319–24.

Johnson, Timothy. *Winfield Scott: The Quest for Military Glory.* Lawrence: University Press of Kansas, 1998.

Johnston, Terry A. "Failure before Knoxville: Longstreet's Attack on Fort Sanders, November 29, 1863." *North and South: The Magazine of Civil War Conflict* 2, no. 7 (September 1999): 56–75.

Jones, Archer. *Civil War Command and Strategy: The Process of Victory and Defeat.* New York: Free Press, 1992.

Jones, Kenneth. "The Fourth Alabama Infantry: A Fighting Legion." *Alabama Historical Quarterly* 38, no. 3 (1976): 171–203.

Kegley, Tracy M. "Bushrod Rust Johnson, Soldier and Teacher." *Tennessee Historical Quarterly* 7 (1948): 249–58.

King, Alvy L. *Louis T. Wigfall: Southern Fire-Eater.* Baton Rouge: Louisiana State University Press, 1970.

Klein, Maury. *Days of Defiance: Sumter, Secession, and the Coming of the Civil War.* New York: Alfred Knopf, 1997.

———. *Edward Porter Alexander.* Athens: University of Georgia Press, 1971.

———. "The Knoxville Campaign." *Civil War Times Illustrated* 10 (October 1971): 4–10, 40–47.

Krick, Robert K. *Lee's Colonels: A Biographical Register of the Field Officers of the Army of Northern Virginia.* Dayton, Ohio: Morningside, 1992.

———. *Parker's Virginia Battery, C.S.A.* Berryville, Va.: Virginia Book, 1975.

———. *The Smoothbore Volley that Doomed the Confederacy: The Death of Stonewall Jackson and other Chapters on the Army of Northern Virginia.* Baton Rouge: Louisiana State University, 2002.

Krolick, Marshall D. "Lee and Longstreet at Gettysburg." *Virginia Country's Civil War* 5 (1986): 32–47.

Kruman, Marc W. "Dissent in the Confederacy: The North Carolina Experience." *Civil War History* 27, no. 4 (December 1981): 300–313.

Laine, J. Gary, and Morris M. Penny. *Law's Alabama Brigade in the War between the Union and the Confederacy.* Shippensburg, Pa.: White Mane, 1996.

Lambert, Dobbie Edward. *Grumble: The W. E. Jones Brigade of 1863–1864.* Wahiawa, Hawaii: Lambert Enterprises, 1992.

Lamers, William M. *The Edge of Glory: A Biography of General William S. Rosecrans, U.S.A.* New York: Harcourt, Brace, and World, 1961.

Longacre, Edward G. *A Soldier to the Last: Maj. General Joseph P. Wheeler in Blue and Gray.* Washington, D.C.: Potomac Books, 2006.

Longstreet, Helen Dortch. "The Great American: General James Longstreet." *Mark Twain Quarterly* 9 (1953): 5–10.

——. *Lee and Longstreet at High Tide: Gettysburg in Light of the Official Records.* Wilmington, N.C.: Broadfoot, 1989.

Losson, Christopher. *Tennessee's Forgotten Warriors: Frank Cheatham and His Confederate Division.* Knoxville: University of Tennessee Press, 1989.

Madden, David. "Unionist Resistance to Confederate Occupation: The Bridge Burners of East Tennessee." *East Tennessee Historical Society's Publications* 52 (1980–81): 22–39.

Marszalek, John F. *Sherman: A Soldier's Passion for Order.* New York: Free Press, 1993.

Martin, David. *General James Longstreet and His New Jersey Relations: A Brief Genealogical History of the Families and Common Ancestry of Jonathan Longstreet of Holmdel, New Jersey, and Confederate General James Longstreet.* Highstown, N.J.: Longstreet House, 1998.

——. *Gettysburg July 1.* Conshohocken, Pa.: Combined Books, 1996.

Marvel, William. *Burnside.* Chapel Hill: University of North Carolina Press, 1991.

McDonough, James Lee. *Chattanooga: A Death Grip on the Confederacy.* Knoxville: University of Tennessee Press, 1984.

——. *War in Kentucky: From Shiloh to Perryville.* Knoxville: University of Tennessee Press, 1994.

McDowell, John E., and William C. Davis. "General Joseph B. Kershaw." *Civil War Times Illustrated* 7 (February 1970): 35–44.

McFeely, William. *Grant: A Biography.* New York: W. W. Norton, 1981.

McKinney, Francis. *Education in Violence: The Life of George H. Thomas and the History of the Army of the Cumberland.* Chicago: Americana House, 1991.

McKinney, Gordon B. *Zeb Vance: North Carolina's Civil War Governor and Gilded Age Political Leader.* Chapel Hill: University of North Carolina Press, 2004.

McMurry, Richard M. *Atlanta 1864.* Lincoln: University of Nebraska Press, 2000.

——. "The Enemy at Richmond: Joseph E. Johnston and the Confederate Government." *Civil War History* 27, no. 1 (March 1981): 6–31.

——. *John Bell Hood and the War of Southern Independence.* Lexington: University Press of Kentucky, 1982.

———. *Two Great Rebel Armies: An Essay in Confederate Military History.* Chapel Hill: University of North Carolina Press, 1989.

McPherson, James M. *For Cause and Comrades: Why Men Fought in the Civil War.* New York: Oxford University Press, 1997.

McWhiney, Grady. *Braxton Bragg and Confederate Defeat.* Vol. 1. New York: Columbia University Press, 1969.

McWhiney, Grady, and Perry D. Jamieson. *Attack and Die: Civil War Military Tactics and the Southern Heritage.* Tuscaloosa: University of Alabama Press, 1982.

Moore, Jerrold Northrop. *Confederate Commissary General: Lucius Bellinger Northrop and the Subsistence Bureau of the Southern Army.* Shippensburg, Pa.: White Mane, 1999.

Morris, Roy. "That Improbable, Praiseworthy Paper: *The Chattanooga Daily Rebel.*" *Civil War Times Illustrated* 23, no. 7 (1984): 16–24.

Morrison, James L. *"The Best School in the World": West Point, the Pre–Civil War Years, 1833–1866.* Kent, Ohio: Kent State University Press, 1986.

Neal, Diane, and Thomas Kremm. *The Lion of the South: General Thomas C. Hindman.* Macon, Ga.: Mercer University Press, 1993.

Newton, Steven H. *The Battle of Seven Pines, May 31–June 1, 1862.* Lynchburg, Va.: H. E. Howard, 1993.

———. *Joseph E. Johnston and the Defense of Richmond.* Lawrence: University Press of Kansas, 1998.

———. *Lost for the Cause: The Confederate Army in 1864.* Mason City, Calif.: Savas, 2000.

Noblitt, Phil. "A Flank Unturned at Chickamauga." *America's Civil War* 9, no. 5 (1996): 34–40.

Nolan, Alan T. *Lee Considered: General Robert E. Lee and Civil War History.* Chapel Hill: University of North Carolina Press, 1991.

O'Brien, Sean Michael. *Mountain Partisans: Guerrilla Warfare in the Southern Appalachians, 1861–1865.* Westport, Conn.: Praeger, 1999.

Osborne, Charles. *Jubal: The Life and Times of Jubal A. Early, C.S.A.* Chapel Hill: University of North Carolina Press, 1992.

Parks, Joseph. *General Edmund Kirby Smith, C.S.A.* Baton Rouge: Louisiana State University Press, 1954.

———. *General Leonidas Polk, C.S.A.: Fighting Bishop.* Baton Rouge: Louisiana State University Press, 1962.

Pearce, Haywood Jefferson. "Longstreet's Responsibility on the Second Day at Gettysburg." *Georgia Historical Quarterly* 10 (1926): 26–45.

Peebles, Ruth. *There Never Were Such Men Before: The Civil War Soldiers and Veterans of Polk County, TX, 1861–1865.* Livingston, Tex.: Polk County Historical Commission, 1987.

Perry, James M. *A Bohemian Brigade: The Civil War Correspondents Mostly Rough, Sometimes Ready.* New York: John Wiley and Sons, 2000.

Pfanz, Donald C. *Ewell: A Soldier's Life.* Chapel Hill: University of North Carolina Press, 1998.

Pfanz, Harry W. *Gettysburg: The First Day.* Chapel Hill: University of North Carolina Press, 2001.

———. *Gettysburg: The Second Day.* Chapel Hill: University of North Carolina Press, 2003.

Pickenpaugh, Roger. *Rescue by Rail: Troop Transfer and the Civil War in the West, 1863.* Lincoln: University of Nebraska Press, 1998.

Piston, William Garrett. *Lee's Tarnished Lieutenant: James Longstreet and His Place in Southern History.* Athens: University of Georgia Press, 1987.

Polk, William M. *Leonidas Polk: Bishop and General.* 2 vols. New York: Longmans, Green, 1915.

Power, J. Tracy. *Lee's Miserables: Life in the Army of Northern Virginia from the Wilderness to Appomattox.* Chapel Hill: University of North Carolina Press, 1998.

Prushankin, Jeffery S. *A Crisis in Confederate Command: Edmund Kirby Smith, Richard Taylor, and the Army of the Trans-Mississippi.* Baton Rouge: Louisiana State University Press, 2005.

Rable, George C. *Fredericksburg! Fredericksburg!* Chapel Hill: University of North Carolina Press, 2001.

Rafuse, Ethan S. *A Single Grand Victory: The First Campaign and Battle of Manassas.* Wilmington, Del.: Scholarly Research, 2002.

Rhea, Gordon C. *The Battle of the Wilderness, May 5–6, 1864.* Baton Rouge: Louisiana State University Press 1994.

Robertson, James I. *Soldiers Blue and Gray.* Columbia: University of South Carolina Press, 1988.

———. *Stonewall Jackson: The Man, the Soldier, the Legend.* New York: Macmillan, 1997.

Robertson, William Glenn. "Rails to the River of Death: Railroads in the Chickamauga Campaign." *Civil War Magazine* 9, no. 6 (1991): 50–71.

Rubin, Anne Sarah. *A Shattered Nation: The Rise and Fall of the Confederacy, 1861–1868.* Chapel Hill: University of North Carolina Press, 2005.

Sanger, Donald B. *The Story of Old Fort Bliss.* El Paso: Buie, 1933.

———. "Was Longstreet a Scapegoat?" *Infantry Journal* 26 (1936): 39–46.

Sanger, Donald B., and Thomas R. Hay. *James Longstreet: Soldier, Politician, Officeholder, and Writer.* Baton Rouge: Louisiana State University Press, 1952.

Sears, Stephen W. *Chancellorsville.* New York: Ticknor & Fields, 1996.

———. *Gettysburg.* New York: Houghton Mifflin, 2003.

———. *Landscape Turned Red: The Battle of Antietam.* New York: Ticknor & Fields 1983.

———. *To the Gates of Richmond: The Peninsula Campaign.* New York: Ticknor & Fields, 1992.

Seitz, Don. *Braxton Bragg, General of the Confederacy.* Columbia: University of South Carolina Press, 1924.

Seymour, Digby Gordon. *Divided Loyalties: Fort Sanders and the Civil War in East Tennessee.* Knoxville: University of Tennessee Press, 1963.

Sheehan-Dean, Aaron C. *The View from the Ground: Experiences of Civil War Soldiers.* Lexington: University of Kentucky Press, 2007.

Siegel, Frederick F. *The Roots of Southern Distinctiveness: Tobacco and Society in Danville, Virginia.* Chapel Hill: University of North Carolina Press, 1987.

Simpson, Brooks D. *Ulysses S. Grant: Triumph over Adversity, 1822–1865.* New York: Houghton Mifflin, 1999.

Simpson, Harold B. *Hood's Texas Brigade: Lee's Grenadier Guard.* Waco: Texian, 1970.

Skelton, William B. *An American Profession of Arms: The Army Officer Corps, 1784–1861.* Lawrence: University Press of Kansas, 1992.

Skoch, George. "War along Southern Rails: A Test of Rebel Rails." *Civil War Times Illustrated* 25, no. 8 (1986): 12–18.

Smith, David C. *Campaign to Nowhere: The Results of General Longstreet's Move into Upper Tennessee.* Rogersville: East Tennessee Printing, 1999.

Smith, Jean Edward. *Grant.* New York: Simon & Schuster, 2000.

Stevens, John K. "Of Mules and Men: The Night Fight at Wauhatchie Station." *South Carolina Historical Magazine* 90 (October 1989): 282–98.

Stickles, Arndt M. *Simon Bolivar Buckner: Borderland Knight.* Chapel Hill: University of North Carolina Press, 1940.

Sutherland, Daniel E. *Fredericksburg and Chancellorsville: The Dare Mark Campaign.* Lincoln: University of Nebraska Press, 1998.

———. *Guerrillas, Unionists, and Violence on the Confederate Homefront.* Fayetteville: University of Arkansas Press, 1999.

Swanson, Guy R., and Timothy D. Johnson. "Conflict in East Tennessee: Generals Law, Jenkins, and Longstreet." *Civil War History* 31, no. 2 (June 1985): 101–110.

Swisher, James K. *The Prince of Edisto: Brigadier General Micah Jenkins, C.S.A.* Berryville, Va.: Rockbridge, 1996.

Sword, Wiley. *Mountains Touched with Fire: Chattanooga Besieged, 1863.* New York: St. Martin's, 1995.

———. *Southern Invincibility: A History of the Confederate Heart.* New York: St. Martin's, 1999.

Symonds, Craig. *Joseph E. Johnston: A Civil War Biography.* New York: W. W. Norton, 1992.

———. *Stonewall of the West: Patrick Cleburne and the Civil War.* Lawrence: University Press of Kansas, 1997.

Thomas, Earl Holley. *Company F, Thomson Guards, Tenth Regiment, Georgia Volunteers, Army of Northern Virginia, Confederate States of America.* Fernandina Beach, Fla.: Wolfe, 2000.

Thomas, Emory. *Bold Dragoon: The Life of J. E. B. Stuart.* New York: Harper and Row, 1986.

———. *The Confederate Nation, 1861–1865.* New York: Harper and Row, 1977.

———. *Robert E. Lee: A Biography.* New York: W. W. Norton, 1995.

Thomas, John P. *Career and Character of Micah Jenkins, C.S.A.* Columbia, S.C.: State, 1905.

Thomas, Wilbur. *General James "Pete" Longstreet: Lee's "Old War Horse," Scapegoat for Gettysburg.* Parsons, W.Va.: McClain Printing, 1979.

Tucker, Glenn. *Chickamauga: Bloody Battle in the West.* New York: Konecky and Konecky, 1961.

———. *Lee and Longstreet at Gettysburg.* Indianapolis: Bobbs-Merrill, 1968.

———. "Longstreet: Culprit or Scapegoat?" *Civil War Times Illustrated* 1, no.1 (1962): 5–7, 39–44.

———. *Zeb Vance: Champion of Personal Freedom.* New York: Bobbs-Merrill, 1965.

Utley, Robert M. *Frontiersmen in Blue: The United States Army and the Indian, 1848–1865.* New York: Macmillan, 1976.

Vandiver, Frank E. "Jefferson Davis and Unified Army Command." *Louisiana Historical Quarterly* 38 (1955): 26–30.

Wade, John D. *Augustus B. Longstreet: A Study of the Development of the Culture of the South.* Athens: University of Georgia Press, 1969.

Warner, Ezra J. *Generals in Blue: Lives of the Union Commanders.* Baton Rouge: Louisiana State University Press, 1964.

———. *Generals in Gray: Lives of the Confederate Commanders.* Baton Rouge: Louisiana State University Press, 1959.

Weigley, Russell F. *A Great Civil War: A Military and Political History, 1861–1865.* Bloomington: Indiana University Press, 2001.

Weitz, Mark A. *A Higher Duty: Desertion among Georgia Troops during the Civil War.* Lincoln: University of Nebraska Press, 2000.

———. *More Damning than Slaughter: Desertion in the Confederate Army.* Lincoln: University of Nebraska Press, 2005.

Wert, Jeffry D. *General James Longstreet: The Confederacy's Most Controversial Soldier—A Biography.* New York: Simon & Schuster, 1993.

———. *Gettysburg: Day Three.* New York: Simon & Schuster, 2001.

———. "You Had Done Me a Great Injustice." *Civil War Times Illustrated* 32, no. 1 (March–April 1993): 40–48.

Wiley, Bell Irvin. *The Life of Johnny Reb: The Common Soldier of the Confederacy.* Baton Rouge: Louisiana State University Press, 1943.

Wilkinson, Warren, and Steven E. Woodworth. *A Scythe of Fire: A Civil War Story of the Eighth Georgia Infantry Regiment.* New York: William Morrow, 2002.

Williams, T. Harry. *Lincoln and His Generals.* New York: Alfred A. Knopf, 1952.

———. *P. G. T. Beauregard: Napoleon in Gray.* Baton Rouge: Louisiana State University Press, 1954.

Wills, Brian Steel. *The Confederacy's Greatest Cavalryman: Nathan Bedford Forrest.* Lawrence: University Press of Kansas, 1992.

———. *The War Hits Home: The Civil War in Southeastern Virginia.* Charlottesville: University of Virginia Press, 2001.

Winders, Richard Bruce. *Mr. Polk's Army: The American Military Experience in the U.S.–Mexican War.* College Station: Texas A&M University Press, 1997.

Wood, W. J. *Civil War Generalship: The Art of Command.* Westport, Conn.: Praeger, 1997.

Woodworth, Steven E., ed. *The Art of Command in the Civil War.* Lincoln: University of Nebraska Press, 1998.

———, ed. *Civil War Generals in Defeat.* Lawrence: University Press of Kansas, 1999.

————. "Dark Portents: Confederate Command in Williamsburg." In *The Peninsula Campaign of 1862: Yorktown to the Seven Days,* edited by William J. Miller. Vol. 3. Campbell, Calif.: Savas, 1997.

————. *Davis and Lee at War.* Lawrence: University Press of Kansas, 1996.

————. *A Deep, Steady Thunder: The Battle of Chickamauga.* Fort Worth: Ryan's Place, 1996.

————, ed. *Grant's Lieutenants: From Cairo to Vicksburg.* Lawrence: University Press of Kansas, 2001.

————. *Jefferson Davis and His Generals: The Failure of Confederate Command in the West.* Lawrence: University Press of Kansas, 1990.

————, ed. *Leadership and Command in the American Civil War.* Campbell, Calif.: Savas Woodbury, 1995.

————, ed. *No Band of Brothers: Problems in the Rebel High Command.* Columbia: University of Missouri Press, 1999.

————. *Six Armies in Tennessee: The Chickamauga and Chattanooga Campaigns.* Lincoln: University of Nebraska Press, 1998.

————. *This Grand Spectacle: The Battle of Chattanooga.* Fort Worth: McWhiney Foundation, 1999.

————. *While God Is Marching On: The Religious World of Civil War Soldiers.* Lawrence: University Press of Kansas, 2001.

Wyatt-Brown, Bertram. *Southern Honor: Ethics and Behavior in the Old South.* New York: Oxford University Press, 1982.

Wyckoff, Mac. *A History of the Second South Carolina Infantry, 1861–1865.* Fredericksburg, Va.: Sergeant Kirkland's Museum and Historical Society, 1994.

————. *A History of the Third South Carolina Infantry, 1861–1865.* Fredericksburg, Va.: Sergeant Kirkland's Museum and Historical Society, 1995.

Wyeth, John Allan. *That Devil Forrest: The Life of General Nathan Bedford Forrest.* New York: Harper & Brothers, 1899.

Yates, Richard E. "Governor Vance and the Peace Movement." *The North Carolina Historical Review* 17, no. 1 (January 1940): 1–25.

Theses and Dissertations

Bryan, Charles Faulkner. "The Civil War in East Tennessee: A Social, Political, and Economic Study." PhD diss., University of Tennessee, 1978.

Grear, Charles D. "Texans to the Front: Why Texans Fought in the Civil War." PhD diss., Texas Christian University, 2005.

Hood, Jonathan D. "A Yellow Rose in Old Dominion: The Civil War Reminiscences of Orlando T. Hanks." M.A. thesis, Stephen F. Austin State University, 1997.

Kinder, Don R. "Secession and Civil War in Jefferson County, Tennessee, 1860–1865." M.A. thesis, East Tennessee State University, 1973.

Peacock, John R. "Keeping the Faith: Douglas Southall Freeman, 1886–1953." PhD diss., Louisiana State University and Agricultural and Mechanical College, 1990.

Piston, William G. "Lee's Tarnished Lieutenant: James Longstreet and His Image in American Society." PhD diss., University of South Carolina, 1982.

Sozonsky, Philip M. "A Mystical Sense of Community: Hood's Texas Brigade and the Social, Cultural, and Environmental Dimensions of Combat Success in the Army of Northern Virginia." M.A. thesis, Texas State University, 2006.

Miscellaneous

Hamilton, D. H. "History of Company M, First Texas Volunteer Infantry, Hood's Brigade, Longstreet's Corps, Army of the Confederate States of America." 1925. Unpublished manuscript, copy in possession of the author.

INDEX

Abingdon, Virginia, 157, 180
Alexander, Col. Edward P., 29, 82, 107, 114, 117, 120, 122, 129, 130, 131–32, 148, 159, 175
Alexander's Bridge, 41
Anderson, Col. Archer, 64, 192
Anderson, Brig. Gen. George T., 29, 119–21, 154
Andrews, Maj. Garnett, 154
Antietam campaign, 16
Army of Northern Virginia, 14, 15, 18, 22, 23, 25, 59, 197–99
Army of Observation, 3
Army of Tennessee, 20, 27, 37, 40, 48, 50, 51, 54, 60, 77, 80, 83, 106, 108, 135; compared to Army of Northern Virginia, 76–77; discord in, 53, 56–61, 63–66, 201, 204; and Kentucky invasion, 57
Army of the Cumberland, 27, 49, 50, 54, 60, 79, 83, 89, 100, 104, 108, 142
Army of the Ohio, 27, 173–174
Army of the Potomac (Confederate), 10
Army of the Potomac (Union), 12, 14, 19, 22, 197
Army of the Tennessee (Union), 142, 177
Averell, Brig. Gen. William, 174

Beauregard, Maj. Gen. Pierre G. T., 8, 10, 180–81, 202
Bean's Station, Tennessee, 144–45, 148, 153, 155, 167, 192; Battle of, 145–47, 173
Benning's Brigade, 32, 44
Benning, Brig. Gen. Henry L., 29, 32, 44, 110, 120, 153
Blackburn's Ford action, 9–10, 11, 15
Blackford, Capt. Charles, 78, 83, 195
Blain's Crossroads, Tennessee, 147
Bragg, Gen. Braxton, 1, 20, 22, 36–38, 41,

49, 57–59, 69, 80, 98, 107, 115, 152, 157–58, 169, 202–03, 208; background of, 56–57; correspondence with Davis, 55, 61, 65, 102–103, 105, 109–10, 116, 166; communication with Longstreet, 37–38, 46–47, 71, 112, 113, 128–29; criticism of, 50, 51–61, 69, 77–78, 109, 113–14; friction with Longstreet, 51–52, 72, 97–98, 102, 109, 113, 123–24, 166, 202; petition against, 64–65; relationship with subordinates, 58–61, 65, 70–71; removal of Polk, 63–65; strategy of, 36, 37, 38, 47–48, 57, 93, 98, 105–06, 108
Brannan, Brig. Gen. John M., 42
Bratton, Col. John, 83, 98, 99, 119–21, 125, 140, 172, 189
Breckinridge, Maj. Gen. John C., 41, 49, 59, 60, 76, 105
Brent, Col. George, 55, 70, 93, 99, 114
Bridgeport, Alabama, 78, 79, 89, 95, 97, 105, 108
Bristol, Alabama, 28, 142, 172, 197–98
Brotherton Farm, 39
Brotherton House, 43, 46
Brotherton Road, 39
Brotherton, Tom, 39
Brown, Brig. Gen. John C., 39
Brown's Ferry, 79, 89–91, 95–96, 98; engagement at, 95–96, 110
Bryan, Goode, 29
Buckner, Maj. Gen. Simon Bolivar, 27, 40, 46, 60, 67–69, 107, 109, 113, 154, 156
Buell, Maj. Gen. Don Carlos, 57
Bull's Gap, Tennessee, 179, 197
Burnside, Maj. Gen. Ambrose, 19, 27, 105–06, 116, 120–121, 123, 128, 140, 142, 208

Campbell's Station, Battle of, 120–21
Castel, Albert, 137
Catoosa Station, 34, 36
Centreville, Virginia, 10
Chancellorsville, Battle of, 22
Chapultepec, Battle of, 4–5
Charleston and Memphis Railroad, 80
Chattanooga campaign, 80–103, 131, 142
Chattanooga, Tennessee, 20, 37, 50, 54,
    78–79, 89, 104, 142, 169, 174; siege
    of, 82–84, 131, 209
Chattanooga Creek, 80, 84
Cheatham, Maj. Gen. Benjamin Franklin,
    55, 67, 69, 108
Cherokee Heights, 129
Chesnut, Col. James, 65, 102
Chesnut, Mary, 49, 56
Chickamauga, Battle of, 36–49, 53–54
Chickamauga Creek, 36, 41, 47, 50, 106
Churrubusco, Battle of, 3–4, 136
Cleveland, Tennessee, 115
Clinch Mountain, 144–46, 172
Columbus, Georgia, 190
Connelly, Thomas Lawrence, 20, 109
Conrad, Bryan, xviii
Cooper, Gen. Samuel, 10, 33, 116, 150,
    153–54, 158–59, 161, 165–66,
    168–69, 189, 197
Cozzens, Peter, xix–xx
Cumberland Gap, 108, 137, 142–43, 179
Cumberland Mountains, 179
Curry, Jabez L. M., 5, 719

Dalton, Georgia, 28, 137, 142–43, 180
Dandridge, Tennessee, 172, 174–76;
    engagement at, 175–76
Davis, Jefferson, 6, 7, 10, 23–25, 66, 85,
    142, 162–63, 169, 180, 196, 201, 208;
    antiBragg sentiment and, 58–60,
    65–69; Beauregard's conflict
    with, 68, 73; strategy of, 10–11,
    12, 23–24, 25, 27, 102–03, 105–06,
    109–10, 179–81, 197; Johnston's
    conflict with, 10, 19–20, 58, 73, 201;
    Longstreet's communication with,
    68, 143, 165; military conference
    with Army of Tennessee, 67;
    relationship with Polk, 58, 65;
    Wigfall's conflict with, 11, 18

Department of East Tennessee, 60, 172
Department of the West, 16–17, 19, 74
Dibrell, Col. George G., 179, 197
Dillard, Col. F. W., 189
District of Southwestern Virginia and
    Tennessee, 142
Dry Valley Road, 36, 43, 48, 100, 104, 108
Dyer Farm, 43
Dyer Field, 43–45
Dyer House, 46
Dyer Road, 43

East Tennessee, 34, 105–06, 112–13, 148,
    168, 181–182
East Tennessee and Georgia Railroad, 28,
    108, 117–18
East Tennessee and Virginia Railroad, 108,
    138, 148, 172, 174
Eighth Infantry Regiment, U.S., 3
Ewell, Maj. Gen. Richard S., 23, 111, 153,
    199

Fair Garden, Tennessee, 176
Fairfax Court House, 10
Fairfax, Maj. John W., 129
Fairfax, Col. Walter, 195
Feagin, Capt. Noah, 95–96
Field, Maj. Gen. Charles, 154, 165, 199;
    background of, 166–67; and First
    Corps, 165–67
First Corps, Army of Northern Virginia, 16,
    19, 33–34, 75, 103, 109, 117, 137, 143,
    161, 180; acknowledgements of, 192;
    acquisition of horses, 183; biases
    of, 172; and clothing, 188–189;
    desertion, 85, 189–191; discord
    in, 110–112, 122, 136, 141, 147–150,
    164, 167, 169, 171, 202–203; food,
    184–187; foraging, 177, 184–186;
    and furloughs, 191; hardships of,
    29–30, 30–31, 34, 54, 80–81, 83–84,
    124–125, 138–40, 185–86, 189, 192,
    203; loyalty of, 33–34, 203; and
    mail, 193; morale of, 69, 74, 81–82,
    84–85, 103, 114–15, 125–26, 150,
    171, 176, 192; and newspapers, 183;
    opinion of Army of Tennessee,
    75–77; organization of, 16; religion
    and, 28–29, 196; return to Army

of Northern Virginia, 140, 177, 197–99; rumors, 183; and shoes, 189; socializing of, 194–95; and Unionists, 193–194; and weather, 187–88; western transfer of, 1–2, 24–25, 29, 51, 105, 106–10, 112

First Manassas, 9–10

Forrest, Brig. Gen. Nathan Bedford, 45, 54

Fort Sanders, 4, 127–28, 132, 137, 143, 149, 171, 203; assault on, 133–36

Fort Stanley, 129

Fort Sumter, 6

Foster, Brig. Gen. John G. Foster, 142, 173

Foy, Lt. Col. James, 96

Fredericksburg campaign, 19

Freeman, Douglas Southall, xvii–xviii

French Broad River, 172, 175–76

Ganahl, Joseph, 154

Garland, Maria Louisa, see Longstreet, Maria Louisa Garland ("Louise")

Garland, Col. John, 3, 5, 201

Garrard, Col. Israel, 175

Geary, Brig. Gen. John, 98–99

Gettysburg, campaign and battle of, 22–24, 29, 34

Giltner, Col. Henry L., 143

Goggin, Capt. James, 135

Goree, Maj. Thomas J., 6, 11

Gracie, Brig. Gen. Archibald, 130, 144–45

Granger, Maj. Gen. Gordon, 147, 175

Grant, Maj. Gen. Ulysses S., 14, 22, 88, 90–91, 116–17, 138, 141, 163, 173, 179, 197, 199, 201, 209

Great Smoky Mountains, 172

Greeneville, Tennessee, 172, 179

Gregg, Brig. Gen. John, 43, 154

Grigsby, Maj. Gen. Warren, 92–93

Hallock, Judith Lee, xix, 72–73

Hardee, Lt. Gen. William J., 105, 107

Hart, Col. John, 119

Hartranft, Col John F., 119

Hay, Thomas Robson, xviii

Hazen, Brig. Gen. William B., 95

Hill, Lt. Gen. Ambrose Powell, 23, 111, 199

Hill, Lt. Gen. Daniel Harvey, 38, 41, 55, 60, 64, 67, 76, 113, 150, 164, 168, 181; conflict with Bragg, 64, 68–69, 168

Hindman, Maj. Gen. Thomas C., 38, 42, 55

Holden, William Woods, 32

Holston River, 125, 138, 144–45, 148, 172

Holston Valley, 143, 149, 171–72, 174

Hood, Maj. Gen. John Bell, 29, 38, 42, 43, 44–46, 76–77, 86, 92, 107, 152, 201

Hooker, Maj. Gen. Joseph, 89, 97, 98

Horseshoe Ridge, 46–48

Huger, Maj. Gen. Benjamin, 12; Longstreet's feud with, 12–13, 17–18

Humphreys, Brig. Gen. Benjamin, 29, 38, 45, 154, 162

Jackson, Brig. Gen. Alfred E., 144

Jackson, Lt. Gen. Thomas J. "Stonewall," 14–15, 22, 202, 207

Jenkins, Brig. Gen. Micah, 29, 80, 95, 99, 104–05, 117, 138, 145–49, 152, 155, 166, 172, 201; background of, 85–87; at Campbell's Station, 119–22; at Knoxville, 131–33; relationship with Longstreet, 85–86; rivalry with Law, 85–88, 95, 100–01, 110, 121–22, 160, 165; at Wauhatchie, 98–100; wounding of, 199

Johnson, Maj. Gen. Bushrod R., 36, 38, 43, 45, 130, 135, 144–46, 148

Johnston, Gen. Albert Sidney, 10, 57, 201

Johnston, Gen. Joseph E., 10, 12, 19, 58–59, 164–65, 169, 178, 180, 197, 207–08; Army of Tennessee and, 59, 169; background of, 10; Davis's conflict with, 10, 20, 58–59, 169; Department of the West, head of, 19–20, 58; Longstreet's correspondence with, 16–17, 180; Longstreet's relationship with, 12, 17–18, 180; personality of, 17–18, 20, 58, 59; "Western Concentration Bloc" and, 20; Wigfall and, 12, 20

Jones, Archer, 20

Jones, Maj. Gen. Sam, 105, 108, 173

Jones, Brig. Gen. William E. "Grumble," 143, 145, 148

Jordan, Brig. Gen. Thomas, 181

Kelly Field, 45

Kelly, Brig. Gen. John H., 92

Kempner, Brig. Gen. James L. Kempner, 154

Kentucky campaign, 57–58
Kershaw's Brigade, 45
Kershaw, Brig. Gen. Joseph, 38, 45, 164, 199
Kingston Road, 118–121, 125
Knoxville, Tennessee, 27, 105, 114, 116–17, 123, 125–26, 128, 137, 141–42, 145, 172, 174, 177, 179, 197
Knoxville campaign, 107–40, 148, 205–06, 208–09

La Fayette, Georgia, 1, 27, 36
La Fayette Road, 36, 39, 42–43
Lamar, Lucius Q. C., 11
Law's Brigade, 160–61, 168–70
Law, Brig. Gen. Evander, 29, 34, 45, 87, 95, 110, 129, 158, 162, 164, 170, 201; alliance with McLaws, 163–64, 166; at Bean's Station, 146–49; at Campbell's Station, 119–23; at Chattanooga, 84–101; background, 87; conflict with Longstreet, 87, 122–23, 147–49; criticism of, 87, 121–22; friendship with Hood, 92, 160; resignation of, 160–61; rivalry with Jenkins, 85–88, 100–01, 110, 121–22, 160, 165; at Wauhatchie, 98–100
Leadbetter, Brig. Gen. Danville, 129–30
Lee, Maj. Pollock, 42
Lee, Gen. Robert E., 10, 12, 14–16, 22–25, 32, 72, 76, 85, 102, 111, 153, 159, 164, 180, 198, 200, 208; background of, 14; Davis's relationship with, 24–25, 72; Longstreet's correspondence with, 22, 62, 72, 163, 177, 179–180; Longstreet's relationship with, 14, 16; strategy of, 16, 22–23, 27, 29, 178–82
Lenoir's Station, Tennessee, 117–118
Leyden, Maj. Austin, 107
Liddell, Brig. Gen. St. John R., 50, 64, 70, 97, 114
Lincoln, Abraham, 5, 181–182
Longstreet, Augustus Baldwin (uncle), 24
Longstreet, Lt. Gen. James, 1–2, 18–19, 31, 35, 39, 44–45, 49, 64, 67, 69, 76, 105, 106–07, 115, 117–18, 132–33, 135, 137–38, 140, 145, 147, 160–64, 173–76, 189, 200; ambition of, 2, 5, 6–7, 13–14, 16–18, 20–21, 24–26, 32, 62–63, 94–95; anti-Bragg faction, participation in, 61–63, 64–69, 72, 202–05; background of, 1–2; Bragg's relationship with, 24, 36, 52, 72, 112; and Campbell's Station, battle of, 118–23; and Chattanooga campaign, 80–103; and Chickamauga campaign, 38–52; communication with Bragg, 41, 46–47, 49, 94, 97, 104–05, 112–13, 115–16, 128–29; confidence of, 1, 9, 14, 19, 44, 46, 94, 102, 113, 124, 129–30, 136, 143, 148, 153, 169–70, 181–82, 205; conflict with Huger, 13–14; conflict with McLaws, 94, 111–12, 141, 157–58; conflict with Law, 87, 101, 122, 141, 147–49, 161–63; correspondence with Davis, 135, 165, 180–181; correspondence with Johnston, 16–17, 180; correspondence with Lee, 20, 24, 31, 62, 72, 162, 177, 179–180, 197; correspondence with Seddon, 24, 62; correspondence with Wigfall, 18, 20, 22–23, 24, 31, 53, 71; Davis's relationship with, 11, 70, 73; and desertion, 190; differences with Bragg, 49, 52, 53, 62–63, 97, 102, 152; and East Tennessee campaign, 143–170, 172–82; and Gettysburg campaign, 22–24, 111–12; Johnston's relationship with, 10–12, 14, 16–17, 21, 180; and Knoxville campaign, 112–43; and Law's removal, 161–63; Lee's relationship with, 16, 21, 31–32, 72; loss of Brown's Ferry, 90–97; and McLaws's removal, 150–51; nicknames of, 2, 52, 125, 150, 200; opinions of, 11, 18, 19, 20, 22–24, 31, 51, 53, 62, 71–72, 86; personality of, 7–8, 11, 22–23, 73, 89; relationship with McLaws, 111–12, 164; strategy and tactics of, 20, 22–24, 29, 31, 39–40, 47–48, 97–99, 101–02, 120, 132, 135–36, 149, 178–82, 197, 205, 207–08; weaknesses of, 206–07; wounded at Wilderness, 164, 199

Longstreet, Maria Louisa ("Louise"), 5, 89, 180
Lookout Creek, 96
Lookout Mountain, 78–80, 82, 89, 96, 102, 104–05
Lookout Valley, 79, 92, 97–98, 101, 104, 108
Lost Cause myth, 1–2, 209
Lowther, Col. Alexander, 161
Loudon, Tennessee, 105–06, 116–17, 144

Mabry's Hill, 126, 130
Mackall, Brig. Gen. William, 63–64, 70–71, 85
Magruder, Maj. Gen. John B., 156
Mahan, Dennis Hart, 57
Manassas, see First Manassas, Battle of; Second Manassas, campaign and Battle of
Manigault, Brig. Gen. Arthur M., 43
Martin, Brig. Gen. William, 137–38, 143, 146–47, 174–76, 179; conflict with Longstreet, 177–78
Marysville, Tennessee, 116–17
McClellan, Maj. Gen. George B., 12
McDonough, James Lee, xix, 99
McLaws, Abram Huguenin ("Hu"), 157
McLaws, Maj. Gen. Lafayette, 29, 31, 50, 63, 80, 83, 107, 117, 119, 132–33, 138, 153–55, 164; alliance with Law, 163–64, 166; at Bean's Station, 145, 147–49; at Campbell's Station, 118–23; at Chattanooga, 80; background of, 111; conflict with Longstreet, 111–12, 123, 157–58, 167, 202; correspondence with Bragg, 157–58; court martial of, 150–51, 158–59; Knoxville campaign and, 123–35; Longstreet's relief of, 150–51; relationship with Lee, 111; relationship with Longstreet, 111–12, 164; transfer of, 159
McLemore's Cove, 37, 55
McNair, Brig. Gen. Evander, 43
McWhiney, Grady, 57
Meade, Maj. Gen. George G., 197
Mexican-American War, 3–5, 136
Missionary Ridge, 51, 79
Moccasin Point, 91, 104
Monterrey, Battle of, 3, 56

Moore, Andrew B., 6–7
Morristown, Tennessee, 145, 172, 177, 179
Moses, Maj. Raphael J., 115, 125, 184
Mossy Creek, Tennessee, 174–175
Mott, Col. Samuel, 174

New Market, Tennessee, 179
Nichols, Brig. Gen. Francis T., 154
Nolichucky River, 17
North Carolina Standard, 32–33
Northrop, Col. Lucius B., 83

Oates, Col William C., 39, 95
Owen, Maj. William Miller, 46

Parke, Maj. Gen. John, 142, 144, 175
Parker's Virginia Battery, 145–46
Pemberton, Maj. Gen. John C., 20, 23, 66
Peninsula campaign, 12–15
Perry, Col. William, 160
Perryville, Battle of, 58
Pickett, Maj. Gen. George E., 23, 29
Piston, William Garrett, xvii,
Poe, Capt. Orlando, 119, 127
Polk, Maj. Gen. Leonidas, 38–41, 54–55, 58, 65, 73; conflict with Bragg, 55, 58–59, 63, 65
Polley, Corp. Joseph, 76
Pope, Maj. Gen. John, 15
Preston, Brig. Gen. William, 38, 40, 43, 48

Raccoon Mountain, 78, 80, 100
Raleigh Progress, 33
Randolph, George W., 12–13
Ransom, Maj. Gen. Robert, 142, 144, 164, 175
Rapidan River, 164, 199
Reynolds, Maj. Gen. Joseph J., 42
Ringgold, Virginia, 34–35
Robertson, Maj. Felix, 39
Robertson, Brig. Gen. Jerome B., 29, 44, 98, 110, 120, 152, 203; conflict with Longstreet, 110, 147–49; court martial of, 153, 155–56
Rogersville, Tennessee, 116, 143, 145, 148
Rosecrans, Maj. Gen. William Starke, 25, 27, 36, 37, 41–42, 46, 54, 58, 80, 88
Russellville, Tennessee, 148, 153, 172, 177
Rutledge, Tennessee, 144, 146, 172

Sand Mountain, 78
Sanger, Donald B., xviii
Santa Anna, Gen. Antonio López de, 3
Scott, Maj. Gen. Winfield, 3, 4, 8
Schurz, Carl, 100
secession, 5–6
Second Manassas, Battle of, 15–16
Seddon, James, 2, 20, 22, 24, 32, 156, 160, 162
Seven Days campaign, 14–15
Seven Pines, Battle of, 12–14
Sevierville, Tennessee, 177
Shackelford, Brig. Gen. James, 142–43, 144–46
Shellmound, Tennessee, 98
Shepherd, Lt. Col. William S., 33–34
Sherman, Maj. Gen. William T., 89, 116, 142–43, 179, 202
Shiloh, Battle of, 57
Smith, Maj. Gen. Edmund Kirby, 57, 172
Smith, Maj. Gen. Gustavus W., 10, 13, 160
Smith, Brig. Gen. William F., 89, 95
Snodgrass Hill, 45–46, 49
Sorrel, Col. G. Moxley, 29, 35, 48, 93, 121–22, 132, 148, 187, 193
Southern Historical Association, 209
State Journal, 33
Stephens, Alexander, 19
Stevenson, Alabama, 80, 105
Stevenson, Maj. Gen. Carter, 105, 108, 113, 116
Stewart, Maj. Gen. Alexander P., 38–39, 42, 48
Stones River, Battle of, 58
Strawberry Plains, Tennessee, 156, 173, 176, 179
Stuart, Maj. Gen. James Ewell Brown "Jeb," 191
Sturgis, Brig. Gen. Samuel, 174–175, 177
sutlers, 186
Sweetwater, Tennessee, 115, 125
Symonds, Craig L., 13, 59

Talbot's Station, Tennessee, 174
Taylor, Col. Walter H., 29, 198, 209
Taylor, Maj. Gen. Zachary, 3, 4, 8
Tennessee River, 78–79, 90–91, 117, 142

Texas Brigade, 36, 44, 76, 110, 152
Thedford's Ford, 36, 41
Thomas, Maj. Gen. George H., 42, 46–48, 89
Thomas, Wilbur, xviii
Toombs, Robert, 19
Trenton, Georgia, 91–92, 97
Turchin, Brig. Gen. John, 95
Tyner's Station, Tennessee, 114, 115

United States Military Academy (West Point), 2, 5, 7, 57, 58, 201

Vaughan, Brig. Gen. John Crawford, 142, 144
Vance, Zebulon, 32–34
Vicksburg campaign, 25
Virginia and East Tennessee Railroad, 78

Walden's Ridge, 79, 83, 89–90
Walker, Leroy P., 6
Walker, Brig. Gen. William H. T., 60
Wauhatchie, 78, 99, 100; engagement at, 98–100, 110
Wert, Jeffry D., xviii, xx, 7, 15
Western and Atlantic Railroad, 29, 31, 78, 83, 108
"Western Concentration Bloc," 1, 20, 23, 27, 67
Wharton, Brig. Gen. Gabriel, 144
Wheeler, Maj. Gen. Joseph, 44, 70, 92, 107, 112, 116, 137
White, Brig. Gen. Julius, 117
Whiting, Maj. Gen. Henry Chase, 164
Widow Glenn House, 43
Wigfall, Louis, 2, 11, 201; Davis's conflict with, 11–12, 18, 20; Johnston's alliance with, 12; Longstreet's correspondence with, 18, 20, 22–24, 53
Wilder, Brig. Gen. John T., 43–44
Wilderness, Battle of, 164, 199
Wofford, William T., 29
Wood, Thomas J., 42–43
Woodworth, Steven E., xix, 182
Wofford, Brig. Gen. William T., 175
Worth, Col. David, 3, 4